Pot Politics

Pot Politics

Marijuana and the Costs of Prohibition

Edited by Mitch Earleywine

OXFORD
UNIVERSITY PRESS

2007

OXFORD
UNIVERSITY PRESS

Oxford University Press, Inc., publishes works that further
Oxford University's objective of excellence
in research, scholarship, and education.

Oxford   New York
Auckland   Cape Town   Dar es Salaam   Hong Kong   Karachi
Kuala Lumpur   Madrid   Melbourne   Mexico City   Nairobi
New Delhi   Shanghai   Taipei   Toronto

With offices in
Argentina   Austria   Brazil   Chile   Czech Republic   France   Greece
Guatemala   Hungary   Italy   Japan   Poland   Portugal   Singapore
South Korea   Switzerland   Thailand   Turkey   Ukraine   Vietnam

Published by Oxford University Press, Inc.
198 Madison Avenue, New York, New York 10016

www.oup.com

Oxford is a registered trademark of Oxford University Press

Library of Congress Cataloging-in-Publication Data
Pot politics : marijuana and the costs of prohibition / edited by
Mitch Earleywine.
    p. cm.
Includes bibliographical references and index.
ISBN-13 978-0-19-518802-8
ISBN 0-19-518802-0
1. Marijuana—Government policy.   2. Marijuana—Social aspects.
3. Marijuana abuse.
I. Earleywine, Mitchell.
HV5822.M3P68 2006
362.29'5561—dc22   2006001434

9 8 7 6 5 4 3 2 1

Printed in the United States of America
on acid-free paper

FOREWORD

Allen F. St. Pierre

Epiphanies are rare. Paradigm-shifting epiphanies are even more so. Some epiphanies leave one with a sense of bewilderment, grasping outward to an unforeseen future. In other cases, an epiphanic moment can instantly replace a vexing conundrum with a crystalline and self-evident solution.

In my 15-year tenure in various leadership positions at the National Organization for the Reform of Marijuana Laws (NORML), I've been exposed to my fair share of unconventional thinking. The staff and board of directors of NORML and our allies have worked hard and creatively for 35 years to reform marijuana laws so that the responsible use of marijuana by an adult will no longer be a criminal or civil offense.

I've participated in long, intellectual retreats on mountaintops, suffered through multihour conference calls, participated in moot courts and legislatures, and attended dozens of conferences and symposiums all directed toward ending marijuana prohibition. Additionally, NORML has one of the largest archives in the world relating to cannabis, and I've read almost every academic paper, report, and book in its extensive collection.

However, a few years ago, I learned more about marijuana's prohibition and the urgent need to reform America's arcane laws from a 30-second interaction than I had at all the intellectual and academic meetings I'd attended or from the books I'd read regarding marijuana and criminal justice policy.

This fortuitous meeting serves as the epiphany that drives and greatly inspires my full-time advocacy for legally controlling marijuana through a taxation policy rather than the expensive and self-evidently failing public policy of marijuana prohibition.

"THE POWER TO TAX IS THE POWER TO CREATE, OR TO DESTROY"

It should go without saying that both reformers and prohibitionists do not want children to have any greater access to currently illegal drugs, including marijuana, than they have under prohibition. For nearly 70 years, the government policy concerning marijuana has principally been one of total prohibition with the expressed goal of diminishing youth access. With marijuana increasingly showing up on youth drug use surveys in greater numbers than such legal and taxed drugs as alcohol and tobacco, one can strongly argue that prohibition fails at its core mission: protecting youth from and limiting youth access to marijuana.

According to the NORML Foundation's report "Crimes of Indiscretion," published in 2005, more than 1 million American children annually sell or resell marijuana. I've always been vexed by prohibitionists who fail to see that the government's abandonment of its generally accepted duty to tax commerce—in this case, the responsible use of marijuana by adults—creates most of the social harms so readily identifiable with marijuana and other illicit drug use. These social harms include: unfettered youth access; misleading and confusing public educational campaigns; lack of genuine controls for age and product quality on production, sales and use; and racial, age, and class disparity in the government's enforcement of marijuana prohibition.

From my perspective, the federal, state, and local governments should tax the legal sale and use of marijuana. Doing so would create a viable and consistent revenue source and a system of monitoring incorporated businesses that grow or sell marijuana. It would send a consistent and credible message to youth regarding "drugs" and would strongly encourage personal and corporate responsibility concerning marijuana. It would also allow benefits to flow from genuine economic back-linkages in the geographical areas where cannabis is cultivated, sold, and consumed (similar to the economic benefits derived from alcohol, tobacco, and caffeine products).

Taxing and legally controlling marijuana will likely destroy most of the social and health concerns associated with it, which have been created principally by the prohibition of cannabis and not by the use of the drug itself. This, of course, is the monumental lesson learned from America's great and failed social experiment: alcohol prohibition.

BEING THERE

I believe Woody Allen says that 98 percent of success is simply showing up. Therefore, when I received complimentary tickets a few years ago to the re-opening of a venerable music venue in the District of Columbia, I could not have foreseen the remarkable event that was going to transpire that evening or the profound effects it would have on my public advocacy regarding ending marijuana prohibition.

I had to wait in line more than an hour before entering the club because security guards were carefully scrutinizing government-issued identification cards (i.e., driver's licenses, passports, and alcohol-ID cards) in an effort to deter youth access to alcohol at this very crowded all-age show. Accompanying me were two sisters, who, like me, were over thirty years old and had graying hair. Once inside, we were issued tight wristbands designating our access to one of America's most deadly, addicting, and problematic drugs: alcohol.

The club was well managed, with plenty of security guards and informal "bouncers." After the warm-up act left the stage, I offered to get refills of our beers. I patiently stood in line with other drug users, I mean, beer drinkers, and when it was my turn to order the three refills I was informed by the drug dealer, I mean bartender, that club rules allowed patrons to procure a maximum of two alcoholic drinks at a time. I inquired, "Why?" and the bartender indicated that limiting the number of drinks purchased at the bar by adult patrons helps limit diversion of alcohol to underage youths at their all-age shows.

I shrugged my shoulders in acknowledgment of her explanation, and I purchased two units of the desired drug, beer. As I made my way out of the beer line, I was approached by two youths sporting wristbands in a color that indicated they were under 21. With a squeaky adolescent voice, one of them asked if he could "ask me something." He looked furtively around and unfurled from his hand before me a large, sweat-stained and unevenly rolled marijuana cigarette (aka, a joint).

"We'll trade you this joint for those two beers."

Then and there, with the requisite brilliance of light and angelic music all around me signaling this epiphanic moment, I looked deeply into the youthful eyes of this impromptu salesman, then turned entirely around to see gallons and gallons of taxed, legally controlled beer pour prodigiously from ever-flowing taps.

I thought to myself: "There is the answer to the U.S. government's great cannabis quandary concerning youth access to marijuana. Taxation and regulation will genuinely control youth access to cannabis in the same manner as it generally does with alcohol products."

Suddenly, the entire juxtaposition of our country's hypercritical and failed cannabis policy versus its tolerant and pragmatic alcohol policy became forever crystal clear in my mind. Though imperfect, controls and regulations for alcohol use far outperform prohibition as a viable means for enhancing public health, especially in reducing youth access.

My mind raced through all the regulatory and licensing concerns and the many corporate liabilities that commercial establishments selling alcohol have to assume in modern-day America.

I looked over the boys' heads and panned the full house of exuberant patrons. I instantly thought about the many social and legal controls that exist today in America for alcohol, again with a strong emphasis on prohibiting youth access, which, in the case of marijuana, the government has abandoned to the vagaries of an unregulated black market. Rather than controls, the marijuana sales industry has no established hours of business; no licensing from a government agency; no consumer age limit; no identification card system or training for retail distributors; no ability to enforce product quality control and purity; no means to regulate potency; and no corporate or personal responsibility or compliance with existing social mores and values.

I looked back into the eyes of the young, but illicit entrepreneur. I looked back again at the overwhelmed bartender trying to efficiently and legally serve her customers. I even got lost for a brief moment in a neon sign above the cash register that alternatively flashed between "Drink Responsibly" and "Stay Alive . . . Don't Drink and Drive."

I already had cannabis on my person, in fact NORML-director-quality cannabis. However, at that moment, I couldn't resist the thought that I would likely make this uneven trade for this desirable contraband if I were not already holding. That thought greatly disturbed me then, and it still does all these years later.

I finally turned to the boys and informed them that I couldn't make the trade. They responded by trying to sweeten the deal: "We'll give you two joints instead." I'm sure I presented them an odd smile as I thanked them for offering me their wares. I walked the two drug units (pints of beer) down to the dance floor where my waiting revelers rejoiced upon my successful beer run. Wanting my own beer to imbibe, I was left to trudge back upstairs to stand in the ever-present line for beer.

While standing in line again, it was hard not to feel bad for these two boys who were still haplessly trying to exchange, with a willing and irresponsible adult, their prohibition-purchased marijuana for the legally purchased and taxed alcohol products that were teasingly only an arm's length away from them.

The fundamental question is, When will elected policy makers recognize that social controls and fiscal benefits of legalizing cannabis, though imperfect, are far better public policy than the outright abandonment by

the government of its responsibility to tax commerce, case at hand here cannabis, thereby creating greater and unchecked access of cannabis by youths?

The power to tax is indeed the power to create or to destroy.

Allen F. St. Pierre is the executive director of NORML
and the NORML Foundation, Washington, DC

ACKNOWLEDGMENTS

My hearty thanks go first to all the authors who appear in this volume. Obviously, the book wouldn't exist without them. Despite numerous calls and e-mails to every anti-drug agency and agent, I could find only one person brave enough to write in support of current prohibitions against marijuana, so a special commendation goes to Kevin Sabet.

I thank everyone at Oxford who helped make this work possible, with particular gratitude to Catharine Carlin, Stacey Hamilton, Jennifer Rappaport, John Rauschenberg, Rudy Faust, and Niko Pfund. My colleagues at the University of Southern California have shown surprising generosity in support of this work, and I thank all my new friends at the University at Albany for taking a gamble on a guy with a reputation for the controversial.

Enthusiastic thanks to all of the following for reasons they already know: Norman Miller and Vicki Pollock, Mark Myers and Tamar Golan, Jim Moore, Jill Nevin, Rick Ross, Sara Smucker Barnwell, Ashley Borders, Archana Jajodia, Sherry Span, Joe LaBrie, Jason Schiffman, Jed Grodin, Joel Erblich, Suzy Luczak, Mona Devich-Navarro, Boaz Levy, Joe Earleywine, Bob Earleywine, Clark and Suzy Van Scoyk, David and Felice Gordis, Rob Kampia, Bruce Mirken, Francis DellaVecchia, Ethan Nadelmann, Stanton Peele, Marsha Rosenbaum, Jeanette Irwin, Allen St. Pierre, Keith Stroup, Kris Krane, Alison Looby, Archana Jajodia, Sara Smucker Barnwell, Sarah Harrison, and Domenico Scarlatti.

My daughters, Dahlia and Maya, endured countless hours without me during the preparation of this work, so I thank them with gusto. Let's hope they grow up in a land where punishments fit crimes.

As always, I dedicate this work to my wife, Elana Gordis. She endured countless bouts of PMS (pot manuscript syndrome) and continues to tolerate other atrocities that go well beyond her vows. Nothing I could say would do justice to her.

CONTENTS

Section VII: A Call to Action

CONTRIBUTORS

Sara Smucker Barnwell
Department of Psychology
University of Southern California

Peter Cohen
Center for Drug Research
University of Amsterdam

Rabbi Elliot N. Dorff
Philosophy and Bioethics
University of Judaism

Mitch Earleywine
Department of Psychology
University at Albany
State University of New York

Daniel Egan
Department of Economics
Boston University

Robert Gore
Department of Psychology
University of Southern California

Wayne Hall
Office of Public Policy and Ethics
Institute for Molecular
    Bioscience
University of Queensland

Douglas Husak
Department of Philosophy
Rutgers University

Anthony Liguori
Department of Physiology and
    Pharmacology
Wake Forest University School
    of Medicine

Bruce Mirken
Director of Communications
Marijuana Policy Project

Jeffrey A. Miron
Department of Economics
Harvard University

Anne Nicoll
School of Social Work
University of Washington

Mary Ann Pentz
Departments of Preventive
    Medicine and Psychology
University of Southern California

Craig Reinarman
Department of Sociology
University of California,
    Santa Cruz

Roger A. Roffman
School of Social Work
University of Washington

Kevin A. Sabet
Department of Social Policy and
    Social Work
Oxford University

Allen F. St. Pierre
Executive Director
NORML/NORML Foundation

Rodney Skager
Graduate School of Education and
    Information Studies
University of California, Los
    Angeles

Steve Sussman
Departments of Preventive
    Medicine and Psychology
University of Southern
    California

Charles Thomas
Executive Director
Interfaith Drug Policy Initiative
    Foundation

Pot Politics

1   Thinking Clearly About Marijuana Policy

Mitch Earleywine

Few people realize that they have been misled about marijuana, marijuana policy, and the effects of both on their lives. Hundreds of millions of people have never even seen marijuana and believe they don't know anyone who has used it, but marijuana policy still affects them. Supporters and detractors of marijuana prohibition agree that the plant and the policies designed to control it generate costs. Both sides of the prohibition argument would like to see the plant remain out of the hands of children. Both sides want to ensure that no one drives while impaired. Both sides want problem users of any drug to receive help. Both want to see anyone with a medical condition receive appropriate, inexpensive treatment. Both sides want to end these troubles without sacrificing civil rights, respect for the law, or quality of life. The question is: How? Resources are limited. The medical, ethical, religious, legal, and economic issues surrounding marijuana policy are remarkably complex.

Even those who have never given marijuana policy much thought would agree that the only way to think about it is to think clearly. Most of us lean a bit toward change or a bit toward the status quo. Many others have strong feelings about tightening enforcement and increasing penalties or dropping prohibition completely. All tend to agree, though, that logical arguments are the best. Those who've seen the discourse on this topic also agree that it's riddled with illogical arguments. Although rationality may not be the answer to every human problem, troubles related to marijuana policy would surely benefit from the judicious use of reason.

A huge volume of research supports the idea that certain critical errors in thinking lead to depression, as we have suspected for more than 40 years (Beck, 1963). Unfortunately, some of these errors have crept into the debate on marijuana laws, leaving proponents of new laws as well as fans of the status quo feeling less vital and energetic than they might. The first step to improving arguments (and moods) requires identifying these errors with genuine vigilance. No one is immune to these. Many of the errors here come directly from the work of depression researchers, but their application to policy arguments is striking. This list is hardly exhaustive, but the few mistakes detailed here are certainly rampant. Eliminating these glitches in logic will improve the debate on marijuana policy and restore the verve of many people who care so much about this important topic.

OVERGENERALIZING FROM INDIVIDUAL CASES

The first error concerns taking a single example as if it were proof of a worldwide trend.

"I know a man who smoked pot once and died of a heart attack!"

"I know a man who smokes pot every day, and he's a millionaire!"

Both prohibitionists and reformers have learned that the public responds to memorable stories of individuals. A graphic tale about one real person grips audiences more than a superb longitudinal study of hundreds. Nevertheless, a single case is a poor argument that marijuana serves as a cause. To prove that marijuana causes any result, we need association, temporal antecedence, and isolation. We have to show an association between marijuana and the result, show that marijuana use preceded the result, and rule out all other potential causes by isolating marijuana as the lone source of the result (see Earleywine, 2002; Hume, 1739/1978). Only a large experiment with randomly assigned participants can support a causal argument. Huge samples of people chosen at random to either use the plant regularly or abstain completely might answer some of the central questions that appear and reappear in the policy debate.

Individual cases cannot prove that marijuana creates any result. A single marijuana user is not proof that marijuana either impairs or enhances accomplishments. Thus, any references to individual users, no matter how famous or notorious, can only serve as examples. Since at least a third of Americans have tried the drug at least once, it should be no surprise that many well-known folks, from philanthropists to criminals, have used the plant. The best way to avoid this error may be to emphasize that no single case can generalize to all cases. If every salient example contained this

caveat, we'd make some progress. If we reasoned from large experiments instead of individual cases, we could start an intelligent, rational conversation about policy.

BIASED SAMPLING

An error related to overgeneralizing concerns biased sampling. It's easy to assume that information about a select group of accomplished recreational users or troubled addicts applies to the whole world. People for and against new policy have fallen into this trap. I recently spoke at an anti-prohibition gathering with a very brave physician who emphasized that adolescents can run into problems with the plant. One member of the audience turned to the others and said, "How many of you successful people started smoking in your teens?" Of course, the question led to wild applause, but this dramatic demonstration is no proof of marijuana's harmlessness. The users who have troubles with the plant simply weren't in the audience.

Prohibitionists make the same error. Many point to large groups of recovering addicts and say, "How many of you started with marijuana?" But again, this biased sample neglects the millions of people who have used the plant without negative consequences. The only way to establish rates of harm or benefit from the plant requires large samples that include a whole range of folks from all walks of life. Such studies show that 9 out of 10 users do not have problems in their use of marijuana (Weller & Halikas, 1980). The same steps for avoiding problems with individual cases apply here as well: Acknowledge the limitations of our samples, and we can have a rational discussion.

"IT'S NATURAL"

The occasional argument for marijuana's harmlessness rests on the idea that the plant is a simple part of nature that requires no processing or alteration for its use. Therefore, it must be innocuous. This approach shows poor reasoning, and anti-prohibitionists should turn to data documenting marijuana's safety (see Earleywine, 2002) rather than resort to such an argument. Poisonous plants are numerous and deadly despite their natural, unadulterated, unprocessed state. The Death Cap mushroom (*Amanita palloides*), hemlock, and mistletoe all serve as examples of toxic plants that should put this argument to rest (see Riordan, Rylance, & Berry, 2002). In addition, many synthesized medicines have few negative effects despite being unavailable in anyone's backyard.

ALL-OR-NOTHING THINKING

As I've mentioned elsewhere (Earleywine, 2002), decisions are easier when everything is black and white. Some things really are horrible, and others really are splendid, but most fall in-between. Fire warms some and burns others. Aspirin heals pain or damages livers. Marijuana really is a source of joy for some and trouble for others. Almost every potential marijuana policy has advantages and disadvantages. Where the debate runs into trouble is when a single pro or con is considered reason to dismiss an entire proposal. Few laws are perfect. That's why we can change them. The tacit assumption that any policy must bring us divine perfection or else it is an egregious mistake will drive us all crazy. The best way to dispute this error may require consistent emphasis that some areas are gray rather than all black or all white. We all must be particularly vigilant to catch this type of reasoning in our own arguments.

JUMPING TO CONCLUSIONS

A small but extremely vocal set of debaters often leaps from one simple idea to extreme assertions without any genuine support for their arguments. Both sides fall for this error. Prohibitionists often claim that after decriminalization, marijuana will be sold next to the candy bars at the corner store. Reformers sometimes claim that current laws will soon force a third of Americans into jail. Assertions like these make great sound bites for brief media reports (see Mirken, chap. 7, in this volume), but these leaps are no way to decide the fate of a nation. Disputing this error requires asking simple questions about how one step leads to the next. How would decriminalization lead to marijuana in a candy store? How would prohibition imprison a third of America? Walking through these steps will reveal the absurdity of these assertions, and help avoid these jumps to conclusions.

Several notorious "slippery slope" arguments fall into this category of jumping to conclusions. I once heard a former Drug Enforcement Administration agent assert that if cannabis becomes legal, the next generation will want Ecstasy to be legal, and soon we'll have a generation that wants heroin legal. He implied that all Americans would soon be opiate addicts. Note how this argument leaps from one topic to the next as if the jumps are simple, logical progressions, when in fact they aren't simple at all. Altering cannabis laws may make voters question policies about other drugs, and I'm happy to list this outcome among the pros and cons of the policy. Nevertheless, assuming that changing cannabis laws will lead to a nation of opiate addicts is simply too far a jump.

CONFUSING CORRELATES WITH CAUSES

A great many conclusions about drugs are actually erroneous misunderstandings based on simple correlations. It's perfectly human to think that if two things go together, one must have caused the other, but proof of causality requires more than that. One of my favorite examples concerns the correlation between the number of churches in a city and the city's crime rate. Churches and crime correlate highly across U.S. cities. The more churches, the more crime. But churches don't cause crime. Being a victim of a crime doesn't even inspire a lot of folks to open a church. In fact, a third variable accounts for this association: the size of the city. As cities get bigger, they have more crime and more churches. Neither causes the other.

Note how this ridiculous example of confusing correlation for cause seems obvious, but when the same correlation fits our stereotypes, it's harder to recognize the error. People who drink more alcohol also have more unsafe sex. Here's a correlation that seems to cry out for a causal explanation. Yes, it must be that these people get drunk and forget to use a condom. We all can conceive how alcohol can do that. Nevertheless, a close look at individual sexual events reveals that this intuitively appealing causal explanation isn't true. People who like to drink a lot happen to have unsafe sex, but they don't seem to get drunk and then do it. The unsafe sex doesn't seem to occur any more often after drinking than not after drinking. Clearly, some sort of personal preference for taking risks must account for the two behaviors, just as the size of the city accounts for the link between crime and churches (Leigh, 1993).

The confusion of correlation and cause gets particularly insidious with arguments for the so-called "gateway theory." The mistaken notion that marijuana creates an urge for hard drugs the way eating salt makes people thirsty has no support from research. Unfortunately, a study in the *Journal of the American Medical Association* (Lynskey et al., 2003) has been misinterpreted to suggest that marijuana causes hard drug use. A close look at the study tells a very different story.

Australian researchers found 311 pairs of same-sex twins in which one had tried marijuana before age 17 but the other had not. The fact that the researchers studied twins is a bit of a red herring. Whether the twins were identical or fraternal, the ones who tried marijuana early were more likely to try other drugs and develop drug problems later in life. If we believe that these data mean that marijuana causes hard drug use, we're sadly mistaken. (The authors of the research even say so, with considerable emphasis.) The analyses actually reveal that early tobacco and alcohol use were also significant predictors of drug problems. Undoubtedly, most people use these legal substances before marijuana. They're simply more available. But the idea

that these legal drugs are the gateway never appears in the study or in the subsequent hullabaloo in the media.

In addition, anyone who used a hard drug before using marijuana was dropped from the analyses. That's right. People who took downers or snorted cocaine before they tried marijuana, or did anything else counter to the gateway theory, were omitted from the study. Other research shows that as many as a third of people in treatment for drug problems used hard drugs before they used marijuana (Blaze-Temple & Lo, 1992). But in short, the deck was stacked so that the gateway theory couldn't be disproved.

Whatever led one twin to try marijuana early also contributed to the other results. The study does not reveal what would make teens try marijuana when their identical twins would not. Obviously, it's not genetics, given that they have the same genes. Nevertheless, anyone who knows identical twins will attest that they are not two copies of the same person. One source of the difference might be the same risk-taking personality discussed with alcohol and unsafe sex. Risk takers like to ride in the front of the roller-coaster, parachute from airplanes, and experiment with drugs. The trait is not completely heritable, and it may account for why one person might smoke marijuana before his or her identical twin. The fact that some people use marijuana early in life and later develop drug problems probably says more about people than it says about marijuana. We all know troubled souls who use a lot of different drugs, drive without seatbelts, have unsafe sex, and engage in a lot of other deviant behaviors. The marijuana does not cause their use of other drugs. They simply use marijuana first because it's the most available substance. In fact, in neighborhoods where crack is more available than marijuana, they use crack first. Surely no one thinks that crack is a gateway drug to marijuana.

The only way to combat this confusion is to require that any purported cause not only correlate with a purported outcome, but also precede it and separate completely from all other potential causes. A step in the right direction would include reanalyzing the Lynskey data while including the participants who used a hard drug before they used marijuana. I'm not going to hold my breath waiting for that to happen.

UNFALSIFIABLE ARGUMENTS

A great many assertions in drug policy debates can neither be proved nor disproved. "Legalization sends the wrong message to our youth" and "marijuana liberates the spirit" serve as prime examples. Both of these statements would require some extensive definitions before evidence could offer any support. What makes a message wrong? (And as I age, I can't help but wonder, who are "our youth"?) What does it mean to liberate the spirit? These assertions can't be disputed or verified because they rely on vague ideas. The

only way to proceed with any clarity is to define terms precisely. The only defense against assertions like these may be a simple question: "What does that mean?"

Unfortunately, asking folks to define their terms has become some kind of symbol of ignorance. In a recent debate I heard a prohibitionist assert that marijuana "corrupts the moral fiber of youth." When I asked what that meant, the speaker rolled his eyes in disdain, as if my question were proof that I had no moral fiber. I have seen anti-prohibitionists make comparable gaffs, particularly when they assert that they can't explain marijuana's bene-fits to anyone who hasn't tried it. The solution to this problem is also quite simple: Define terms. We can't understand each other's arguments unless we define our terms.

EMOTIONAL REASONING

The prime example of emotional reasoning is "I feel it, so it must be so." Marijuana policy stirs a lot of strong feelings, but the feelings are no indica-tor of right or wrong. Our feelings about this very fact can tell a great deal. Just the idea that our emotions aren't accurate indicators of the truth can make some people angry as hell. The feelings can serve as superb motivators to take action; the anger, frustration, sadness, or disgust anyone experiences in response to any situation can be a great indicator that changes are neces-sary. But the feelings alone are not a sufficient ground for national policy.

This error gets particularly troublesome in arguments that purport to be moral. Former drug czar William Bennett uses moral explanations in his work. "The simple fact is that drug use is wrong. And the moral argument, in the end, is the most compelling argument" (Bennett, 1991). The ironies of Mr. Bennett's own life aside, I assume he means that the use of intoxicating drugs is wrong. (I doubt he's upset about the morality of aspirin or coffee.) The reasons marijuana consumption is wrong often rely on incontestable ethical insight (Husak, 1998; see also Husak, chap. 10, in this volume). When asked what, exactly, is wrong with drug use, prohibitionists frequently fall into circular arguments that cannot be disproved. Drug use is wrong be-cause it is immoral; it is immoral because it is wrong. They sometimes turn to other unfalsifiable ideas as evidence. "Drug use is wrong because it drains the human spirit," or some such thing. These arguments often allude to the negative consequences of drugs, leading one to wonder if drug use would still be immoral if it did not lead to problems. When pressed, many state flatly that drug use feels wrong, so it must be wrong. This argument is emo-tional reasoning incarnate.

Reformers make comparable errors. I've said myself: "It is wrong for any-one to go to jail for owning a plant." But what, exactly, is wrong? I can spin an

argument about how punishments should be proportional to the severity of the crime (though not as well as Husak, chap. 10). But the point is that I can't simply argue that something is wrong because I feel it is wrong, or even because many people feel it is. And though it certainly feels wrong to me, the feeling is not enough. There most be a genuine argument, not just a feeling. (See Dorff, chap. 11, and Husak in this volume for better moral arguments.)

CONFUSING THE EFFECTS OF PROHIBITION WITH THE EFFECTS OF MARIJUANA

Many arguments about marijuana policy confuse the effects of marijuana with the effects of laws. Legal policies cause outcomes that are not the effect of any drug. For example, in a legislative hearing in a state that was considering altering its policies, a law enforcement officer mentioned the shooting deaths of four members of the Royal Canadian Mounted Police as they raided a marijuana field. The tacit assumption behind mention of these deaths was that marijuana caused this violence. Marijuana intoxication does not increase aggression (see Earleywine, 2002, for a review), and it's unclear if those who shot these officers had used the plant. In fact, prohibition created illegal marijuana fields. Just as alcohol prohibition created enormous jumps in murder rates in the United States in the 1920s and early 1930s, prohibition of other drugs has led to tremendous potential for profits and accompanying competition for market share that includes violence. A licit market, taxed and regulated, has the potential to minimize confrontations between police and criminals, as well as hostile turf wars between underground dealers.

The solution to this logical error requires some genuine reflection. We have to ask: Is this an effect of the drug or an effect of the laws?

CONFUSING METABOLITES WITH INTOXICATION

A single dose of marijuana does not create a 14-day high. I recently spoke before state representatives on a committee examining marijuana laws. One representative had learned that marijuana "stays in your system for weeks" and expressed concern that someone who used the drug over the weekend would create havoc on the road come Monday morning.

Marijuana metabolites remain detectable in the urine for extended periods. One of the best studies on the topic estimates that detectable levels of marijuana metabolites remain for two weeks after a single dose (Huestis & Cone, 1998). A few people apparently think that these results mean that

users remain high for 14 days after a single dose. Others have learned (correctly) that THC metabolites store in fat but think (incorrectly) that THC will somehow leak from fat cells at inopportune times and re-create intoxication. Uninformed citizens often assume that marijuana users will suddenly grow giddy or confused in the middle of landing an airplane or driving a forklift despite days of abstinence from the drug.

Nothing could be further from the truth. Most users report psychoactive effects that last a few hours. There seem to be no hangover effects the morning after use (Chait, Fischman, & Schuster, 1985), much less any psychoactive effect days later. The urine screens frequently employed to detect marijuana can only reveal if the person has used the drug recently; they say nothing about current intoxication. A person who uses marijuana a few hours before the sample is taken can test negative because metabolites have yet to form. In contrast, a person who hasn't used marijuana in days and is experiencing no subjective effects can test positive because of marijuana consumption the week before. (A better alternative would be to test for current impairment for any reason rather than the presence of drugs. See Smucker Barnwell & Earleywine, chap. 3, in this volume.) Prohibitionists, anti-prohibitionists, and established scientists have made this error. This notion that metabolites remain for weeks appears in prohibitionist arguments, but the arguments often imply that intoxication or some sort of impairment lasts for weeks as well.

Anti-prohibitionists can unknowingly refer to research that makes this same error. For example, epidemiological studies suggest that marijuana use has no effect on traffic accidents (Bates & Blakely, 1999; Williams, Peat, & Crouch, 1985), but these data rely on urine screens after accidents. The urine screens could have been negative even if the person was high at the time of the accident (see Liguori, chap. 4, in this volume).

THE MENTAL FILTER

Strong attitudes can alter our perceptions of reality to the extent where we can't absorb information that counters the attitude. We simply see the world differently depending on what we think. Years ago I asked a large group of folks to define words like "shot," "spirits," and "toast." Heavy drinkers explained that a shot is an ounce and a half of booze, spirits are liquor, and a toast is the clinking of glasses before drinking. Light drinkers said that a shot is an injection of medicine from the doctor, spirits are ghosts, and toast is browned bread (Earleywine, 1994). People defined the words in ways that were consistent with their experience.

Prohibitionists and anti-prohibitionists can suffer from comparable filters. Compelling data appear to have little effect on prohibitionist attitudes about medical marijuana, for example. The last 3 drug czars have denied any

medical use for marijuana, despite contrary conclusions by prestigious others, including the Institute of Medicine (1999). Reformers often minimize data on the potential for problems (see Roffman & Nicoll, chap. 8, in this volume). In their zeal to end punishment, they seem to ignore the few who use the plant problematically. It's as if the data don't pass through their mental filter.

The cure for this problem may require more effort than the others. As we examine new data and new ideas, we have to ask ourselves to pay particular attention to those that contradict our own ideas. We have to be as critical of research that supports our ideas as we are of research that opposes it.

KITCHEN SINKING

Many policy debates fly past each other. Folks on one side mention a specific point. Folks on the other side fail to address the point, and instead go into great detail about some other issue. Marital therapists call this "kitchen sinking"; they often see distressed couples yell back and forth at each other without sticking to a single issue, throwing everything, including the kitchen sink, at each other.

"You left your socks on the floor again!"

"Well, your mother can't stop criticizing me."

Note how these two sentences have nothing to do with each other. Policy debates often fall into the same trap.

"More than 700,000 Americans were arrested for marijuana last year!"

"Marijuana smokers report more coughs and bronchitis!"

Note how the second sentence is unrelated to the first. This is not a debate, but a collection of facts from each side. Rather than focus on a single topic, such as arrests or respiratory problems, folks bring out whatever comes to mind and spew it. Part of the problem arises from the needs of the news media. Debaters often have only a few seconds to speak. They have to get their most powerful argument out in a hurry. They can't follow a single train of thought in detail because they have to finish before the next commercial.

The cure for this problem is simple: Argue one point at a time. Although policy issues form a tangled web of implications and outcomes, we can do a much better job and come to rational conclusions by focusing on one issue before we move to the next.

THE CURE

The way to avoid these errors and the depression associated with them requires a few simple steps. First and foremost, we have to identify them in

Table 1.1. The Dirty Dozen: Questions to Ask Before
Debating Marijuana Policy

1. Is this an individual case?
2. Is this a biased sample?
3. Am I arguing that cannabis is harmless because it is natural?
4. Am I dichotomously dividing issues into all or nothing?
5. Am I jumping to conclusions?
6. Am I confusing correlates with causes?
7. Could any data falsify this argument?
8. Am I reasoning from emotion?
9. Is this an effect of prohibition or an effect of marijuana?
10. Am I confusing metabolites with intoxication?
11. Am I filtering out information that's counter to my attitudes?
12. Am I tossing in irrelevant arguments and the kitchen sink?

our own arguments and those of others. Once we have a taxonomy of errors like this one, it's easier to recognize them. Few things are more frustrating than knowing an argument is wrong but being unable to identify what, exactly, is wrong with it. Naming these errors may help.

Once we understand such expressions as "all-or-nothing thinking" and "kitchen sinking," we can identify the errors more readily. Another approach requires asking ourselves questions as we debate. I've summarized the ones mentioned here into a list known affectionately as the dirty dozen (see Table 1.1). If each debate about cannabis policy could begin with these questions, our thinking could grow more rational, and our policies could, too.

REFERENCES

Bates, M. N., & Blakely, T. A. (1999). Role of cannabis in motor vehicle crashes. *Epidemiological Reviews, 21,* 222–232.

Beck, A. T. (1963). Thinking and depression: Idiosyncratic content and cognitive distortions. *Archives of General Psychiatry, 9,* 324–333.

Bennett, W. (1991). The plea to legalize drugs is a siren call to surrender. In M. Lyman & G. Potter (Eds.) *Drugs in society* (p. 339). Cincinnati: Anderson.

Blaze-Temple, D., & Lo, S. K. (1992). Stages of drug use: A community survey of Perth teenagers. *British Journal of Addiction, 87,* 215–225.

Chait, L. D., Fischman, M. W., & Schuster, C. R. (1985) Hangover effects the morning after marijuana smoking. *Drug and Alcohol Dependence, 15,* 229–238.

Earleywine, M. (1994). Cognitive bias covaries with alcohol consumption. *Addictive Behaviors, 19,* 539–544.

Earleywine, M. (2002). *Understanding marijuana.* New York: Oxford University Press.

Huestis, M. A., & Cone, E. J. (1998). Urinary excretion half-life of 11-Nor-9-carboxy-DELTA-9-tetrahydrocannabinol in Humans. *Proceedings of the Fifth International Congress of Therapeutic Drug Monitoring and Clinical Toxicology, 20,* 570–576.

Hume, D. (1978). *A treatise on human nature.* New York: Oxford University Press. (Original work published 1739)

Husak, D. (1998). Two rationales for drug policy: How they shape the content of reform. In J. M. Fish (Ed.), *How to legalize drugs* (pp. 29–60). Northvale, NJ: Jason Aronson.

Institute of Medicine. (1999). *Marijuana and medicine: Assessing the science base.* Washington, DC: National Academy.

Leigh, B. C. (1993). Alcohol consumption and sexual activity as reported with a diary technique. *Journal of Abnormal Psychology, 102,* 490–493.

Lynskey, M., Heath, A., Bucholz, K., Slutske, W., Madden, P., Nelson, E., et al. (2003). Escalation of drug use in early-onset cannabis users vs. co-twin controls. *Journal of the American Medical Association, 289,* 427–433.

Riordan, M., Rylance, G., & Berry, K. (2002). Poisoning in children 4: Household products, plants, and mushrooms. *Archives of Disease in Childhood, 87,* 403–406.

Weller, R. A., & Halikas, J. A. (1980). Objective criteria for the diagnosis of marijuana abuse. *Journal of Nervous and Mental Disease, 176,* 719–725.

Williams, A. F., Peat, M. A., & Crouch, D. J. (1985). Drugs in fatally injured young male drivers. *Public Health Reports, 100,* 19–25.

SECTION I

Costs of Use and Control

Marijuana policies have the potential to create benefits, but always at some sort of cost. Evaluating new ideas requires an assessment of current ones. Daniel Egan and Jeffrey Miron have examined modern estimates of the costs of enforcing current prohibitions. Although few policies can be reduced to dollars and cents, an economic approach to the expense of current laws can help us put alternative plans in perspective. These authors use conservative estimates of the price of law enforcement and find that removing penalties for marijuana sales and use would save billions of dollars' worth of time and effort for police officers, judges, attorneys, and corrections centers nationwide. They add that a taxed and regulated market (comparable to alcohol's or tobacco's) would have its own expenses but potentially could generate billions of tax dollars. The effect on use and associated problems is difficult to guess, but the severity of these is addressed later in this book, along with issues that are not purely economic.

Many citizens are concerned about testing for marijuana use under the current system of marijuana laws. Balancing privacy and the right to know who has used irresponsibly can prove confusing and difficult. Any discussion of relaxing prohibitions invariably leads to concern about the use of marijuana in dangerous settings, including some work conditions and on the road. Employers understandably want the most efficient, healthy, productive workforce that they can afford. But employees frequently assert that their use of marijuana during their free time need not alter the quality or quantity of their work. An outspoken few even suggest that their labor

improves with occasional use outside the workplace, claiming that the relaxation and change of perspective can bring novel insights to difficult problems and renewed patience for difficult tasks.

Medical users typically express considerable concern and assert that relief from symptoms enhances productivity while the tolerance they develop to intoxication eliminates worries about impairment. In chapter 3, Sara Smucker Barnwell and Mitch Earleywine review data on workplace drug testing and find its expense and effect on morale make it less appealing than assessments based on job performance. Productivity can suffer for numerous reasons. Drug testing may lull employers into a false sense of security about their ability to identify employees whose work might suffer. In contrast, assessments based on performance are much more likely to identify the true problem: poor work.

The data on marijuana intoxication and driving are a bit of a mess, as Liguori details in chapter 4. Research seems quite clear, however, that when combined with alcohol, marijuana does alter driving in potentially dangerous ways. A clear separation between acute intoxication and previous use detected in tests of blood and urine is also essential. The current literature contains enough weaknesses to support a call for continued research. Liguori maps out the appropriate steps to make subsequent studies and experiments as informative as possible.

A close look at these economic issues related to the costs of prohibition, drug testing, and driving can improve discussions of alternative policies.

2 The Budgetary Implications of Marijuana Prohibition

Daniel Egan
Jeffrey A. Miron

Government prohibition of marijuana is the subject of ongoing debate. One issue in this debate is the effect of marijuana prohibition on government budgets. Prohibition entails direct enforcement costs and prevents taxation of marijuana production and sale. This chapter examines the budgetary implications of legalizing marijuana—taxing and regulating it like other goods—in all fifty states and at the federal level. We estimate that legalizing marijuana would save almost $8 billion per year in prohibition enforcement costs. We estimate that marijuana legalization would yield tax revenue of more than $2 billion annually if marijuana were taxed at the general merchandise rate and more than $6 billion annually if it were taxed at rates comparable to those on alcohol and tobacco. Whether marijuana legalization is a desirable policy depends on many factors other than the budgetary effects discussed here. But these impacts should be included in a rational debate about marijuana policy.

INTRODUCTION

Advocates of prohibition argue that it reduces marijuana trafficking and use, thereby discouraging crime, improving productivity, and enhancing public health. Critics counter that prohibition has only modest effects on trafficking and use and causes many problems typically attributed to marijuana itself.

Both sides agree, however, that the cost of prohibition enforcement is quite large. And anti-prohibitionists note that prohibition prevents taxation of marijuana production and sale. If marijuana were legal, they argue, enforcement costs would be negligible, and governments could have a rich new source of revenue by levying taxes on the production and sale of marijuana.

This chapter is devoted to estimating these savings and revenue gains. The policy change considered in this chapter, marijuana legalization, is more substantial than marijuana decriminalization, which means repealing criminal penalties against possession but retaining them against trafficking. The budgetary implications of legalization exceed those of decriminalization for three reasons.[1] First, legalization eliminates arrests for trafficking in addition to eliminating arrests for possession. Second, legalization saves prosecutorial, judicial, and incarceration expenses; these savings are minimal in the case of decriminalization. Third, legalization allows taxation of marijuana production and sale.

The specific figures we arrive at in this chapter in figuring the budgetary effects of legalization rely on a range of assumptions, but these probably bias the estimated expenditure reductions and tax revenues downward.

The chapter proceeds as follows. Section II estimates state and local expenditure on marijuana prohibition. Section III estimates federal expenditure on marijuana prohibition. Section IV estimates the tax revenue that would accrue from legalized marijuana. Section V discusses caveats and implications.

STATE AND LOCAL EXPENDITURE FOR DRUG PROHIBITION ENFORCEMENT

The savings in state and local government expenditure that would result from marijuana legalization consists of three main components: the reduction in police resources from elimination of marijuana arrests; the reduction in prosecutorial and judicial resources from elimination of marijuana prosecutions; and the reduction in correctional resources from elimination of marijuana incarcerations.[2] There are other possible savings in government expenditure from legalization, but these are minor or are difficult to estimate with existing data.[3] The omission of these items biases the estimated savings downward.

To estimate the state savings in criminal justice resources, our methodology uses the following procedure. It estimates the percentage of arrests in a state for marijuana violations and multiplies this by the budget for police. It estimates the percentage of prosecutions in a state for marijuana violations and multiplies this by the budget for prosecutors and judges. It estimates the percentage of incarcerations in a state for marijuana violations

and multiplies this by the budget for prisons. It then adds these components to estimate the overall reduction in government expenditure. Under plausible assumptions, this procedure yields a reasonable estimate of the cost savings from marijuana legalization.[4]

The Police Budget Ascribable to Marijuana Prohibition

The first cost of marijuana prohibition we consider is the portion of state police budgets devoted to marijuana arrests.

Table 2.1 calculates the fraction of arrests in each state as a result of the marijuana prohibition. Column 1 gives the total number of arrests for the year 2000.[5] Column 2 gives the number of arrests for marijuana possession violations. Column 3 gives the number of arrests for marijuana sale/manufacturing violations. Columns 4 and 5 give the ratio of column 2 to column 1 and column 3 to column 1, respectively; these are the percentages of arrests for possession and sale/manufacture of marijuana, respectively.

The information in columns 4 and 5 is what is required in the subsequent calculations, subject to one modification. Some arrests for marijuana violations, especially those for possession, occur because the person arrested is under suspicion for a non–drug-related crime but possesses marijuana that is discovered by police during a routine search. This means an arrest for marijuana possession is recorded, along with, or instead of, an arrest on the other charge. If marijuana possession were not a criminal offense, the suspects in such cases would still be arrested on the charge that led to the search, and police resources would be used to approximately the same extent as when marijuana possession is criminal.[6]

In determining which arrests represent a cost of marijuana prohibition, therefore, it is appropriate to count only those that are "stand-alone," meaning those in which a marijuana violation rather than some other charge is the reason for the arrest. This issue arises mainly for possession rather than for trafficking. There are few hard data on the fraction of "stand-alone" possession arrests, but the information in Miron (2002) and Reuter, Hirschfield, and Davies (2001) suggests it is between 33% and 85%.[7] To err on the conservative side, we assume that 50% of possession arrests are solely a result of marijuana possession rather than being incidental to some other crime. Thus, the resources used in making these arrests would be available for other purposes if marijuana possession were legal. Column 6 of Table 2.1 therefore indicates the fraction of possession arrests attributable to marijuana prohibition, taking this adjustment into account.[8]

The first portion of Table 2.2 uses this information to calculate the police budget ascribable to marijuana prohibition in each state. Column 1 gives the total expenditure in 2000 by police for each state. Column 2 gives the

Table 2.1. Percentage of Arrests Ascribable to Marijuana Prohibition

	Total Arrests	MJ Possession	MJ Sale/Man.	Poss %	S/M %	Poss % /2
	1	2	3	4	5	6
Alabama	215,587	11,501	258	0.053	0.001	0.027
Alaska	40,181	1,239	200	0.031	0.005	0.015
Arizona	304,142	16,288	1,233	0.054	0.004	0.027
Arkansas	218,521	6,846	928	0.031	0.004	0.016
California	1,428,248	50,149	12,338	0.035	0.009	0.018
Colorado	282,787	12,067	604	0.043	0.002	0.021
Connecticut	146,992	6,751	773	0.046	0.005	0.023
Delaware	41,515	2,151	131	0.052	0.003	0.026
D.C.*	4,009	32	0	0.008	0.000	0.004
Florida*	0	0	0	0.043	.006	0.022
Georgia	429,674	24,321	4,093	0.057	0.010	0.028
Hawaii	64,463	1,110	167	0.017	0.003	0.009
Idaho	76,032	2,949	219	0.039	0.003	0.019
Illinois*	319,920	0	0	0.043	0.006	0.000
Indiana	270,022	14,484	1,806	0.054	0.007	0.027
Iowa	113,394	6,054	551	0.053	0.005	0.027
Kansas	78,285	3,277	594	0.042	0.008	0.021
Kentucky*	160,899	10,669	1,188	0.066	0.007	0.033
Louisiana	297,098	14,941	2,526	0.050	0.009	0.025
Maine	57,203	3,294	554	0.058	0.010	0.029
Maryland	318,056	17,113	2,711	0.054	0.009	0.027
Massachusetts	160,342	8,975	1,365	0.056	0.009	0.028
Michigan	413,174	14,629	2,050	0.035	0.005	0.018
Minnesota	269,010	9,325	6,782	0.035	0.025	0.017
Mississippi	202,007	9,925	1,054	0.049	0.005	0.025
Missouri	322,775	13,202	1,338	0.041	0.004	0.020
Montana	30,396	384	35	0.013	0.001	0.006
Nebraska	97,324	6,787	326	0.070	0.003	0.035
Nevada	148,656	3,828	933	0.026	0.006	0.013
New Hampshire	50,830	3,706	550	0.073	0.011	0.036
New Jersey	375,049	20,285	3,058	0.054	0.008	0.027
New Mexico	112,829	2,966	325	0.026	0.003	0.013
New York	1,295,374	101,739	11,309	0.079	0.009	0.039
North Carolina	523,920	21,179	2,539	0.040	0.005	0.020
North Dakota	27,846	896	137	0.032	0.005	0.016
Ohio	533,364	25,420	1,863	0.048	0.003	0.024
Oklahoma	166,004	11,198	1,302	0.067	0.008	0.034
Oregon	157,748	6,336	283	0.040	0.002	0.020
Pennsylvania	493,339	16,471	5,057	0.033	0.010	0.017
Rhode Island	35,733	2,200	293	0.062	0.008	0.031
South Carolina	216,451	14,348	2,370	0.066	0.011	0.033
South Dakota	41,615	2,449	153	0.059	0.004	0.029
Tennessee	232,486	12,869	2,586	0.055	0.011	0.028
Texas	1,074,909	55,509	1,926	0.052	0.002	0.026

Table 2.1. (continued)

	Total Arrests	MJ Possession	MJ Sale/Man.	Poss %	S/M %	Poss % /2
	1	2	3	4	5	6
Utah	125,553	4,192	311	0.033	0.002	0.017
Vermont	17,565	632	65	0.036	0.004	0.018
Virginia	303,203	13,140	1,443	0.043	0.005	0.022
Washington	298,474	13,146	1,329	0.044	0.004	0.022
West Virginia	51,452	2,618	248	0.051	0.005	0.025
Wisconsin	322,877	45	16	0.000	0.000	0.000
Wyoming	34,243	1,633	164	0.048	0.005	0.024

*Quoting http://fisher.lib.virginia.edu/collections/stats/crime/2000cb.pdf: "(3) No arrest data were provided for Washington, DC, and Florida. Limited arrest data were available for Illinois and Kentucky."

Source: FBI Uniform Crime Reports accessed at http://fisher.lib.virginia.edu/collections/stats/crime/

product of column 1 with the sum of columns 5 and 6 from Table 2.1. This is the amount spent on arrests for marijuana violations. For 2000, the amount was $1.71 billion.

The Judicial and Legal Budget Ascribable to Marijuana Prohibition

The second main cost of marijuana prohibition is the portion of the prosecutorial and judicial budget devoted to marijuana prosecutions. A reasonable indicator of this percentage is the fraction of felony convictions in state courts for marijuana offenses. Data on this percentage are not available on a state-by-state basis, so this chapter uses the national percentage. Data on the percentage of possession convictions attributable to marijuana are also not available, so this chapter assumes it equals the percentage for trafficking convictions.

In 2000, the percent of felony convictions in state courts for any type of trafficking violation was 22%.[9] Of this total, 2.7% was for trafficking marijuana, 5.9% was for other drugs, and 13.4% was for unspecified substances. This chapter assumes that the fraction of marijuana convictions in the unspecified category equals the fraction for those in which a specific drug is given, or 31.4% [=2.7%/(2.7%+5.9%)]. We also assume that the percentage of possession convictions related to marijuana equals this same fraction. These assumptions jointly imply that the percentage of felony convictions ascribable to marijuana violations equals the fraction of felony convictions ascribable to

Table 2.2. Expenditures Attributable to Marijuana Prohibition ($ in millions)

State	Police Budget		Judicial Budget		Corrections Budget		Total	
	Total	MJ Prohib.	Total	MJ Prohib.	Total	MJ Prohib.	Total	MJ Prohib.
Alabama	656	18.28	262	28.56	404	4.04	1,322	51
Alaska	177	3.61	130	14.17	175	1.75	482	20
Arizona	1,096	33.79	611	66.60	955	9.55	2,662	110
Arkansas	351	6.99	156	17.00	328	3.28	835	27
California	8,703	227.97	6,255	681.80	7,170	71.70	22,128	981
Colorado	830	19.48	329	35.86	820	8.20	1,979	64
Connecticut	682	19.25	430	46.87	554	5.54	1,666	72
Delaware	166	4.82	90	9.81	228	2.28	484	17
Florida	3,738	103.19	1,396	152.16	3,272	32.72	8,406	288
Georgia	1,279	48.38	525	57.23	1,375	13.75	3,179	119
Hawaii	222	2.49	180	19.62	153	1.53	555	24
Idaho	207	4.61	102	11.12	191	1.91	500	18
Illinois	3,053	84.28	961	104.75	1,763	17.63	5,777	207
Indiana	843	28.25	325	35.43	727	7.27	1,895	71
Iowa	426	13.44	253	27.58	298	2.98	977	44
Kansas	430	12.26	206	22.45	349	3.49	985	38
Kentucky	488	19.78	290	31.61	610	6.10	1,388	57
Louisiana	829	27.89	359	39.13	780	7.80	1,968	75
Maine	164	6.31	69	7.52	123	1.23	356	15
Maryland	1,120	39.68	489	53.30	1,104	11.04	2,713	104
Massachusetts	1,479	53.98	628	68.45	795	7.95	2,902	130
Michigan	1,792	40.62	905	98.65	1,853	18.53	4,550	158
Minnesota	874	37.18	442	48.18	591	5.91	1,907	91
Mississippi	404	12.03	154	16.79	292	2.92	850	32
Missouri	886	21.79	359	39.13	627	6.27	1,872	67
Montana	136	1.02	66	7.19	125	1.25	327	9
Nebraska	235	8.98	96	10.46	231	2.31	562	22
Nevada	539	10.32	248	27.03	471	4.71	1,258	42
New Hampshire	187	8.84	92	10.03	115	1.15	394	20
New Jersey	2,231	78.52	948	103.33	1,480	14.80	4,659	197
New Mexico	382	6.12	167	18.20	315	3.15	864	27
New York	5,717	274.42	2,262	246.56	4,392	43.92	12,371	565
North Carolina	1,318	33.03	470	51.23	1,159	11.59	2,947	96
North Dakota	68	1.43	55	6.00	40	0.40	163	8
Ohio	2,124	58.03	1,158	126.22	1,937	19.37	5,219	204
Oklahoma	518	21.53	193	21.04	511	5.11	1,222	48
Oregon	696	15.23	356	38.80	747	7.47	1,799	62
Pennsylvania	2,220	59.82	1,067	116.30	2,221	22.21	5,508	198
Rhode Island	211	8.23	105	11.45	139	1.39	455	21
South Carolina	653	28.79	179	19.51	559	5.59	1,391	54
South Dakota	88	2.91	40	4.36	81	0.81	209	8
Tennessee	940	36.47	399	43.49	604	6.04	1,943	86
Texas	3,204	88.47	1,355	147.70	3,755	37.55	8,314	274

Table 2.2. (continued)

State	Police Budget		Judicial Budget		Corrections Budget		Total	
	Total	MJ Prohib.	Total	MJ Prohib.	Total	MJ Prohib.	Total	MJ Prohib.
Utah	381	7.30	202	22.02	351	3.51	934	33
Vermont	78	1.69	39	4.25	66	0.66	183	7
Virginia	1,176	31.08	513	55.92	1,246	12.46	2,935	99
Washington	1,007	26.66	470	51.23	1,053	10.53	2,530	88
West Virginia	171	5.17	108	11.77	184	1.84	463	19
Wisconsin	1,124	0.13	440	47.96	1,030	10.30	2,594	58
Wyoming	99	2.83	50	5.45	98	0.98	247	9
	56,398	1,707.41	26,984	2941.26	48,447	484.47	131,829	5,133

Sources:
Arrest Data: http://fisher.lib.virginia.edu/collections/stats/crime/
Budget Data: http://www.census.gov/govs/www/state00.html
Judicial Percent: *Pastore and Maguire* (2003), Table 5.42, p. 444
Incarceration Percent: *Pastore and Maguire* (2003), Table 6.30, p. 499

any drug offense (34.6%) multiplied by the percentage of trafficking violations ascribable to marijuana (31.4%). This yields 10.9% (=34.6%×31.4%).[10]

The second portion of Table 2.2 uses this information to calculate the
judicial and legal budget devoted to marijuana prohibition. Column 3 gives
the judicial and legal budget, by state. Column 4 gives the product of column 3 and 10.9%, the percentage of felony convictions resulting from
marijuana violations. This is the judicial and legal budget for marijuana
prosecutions. For 2000, the amount was $2.94 billion.

The Corrections Budget Ascribable to Marijuana Prohibition

The third main cost of marijuana prohibition is the portion of the corrections budget devoted to incarcerating marijuana prisoners. A reasonable indicator of this portion is the fraction of prisoners incarcerated for marijuana
offenses.

As with the percentage of prosecutions ascribable to marijuana, state-
by-state information on the percentage of prisoners incarcerated for marijuana offenses is not available. Appropriate data do exist for a few states,
however, and this percentage is likely to be similar across states. Our procedure is to compute a population-weighted average based on the few states
for which data exist, then to impose this percentage on all states. This percentage is 1%, as documented in Appendix A.

The third portion of Table 2.2 calculates the corrections budget ascribable to marijuana prohibition.[11] Column 5 gives the overall corrections budget, by state. Column 6 gives the product of column 5 and 1%, the estimated fraction of prisoners incarcerated on marijuana charges. This is the corrections budget devoted to marijuana prisoners. For 2000, the amount was $484 million.

Overall State and Local Expenditure for Enforcement of Marijuana Prohibition

As shown at the bottom of Table 2.2, total state and local government expenditure for enforcement of marijuana prohibition was $5.1 billion for 2000. This is an overstatement of the savings in government expenditure that would result from legalization, however, for two reasons. First, under prohibition the police sometimes seize assets from those arrested for marijuana violations (financial accounts, cars, boats, land, houses, and the like), with the proceeds used to fund police and prosecutors.[12] Second, under prohibition some marijuana offenders pay fines, which partially offsets the expenditure required to arrest, convict, and incarcerate these offenders. The calculations in Appendix B, however, show that this offsetting revenue has been at most $100 million per year in recent years at the state and local level. This implies a net savings of criminal justice resources from marijuana legalization of $5 billion in 2000. Adjusting for inflation implies savings of $5.3 billion in 2003.[13,14,15]

FEDERAL EXPENDITURE FOR MARIJUANA PROHIBITION ENFORCEMENT

This section estimates federal expenditure for marijuana prohibition enforcement. There are no data available on expenditure for marijuana interdiction per se; existing data report expenditure on interdiction of all drugs, without separately identifying expenditure aimed at marijuana. It is nevertheless possible to estimate the portion devoted to marijuana prohibition using the following procedure:

1. Estimate federal expenditure for all drug interdiction;
2. Estimate the fraction of this expenditure related to marijuana interdiction based on the fraction of federal prosecutions for marijuana;
3. Multiply the first estimate by the second estimate.

This provides a reasonable estimate of federal expenditure for marijuana interdiction so long as this expenditure is roughly proportional to the variable

Table 2.3. Federal Expenditure on Marijuana Prohibition, 2002

1. Prohibition Enforcement, All Drugs		$13.6 billion
2. Marijuana Use Rate, Past Year, 2002	11.0%	
3. Any Illicit Drug Use Rate, Past Year, 2002	14.9%	
4. Ratio	74%	
5. Ratio × Line 1		$10.0 billion
6. Percent of All Drug Arrests for MJ, 2001	46.0%	
7. Line 6 × Line 1		$6.3 billion
8. Percent of All Trafficking Arrests for MJ, 2001	26%	
9. Line 8 × Line 1		$3.6 billion
10. Percent of DEA Drug Arrests for MJ, 2002	18.6%	
11. Line 10 × Line 1		$2.5 billion
12. Percent of DEA Drug Convictions for MJ, 2002	19.9%	
13. Line 12 × Line 1		$2.7 billion

Sources:
Line 1: Miron 2003b, p. 10.
Lines 2–3: SAMHSA, Office of Applied Statistics, National Survey on Drug Use and Health, 2002,
http://www.samhsa.gov/oas/nhsda/2k2nsduh/Results/apph.htm#tabh.2
Lines 6 and 8: Sourcebook of Criminal Justice Statistics Online,
http://www.albany.edu/sourcebook/1995/pdf/t429.pdf/
Line 10: Sourcebook of Criminal Justice Statistics Online,
http://www.albany.edu/sourcebook/1995/pdf/t440.pdf/
Line 12: Sourcebook of Criminal Justice Statistics Online,
http://www.albany.edu/sourcebook/1995/pdf/t538.pdf

being used to determine the fraction of total interdiction devoted to marijuana.[16]

Table 2.3 displays federal expenditure for drug interdiction. This was $13.6 billion in 2002 (Miron 2003b), and it is the figure that applies for all drugs.[17,18,19] To determine expenditure for marijuana interdiction, it is necessary to adjust for the fraction of federal expenditure devoted to marijuana as opposed to other drugs.

Table 2.3 next shows possible indicators of the relative magnitude of marijuana interdiction as compared to other-drug interdiction. These indicators include use rates, arrest rates, and felony convictions for marijuana versus other drugs. For the purposes here, the most appropriate indicator is the percentage of DEA arrests or convictions for marijuana as opposed to other drugs.[20]

The data therefore indicate that $2.6 billion is a reasonable estimate of the federal government expenditure to enforce marijuana prohibition in 2002.

As with state and local revenue, this figure must be adjusted downward by the revenue from seizures and fines. Appendix B indicates that this amount has been, at most, $214.2 million in recent years, implying a net savings of about $2.39 million. Adjusting for inflation implies federal expenditure for enforcement of marijuana prohibition of $2.4 billion in 2003.[21]

THE TAX REVENUE FROM
LEGALIZED MARIJUANA

To estimate tax revenue from the legal production and sale of marijuana, our method uses the following procedure. First, it estimates current expenditure on marijuana at the national level. Second, it estimates the expenditure likely to occur under legalization. Third, it estimates the tax revenue that would result from this expenditure based on assumptions about the kinds of taxes that would apply to legalized marijuana. Fourth, it provides illustrative calculations of the portion of the revenue that would accrue to each state.

Expenditure on Marijuana Under Current Prohibition

The first step in determining the tax revenue under legalization is to estimate current expenditure on marijuana for personal use. The Office of National Drug Control Policy ([ONDCP], 2001b, Table 1, p. 3) estimates that in 2000, U.S. residents spent $10.5 billion on marijuana. This estimate relies on a range of assumptions about the marijuana market, and modification of these assumptions might produce a higher or lower estimate. There is no obvious reason, however, why alternative assumptions would imply a dramatically different estimate of current expenditure on marijuana. This chapter therefore uses the $10.5 billion figure as the starting point for the revenue estimates presented here.

Expenditure on Marijuana Under Legalization

The second step in estimating the tax revenue that would occur under legalization is to determine how expenditure on marijuana would change as the result of legalization. A simple framework in which to consider various assumptions is the standard supply-and-demand model. To use this model to assess legalization's effect on marijuana expenditure, it is necessary to state what effect legalization would have on the demand and supply curves for marijuana.

This chapter assumes there would be no change in the demand for marijuana.[22] This assumption likely errs in the direction of understating the tax revenue from legalized marijuana, since the penalties for possession probably deter some persons from consuming. But any increase in demand from legalization would plausibly come from casual users, whose marijuana use would likely be modest. Any increase in use might also come from decreased

consumption of alcohol, tobacco, or other goods, so increased tax revenue from legal marijuana would be partially offset by decreased tax revenue from other goods. And there might be a forbidden fruit effect from prohibition that would offset any decrease in demand created by penalties for possession. Thus, the assumption of no change in demand is plausible, and it likely biases the estimated tax revenue downward.

Under the assumption that demand will not shift because of legalization, any change in the quantity and price would result from changes in supply conditions. There are two main effects that would operate (Miron, 2003c). On the one hand, marijuana suppliers in a legal market would not incur the costs imposed by prohibition, such as the threat of arrest, incarceration, fines, asset seizure, and the like. This means, other things equal, that costs and therefore prices would be lower under legalization. On the other hand, marijuana suppliers in a legal market would bear the costs of tax and regulatory policies that apply to legal goods but that black market suppliers normally avoid.[23] This implies an offset to the cost reductions resulting from legalization. Further, changes in competition and advertising under legalization can potentially yield higher prices than under prohibition.

It is thus an empirical question as to how prices under legalization would compare to prices under current prohibition. The best evidence available on this question comes from comparisons of marijuana prices in the United States and the Netherlands. Although marijuana is still technically illegal in the Netherlands, the degree of enforcement is substantially below that in the United States, and the sale of marijuana in coffee shops is officially tolerated. The regime thus approximates de facto legalization. Existing data suggest that retail prices in the Netherlands are roughly 50% to 100% of U.S. prices.[24,25]

The effect of any price decline that occurs as a result of legalization depends on the elasticity of demand for marijuana. Evidence on this elasticity is limited because appropriate data on marijuana price and consumption are not readily available. Existing estimates, however, suggest an elasticity of at least –0.5 and plausibly more than –1.0 (Nisbet & Vakil, 1972).[26,27]

If the price decline under legalization is minimal, then expenditure will not change regardless of the demand elasticity. If the price decline is noticeable, but the demand elasticity is greater than or equal to 1.0 in absolute value, then expenditure will remain constant or increase. If the price decline is noticeable and the demand elasticity is less than 1.0, then expenditure will decline. Since the decline in price is unlikely to exceed 50%, and the demand elasticity is likely to be at least –0.5, the plausible decline in expenditure is approximately 25%. Given the estimate of $10.5 billion in expenditure on marijuana under current prohibition, this implies expenditure under legalization of about $7.9 billion.[28]

Tax Revenue From Legalized Marijuana

To estimate the tax revenue that would result from marijuana legalization, it is necessary to assume a particular tax rate. We consider two assumptions that plausibly bracket the range of reasonable possibilities.

The first assumption is that tax policy would treat legalized marijuana identically to most other goods. In that case, tax revenue as a fraction of expenditure would be approximately 30%, implying tax revenue from legalized marijuana of $2.4 billion.[29] The amount of revenue would be lower if substantial home production occurred under legalization.[30] The evidence suggests, however, that the magnitude of such production would be minimal. Alcohol production switched mostly from the black market to the licit market after repeal of Prohibition in 1933.

The second assumption is that tax policy would treat legalized marijuana as it does alcohol or tobacco, imposing a "sin tax" in excess of any tax applicable to other goods.[31] Imposing a high sin tax can force a market underground, thereby reducing rather than increasing tax revenue. Existing evidence, however, suggests that relatively high rates of sin taxation are possible without generating a black market. For example, cigarette taxes in many European countries account for 75% to 85% of the price (U.S. Department of Health and Human Services [DHHS], 2000).

One benchmark, therefore, is to assume that an excise tax on legalized marijuana would double the price. If general taxation were to account for 30% of the price, this additional tax would then make tax revenue account for 80% of the price. This doubling of the price, given an elasticity of -0.5, would cause roughly a 50% increase in expenditure, implying total expenditure on marijuana of $11.85 billion (=$7.9×1.5). Tax revenue would equal 80% of this total, or $9.5 billion. This includes any standard taxation that would be applied to marijuana income as well as the sin tax on marijuana sales.

The $9.5 billion figure is not necessarily attainable given the characteristics of marijuana production, however. Small-scale, efficient production is possible and occurs widely now, so the imposition of a substantial tax wedge might encourage a substantial fraction of the market to remain underground. The assumption of a constant demand elasticity in response to a price change of this magnitude is also debatable; more plausibly, the elasticity would increase as the price rose, implying a larger decline in consumption and thus less revenue from excise taxation. The $9.5 billion figure should therefore be considered an upper bound.

These calculations nevertheless indicate the potential for substantial revenue from marijuana taxation. A more modest excise tax, such as one that raises the price 50%, would produce revenue on legalized marijuana of $6.2 billion per year.

Distribution of the Marijuana Tax Revenue

The estimates of tax revenue discussed so far indicate the total amount that could be collected by all levels of government. In practice, this total would be divided between state and federal governments. It is therefore useful to estimate how much revenue would accrue to each state, and to state governments versus the federal government, under plausible assumptions.

Table 2.4a indicates the tax revenue that would accrue to each state and to the federal government if each state collected revenue equal to 10% of the income generated by legalized marijuana and the federal government collected income equal to 20%. This is approximately what occurs now for the economy overall, except that the ratio of tax revenues to income varies across states from the 10% figure assumed here. The table indicates that under these assumptions, the federal government would collect $1.6 billion in additional revenue, each state would on average collect $16 million in additional tax revenue.

These calculations ignore the fact that marijuana use rates differ across states, so application of identical policies would yield different amounts of revenue per capita. Wright (2002, Table A.4, p. 82), for example, indicates that the percent of those 12 and over reporting marijuana use in the past month ranged in 1999–2000 from a low of 2.79% in Iowa to a high of 9.03% in Massachusetts. Table 2.4b therefore shows the breakdown of revenue by state under the assumption that tax revenue is proportional to state marijuana use rates. A third possibility, which cannot easily be examined with existing data, is that revenue by state differs depending on the distribution of marijuana production.

SUMMARY

In this chapter, we have estimated the budgetary implications of legalizing marijuana and taxing and regulating it like other goods. According to the calculations here, legalization would reduce government expenditure by $5.3 billion at the state and local level and by $2.4 billion at the federal level. In addition, marijuana legalization would generate tax revenue of $2.4 billion annually if marijuana were taxed like all other goods and $6.2 billion annually if marijuana were taxed at rates comparable to those on alcohol and tobacco.

Funded by the grants program administered by the Marijuana Policy Project in Washington, D.C.

Table 2.4a. State Marijuana Tax Revenue—Population Method

	Population	Proportion	Tax Revenue
Alabama	4,447,100	0.016	12.6
Alaska	626,932	0.002	1.8
Arizona	5,130,632	0.018	14.6
Arkansas	2,673,400	0.009	7.6
California	33,871,648	0.120	96.3
Colorado	4,301,261	0.015	12.2
Connecticut	3,405,565	0.012	9.7
Delaware	783,600	0.003	2.2
Dist. Columbia	572,059	0.002	1.6
Florida	15,982,378	0.057	45.4
Georgia	8,186,453	0.029	23.3
Hawaii	1,211,537	0.004	3.4
Idaho	1,293,953	0.005	3.7
Illinois	12,419,293	0.044	35.3
Indiana	6,080,485	0.022	17.3
Iowa	2,926,324	0.010	8.3
Kansas	2,688,418	0.010	7.6
Kentucky	4,041,769	0.014	11.5
Louisiana	4,468,976	0.016	12.7
Maine	1,274,923	0.005	3.6
Maryland	5,296,486	0.019	15.1
Massachusetts	6,349,097	0.023	18.0
Michigan	9,938,444	0.035	28.3
Minnesota	4,919,479	0.017	14.0
Mississippi	2,844,658	0.010	8.1
Missouri	5,595,211	0.020	15.9
Montana	902,195	0.003	2.6
Nebraska	1,711,263	0.006	4.9
Nevada	1,998,257	0.007	5.7
New Hampshire	1,235,786	0.004	3.5
New Jersey	8,414,350	0.030	23.9
New Mexico	1,819,046	0.006	5.2
New York	18,976,457	0.067	53.9
North Carolina	8,049,313	0.029	22.9
North Dakota	642,200	0.002	1.8
Ohio	11,353,140	0.040	32.3
Oklahoma	3,450,654	0.012	9.8
Oregon	3,421,399	0.012	9.7
Pennsylvania	12,281,054	0.044	34.9
Rhode Island	1,048,319	0.004	3.0
South Carolina	4,012,012	0.014	11.4
South Dakota	754,844	0.003	2.1
Tennessee	5,689,283	0.020	16.2
Texas	20,851,820	0.074	59.3
Utah	2,233,169	0.008	6.3
Vermont	608,827	0.002	1.7
Virginia	7,078,515	0.025	20.1
Washington	5,894,121	0.021	16.8
West Virginia	1,808,344	0.006	5.1
Wisconsin	5,363,675	0.019	15.2
Wyoming	493,782	0.002	1.4

Source: State Populations: http://www.census.gov/popest/states/NST
-EST2003-ann-est.html

Table 2.4b. State Marijuana Tax Revenue—Consumption Method

	Use Rate†	User Population	Use Proportion	Tax Revenue
Alabama	0.044	193,449	0.011	8.9
Alaska	0.098	61,251	0.004	2.8
Arizona	0.055	284,237	0.016	13.0
Arkansas	0.054	145,166	0.008	6.7
California	0.068	2,296,498	0.132	105.4
Colorado	0.089	383,672	0.022	17.6
Connecticut	0.063	213,529	0.012	9.8
Delaware	0.068	53,206	0.003	2.4
Dist. Columbia	0.108	61,897	0.004	2.8
Florida	0.066	1,051,640	0.060	48.2
Georgia	0.051	420,784	0.024	19.3
Hawaii	0.072	87,110	0.005	4.0
Idaho	0.056	72,461	0.004	3.3
Illinois	0.056	689,271	0.040	31.6
Indiana	0.064	388,543	0.022	17.8
Iowa	0.046	135,489	0.008	6.2
Kansas	0.053	143,024	0.008	6.6
Kentucky	0.055	221,489	0.013	10.2
Louisiana	0.064	284,227	0.016	13.0
Maine	0.069	88,352	0.005	4.1
Maryland	0.057	302,959	0.017	13.9
Massachusetts	0.063	401,263	0.023	18.4
Michigan	0.071	705,630	0.040	32.4
Minnesota	0.063	311,403	0.018	14.3
Mississippi	0.050	142,802	0.008	6.6
Missouri	0.061	339,070	0.019	15.6
Montana	0.087	78,581	0.005	3.6
Nebraska	0.064	109,179	0.006	5.0
Nevada	0.086	172,450	0.010	7.9
New Hampshire	0.099	121,725	0.007	5.6
New Jersey	0.050	420,718	0.024	19.3
New Mexico	0.059	106,596	0.006	4.9
New York	0.075	1,427,030	0.082	65.5
North Carolina	0.056	448,347	0.026	20.6
North Dakota	0.056	35,771	0.002	1.6
Ohio	0.067	759,525	0.044	34.8
Oklahoma	0.052	180,469	0.010	8.3
Oregon	0.090	306,557	0.018	14.1
Pennsylvania	0.054	664,405	0.038	30.5
Rhode Island	0.095	99,485	0.006	4.6
South Carolina	0.050	198,996	0.011	9.1
South Dakota	0.057	42,875	0.002	2.0
Tennessee	0.047	266,827	0.015	12.2
Texas	0.049	1,015,484	0.058	46.6
Utah	0.046	102,502	0.006	4.7
Vermont	0.100	61,126	0.004	2.8
Virginia	0.064	455,149	0.026	20.9
Washington	0.081	479,192	0.027	22.0
West Virginia	0.050	90,056	0.005	4.1
Wisconsin	0.054	291,784	0.017	13.4
Wyoming	0.052	25,578	0.001	1.2

†Marijuana Use Rates: http://oas.samhsa.gov/2k2State/html/appA.htm#taba.1

APPENDIX A: PERCENTAGE OF CORRECTIONS POPULATION INCARCERATED ON MARIJUANA CHARGES

State-by-state data on the fraction of prisoners incarcerated on marijuana charges are not available, but data for a few states provide reasonable estimates of this fraction. Table 2A.1 displays the available information.

APPENDIX B: REVENUE UNDER PROHIBITION FROM SEIZURES AND FINES

State-by-state data on fines and seizures are not available. There is sufficient information, however, to estimate an upper bound on the revenue from fines and seizures. There are also data on federal fines and seizures.

Seizures

The two main sources of federal seizure revenue are the Drug Enforcement Administration (DEA) and the U.S. Customs Service. In 2002, the DEA made seizures totaling $438 million. (See http://www.albany.edu/sourcebook/1995/pdf/t442.pdf.)

In 2001, the U.S. Customs Service seized property valued at $592 million. (See http://www.albany.edu/sourcebook/1995/pdf/t444.pdf.) These figures

Table 2A.1

State	Year	% Incarcerated for MJ Violation	Population	Pop %	Weighted Share
California	2003	0.008	33,871,648	0.568	0.005
Georgia	2000	0.014	8,186,453	0.137	0.002
Massachusetts	2000	0.017	6,349,097	0.107	0.002
Michigan	2001	0.006	9,938,444	0.167	0.001
New Hampshire	2002	0.016	1,235,786	0.021	0.000
Total		0.061	59,581,428		
Average		0.012			
Weighted Average					0.010

Sources:
New Hampshire: http://www.state.nh.us/doc/population.html
California: http://www.corr.ca.gov/OffenderInfoServices/Reports/Annual/CensusArchive.asp
Michigan: http://www.michigan.gov/documents/2001Stat_79881_7.pdf
Georgia: http://www.dcor.state.ga.us/pdf/inms03-12.pdf
Massachusetts: Miron 2002, pp. 4–5.

overstate revenue since some defendants recovered their seized property. The customs seizures overstate revenue related to drugs because the figure includes seizures for all reasons, such as violation of gun laws, intellectual property laws, and the like. There may also be double-counting between the DEA seizures and the customs seizures.

Adding the two components yields $1,030 million (=$438+$592 million) as the seizure revenue that results from enforcement of drug laws. This figure must be adjusted downward, however, to separate out the portion specifically attributable to violation of marijuana laws. As shown in Table 2.3, approximately 20% of the federal drug enforcement budget is attributable to marijuana, so it is reasonable to assume that approximately 20% of the fines and seizures correspond to enforcement of marijuana laws.

Thus, seizure revenue at the federal level ascribable to marijuana prosecutions is roughly $206 million annually.

State and local data on forfeiture revenue are not readily available for all states. Baicker and Jacobson (2004), however, use a sample of states to estimate that state forfeiture revenue per capita was roughly $1.14 during the 1994–2001 period. This implies aggregate state forfeiture revenue of $342 million. Deflating by 26%, the fraction of all drug trafficking arrests ascribable to marijuana, implies that marijuana seizures yield $89 million to state governments.

Fines

In 2001, the total quantity of fines and restitutions ordered for drug offense cases in U.S. district courts was a little less than $41 million (see http://www.albany.edu/sourcebook/1995/pdf/t531.pdf). Adjusting this by the 20% figure implies $8.2 million from marijuana cases. Assuming the ratio of state/local to federal fine revenue is similar to ratio of state/local to federal seizure revenue implies that state and local fines/restitution from marijuana cases is about $3.5 million.

NOTES

1. See, for example, the estimates in Miron (2002) versus those in Miron (2003a).

2. This chapter addresses only the criminal justice costs of enforcing marijuana prohibition; it does not address any possible changes in prevention, education, or treatment expenses that might accompany marijuana legalization. The narrower approach is appropriate because the decision to prohibit marijuana is separate from the decision to subsidize prevention,

education, and treatment activities. Marijuana legalization might neverthe-less cause some reduction in government expenditure for demand-side poli-cies. For example, legalization would likely mean reduced criminal justice referrals of marijuana offenders to treatment; this category accounted for 58.1% of marijuana treatment referrals in 2002 (DHHS, 2004, Table 4, p. 15). Thus, the approach adopted here implies a conservative estimate of the reduction in government expenditure from marijuana legalization.

3. For example, under current rules regarding parole and probation, a positive urine test for marijuana can send a parolee or probationer to prison, regardless of the original offense. These rules might change under legaliza-tion, implying additional reductions in government expenditure.

4. The key assumption is that average costs equal marginal costs. This equivalence is not necessarily accurate in the short run or for very small communities but is likely a good approximation overall.

5. This part of our chapter relies on data for 2000 since that is the last year for which complete information on arrests is available. After esti-mating expenditure for 2000, we adjust for inflation between 2000 and 2003.

6. To the extent that it takes additional resources to process someone on multiple charges rather than on a single charge, there is still a net cost in police resources in such cases because of prohibition. In addition, a lab test is typically done to determine the precise content of any drugs seized when there is an arrest on drug charges, which takes yet more resources. A differ-ent issue is that in some cases, police stops for nondrug charges result in ar-rests on drugs charges alone (e.g., because of insufficient evidence to support any other charges).

7. Lewis (2004) reports that the fraction of stand-alone arrests on all drug charges in the city of Syracuse, New York, was 90.5% in 2002.

8. Gettman and Fuller (2003) obtain a similar estimate to that re-ported here for Virginia in 2001.

9. The data on felony convictions are from Durose and Langan (2003, Table 1, p. 2).

10. The fraction of felony convictions for any type of drug is from Durose and Langan (2003, Table 1, p. 2).

11. This chapter excludes the capital outlays portion of the corrections budget, since the available data do not indicate the average rate of such ex-penditures. This biases the estimates downward.

12. Most seized assets are ultimately forfeited.

13. Inflation rate data are for the Consumer Price Indices—All Urban Consumers (Bureau of Labor Statistics, U.S. Department of Labor, http://www.bls.gov/cpi/home.htm#data).

14. The figure here for Massachusetts exceeds that in Miron (2003a) because this chapter assumes that 50% of possession arrests are for mari-juana, whereas the earlier report assumed that 33% were. The 50% figure is more appropriate here because the analysis covers all states rather than just Massachusetts.

15. As a check, it is useful to compare the $5.1 billion figure provided here to that derived from an alternative methodology. The ONDCP (1993) reports survey evidence on drug prohibition enforcement by state and local authorities for the years 1990/1991. Adjusting these data for inflation and the percent attributable to marijuana prohibition yields an estimate similar to that reported above.

16. The approach used here differs from that employed in the case of state and local expenditure because of differences in the kinds of data available. Using an approach that is similar to the extent possible yields an estimate of federal marijuana enforcement expenditure that is similar to the estimate provided in the text.

17. This consists of expenditure in the following categories: D.C. Court Services and Offender Supervision ($86.4 million); Department of Defense ($1 billion); Intelligence Community Management Account ($42.8 million); The Judiciary ($819.7 million); Department of Justice ($8.14 billion); ONDCP ($533.3 million); Department of State ($832.6 million); Department of Transportation ($591.4 million); and Department of Treasury ($1.55 billion). See ONDCP (2002), pp. 29–31.

18. Murphy, Davis, Liston, Thaler, and Webb (2000) examine the methods used by the ONDCP to estimate this expenditure. They conclude that methodological problems render parts of the estimates biased, in some cases by substantial amounts. These issues do not imply major qualifications to the data considered here, however. Murphy et al. find that the antidrug budgets of the Coast Guard and the Bureau of Prisons are accurate reflections of the resources expended and that the reported expenditure of the Department of Defense probably underestimates its antidrug budget. The overestimates that they identify occur for demand-side activities.

19. The 2003 *National Drug Control Strategy* adopts a new methodology for estimating the federal drug-control budget. This new methodology implies a substantial reduction in supply side expenditure (ONDCP, 2002, pp. 33–34). For the purposes of this chapter, the old methodology is more appropriate. For example, the new approach excludes expenditures on incarceration of persons imprisoned for drug crimes.

20. The percentage of prisoners whose primary offense was a marijuana charge would also be relevant, but data are not readily available. Since most convictions at the federal level result in prison terms, incarceration data would imply a result similar to that provided above.

21. Inflation rate data are for the CPI—All Urban Consumers (Bureau of Labor Statistics, U.S. Department of Labor, http://www.bls.gov/cpi/home.htm#data).

22. To be explicit, the assumption is that there is no shift in the demand curve. If the supply curve shifts, there will be a change in the quantity demanded.

23. The underlying assumption is that the marginal costs of evading tax and regulatory costs is zero for black market suppliers who are already conducting their activities in secret.

24. MacCoun and Reuter (1997) report gram prices of $2.50–$12.50 in the Netherlands and $1.50–$15.00 in the United States. They speculate that the surprisingly high prices in the Netherlands may reflect enforcement aimed at large-scale trafficking. Harrison, Backenheimer, and Inciardi (1995) note that ONDCP data on drug prices in the U.S. are very similar to prices charged in Dutch coffee shops. The ONDCP (2001a) reports a price per gram for small-scale purchases of roughly $9 per gram in the second quarter of 2000, whereas the European Monitoring Center for Drugs and Drug Addiction (2002) suggests a price of 2–8 Euros per gram, which is roughly $6 on average. Various websites that discuss the coffee shops in Amsterdam suggest prices of $5–$11 per gram in recent years. These comparisons do not adjust for potency or other dimensions of quality.

25. Clements and Daryal (2001) report marijuana prices for Australia that are similar to or higher than those in the United States. Since Australian marijuana policy is noticeably less strict than U.S. policy, this observation is consistent with the view that legalization would not produce a dramatic fall in price.

26. The Nisbet and Vakil estimates that use survey data imply price elasticities of −0.365 or −0.51 in the log and linear specifications, respectively, while the purchase data imply price elasticities of −1.013 and −1.51. The estimates based on purchase data are plausibly more reliable. Moreover, as they note, these estimates are likely biased downward by standard simultaneous equations bias. Clemens and Daryal (2001) estimate a price elasticity of −0.5 for marijuana using Australian data. Estimates of the demand for "similar" goods (e.g., alcohol, cocaine, heroin, or tobacco) suggest similar elasticities.

27. Pacula et al. (2000) summarize the literature on the relation between marijuana use and factors that can affect use, such as legal penalties. They conclude the evidence is mixed but overall indicates a moderate response of marijuana consumption to "price." The papers summarized do not provide measures of the price elasticity. The results reported by Pacula et al. suggest an elasticity of marijuana participation between 0 and −0.5; this understates the total elasticity, which includes any change in consumption conditional on participation. The literature since Nisbet and Vakil is thus consistent with the elasticity estimate assumed above.

28. Given the uncertainties involved in calculating the tax revenue from marijuana legalization and the possibility that declines in marijuana prices have offset general inflation since 2000, this chapter omits any adjustment of the tax revenue for inflation. Such an adjustment would make only a small difference in any case.

29. In 2001, total government receipts divided by the gross domestic product equaled 29.7%. See the *2003 Economic Report of the President* online, http://w3.access.gpo.gov/usbudget/fy2004/pdf/2003_erp.pdf, Tables B-1 and B-92, pp. 276 and 373.

30. Whether such production is illicit depends on the details of a legalization law. Plausibly, growing small amounts for personal use would not be

subject to taxation or regulation, just as growing small amounts of vegetables or herbs, or brewing beer for personal consumption, is not subject to taxation or regulation.

31. Schwer, Riddel, and Henderson (2002) estimate the tax revenue from marijuana legalization in Nevada assuming "sin taxation." Their estimates are not readily comparable to those presented here because they consider the situation in which one state legalizes marijuana while other states and the federal government prohibit marijuana. The same comment applies to Bates (2004), who estimates the tax revenue from marijuana legalization in Alaska. Easton (2004) estimates the tax revenue from marijuana legalization in Canada under the assumption of sin taxation. His estimates are comparable but modestly higher than those presented here, adjusted for the different size of the U.S. and Canadian economies. Caputo and Ostrom (1994) provide estimates for the overall economy that are similar to those obtained here.

REFERENCES

Baicker, K., & Jacobson, M. (2004). Finders keepers: Forfeiture laws, policing incentives, and local budgets (*NBER Working Paper*, 10484). Cambridge, MA: National Bureau of Economic Research.

Bates, S. W. (2004). The economic implications of marijuana legalization in Alaska. Fairbanks, AK: Alaskans for Rights & Revenue.

Caputo, M. R., & Ostrom, B. J. (1994). Potential tax revenue from a regulated marijuana market: A meaningful revenue source. *American Journal of Economics and Sociology, 53,* 475–490.

Clements, K. W., & Daryal, M. (2001). Marijuana prices in Australia in 1990s (Discussion Paper No 01.01). Australia: University of Western Australia, Economic Research Centre, Department of Economics.

Durose, M., & Patrick A. L. (2003). *Felony sentences in state courts, 2000* (NCJ 198821). Washington, DC: U.S. Department of Justice, Bureau of Justice Statistics, Office of Justices Programs.

Easton, S. T. (2004). *Marijuana growth in British Columbia* (Fraser Institute Occasional Paper #74). Vancouver, BC: Public Policy Sources.

European Monitoring Center for Drugs and Drug Addiction (2002). *Annual report 2002.* Retrieved January 12, 2005, from http://annualreport.emcdda.eu.int/pdfs/2002_0458_EN.pdf.

Gettman, J. B., & Fuller, S. S. (2003). Estimation of the budgetary costs of marijuana possession arrests in the Commonwealth of Virginia. Arlington, VA: George Mason University, Center for Regional Analysis.

Harrison, L. D., Backenheimer, M., & Inciardi, J. A. (1995). Cannabis use in the United States: Implications for policy. In P. Cohen & A. Sas (Eds.), *Cannabisbeleid in Duitsland, Frankrijk en do Verenigde Staten* (231–236). Amsterdam: Centrum voor Drugsonderzoek, University of Amsterdam.

Lewis, M. (2004). *Report on the Syracuse Police Department activity for the year ended June 30, 2002.* Syracuse, NY: City of Syracuse, Department of Audit.

MacCoun, R., & Reuter, P. (1997). Interpreting Dutch cannabis policy: Reasoning by analogy in the legalization debate. *Science, 278,* 47–52.

Miron, J. A. (2002). The effect of marijuana decriminalization on the budgets of Massachusetts governments, with a discussion of decriminalization's effect on marijuana use. *Report to the Drug Policy Forum of Massachusetts.*

Miron, J. A. (2003a). The budgetary implications of marijuana legalization in Massachusetts. Greenfield, MA: *Change the Climate.*

Miron, J. A. (2003b). A critique of estimates of the economic costs of drug abuse. New York: *Drug Policy Alliance.*

Miron, J.A. (2003c). Do prohibitions raise prices? Evidence from the markets for cocaine and heroin. *Review of Economics and Statistics, 85*(3), 522–530.

Murphy, P., Davis, L. E., Liston, T., Thaler, D., & Webb, K. (2000). *Improving anti-drug budgeting.* Santa Monica, CA: Rand.

Nisbet, C. T., & Vakil, F. (1972). Some estimates of price and expenditure elasticities of demand for marijuana among U.C.L.A. students. *Review of Economics and Statistics, 54,* 473–475.

Office of National Drug Control Policy. (1993). *State and local spending on drug control activities.* Washington, DC: Author.

Office of National Drug Control Policy. (2001a). *The price of illicit drugs: 1981 through second quarter of 2000.* Washington, DC: Abt Associates.

Office of National Drug Control Policy. (2001b). *What America's users spend on illegal drugs.* Cambridge, MA: Abt Associates.

Office of National Drug Control Policy. (2002). *National drug control strategy.* Washington, DC: Author.

Pacula, R. L., Grossman, M., Chaloupka, F. J., O'Malley, P. M., Johnston, L. D., & Farrelly, M. C. (2000). *Marijuana and youth* (NBER WP #7703). Los Angeles: RAND.

Pastore, A. L., & Maguire, K. (2003). *Sourcebook of criminal justice statistics.* Washington, DC: U.S. Department of Justice, Bureau of Justice Statistics.

Reuter, P., Hirschfield, P., & Davies, C. (2001). *Assessing the crack-down on marijuana in Maryland.* Baltimore: The Abell Foundation.

Schwer, R. K., Riddel, M., & Henderson, J. (2002). *Fiscal impact of Question 9: Potential state-revenue implications.* Las Vegas: University of Nevada, Center for Business and Economic Research.

U.S. Department of Health and Humans Services. (2000). *Reducing tobacco use: A report of the surgeon general, tobacco taxation fact sheet.* Retrieved January 5, 2005, from http://www.cdc.gov/tobacco/sgr/sgr_2000/factsheets/factsheets_taxation.htm

U.S. Department of Health and Human Services. (2004). *Treatment episode data set (TEDS) highlights—2002.* Washington, DC: Substance Abuse and Mental Health Services Administration, Office of Applied Statistics.

Wright, D. (2002). *State estimates of substance use from the 2000 National Household Survey on Drug Abuse: Vol. 1. Findings* (DHHS Publication No. SMA 02–3731, NHSDA Series H-15). Rockville, MD: Substance Abuse and Mental Health Services Administration, Office of Applied Statistics.

3 Is Drug Testing in the Workplace Worthwhile?

Sara Smucker Barnwell
Mitch Earleywine

DRUG PREVALENCE AND RELATED PROBLEMS IN THE U.S. WORKFORCE

The accuracy, costs, and effectiveness of drug testing in the workplace bears implications for the welfare of American business and the well-being of its workers. Numerous studies find that alcohol and illicit substance use threaten employee health, safety, and productivity (Roman & Blum, 1995; Sindelar, 1998), and may interfere with companies' capacity to compete in domestic and global markets (Frone, 2004). More than 4 million injuries occur among American workers annually (Bureau of Labor Statistics, 2004). Estimates of the percentage of these accidents attributable to substance use vary widely (e.g., 47%, United States Department of Labor, 2006; 36%, The Hartford, 2004). Post-accident drug testing identifies positive results for illicit substances among 4% of individuals with dangerous or "safety-sensitive" jobs (e.g., heavy machinery operation) and 6% of general workforce employees involved in accidents (Frone, 2004). Not surprisingly, drug use is a primary concern of human resource departments (Gust & Walsh, 1989). Cannabis use on the job, however, seems to have little to do with any of these accidents, making the value of drug testing questionable.

In 1999, the U.S. Department of Health and Human Services Substance Abuse and Mental Health Services Administration's (SAMHSA) National Household Survey on Drug Abuse in the Workforce suggested that 77% of illicit drug users participate in the workforce. Approximately 7% of the full-time

workforce uses illicit drugs, while 9% of the part-time workforce reports illicit drug use. Nine percent of employed adults report having used cannabis in their lifetimes, and approximately 5% used cannabis in the 30 days preceding the survey (National Household Survey on Drug Abuse, 1999). Estimates suggest that 20 million American workers will experience moderate to serious problems related to drug use in their work lives (Martin, Kraft, & Roman, 1994). Thus the implicated role of substance use in lost employee productivity, diminished workplace safety and the health of the workforce is a relevant topic for consideration.

Drug testing emerges as many employers' answer to the problem of employee substance use. Drug-testing programs seek to provide an objective basis for mandatory employee referral to treatment programs, prevent the onset of drug use among abstaining workers, diminish productivity losses and workplace accidents ascribable to substance use, minimize cost increases for employer-paid health care expenses, and decrease drug-related work turnover (Marshman, 1994). In short, drug testing endeavors to identify or prevent the development of problems to maintain a healthy and safe workforce. Despite these admirable goals, drug testing programs do not appear to accomplish these aims and require considerable expense. To understand how drug testing promotes worker health and safety, the present discussion examines the literature on the effectiveness of drug testing in the identification of workers whose substance use impairs job performance.

HISTORY OF DRUG TESTING

Although institutional attention to drug use in the workplace via blood- or urine-based drug testing emerged in the past two decades, American workplace drug testing existed long beforehand (Tunnell, 2004). In 1914, Ford Motor Company joined forces with the U.S. Sociological Department to arrange visits to workers' homes to evaluate their lifestyles. Workers whose values did not align with Ford and Sociological Department ideals (e.g., sobriety) were suspended without compensation until they were able to alter these perceived deficiencies (SAMSHA, 2004). In the 1960s and 1970s, relatively few companies possessed drug-testing programs, despite a boom in rates of drug use in the workforce.

The mid-1980s ushered in a time of decreasing substance use, increasingly conservative public attitudes towards illicit drugs, media attention to several high-profile overdoses and increased awareness of drug-related workplace accidents (Tunnell, 2004). Government policies reflected growing public disapproval of illicit substance use (Strossen, Glasser, & Clark, 1999). In 1986, President Ronald Reagan introduced the Drug-Free Workplace Act,

which cited illegal substance use as the cause of millions of dollars of lost productivity and safety risks (Executive Order No. 12,564, 1986). The Reagan administration required federal agencies to institute urine testing to promote a drug-free workplace, and it encouraged American businesses to do the same. A surge in employer-sponsored drug testing programs followed (Tunnell, 2004).

By 2001, more than 65% of the largest American companies tested employees for drugs or alcohol (American Management Association, 2001). Larger companies are more likely to adopt drug-testing programs (Knudsen, Roman, & Johnson, 2003; Tunnell, 2004). Blue-collar positions are more likely to be drug tested than white-collar positions (Tunnell, 2004). Drug testing is mandatory for numerous safety-sensitive jobs and many other positions as well. Companies with more than $25,000 in contracts with the United States government must test all employees for drug use (Allison & Stahlhut, 1995). Federal drug-testing efforts focus on about 400,000 employees whose jobs involve security clearances, firearms, public or national safety, or presidential appointment (SAMSHA, 2004).

RESEARCH SUPPORTING DRUG-TESTING POLICIES

Data supporting the Drug-Free Workplace Act and comparable public perceptions of substance use's deleterious effects on the American workplace are spurious at best. Policy makers often cite the so-called Firestone Study. In the early 1970s, the Employee Assistance Program of the Firestone Tire and Rubber Company brought someone in to speak to human resources personnel about medical behavior problems among workers. Although the speaker offered no information on the source of his data or on his study methods, he reported that individuals with medical behavior problems cost companies far more than other employees because of their absences, medical needs, and accidents and injuries. The speech focused primarily on alcoholism, but it cited illicit drug abuse as a potentially complicating additional problem. Facts from the speech transcript appeared as accredited scientific findings in the nationally distributed *Drug Abuse and Alcoholism Newsletter* (Strossen et al., 1999).

There never was a Firestone Study. Information from a misunderstood and unvalidated speech intended for a company's human resources department in Ohio developed a life of its own (Strossen et al., 1999). Numerous government initiatives (e.g., Drug-Free Workplace Act; Executive Order No. 12,564, 1986) and private business policies cite the fictitious study. Thus numerous policies regarding substance use's negative impacts on the workforce

derived from unsubstantiated research claims. In short, the Drug-Free Workplace Act and other drug-testing policies rely on a lie.

In 1984, the Research Triangle Institute conducted a study that has since been frequently cited. The institute employed National Household Drug Survey data to examine incomes among families with a member who acknowledges using, or having used, cannabis daily. Households with a daily cannabis user possessed lower incomes than households whose members reported never using cannabis daily. Yet the research failed to establish a causal relationship between cannabis use and diminished income. The researchers also failed to report discrepancies in the data. Most notably, households with current cannabis users did not differ in income from those with nonusers. Instead, the researchers multiplied income discrepancies between households by the average number of daily cannabis users in the workforce to arrive at a figure of $33 billion in lost income among cannabis users. This figure endures as a purportedly reliable estimate of cannabis-related work loss and is regularly adjusted for inflation to reflect current costs of cannabis use to the American workforce. The potentially erroneous estimates of lost productivity ascribable to cannabis use in 1999 equaled $100 billion (Strossen et al., 1999). Again, statistical hand waving and mental gymnastics have created bogus statistics to support an expensive idea.

Though the foundations of the drug-testing movement may have relied on poor data, more methodologically sound, empirically based studies do connect workplace drug intoxication to increases in workplace accidents (e.g., Mangione et al., 1999; Zwerling, Ryan, & Orav, 1990), injuries (e.g., Bass et al., 1996; Moore, Grunberg, & Greenberg, 1998), absences (e.g., Normand, Salyards, & Mahoney, 1990; Zwerling et al., 1992) and myriad other behavioral problems (e.g., antagonistic behaviors; Lehman & Simpson, 1992). Impairment because of intoxication could pose a significant barrier to a safe work environment, especially among safety-sensitive jobs that require mental acuity (e.g., operation of heavy machinery, use of advanced equipment).

An important distinction in the literature arises: on-the-job drug use versus off-the-job drug use. Little consistency exists regarding prevalence rates for intoxication in the workplace (Frone, 2004). For example, some individuals consume cannabis and work at their jobs while intoxicated (the estimated range is 1%–39%; Frone, 2004). Newcomb (1988) found that on-the-job drug use correlated with more severe off-the-job drug problems as well (e.g., accidents related to drug use). Thus on-the-job intoxication poses a more serious threat to worker competence, especially in safety-sensitive positions. To understand the potential dangers of cannabis to worker well-being, we examine the literature on the effects of cannabis use and intoxication on workers.

CANNABIS EFFECTS AND THE RELEVANCE
OF DRUG TESTING

In the context of cannabis use, an accurate understanding of the effectiveness and relevance of workplace drug testing is particularly important. Marijuana is the most popular illicit drug in the United States. In 1999, one-third (76 million) of adults in the United States reported smoking cannabis at least once in their lifetime (SAMSHA, 2000). Approximately 7% of females and 11% of males over age 12 report using the drug within the past year (Greenfield & O'Leary, 1999). Recall that 5% of the workforce reports using cannabis in the past month. Eighty percent of illicit substance users report consuming cannabis in some form in their lifetime (National Household Survey on Drug Abuse, 1999).

Cannabis is also the substance most frequently identified through drug testing, accounting for more than 40% of all positive test results (Tunnell, 2004). Yet surprisingly little is known regarding the actual effects of cannabis on the average worker. Many studies examining the roles of substance use on worker productivity do not distinguish among specific substances (e.g., Lehman & Simpson, 1992). Among those studies that do distinguish drug types, many focus on drugs with high dependence rates, such as alcohol (e.g., Mangione et al., 1999) and cocaine (e.g., Walsh, Hingson, Merrigan, & Cupples, 1991). Considerably fewer studies address cannabis use, despite its high prevalence among Americans (Paronto, Truxillo, Bauer, & Leo, 2002). As will be discussed later in this report, chemical properties unique to cannabis limit interpretations of positive drug-test results for cannabis. To explore the role of cannabis use and intoxication in worker problems, we examine the specific effects of the drug on the user.

EFFECTS OF CANNABIS USE ON WORKERS

Research on the most straightforward constructs associated with job competence (e.g., wages, general productivity, turnover/firings) fail to offer consistent evidence linking cannabis use with problematic employees. The casual cannabis user's employment record better resembles that of the nonuser than the problem user (French, Roebuck, & Alexandre, 2001). Cannabis use does not appear to relate to wages or job turnover. An examination of more than 8,000 young adults in various fields suggests that frequent cannabis users earn higher wages than abstainers (Kaestner, 1994). Other studies simply suggest comparable wages for cannabis users and abstainers (Earleywine, 2002). Marijuana smokers are no more likely to be fired from their jobs than are nonsmokers (Normand et al. 1990; Parish, 1989). Laboratory- and field-based studies suggest that cannabis users work as hard, if not harder, than

nonusers (Strossen et al., 1999). Though cannabis users tend to occupy lower status positions (Mensch & Kandel, 1988; Voss, 1989), some research suggests that they are extremely productive in these positions (Kagel, Battalio, & Miles, 1980). A study of cannabis's long-term effects on workers suggests few if any residual effects of cannabis use on job performance (Kandel & Davies, 1996).

Furthermore, cannabis users may be as cognitively capable as nonusers. Several studies connect low focus among users with repeated cannabis use, citing possible neurological causes (McGlothlin & West, 1968; Smith, 1968), but others show that repeated cannabis use bears no effect on motivation, productivity, and clarity in work tasks (Cohen, 1976). Despite the popularity of reported connections between cannabis use and cognitive deficits, the majority of research available suggests no significant long-term differences between chronic cannabis users and nonusers on indices of cognitive ability, including intelligence, memory, and capacity to learn (Earleywine, 2002). Indeed there is no evidence that cannabis use causes decreased productivity in the workplace (DiNardo, 1994), and even chronic use appears to bear few decrements on the job (U.S. Secretary of Health, Education, and Welfare, 1980).

Absenteeism arises as one domain in which cannabis users differ from nonusers. Just as employees using illicit drugs report greater numbers of absences (Basset al., 1996), workers consuming cannabis heavily are more frequently absent than those consuming less (Strossen et al., 1999; Zwerling et al., 1992). However, these studies often fail to control for important demographic variables. Age and gender are key components to understanding cannabis use (Martin et al., 1994; Strossen et al., 1999). Individuals 18–25 years old are almost twice as likely as to use cannabis as workers 26–34 years old, and are almost six times as likely to consume cannabis as are adults over 35. Young workers take significantly more unapproved leaves from work. Men are twice as likely as women to use cannabis (National Household Survey on Drug Abuse, 1996). In addition, men are significantly more likely to have unscheduled absences than are female workers (Morgan, 1988; Strossen et al, 1999). Thus the demographic groups most likely to consume cannabis are also the groups most likely to take unapproved absences regardless of substance use. Though it is possible that cannabis use accounts for unique variance in this equation, it is also plausible that a common variable (e.g., age, gender, or sensation seeking) underlies both phenomena. Though cannabis use could act as a proxy in the identification of other behavioral problems, employers are well advised not to target specific employee demographics as problematic.

Concerned safety advocates may wonder whether cannabis users suffer cognitive problems that impair mental acuity requisite to job safety. Relatively few studies make the important distinction between drugs well known to cause impairments of cognitive and motor abilities (e.g., alcohol: Ravaglia, Costa, Ratti, Savoldi, Bo, & Moglia, 2002; heroin and cocaine:

Margolin, Avants, Warburton, & Hawkins, 2002) and cannabis, which has considerably less severe effects on cognitive and motor abilities (Earleywine, 2002). The majority of studies connecting positive drug-test results with workplace accidents address correlation but not causation. Thus the conceptual and methodological limitations of the research limit the precision of conclusions that can drawn from the data (Frone, 2004).

EFFECTS OF CANNABIS INTOXICATION ON WORKERS

Not surprisingly, research on workplace cannabis intoxication suggests that on-the-job cannabis intoxication has more negative consequences than cannabis use in general. Indeed, research links cannabis intoxication with decreased worker safety (Zwerling et al., 1992). A study of post-accident postal workers found that although the vast majority (96%) tested negative for illicit substances, some did test positive for previous cannabis use (Strossen et al., 1999). However, most researchers are hesitant to suggest a causal relationship between positive drug test results and accidents (e.g., Frone, 2004), given the tests' inability to detect intoxication.

On-the-job cannabis intoxication can be expected to have implications for safety-sensitive workers in particular. Cannabis intoxication evidences little impact on the most basic cognitive processes, such as simple learning (Chait & Pierri, 1992; Hooker & Jones, 1987), remote memory (Tart, 1971; Wetzel, Janowsky, & Clopton, 1982) and simple reaction times (Chait & Pierri, 1992). Intoxication, does, however, affect complex reaction times, basic learning (Earleywine, 2002), perceptual-motor tasks and decision-making processes (Coambs & McAndrews, 1994). Intoxicated employees whose jobs require fast reaction times, timely decision making or high levels of motor coordination could be affected, increasing the potential for accident and injury.

Mensch and Kandel (1988) examined job characteristics that correlate with on-the-job cannabis use. On-the-job cannabis use correlated with domains irrelevant to worker safety: little decision-making authority, low job complexity, and rigorous physical demands. Among men, cannabis use on the job correlated with exposure to hazardous and potentially dangerous work situations. Thus the question of how best to identify intoxicated individuals in the workplace remains vital, particularly among male workers.

Given the dearth of research connecting cannabis use outside of the workplace with diminished employee safety, individuals who are intoxicated outside of work hours likely demonstrate comparable job fitness and work safety as nonusers. The lack of a demonstrated connection between cannabis intoxication and impairment on low-level learning, memory, and performance tasks suggests that cannabis intoxication is not likely to dimin-

ish workplace safety in nonsafety sensitive positions requiring less mental acuity. However, the data do suggest that on-the-job intoxication can impair worker safety, especially among those in safety-sensitive positions.

HEALTH EFFECTS OF CANNABIS ON THE WORKER

Employers may use drug testing to address cannabis's deleterious effects on worker health and associated costs to employee health insurance plans. The inhalation of cannabis smoke can bring on symptoms of respiratory illness (Tashkin, Simmons, Sherrill, & Coulson, 1997). Cannabis users report greater incidence of coughing and wheezing (Earleywine & Smucker Barnwell, in preparation; Zimmer & Morgan, 1997). These effects parallel symptoms associated with tobacco consumption (Bloom, Kaltenborn, Paoletti, Camilli, & Leibowitz, 1987). Marijuana cigarettes possess high levels of tar and are inhaled deeply. Although they are less frequently consumed than tobacco, cannabis cigarettes are often used in conjunction with tobacco. Research suggests that tobacco consumption increases negative respiratory effects associated with cannabis use (e.g., greater coughing and wheezing; Earleywine & Smucker Barnwell, in preparation). Some studies find little connection between lung cancer and cannabis consumption (Sidney, Beck, Tekawa, Quesenberry, & Friedman 1997), whereas other studies suggest that chronic heavy use may result in cancer or related symptoms (Earleywine, 2002). Overall, tobacco represents a greater risk for lung cancer and cost to employer health plans (Centers for Disease Control and Prevention, 2000), inducing more severe symptoms of respiratory illness (Earleywine & Smucker Barnwell, in preparation). Yet companies typically do not test for nicotine use among workers.

Cannabis users do not incur greater costs to employers via health care service utilization. A large-scale examination of California's largest health maintenance organization found that heavy cannabis users' medical insurance claims cost employers no more than nonusers (Polen, 1993; Strossen et al., 1999).[1] Some might argue that cannabis users' true cost to employers exists in lost work and rehabilitation for substance-abusing employees. The fourth edition of the *American Psychiatric Association's Diagnostic Statistical Manual* (1994) includes a failure to fulfill major role obligations in the workplace among the diagnostic criteria for cannabis abuse. Individuals attending work while intoxicated are not only more likely to be impaired while at work, but also to possess a constellation of behaviors and traits that merit an abuse or dependence diagnosis. Decreasing cannabis consumption in the workforce clearly could cut employer costs.

However, it is important to consider the relatively low rates of progression from cannabis use to dependence (Earleywine, 2002; Weller & Halikas,

1980). Few cannabis users develop problems with the drug that affect every-day functioning (Earleywine, 2002). The Grant and Pickering (1998) study of more than 42,000 people focused on individuals who used cannabis over the past year, and found that approximately 6% met criteria for a dependence diagnosis. Indeed, the most chronic substance abusers suffering impaired functioning tend to be unemployed people with little education (Currie, 1997; Frone, 2004). Given the relatively low rates of problem cannabis use generally and in the workforce, the issue of rehabilitation cost seems to be less of a problem for employers. As will be discussed later in the chapter, the vast majority of workers testing positive for cannabis may neither require nor benefit from costly rehabilitation efforts, and those in greatest need of assistance may best be able to confuse the test.

EFFECTS OF COMORBID ALCOHOL ON WORKERS

Just as cigarettes pose a far greater threat to worker health than cannabis, alcohol may represent a far more significant risk to worker safety, well-being, and productivity. Newcomb (1988) examined drug use in the workplace and concluded that the use of potentially intoxicating substances in the workplace frequently involved more than one substance. Individuals caught using cannabis are likely to have also used alcohol on the job. Indeed, comorbid heavy alcohol and cannabis use is linked with a number of problems that impede workplace productivity, including accidents (Stein, 1986) and performance problems (Huestis, 2002). A study of chronic cannabis users reporting low motivation and little energy found that the majority consumed alcohol simultaneously and even reported problems with alcohol (Reilly, Didcott, Swift, & Hall, 1998). Heavy alcohol consumption is a leading cause of work loss (e.g., days ill, job termination) (Frone, 2004), a significant barrier to entry into the workforce for the unemployed, and the most commonly abused drug among workers (Arons, Greene Foster, & Smucker, 2003). Alcohol use is directly connected to absenteeism (Strossen et al., 1999) and decreased worker efficacy (Frone, 2004). Approximately two thirds (64%) of the American workforce reports using alcohol, and more than one third (35%) binge in their drinking (e.g., consume five or more drinks on a single occasion; Department of Health and Human Services, 1999)[2].

Considerable evidence links workplace alcohol intoxication with negative outcomes for the affected workers, but few credible data sources exist on the rates of on-the-job alcohol intoxication. Estimates of the proportion of workers who are under the influence of alcohol at the workplace range from less than 1% to almost 34% (Frone, 2004). A study of on-the-job alcohol use among shipyard workers found that alcohol accounted for more than one

third of nonfatal injuries (Moll van Charante & Mulder, 1990). Beaumont and Allsop (1983) found that more than three quarters (76%) of alcohol-related workplace accidents in industrial settings occurred from 8 to 10 a.m. and 1 to 2 p.m.—immediately after times when workers had an opportunity to drink alcohol. Yet cannabis is more frequently targeted though drug testing (Tunnell, 2004). Given the relatively stable body of evidence linking problematic alcohol use with work loss (Arons, Greene Foster, & Smucker, 2003), accidents, injuries, lost productivity (Fisher, Hoffman, Austin-Lane, & Kao, 2000), and financial costs to employers (McCeney, 1995), such testing disparities are somewhat surprising.

Perhaps employers are more likely to accept the use and misuse of a legal substance, alcohol, rather than an illicit drug such as cannabis. Alcohol abusers are defined as a medically protected group by the Americans With Disabilities Act (1990); employees with alcohol abuse problems tend to receive less severe forms of reprimand compared with illicit substance users. Indeed, individuals with identified alcohol problems typically receive employer-sponsored counseling or formal rehabilitation efforts, whereas illicit substance users more commonly receive dismissal (Tunnell, 2004). Although testing for cannabis use may correctly identify users, it does not successfully identify those comorbid alcohol problems linked with myriad work-interfering behaviors.

THE RELEVANCE OF DRUG TESTING FOR IDENTIFYING PROBLEMATIC CANNABIS USERS

To what extent does employee drug testing accurately identify problem behaviors, delivering benefits that outweigh costs? Numerous studies suggest that drug-testing programs increase worker safety and productivity (Strossen et al., 1999). Yet some data suggest that companies with no drug testing enjoy greater productivity than those with programs (Shepard & Clifton, 1998b), and that drug testing may actually diminish company productivity (Konovsky & Cropanzano, 1991; Shepard & Clifton, 1998a; Shepard & Clifton, 1998b). An examination of the data surrounding worker productivity, safety, and substance use is merited. To address this question, one must examine the tests' procedures, accuracy, and relative costs and benefits to an employer.

Test Procedures

Employers primarily focus drug-testing efforts on three fronts: pre-employment testing, random employee testing, and reasonable cause/post-accident testing. Pre-employment drug testing as a contingency of hiring seeks to screen out

potentially problematic applicants with substance problems. Among companies with drug-testing policies, more than three quarters use pre-employment test strategies, and positively identify approximately 4% of applicants as substance users (*Drug Abuse and the Workplace Demographics,* 2001).

The most controversial of substance use testing, random employee drug testing, purportedly assists companies in monitoring employee stability and safety (Tunnell, 2004). Random drug testing yields approximately 3% positive findings among workers (Drug Abuse and the Workplace Demographics, 2001). Periodic drug tests administered with advance notice to employees is less popular among companies (e.g., 14%) and yields fewer positives (e.g., 1.7%; Drug Testing Index, 1999; Tunnell, 2004).

Finally, companies test a worker when the worker's behavior raises substance abuse concerns (Tunnell, 2004). More than one third of companies with drug testing policies use this general strategy (Hartwell, Steele, French & Rodman, 1996), and 14% of employees tested on that basis return positive results for illicit substances (Drug Testing Index, 1999). Approximately one quarter of companies use a different type of reasonable-cause testing: post-accident testing. Three and a half percent of post-accident tests return positive results (Hartwell et al., 1996; Tunnell, 2004).

Test Accuracy

Traditional on-site workplace drug testing requires the collection of a urine sample (Armbruster, 2002; Tunnell, 2004). Approximately 81% of companies use urine tests; 13% use blood tests; 1% test hair; and another 1% use performance testing. Some workplaces possess the technology for on-site drug screening, but most ship specimens for laboratory-based testing (Armbruster, 2002; Tunnell, 2004). Immunoassay test and chromatography are the two predominant forms of drug testing. Immunoassay tests are the most popular, with accuracy levels between 95% and over 99% (e.g., 99.2% in Kravitz & Brock, 1997). Several of the most popular immunoassay tests include the Enzyme Multiplied Immunoassay Technique (EMIT), the Enzyme-Linked Immunosorbent Assay (ELISA) test, and the Radioimmunoassay (RIA) test. Employee urine samples are processed by comparing them with a calibrator measuring a known amount of a given drug. If the sample is equal to or higher than the known amount, the test is positive (Tunnell, 2004).

Chromatography tests rank second in popularity after immunoassay tests because of higher costs. Gas Chromatography/Mass Spectrometry (GC/MS) is the most popular chromatography test. This test detects the presence of drugs in bodily fluids (e.g., urine or blood) by employing a gas (e.g., helium or nitrogen) to volatize a sample to decipher its components (Kapur, 1994; Tunnell, 2004). Other types of chromatography tests include

Thin-Layer Chromatography (TLC) and Liquid Chromatography (HPLC). Thin-Layer Chromatography offers higher specificity; Liquid Chromatography tends to be less costly but also less sensitive (Kapur, 1994; Tunnell, 2004). Chromatography tests offer even more accurate findings (e.g., 99.7% accuracy, according to Kravitz & Brock, 1997). Accuracy rates do not account for potential human error introduced in the testing process and operation of the highly sophisticated machinery. Thus some researchers estimate that actual accuracy rates may be lower (Butler & Tranter, 1994; Kapur, 1994; Tunnell, 2004).

Despite relatively low margins of error, drug testing is far from infallible. The most popular screening procedures demonstrate problems with cross-reactivity—the tendency to mistake a legal substance for an illicit one. Popular immunoassay tests may confuse substances such as ibuprofen, antiulcer drugs (Tunnell, 2004), appetite enhancers for AIDS sufferers, and nausea suppressants for cancer patients (Strossen et al., 1999) for cannabis metabolites, creating a false positive. Both immunoassay and chromatography testing accuracy also rely on the urine's temperature and pH (Tunnell, 2004). Failure to store samples correctly may introduce additional human error to the testing procedures, potentially creating false positives or negatives (Kapur, 1994; Tunnell, 2004).

Other, more expensive forms of testing do not offer failsafe options. Tests examining hair samples tend to find false positives among dark-haired employees and especially African Americans. Hair that is passively exposed to cannabis smoke is significantly more likely to test positive (Strossen et al., 1999; Tunnell, 2004). Saliva tests have lower error rates than urine tests, but are subject to high rates of cross-reactivity (e.g., Yacoubian & Wish, 2002). Blood tests are among the most accurate, but they are also the most expensive, invasive, difficult to administer, and potentially hazardous for the subject (i.e., by causing infections; Tunnell, 2004). Tunnell (2004) provides a thorough review of drug testing methodology and relative effectiveness.

Counter-Industry for Drug Testing

As the drug-testing industry in the United States grew, a counterindustry designed to obfuscate testing results and decrease test accuracy grew in parallel. Given the prevalence of cannabis use, it is unsurprising that the vast majority of companies offering detoxification products focus on marijuana. The detoxification industry offers advice on how best to purge cannabis metabolites from the system or generate a false positive via masking the presence of a drug or altering a urine sample. Though detoxification products have long been available at local health food and other various specialty stores, the

advent of the Internet has permitted this industry to grow exponentially (Tunnell, 2004).

The detoxification industry offers extensive resources, including information guides to achieving false negatives with simple methods. These conventional methods of duping a drug test enjoy moderate success rates. Substituting one's own urine with a clean urine sample is the most straightforward and effective method. Clean urine samples may be purchased through a vast underground market. Drinking large quantities of water prior to urine testing or consuming over-the-counter diuretics to flush cannabis metabolites assist the body in expelling cannabis metabolites at an increased rate. Individuals attempting this method are advised to take B-complex vitamins prior to testing to ensure proper coloration of the sample. However, this method is well known to many drug-testing laboratories. The National Institute on Drug Abuse has suggested strict limitations on the amount of water that may be consumed immediately prior to drug testing to ensure test accuracy (Tunnell, 2004).

Others attempting to confound urine testing may dilute their specimen with water. As a result, invasive security measures often accompany drug testing. Employee complaints recount scenarios in which the sample must be deposited under the supervision of a drug-testing authority (Strossen et al., 1999). Aware of dilution practices, drug testing companies developed technology to detect abnormally diluted samples. Such procedures require relatively advanced machinery, and impose significant increases in cost for employers (Tunnell, 2004). Still, the detoxification industry met this challenge. Numerous products provide clean urine or assist in urine dilution via devices that attach underneath an employee's clothing. Thus even when monitored closely, an employee could provide a clean urine sample with help from the underground detoxification market.

Various everyday household items, such as table salt, bleach, or hydrogen peroxide, when added to a urine sample, may mask the presence of cannabis metabolites. Detoxification guides instruct employees to store these products under one's fingernails (Tunnell, 2004), on a saturated cotton ball or even soaked in one's clothing. Various detoxification regimens, including regular trips to the sauna, ample hydration, and vitamin supplements are also commonly attempted methods at beating the tests. Alternatively, materials purchased through the detoxification industry may advise employees to list a variety of legal drugs known to mimic cannabis metabolites to offer an explanation for positive results (Tunnell, 2004).

The underground detoxification industry's primary source of revenue, however, comes from an array of designer products created to muddle test results. Natural herbal remedies such as goldenseal appear in products like Detoxification brew, an herbal tea designed to help purge toxins from the body. Yet products such as these do not consistently achieve test-negative re-

sults. More costly manufactured products such as urine additives, pretest flushing agents, drinks designed to prevent cannabis metabolites' release into the body's waste, and shampoos offer superior results. Tunnell (2004) provides a comprehensive review of products offered and the companies behind them. The science behind the widely available products varies.

Whom Do Drug Tests Identify?

Beyond the issue of test reliability, however, remains the fundamental question of precisely whom the drug test identifies with a true positive result. High rates of positive test results among cannabis users reflect both its relatively prevalent use among the workforce (e.g., 9% in the National Household Survey on Drug Abuse, 1999) and the drug's chemical properties. Concentrations of the active ingredient in marijuana, δ^9-tetrahydrocannabinol (THC), accumulate in fat cells, and release into bodily fluids (e.g., urine, blood) over time (Kapur, 1994). Cannabis metabolites remain detectable in the users' urine weeks after the last use. Among chronic users, metabolites may be detectable up to 60 days after use (Dackis, Pottash, Annitto, & Gold, 1982). Because cannabis metabolites take considerable time to process through the body, the test is unlikely to respond to the individual consuming cannabis immediately prior to the test (Tunnell, 2004). Instead, the test may identify more distal use. Accurate tests of on-the-job cannabis intoxication require more sophisticated laboratory procedures (Kapur, 1994).

As previously discussed, cannabis intoxication of those occupying safety-sensitive positions could impair worker abilities. However, traditional drug-testing technology does not have the capacity to identify workers presently intoxicated from cannabis. Positive drug tests do not distinguish problematic workplace intoxication from past recreational use. Recall that a primary goal of drug testing is to identify the substance abuser whose problem diminishes his work performance. If test sensitivity responds to use in the distal past rather than employee intoxication at the time of testing, the question of whether the tests have identified a problematic abuser or occasional user remains. Given the dearth of data supporting a connection between past cannabis use and workplace impairment, the drug test's identification of past cannabis use does not appear as critical to worker health, workplace safety, or employer costs. More relevant to employers and clinicians alike is the issue of cannabis use versus abuse. Yet drug testing is incapable of distinguishing the occasional user with whom few workplace problems are associated from the problematic user who is experiencing negative off-the-job consequences or even on-the-job substance impairments (Frone, 2004; Tunnell, 2004).

PROBLEM CANNABIS USERS' FINANCIAL
COSTS TO EMPLOYERS

The administration, processing, and reporting of drug tests incur high costs for employers. Federal programs offer financial incentives to companies implementing drug testing (Allison & Stahlhut, 1995), but these do not offset the considerable financial burdens that employers' bear. The average laboratory or on-site urine-based drug test costs $15 per test (Armbruster, 2002), but they can cost more than $50 per test. Quality assurance measures may incur higher costs (Kapur, 1994). A positive result, true or false, incurs more cost via expensive confirmatory tests. If false positives are obtained, due diligence mandates costly retesting procedures. Associated costs arise from work loss during testing, test administration, and resulting grievances (Strossen et al., 1999).

Other types of test incur greater costs. The GC/MS test machinery is costly (e.g., $75,000 for GC/MS Hewlett Packard machinery [Tunnel, 2004]; $120,000–$200,000 [Kapur, 1994]), and requires prohibitively expensive confirmatory tests that range from $40 to $75 per test. Tests examining hair samples (e.g., $70 per test) and saliva samples are costly (e.g., at least $30; Craig Medical Distribution, 2005), impose higher costs than urine tests, and also require confirmatory testing.

Findings from the federal government's employee drug-testing program suggest that identifying a single drug user costs more than $75,000 (Focus on Federal Drug Testing, 1991; Strossen et al., 1999). In one of America's largest and most prominent electronics companies, drug testing of 10,000 workers cost more than $1 million. In 1991, the federal government spent an estimated $11.7 million on drug testing at 38 agencies and found only a 0.5% rate of positive results (Strossen et al., 1999). For some small businesses, the costs associated with workplace drug testing are prohibitive. If these costs are not offset by the success of drug testing in accurately identifying those workers that pose the greatest risk and financial burden to employers, one must question their value.

Indeed, large-scale examinations of drug-testing program costs versus benefits find that drug tests' financial costs do not outweigh benefits delivered from recovered productivity, worker retention, or increases in workforce health (Marshman, 1994). It is perhaps unsurprising that many companies that implemented drug testing programs in the 1980s did not maintain them. One third of companies that had drug testing programs in 1988 had discontinued them by 1990. Approximately 10% of large companies and almost 50% of small businesses found that the benefits of drug testing did not offset the high costs (Hayghe, 1991).

If drug testing fails to distinguish the recreational drug user from the problematic drug abuser, then not all individuals testing positive for substances

will benefit from substance abuse rehabilitation efforts (Normand et al., 1990). Whereas a positive drug test may result in employee participation in an employer-sponsored rehabilitation program as a condition of continued employment, the incorporation of drug testing may result in numerous inappropriate rehabilitation referrals (Jacob & Zimmer, 1991). Substance abuse rehabilitation services can incur costs of more than $12,000 per employee (Bahls, 1998). Thus a company that endeavors to treat employee substance abuse using positive drug test results as a criterion may inadvertently refer inappropriate candidates at considerable expense.

Given the wide availability of products designed to mask positive test results, the most seasoned substance abusers may escape helpful rehabilitation, and continue to suffer negative health consequences and incur company costs via lost productivity. Perhaps most important, although cannabis is the most popular illicit substance, dependence rates remain low (Earleywine, 2002). Recall that cannabis is the most frequently identified substance via workplace drug testing (Tunnell, 2004). Thus, referring individuals testing positive for cannabis to employee-sponsored rehabilitation programs may reflect poorly conceived employee policies and unwise expenditures.

HUMAN RESOURCE AND PRODUCTIVITY COSTS

Aside from its financial costs, drug testing may pose costs in terms of employer-employee relations. Employers may lose more than money on drug testing: They may also sacrifice morale. Millions of American jobs require preemptive drug testing as a condition of initial and sustained employment (Strossen et al., 1999). Concerns regarding test accuracy, result privacy, and general work environment may prevent potentially productive workers from entering companies with drug testing policies. Among existing employees, introduction of a drug-testing program may tarnish employee perceptions of a just workplace (Kravitz & Brock, 1997), an attribute linked with better worker attitudes, behavior, and performance (Crant & Bateman, 1989; Konovsky & Cropanzano, 1991). Workers perceive testing for safety-sensitive positions as an acceptable precaution but tend to regard company-wide testing as intrusive (Hanson, 1990; Paronto et al., 2002). Fear of inaccurate test results introduce worker uncertainty and distress, and may engender poor retention of workers without substance problems (Kravitz & Brock, 1997). Alternatively, lack of trust in the workplace could discourage workers with drug problems from entering employer-sponsored drug treatment programs.

The effects of worker attitudes about drug testing may extend beyond individual employee satisfaction, acquisition, and retention rates.

The implementation of drug-testing programs may affect company productivity on a larger organizational scale. An examination of 63 technology companies found that drug testing had reduced employee productivity between 15%–30% across numerous domains (e.g., in wasted resources and low morale). Shepard and Clifton (1998b) contend that these effects may relate to poor management, a correlate of the type of company most likely to adopt drug-testing programs that are ill suited to identify problem drug users. Though the authors caution that the sample was relatively small, they note that the findings cast serious doubt on the effectiveness of drug testing in promoting productivity. Indeed, numerous researchers suggest that the seemingly paradoxical effect of drug testing—that is, though it is instituted to increase employee productivity, it in fact reduces productivity—is indicative of workers' negative perception of employers (e.g., Konovsky & Cropanzano, 1991). Again, perceived lack of respect and justice among employees predicts poor productivity outcomes and lost capital for employers.

GENERAL ALTERNATIVES TO DRUG TESTING

Clearly, employers are well advised to ascertain employee fitness for work, especially in safety-sensitive positions. Yet the extent that drug tests accurately achieve these goals is unclear. Numerous practical, financial, and ideological problems associated with traditional drug testing merit an examination of alternatives. Creating payment schedules contingent on workplace safety and competent performance reduces workplace accidents (Zacharatos & Barling, 2004) and overall injuries (Austin, Kessler, Riccobono, & Bailey, 1996; Haynes, Pine, & Fitch, 1982). Rewarding safety may achieve the stated goals of drug testing without the same expense. Employee assistance programs and health promotion programs and policies offer viable options for maintaining employee well-being and reducing substance-related costs (Shain, 1994). Numerous programs offer effective and cost-efficient options for employers (Browne Miller, 1988; Kertesz, 1989).

Some individuals with cannabis or other substance problems will not volunteer for treatment. When individuals experiencing work-disrupting substance abuse occupy safety-sensitive positions, employers and many employees agree that identification and treatment is imperative (Konovsky & Cropanzano, 1991; Paronto et al., 2002). Once more, drug tests may fail to identify those in need of assistance or likely to pose safety threats. For these individuals, behavioral tests of fitness for work emerge as an effective way of assessing employee work readiness.

BEHAVIORAL ASSESSMENT PROGRAMS
OF WORK READINESS

Several behavioral programs emerge as cost-effective ways to identify problematic workers suffering from work-disrupting problems (e.g., lack of sleep, substance abuse problems, other medical impairments). Butler and Tranter (1994) review behavioral assessments of work readiness tests to monitor drug use and other impairments. For example, the Drug Evaluation and Classification (DEC) program combines performance-based tests with sobriety testing. Supervisors monitor employee appearance, behavior, and job performance. When a problem is suspected, the employee completes an interview assessing general job performance, medical history, and drug use. The employee completes a test for physiological impairments indicative of substance abuse (e.g., vital signs, pupils dilation), and then completes a battery of behavioral tests to assess psychomotor performance. Empirical studies of the DEC program suggest that the program demonstrates considerable success in identifying problematic drug users and others unfit for safety-sensitive work (Butler & Tranter, 1994). In the detection of cannabis intoxication specifically, the test demonstrated moderate success (e.g., sensitivity 61.4%, specificity 93.3%, false positives 6.7%, false negatives 38.6%, efficiency 82.7%; Heishman, Singleton, & Crouch, 1998). Note that this approach can identify workers who are impaired for any reason. Some employers may be just as interested in workers who cannot work because of fatigue, illness, or the side effects of cold medicine as they are in identifying illicit drug use.

COMPUTERIZED BEHAVIORAL ASSESSMENT
PROGRAMS OF WORK READINESS

Critics of programs such as DEC and other supervisor-administered behavioral assessments of substance use argue that supervisor participation may introduce greater error rates, or that a seasoned substance abuser may subvert such a program. When supervisors identify an individual for testing without proving probable cause, legal complications may arise (DuPont, 1990). Supervisors may abuse their discretion, harassing employees with threats of testing (Segal, 1989).

Computerized performance tests offer more regulated alternatives to assessing employee fitness for work (Butler & Tranter, 1994). A computerized test provides a reliable way to measure capacity to perform a given task at a standardized level of performance. Many biological, physiological, psychological, social, and environmental factors outside of drug intoxication

may affect performance. Thus creating a straightforward, failsafe, computerized test that assesses multiple domains of work fitness may prove extremely challenging. At present, three computerized methods of assessing performance have been developed and widely implemented in the workplace: reaction time tasks, critical tracking tasks, and divided-attention tests (Butler & Tranter, 1994). Recall that employees intoxicated with cannabis may experience diminished reaction times, decision making, or motor coordination. Each class of computerized test possesses merits and weaknesses, and no one test has been widely accepted by critics.

First, computerized reaction-time tests present an employee with a stimulus and require that she respond as quickly as possible. Such tests are typically easy to administer and involve less potential for human error than tests involving supervisors or specimen collection. Reaction-time tests typically require the individual to demonstrate the ability to react to visual stimuli, but some require response to an auditory cue (Lisper, Dureman, Ericsson, & Karlsson, 1971). Tests may be administered at the beginning of shifts to demonstrate work competence. Reaction time tasks capture drug intoxication (e.g., alcohol; cannabis [Bird et al., 1980]) and other work-impairing states, such as fatigue (Williamson, Feyer, Mattick, Friswell, & Finlay-Brown, 2001). Critics of the tests note that they are incapable of distinguishing the specific nature of employee impairment (e.g., alcohol, cannabis, etc.), and may be insensitive to some types of intoxication, including cannabis. Individuals who have consumed even large amounts of cannabis may perform relatively well on the test (Dornbush, Fink, & Freeman, 1971; Huestis, 2002; Kvasleth, 1977; Moskowitz, Sharma, & Schapiro, 1972). Nevertheless, if the reaction-time test is a good predictor of work performance, it can separate those who are too impaired to work from all others.

Second, computerized critical tracking tests require an employee to center an object on the computer screen that moves unpredictably. The tests measure hand-eye coordination as well as compensatory reaction time. A critical tracking test may require a worker to center a pointer on a computer screen while the pointer moves in varying directions on the screen (Butler & Tranter, 1994). As in reaction-time tasks, critical tracking tests typically examine reactions to visual stimuli. Poor test performance correlates with both cannabis and alcohol at moderate or high levels but may not help identify low levels of such substances. However, critical tracking tests do appear to be more sensitive to the presence of alcohol and drugs than reaction-time tests (Butler & Tranter, 1994).

An example of a computerized critical tracking test is Performance Factor Incorporated's Factor 1000 critical tracking test. A test taker completes a series of trials in which he must center a cursor on an object in the middle

of the screen. The cursor becomes increasingly difficult to center, requiring fast reaction time and hand-eye coordination. Employees' speed and accuracy are compared both with a general norm, as well as their own previous scores on the test (Comer, 1995). Although the individual's performance may improve over time, a complex algorithm precludes mastery (Maltby, 1990; Stevens, 1990). Compared to traditional drug tests, the test takes less time to administer (about 1 minute), offers frequent testing at lower costs (e.g., $100 per employee per year, according to Fine, 1992), and demonstrates higher rates of accuracy at determining impairment (Flaig, 1990; Frieden, 1990; Maltby, 1990; Stevens, 1990). Similar critical tracking tasks are sensitive to alcohol intoxication at rates up to 100% after several iterative trials (Klein & Jex, 1975). Results are immediately available, and impaired workers may be prevented from working. The test also addresses intentional underperformance, setting the probability of failing all trials at approximately 0.5 percent.

Third, the divided-attention test examines employee ability to attend to two stimuli simultaneously. One such test requires the subject to operate a car and quickly decide between avoiding an oncoming car or a child darting into the street (Mills, 1991). A more complicated task than simple reaction time or critical tracking tests, the divided-attention task may better simulate challenges facing an intoxicated individual experiencing a potentially dangerous situation. The intoxicated employee typically demonstrates far greater difficulty in successfully navigating the divided-attention task. Research suggests that such tests are capable of detecting lower levels of both cannabis and alcohol compared to other types of performance-based assessments (Hindmarch, Kerr, & Sherwood, 1991; Mills & Bisgrove, 1983; Mills, Bisgrove, Hill, Ballard, & Stepney, 1986; Moskowitz & Burns, 1981; Perez-Reyes, Hicks, Bumberry, Jeffcoat, & Cook, 1988).

Stein (1986) reviews a divided-attention task that may be adapted for work fitness testing and found that it successfully detected cannabis intoxication on tasks such as negotiating speed and steering. Yet other tasks did not identify cannabis intoxication, or they identified only higher levels of cannabis use. Empirical reviews of other divided-attention tests suggest that they are sensitive to alcohol intoxication and sleep deprivation, but like many other performance tests may only detect cannabis intoxication at high doses (Huestis, 2002). However, the test is superior to standard drug tests inasmuch as it provides an assessment of on-the-job impairment.

The three basic genres of computerized tests demonstrate considerable sensitivity but lesser specificity. Precise measures of sensitivity and selectivity of these measures vary greatly in the literature and have yet to be standardized across test genres. The lack of these empirically validated data imposes a challenge to the adoption of computerized behavioral assess-

ment. Further research will provide more information. Recall, however, that such tests cannot provide details regarding the employee's specific problem (e.g., alcohol, cannabis, depression, etc.). Thus computerized tests demonstrate limited specificity inasmuch as they offer an indication of worker impairment but little detailed information (Butler & Tranter, 1994). Then again, employers may be markedly more interested in whether an employee can work productively than in the specific cause of diminished productivity.

Computerized behavioral assessments of work readiness provide considerable reliability, but their validity may be called into question. The test is reliable in that it measures the same factors consistently. Because the tests gauge general performance, reliability regarding testing of drug and alcohol impairment may be compromised. However, if employers seek to measure employee general work readiness rather than drug use, computerized behavioral measures are highly reliable. Though some argue that the identification of impairment provides enough information for a safety-conscious employer, others question how generalizable the skills required to pass such tests are to actual work tasks. A new generation of more advanced and specified work readiness computerized tasks may test task-specific readiness more accurately.

PAPER-BASED BEHAVIORAL ASSESSMENTS OF WORK READINESS

Critics of computerized performance tests may suggest that such tests require costly investments in equipment and administration. Installing computers and testing equipment in business where computers are not readily available could impose large costs (e.g., $100 per employee annually, according to Fine, 1994). Although still less costly than drug tests for all employees for large businesses, small businesses may not be able to afford computerized tests.

Generic, paper-based performance tests offer a straightforward and cost-effective way to address fitness for work in safety-sensitive positions. Motor ability tests examine gross/fine motor capabilities, including factors such as balance and dexterity. Adapted roadside sobriety tests evaluate balance, dexterity, and coordination. Reeve et al. (1983, as cited in Huestis, 2002) found that 94% of subjects failed roadside sobriety and coordination tests 90 minutes after smoking marijuana. Learning tests gauge the employee's ability to engage in basic learning tasks. Basic tests of reading comprehension may be used to examine learning (Butler & Tranter, 1994).

Memory tests measure employee ability to remember important information (e.g., WMS-III, 1997). Sensitivity and specificity of such tests have

been conducted in neuropsychological research (e.g., Taylor & Heaton, 2001), potentially providing baseline norms for impairment testing. Decision-making tests will examine their capacity to apply logical reasoning in the job environment quickly (Baddeley, 1968). Huestis and colleagues (1992d) found that individuals who consumed only one cannabis cigarette performed significantly worse on logical reasoning tasks than those who did not.

In their review of behavioral measures of performance, Butler and Tranter (1994) offer procedural recommendations for establishing an effective testing regimen for employee work readiness. The authors recommend task analyses of safety-sensitive positions to determine the levels of information processing and motor coordination critical to competent job performance. They also recommend laboratory-based tests of measurement protocols designed specifically for certain safety-sensitive jobs. Test administrators may then develop a battery of tests (e.g., computerized, general, other) appropriate for a position, and begin preliminary testing in the field to examine validity, practicality, acceptability, and so on. Then employers may maintain the program by modifying as needed (Butler & Tranter, 1994).

Random performance testing or even brief testing prior to the beginning of a shift could ensure greater competence among workers, help in the identification of substance abuse or other employee problems, and decrease costly workplace accidents and impairment. Though such steps may seem time consuming and costly, recall that repeated drug tests cost far more annually and require similar iterative steps.

Given the array of problems associated with traditional drug-testing programs and the sound alternatives available, the question of their popularity remains. Even in safety-sensitive environments, drug testing offers a particularly poor tool for the identification of problematic cannabis users. Instead of identifying workplace intoxication, the tests detect more distal cannabis use. Though some may argue that distal cannabis use is likely representative of a pattern of use behavior suggesting workplace intoxication, the number of cannabis users in the American workplace would suggest that this pattern is unlikely. Whereas traditional drug tests cannot decipher the recreational cannabis user from the individual attending work while intoxicated, the test fails to identify those workers whose use poses potential safety and productivity threats.

Alignment of public opinion and employer practices with sound research could reduce costs to employers, identify and assist those cannabis abusers in need of help, and maintain employee rights to maintain privacy regarding their personal lives. As mentioned early in this chapter, Ford Motor Company once promoted home visitations, evaluations, and subsequent dismissals for employees who failed to meet lifestyle standards unrelated to job performance. Under a modern lens, such practices are laughably

inappropriate and invasive. In time, perhaps the advent of more efficient and effective methods of identifying worker substance abuse problems will lead history to regard modern drug-testing policies as similarly emblematic of a less progressive era.

NOTES

1. Several more general studies find that substance users may incur greater costs to employer health-care plans, whereas others suggest that even problematic drug users do not cost employers significantly more in terms of health benefits than nonusers (e.g., French, Roebuck, McGeary, Chitwood, & McCoy, 2001).

2. It is notable that numerous studies suggest that even heavy alcohol use outside of work hours does not decrease worker safety or productivity (e.g., Veazie & Smith, 2000).

REFERENCES

Allison, L. K., & Stahlhut, E. H. J. (1995). DOT, ADA, and FMLA: Overlap, similarities, and differences with respect to the new alcohol and drug testing rules. *Labor Law Journal, 46*, 153–161.

American Management Association. (2001). *U.S. corporations reduce levels of medical, drug and psychological testing of employees.* New York: Author.

American Psychiatric Association. (1994). *Diagnostic and statistical manual of mental disorders* (4th ed.). Washington, DC: Author.

Americans With Disabilities Act of 1990, 42 U.S.C.A. § 12101 *et seq.* (West 1993).

Armbruster, D. (2002). On-site workplace drug-testing. In A. Jenkins & B. Goldberger (Eds.), *On-site drug testing* (pp. 25–36). Ohio: Forensic Science and Medicine.

Arons, A., Greene Foster, D., & Smucker, S. (2002). *Chronic conditions and barriers to employment in California.* Sacramento: California Department of Social Services.

Austin, J., Kessler, M. L., Riccobono, J. E., & Bailey, J. S. (1996). Using feedback and reinforcement to improve the performance and safety of a roofing crew. *Journal of Organizational Behavior Management, 16*, 49–75.

Baddeley, A. D. (1968). A three minute reasoning test based on grammatical transformation. *Psychonomic Science, 10*, 341–345.

Bahls, J. E. (1998, February). Drugs in the workplace. *HR Magazine, 43*, 81–87.

Bass, A. R., Bharucha-Reid, R., Delaplane-Harris, K., Schork, M. A., Kaufmann, R., McCann, D., et al. (1983). Beverage report. *Occupational Safety and Health, 13*, 25–27.

Bass, A. R., Bharucha-Reid, R., Delaplane-Harris, K., et al. (1996). Employee drug use, demographic characteristics, work reactions, and absenteeism. *Journal of Occupational Health Psychology, 1*, 92–99.

Beaumont, P., & Allsop, S. (1983). Beverage Report. *Occupational Health & Safety*, 25-27

Bird, K. D., Boleyn, T., Chesher, G. B., Jackson, D. M., Starmer, G. A., & Teo, R. K. (1980). Intercannabinoid and cannabinoid-ethanol interactions and their effects on human performance. *Psychopharmacology, 71*, 181–187.

Blank, D., & Fenton, J. (1989). Early employment testing for marijuana: Demographic and employee retention patterns. In S. Gust & J. Walsh (Eds.), *Drugs in the workplace: Research and evaluation data* (monograph 91, pp. 151–167). Rockville, MD: National Institute on Drug Abuse.

Bloom, J. W., Kaltenborn, W. T., Paoletti, I. P., Camilli, A., & Leibowitz, M. D. (1987). Respiratory effects of non-tobacco cigarettes. *British Medical Journal, 295*, 1516–1518.

Browne Miller, A. (1988). New perspectives on chemical dependence treatment evaluation: A case study. *Employee Assistance Quarterly, 4*, 45.

Bureau of Labor Statistics, United States Department of Labor. (2004). *Workplace injuries and illnesses.* Washington, DC: United States Department of Labor.

Butler, B., & Tranter, D. (1994). Behavioral tests to assess performance. In S. Macdonald & P. M. Roman (Eds.), *Drug testing in the workplace: Vol. 11* (pp. 231–256). *Research advances in alcohol and drug problems.* New York: Plenum Press.

Centers for Disease Control and Prevention. (2000). Smoking and lung cancer. Atlanta, GA: Author.

Chait, L. D., & Pierri, J. (1992). Effects of smoked marijuana on human performance: A critical review. In L. Murphy & A. Bartke (Eds.), *Marijuana/cannabinoids: Neurobiology and neurophysiology* (pp. 387–423). Boca Raton, FL: CRC.

Coambs, B. R., & McAndrews, M. P. (1994). The effects of psychoactive substances on workplace performance. In S. Macdonald & P. M. Roman (Eds.), *Drug testing in the workplace: Vol. 11* (pp. 77–96). *Research advances in alcohol and drug problems.* New York: Plenum Press.

Cohen, S. (1976). The 94 day cannabis study. *Annals of the New York Academy of Sciences, 282*, 24–34.

Comer, D. (1995, August 15). *An evaluation of fitness for duty testing.* Paper presented at the 103rd Annual Convention of the American Psychological Association, New York.

Craig Medical Distribution (2005). *Drug tests.* Retrieved March 15, 2005, from http://www.craigmedical.com.

Crant, J. M., & Bateman, T. S. (1989). A model of employee responses to drug testing programs. *Employee Responsibilities and Rights Journal, 2*, 173–190.

Currie, E. (1997). *Reckoning: Drugs, the cities, and the American future.* New York: Hill & Wang.

Dackis, C. A., Pottash, A. L. C., Annitto, W., & Gold, M. S. (1982). Persistence of urinary marijuana levels after supervised abstinence. *American Journal of Psychiatry, 139,* 1196–1198.

Department of Health and Human Services (DHHS). (1999). *Substance abuse and mental health characteristics by employment status.* Washington, DC: U.S. Government Printing Office.

DiNardo, J. (1994). A critical review of the estimates of the costs of alcohol and drug use. In S. Macdonald & P. M. Roman (Eds.), *Drug testing in the workplace: Vol. 11* (pp. 57–73). *Research advances in alcohol and drug problems.* New York: Plenum Press.

Dornbush, R. L., Fink, M., & Freeman, A. M. (1971). Marijuana, memory, and perception. *American Journal of Psychiatry, 128,* 194–197.

Drug abuse and the workplace demographics. (2001). Washington, DC: Office of National Drug Control Policy.

DuPont, R. L. (1990). Mandatory random testing needs to be undertaken at the worksite. In R. C. Engs (Ed.), *Controversies in the addiction field* (pp. 105–111). Dubuque, IA: Kendall/Hunt.

Earleywine, M. (2002). *Understanding marijuana.* New York: Oxford University Press.

Earleywine, M., & Smucker Barnwell, S. V. (in preparation). Cigarettes consumption moderates the link between cannabis use and respiratory symptoms.

Executive Order No. 12,564, 3 C.F.R. 224. (1986), reprinted as amended in 5 USC 7301 (1986).

Fine, C. R. (1992). Video tests are the new frontier in drug detection. *Personnel Journal, 6,* 149–161.

Fisher, C., Hoffman, K. J., Austin-Lane, J., & Kao, T. C. (2000). The relationship between heavy alcohol use and work productivity loss: A secondary analysis for the 1995 DoD Worldwide Survey. *Military Medicine, 165,* 355–361.

Flaig, J. M. (1990). Preserving employee rights during the war on drugs. *Pacific Law Journal, 21,* 995–1033.

Focus on Federal Drug Testing. (1991). *Individual employment rights, BNA.* Forensic Drug Abuse Advisor.

French, M. T., Roebuck, C., & Alexandre, P. K. (2001). Illicit drug use, employment, and labor force participation. *Southern Economic Journal, 68,* 349–368.

French, M. T., Roebuck, M. C., McGeary, K. A., Chitwood, D. D., & McCoy, C. B. (2001). Using the Drug Abuse Screening Test (DAST—10) to analyze health services utilization and cost for substance abusers in a community based setting. *Substance Use and Misuse, 36,* 935–939.

Frieden, J. (1990). America's response to substance abuse. *Business and Health, 8,* 32–42.

Frone, M. R. (2004). Alcohol, drugs, and workplace safety outcomes: A view from a general model of employee substance use and productivity. In J. Barling & M. R. Frone (Eds.), *Psychology of workplace safety* (pp. 127–156). Washington, DC: American Psychological Association.

Gergen, M. K., Gergen, K. J., & Morse, S. J. (1972). Correlates of marijuana use among college students. *Journal of Applied Social Psychology, 2,* 1–16.

Grant, B. F., & Pickering, R. (1998). The relationship between cannabis use and DSM-IV cannabis abuse and dependence: Results from the National Longitudinal Alcohol Epidemiological Survey. *Journal of Substance Abuse, 10,* 255–264.

Greenfield, S. F., & O'Leary, G. (1999). Sex differences in marijuana use in the United States. *Harvard Review of Psychiatry, 6,* 297–303.

Gust, S. W., & Walsh, J. M. (1989). Drugs in the workplace: Research and evaluation data (DHHS publication no. [ADM] 89–1612). Rockville, MD: National Institute on Drug Abuse.

Hanson, M. (1990, July). What employees say about drug testing. *Personnel,* 32–36.

Hartford. (2004). Drug screening and testing. *Loss control technical information paper series.* Hartford publication no. 140.014. Washington, DC: The Hartford.

Hartwell, T. D., Steele, P. D., French, M. T., & Rodman, N. F. (1996, November). Prevalence of drug testing in the workplace. *Monthly Labor Review,* 35–42.

Hayghe, H. V. (1991, April). Anti-drug programs in the workplace: Are they here to stay? *Monthly Labor Review,* 26–29.

Haynes, R. S., Pine, R. C., & Fitch, H. G. (1982). Reducing accidents with organizational behaviour modification. *Academy of Management Journal, 25,* 407–416.

Heishman, S. J., Singleton, E. G., & Crouch, D. J. (1998). Laboratory validation study of drug evaluation and classification program: Alprazolam, *d*-amphetamine, codeine, and marijuana. *Journal on Analytical Toxicology, 22,* 503–510.

Hindmarch, I., Kerr, J. S., & Sherwood, N. (1991). The effects of alcohol and other drugs on psychomotor performance and cognitive function. *Alcohol and Alcoholism, 26,* 7179.

Hooker, W. D., & Jones, R. T. (1987). Increased susceptibility to memory intrusions and the Stroop interference effect during acute marijuana intoxication. *Psychopharmacology, 91,* 20–24.

Huestis, M. A. (2002). Cannabis (marijuana)—Effects on human behavior and performance. *Forensic Science Review, 14,* 16–60.

Huestis, M. A., Sampson, A. H., Holicky, B. J., Henningfield, J. E., & Cone, E. J. (1992d). Characterization of the absorption phase of marijuana smoking. *Clinical Pharmacological Therapy, 52,* 31–36.

Jacobs, J. B., & Zimmer, L. (1991). Drug treatment and workplace drug testing: Politics, symbolism, and organizational dilemmas. *Behavior Sciences and the Law, 9,* 345–360.

Kaestner, R. (1994). The effects of illicit drug use on the labor supply of young adults. *Journal of Human Resources, 29,* 123–136.

Kagel, J. H., Battalio, R. C., & Miles, C. G. (1980). Marihuana and work performance. *Journal of Human Resources, 15,* 373–393.

Kandel, D. B., & Davies, M. (1996). High school students who use crack and other drugs. *Archives of General Psychiatry, 53,* 71–80.

Kapur, B. (1994). Drug testing methods and interpretation of test results. In S. Macdonald & P. M. Roman (Eds.), *Drug testing in the workplace: Vol. 11* (pp. 103–120). *Research advances in alcohol and drug problems.* New York: Plenum Press.

Kertesz, L. (1989). McDonnell Douglas EAP trims health care costs. *Business Insurance, 13,* 56–69.

Klein, R. H., & Jex, H. R. (1975). Effects of alcohol on a critical tracking task. *Journal of Studies on Alcohol, 36,* 11–20.

Knudsen, H. K., Roman, P. M., & Johnson, J. A. (2003). Organizational compatibility and workplace drug testing: Modeling the adoption of innovative social control practices. *Sociological Forum 18,* 621–640.

Konovsky, M. A., & Cropanzano, R. (1991). Perceived fairness of employee drug testing as a predictor of employee attitudes and job performance. *Journal of Applied Psychology, 76,* 698–707.

Kravitz, D. A., & Brock, P. (1997). Evaluations of drug-testing programs. *Employee Responsibilities & Rights Journal, 10,* 65–86.

Kvasleth, T. O. (1977). Effects of marijuana on human reaction time and motor control. *Perceptual Motor Skills, 45,* 935.

Lehman, W. E. K., & Simpson, D. D. (1992). Employee substance use and on-the-job behaviors. *Journal of Applied Psychology, 77,* 309–321.

Lisper, H., Dureman, I., Ericsson, S., & Karlsson, N. G. (1971). Effects of sleep deprivation and prolonged driving on a subsidiary auditory reaction time. *Accident Analysis and Prevention, 2,* 335–341.

Maltby, L. L. (1990). Put performance to the test. *Personnel, 67,* 30–31.

Mangione, T. W., Howland, J., Amick, B., Cote, J., Lee, M., Bell, N., et al. (1999). Employee drinking practices and work performance. *Journal of Studies on Alcohol, 60,* 261–270.

Margolin, A., Avants, S. K., Warburton, L. A., & Hawkins, K. A. (2002). Factors affecting cognitive functioning in a sample of HIV-seropositive injection drug users. *AIDS Patient Care and STDs, 16,* 255–267.

Marshman, J.A. (1994). Evaluation approaches for effectiveness and cost effectiveness for drug testing programs. In S. Macdonald & P. M. Roman (Eds.), *Drug testing in the workplace: Vol. 11* (pp. 121–140). *Research advances in alcohol and drug problems.* New York: Plenum Press.

Martin, J. K., Kraft, J. M., & Roman, P. M. (1994). Extent and impact of alcohol and drug use problems in the workplace: A review of the empirical evidence. In S. Macdonald & P.M. Roman (Eds.), *Drug testing in the workplace: Vol. 11* (pp. 3–26). *Research advances in alcohol and drug problems.* New York: Plenum Press.

McCeney, S. K. (1995). Employer based aftercare and follow-up for the recovering alcoholic employee. *Dissertation Abstracts International Section A: Humanities & Social Sciences, 55,* 2774.

McGlothlin, H. W., & West, L. J. (1968). The marijuana problem: An overview. *American Journal of Psychiatry, 125,* 1126–1134.

Mensch, B. S., & Kandel, D. B. (1988). Do job conditions influence the use of drugs? *Journal of Health and Social Behavior, 29,* 169–184.

Mills, K. (1991). *Behavioral performance test for the assessment of substance abuse in the workplace.* Paper presented at the 1991 Drug-Free Workplace Conference and Exposition, Anaheim, CA.

Mills, K., & Bisgrove, E. Z. (1983). Body sway and divided attention performance under the influence of alcohol: Dose-response differences between males and females. *Alcoholism: Clinical and Experimental Research, 74,* 393–398.

Mills, K., Bisgrove, E. Z., Hill, G., Ballard, F., & Stepney, C. (1986). *A computer test of actual and simulated BAC impairment.* National Institute on Alcohol Abuse and Alcoholism, Small Business Research Grant, Phase 1, 1 R43 AA 06522–01, London, Ontario.

Moll van Charante, A., & Mulder, P. G. (1990). Perceptual acuity and the risk of accidents. *American Journal of Epidemiology, 131*(4), 652–663.

Moore, S., Grunberg, L., & Greenberg, E. (1998). Correlates of drug testing attitudes in a sample of blue collar workers. *The Employee Responsibilities and Rights Journal, 11,* 135–150.

Morgan, J. P. (1988). The "scientific" justification for urine drug testing. *University of Kansas Law Review, 36,* 683–697.

Moskowitz, H., Sharma, S., & Schapiro, M. (1972). The effects of marihuana upon peripheral vision as a function of the information processing demands upon central vision. *Perceptual and Motor Skills, 35,* 875–891.

Moskowitz, H., & Burns, M. (1981). The effects of alcohol and caffeine in combination on driving-related skills. In L. Gildberg (Ed.), *Alcohol, and Traffic Safety* (Vol. 3, pp. 969–983). Stockholm: Almqvist & Wiksell.

National Institute on Drug Abuse. (1996). *National household survey on drug abuse.* Washington DC: U.S. Department of Health and Human Services.

Newcomb, M. D. (1988). *Drug use in the workplace: Risk factors for disruptive substance use among young adults.* Dover, MA: Auburn House.

Normand, J. S., Salyards, S., & Mahoney, J. (1990). An evaluation of preemployment drug testing. *Journal of Applied Psychology, 75,* 629–639.

Parish, D. (1989). Relation of pre-employment drug testing result to employment status: A one-year follow-up. *Journal of General Internal Medicine, 4,* 44–47.

Paronto, M. E., Truxillo, D. M., Bauer, T. N., & Leo, M. C. (2002). Drug testing, drug treatment, and marijuana use: A fairness perspective. *Journal of Applied Psychology, 87,* 1159–1166.

Perez-Reyes, M., Hicks, R. E., Bumberry, J., Jeffcoat, A. R., & Cook, C. E. (1988). Interaction between marihuana and ethanol: Effects on psychomotor performance. *Alcoholism: Clinical and Experimental Research, 12,* 268–276.

Polen, M. R. (1993). Health care use by frequent marijuana smokers who do not smoke tobacco. *Western Journal of Medicine, 158,* 596–601.

Ravaglia, S., Costa, A., Ratti, M. T., Savoldi, F., Bo, P., & Moglia, A. (2002). Cognitive impairment and central motor conduction time in chronic alcoholics. *Functional Neurology, 17,* 83–86.

Reeve, V. C., Robertson, W. B., Grant, J., Soares, J. R., Zimmermann, E. G., Gillespie, H. K., et al. (1983). Hemolyzed blood and serum levels of delta-THC: Effects on the performance of roadside sobriety tests. *Journal of Forensic Science, 28,* 963–987.

Reilly, D., Didcott, P., Swift, W., & Hall, W. (1998). Long-term cannabis use: Characteristics of users in an Australian rural area. *Addiction, 93,* 837–846.

Roman, P. M., & Blum, T. C. (1995). Employers. In R. H. Coombs & D. M. Ziedonis (Eds.), *Handbook on drug abuse prevention: A comprehensive strategy to prevent the abuse of alcohol and other drugs* (pp. 139–158). Boston: Allyn & Bacon.

Segal, J. A. (1989, December). How reasonable is your suspicion? *Personnel Administrator,* 103–104.

Shain, M. (1994). Alternatives to drug testing. In S. Macdonald & P. M. Roman (Eds.), *Drug testing in the workplace: Vol. 11* (pp. 257–287). *Research advances in alcohol and drug problems.* New York: Plenum Press.

Shepard, E., & Clifton, T. (1998a). Drug testing and labor productivity: Estimates applying a production function model. *Le Moyne College Institute of Industrial Relations, 18,* 1–30.

Shepard, E., & Clifton, T. (1998b). Drug testing: Does it really improve labor productivity? *Working USA, 76,* 13–18.

Sidney, S., Beck, J. E., Tekawa, I. S., Quesenberry, C. P., Jr., & Friedman, G. D. (1997). Marijuana use and mortality. *American Journal of Public Health, 87,* 585–590.

Sindelar, J. L. (1998). Social costs of alcohol. *Journal of Drug Issues, 28,* 763–780.

Smith, D. E. (1968). The acute and chronic toxicity of marijuana. *Journal of Psychedelic Drugs, 2,* 37–48.

Smucker Barnwell, S. V., Earleywine, M., & Gordis, E. B. (2005). Alcohol moderates the link between cannabis use and dependence. *Psychology of Addictive Behaviors, 19,* 212–216.

Stein, A. C. (1986, September). *A simulator study of the effects of alcohol and marihuana on driving behavior.* Paper presented at the 10th International Conference on Alcohol, Drugs and Traffic Safety, Amsterdam.

Stevens, W. K. (1990, March 6). Measuring workplace impairment. *New York Times,* B5, B8.

Strossen, N., Glasser, I., & Clark, S. (1999). Drug testing: A bad investment. Washington, DC: ACLU Press.

Substance Abuse and Mental Health Administration (SAMSHA). (2000). *Summary of findings from the 1999 National Household Survey on Drug Abuse.* Rockville, MD: Author.

Substance Abuse and Mental Health Administration (SAMSHA). (2004). *Drug free workplace programs.* Rockville, MD: Author.

Tart, C. T. (1971). *On being stoned.* Palo Alto, CA: Science and Behavior Books.

Tashkin, D. P., Simmons, M. S., Sherrill, D. L., & Coulson, A. H. (1997). Heavy habitual marijuana smoking does not cause an accelerated decline in FEVI age. *American Journal of Respiratory and Critical Care Medicine, 155,* 141–148.

Taylor, M. J., & Heaton, R. K. (2001). Sensitivity and specificity of WAIS–III/WMS–III demographically corrected factor scores in neuropsychological assessment. *Journal of the International Neuropsychological Society, 7,* 867–874.

Tunnell, K. (2004). *Pissing on demand.* New York: New York University Press.

United States Department of Labor. (2006). *Alcohol and drug abuse in America today: General workplace impact.* Washington, DC: Office of the Assistant Secretary for Policy.

United States Secretary of Health, Education and Welfare. (1980). *Marihuana and health: Eighth annual report to the U.S. Congress.* Rockville, MD: National Institute on Drug Abuse.

Veazie, M. A., & Smith, G. S. (2000). Heavy drinking, alcohol dependence, and injuries at work among young workers in the United States labor force. *Alcoholism: Clinical and Experimental Resesearch, 24,* 1811–1819.

Voss, H. (1989). Patterns of drug use: Data from the 1985 National Household Survey. In S. Gust and J. Walsh (Eds.), *Drugs in the workplace: Research and evaluation data* (pp. 33–46). National Institute on Drug Abuse Research Monograph 91. DHHS Pub. No. (ADM) 89–1612. Washington, DC: Supt. of Docs., U.S. Govt. Print. Office.

Walsh, D. C., Hingson, R. W., Merrigan, D. M., & Cupples, L. A., Levenson, S. M., & Coffman, G. A. (1991). Associations between alcohol and cocaine use in a sample of problem-drinking employees. *Journal of Studies on Alcohol, 52,* 17–25.

Weller, R. A., & Halikas, J. A. (1980). Objective criteria for the diagnosis of marijuana abuse. *Journal of Nervous and Mental Disease, 176,* 719–725.

Weschler D. (1997). Weschler Memory Scale-Revised, Third Edition.. San Antonio, TX: Psychological Corporation.

Wetzel, C. D., Janowsky, D. S., & Clopton, P. L. (1982). Remote memory during marijuana intoxication. *Psychopharmacology, 76,* 278–281.

Williamson, A. M., Feyer, A. M., Mattick, R. P., Friswell, R., & Finlay-Brown, S. (2001). Developing measures of fatigue using measure of alcohol to validate effects of fatigue on performance. *Accident Analysis and Prevention, 33,* 313–326.

Yacoubian, E. S., & Wish, E. D. (2002). A comparison of the Intercept Oral Specimen Collection Device (IOSCD)® to laboratory urinalysis among Baltimore City treatment clients. *International Journal of Drug Testing, 3,* 132–145.

Zacharatos, A., & Barling, J. (2004). High-performance work systems and occupational safety. In J. Barling & M. R. Frone (Eds.), *Psychology of workplace safety* (pp. 203–222). Washington, DC: American Psychological Association.

Zimmer, L. & Morgan, J. P. (1997). *Marijuana myths, marijuana facts.* New York: Lindesmith Center.

Zwerling, C., Ryan, J., & Orav, J. E. (1990). The efficacy of preemployment drug screening for marijuana and cocaine in predicting employment outcome. *Journal of the American Medical Association, 264,* 2639–43.

4   Marijuana and Driving: Trends, Design Issues, and Future Recommendations

Anthony Liguori

Marijuana smoking, whether alone or in conjunction with alcohol or other drug use, has frequently been associated with automobile driving. Young marijuana users are particularly at risk for driving while intoxicated. In a 2001 survey of American high school seniors, 15% of respondents reported driving under the influence of marijuana (O'Malley & Johnston, 2003). For comparison, approximately 16% reported driving under the influence of alcohol. In another survey, approximately 50% of marijuana users between 18 and 21 years old reported smoking marijuana while driving, driving under the influence of marijuana, or both (Johnson & White, 1989). The marijuana-driving connection is particularly troublesome in North America, where the likelihood of delta-9-tetrahydrocannabinol (THC) being associated with a fatal collision is approximately five times greater than in other continents (Jones, Shinar, & Walsh, 2003). Across several studies, THC has been present in up to 14% of injured or killed drivers (for review, see Ramaekers, Berghaus, van Laar, & Drummer, 2004). Other surveys have found THC in 30 to 33% of injured or reckless automobile or motorcycle drivers (Brookoff, Cook, Williams, & Mann, 1994; Soderstrom, Dischinger, Kerns, & Trifillis, 1995).

Since 1981, every U.S. president has proclaimed December National Drunk and Drugged Driving Prevention Month. However, in December 2004, marijuana was the only illicit drug specifically targeted for use prevention by the Office of National Drug Control Policy in a campaign entitled "Steer Clear of Pot," suggesting that marijuana is a harmful and impairing

drug particularly among teenagers. Despite this attention and notoriety, the self-reported effects of marijuana on driving vary among users (Neale, 2001). Some drivers report positive effects such as improved vision and decreased propensity to speed or engage in other risky maneuvers. Others report negative effects on driving, including impairments in concentration and vehicular control. One question remains: To what extent does marijuana use directly contribute to a crash?

This chapter summarizes the current state of peer-reviewed research on acute marijuana effects on both actual and simulated driving. Most research on the connection between marijuana use and driving may be divided into three major classes of studies that occasionally overlap. These classes are (1) post-hoc epidemiological surveys examining the extent to which prior marijuana use predicted collision-related injuries; (2) simulated driving studies; and (3) studies of actual on-road driving. While several reviews of the existing literature have drawn comparable conclusions, the available peer-reviewed literature has been marked by several inconsistencies in the methods used and samples recruited. The emphasis of this chapter will be on identifying the strengths and limitations of the procedural approaches within this area of research. In determining the effects of marijuana use on driving, one must study not only results but also experimental design components such as route of administration, dose selection, drugs administered concurrently within the study, realism of driving simulation, and key dependent driving measures. Participant pre-study marijuana and other drug use patterns also must be considered. These characteristics are summarized separately below.

EPIDEMIOLOGICAL SURVEYS

Although necessarily retrospective in approach, urine or blood analyses and regression modeling are often used to determine the frequency and likelihood of THC's role in driving accidents. The frequent prevalence of THC in the bloodstreams of marijuana users who drive might suggest that marijuana use directly or indirectly contributes to automobile collisions. However, other recent surveys have raised conflicting evidence for the direct impairing role of marijuana. In a cohort of nearly 65,000 Californians completing a health checkup, responses to a self-report questionnaire on tobacco, alcohol, and marijuana use were regressed to subsequent hospitalization due to a variety of injuries (Gerberich et al., 2003). Marijuana use was associated with increased rates of hospitalization due to motor vehicle–related injury. Whether this connection is confounded by other illicit drug use or whether any of the accidents were caused by marijuana could not be determined. In a sample of injured drivers presenting to an emergency room in Colorado

within one hour of a crash, toxicological assays and crash reconstructions indicated that marijuana use by itself was not associated with crash responsibility (Lowenstein & Koziol-McLain, 2001). Ultimately, the increased risk of traffic accidents among marijuana users may be more related to personal characteristics of the users rather than the marijuana use itself (Fergusson & Horwood, 2001).

Among these characteristics are alcohol-impaired driving and other risky driving behaviors. In a survey of New Zealand drivers who were asked at the crash site whether they had used marijuana in the prior 3 hours, a significant association between recent marijuana use and car crash injury was reported (Blows et al., 2005). However, the association was rendered insignificant when the authors controlled for other risky behaviors such as alcohol use, increased speed, and drowsy driving. A review of several epidemiological studies that conducted drug tests of drivers concluded that alcohol but not marijuana was more associated with fatal than nonfatal collisions (Macdonald et al., 2003). The authors also concluded that marijuana is relatively less likely than alcohol to cause injuries due to collisions. A longitudinal approach to driving assessment was taken in a study of a cohort of more than 1,000 New Zealand residents who were administered interviews addressing predictive variables and/or driving behaviors at ages 15, 18, 21, and 26 years (Begg, Langley, & Stephenson, 2003). In addition to marijuana dependence before age 21, non–use-related factors such as teenage traffic and nontraffic convictions predicted driving after marijuana use in young adult males. Because risk-taking is often confounded with direct effects of marijuana, the causal role of marijuana has been called into question (Kalant, 2004).

SIMULATED AND ACTUAL DRIVING STUDIES

Several laboratories have investigated THC effects on actual or simulated driving (for reviews, see Ogden & Moskowitz, 2004; Ramaekers et al., 2004; Smiley, 1998). Yet, the peer-reviewed empirical literature on marijuana and driving is surprisingly modest. As might be expected, the driving-related aspects of the studies have varied in their scope, approaches, and validity. Two approaches have dominated the driving literature. The first is an objective approach in which computer-quantified aspects of driving such as reaction times are measured and compared across dose conditions. In one example of this approach (Moskowitz, Hulbert, & McGlothlin, 1976), a car was mounted facing a screen that provided a 160-degree view for the driver. A film was projected on the screen and the driver's use of the brake and gas pedals controlled the speed of the film projection. Some data were counted occurrences (e.g., number of steering reversals of 10 degrees). However,

most of the scores were measured in ratio scales (e.g., average speed, time to first brake, average steering wheel position).

The second common approach is a "checklist" approach in which the occurrence of errors is tabulated and compared across dose conditions. This approach has been favored by researchers from Maastricht University in the Netherlands (Lamers & Ramaekers, 2001; Ramaekers, Robbe, & O'Hanlon, 2000; Robbe, 1998). In a typical study from these laboratories, participants drive an actual vehicle on a closed course. A 90-item list of dichotomous "pass/fail" measures scored by a driving instructor in the passenger seat is used to quantify driver performance. Just as the Moskowitz et al. study used some counted measures, the Maastricht investigators incorporated some computer-quantified items such as standard deviation of lateral position and time out of lane, both of which quantified weaving and lane control.

In addition to the quantification of driving performance, other method-ological aspects have also been highly variable in studies of marijuana use and driving. There is a need for more consistency in research designs that ad-dress the question of marijuana impairment while driving. In order to deter-mine future research needs, the gaps and inconsistencies across existing studies must be identified. The following is an overview of the key questions guiding the review of these studies.

WHO PARTICIPATES IN THESE STUDIES?

Most frequently, the participants are recreational nondependent users who use on a weekly but not daily basis. Like much behavioral research, the study of marijuana and driving has been marked by a noteworthy absence of women, minorities, and older participants. Several studies (Moskowitz et al., 1976; Rafaelsen et al., 1973; Sutton, 1983) used only male participants with no explanation for the exclusion of women. Even in studies with both genders, direct effects of gender have not been analyzed. This is likely be-cause most studies have included relatively small sample sizes (typically 10–20) that preclude adequately powered study of statistically significant gender effects. Women are a minority of marijuana users but represent a large number of Americans. Although men are almost three times more likely to report daily use than women, an estimated 837,000 women were daily marijuana users in 2003 (Office of Applied Studies, 2004). Older adults are similarly underrepresented. The mean age of participants in the existing driving literature has typically been under 30 years, with most par-ticipants not exceeding age 40. Yet approximately 1.4 million of daily mar-ijuana users were aged 26 years or older in 2003 (Office of Applied Studies, 2004).

HOW IS THC GIVEN?

With the noteworthy exception of baked "cannabis cake" containing delta-1-tetrahydrocannabinol resin in one study (Rafaelsen et al., 1973), the THC is typically administered through smoked marijuana cigarettes in empirical studies of driving. The latter approach is the most common route of administration and increases the face validity of the studies. Several studies (Klonoff, 1974; Liguori, Gatto, & Jarrett, 2002; Liguori, Gatto, Jarrett, McCall, & Brown, 2003; Liguori, Gatto, & Robinson, 1998; Moskowitz et al., 1976; Sutton, 1983) have used paced smoking procedures (cf., Higgins & Stitzer, 1986) in which most aspects of smoking topography are subject to time limitations. For example, in one simulator study, participants inhaled for 7 seconds with ad lib duration and puff volume, held the inhalation for 7 seconds, then exhaled, with the next inhalation beginning 23 seconds later (Liguori et al., 2003). This pattern is repeated until the cigarette is fully pyrolized. Unfortunately, such procedures can invite dose manipulation by participants. Because the inhalation duration and puff volume are partially under the control of the participant, a relatively lower volume of smoke may be inhaled when higher potency cigarettes are smoked. Breath-hold duration must be considered carefully in designing studies of driving impairment because variations in puff volume may alter both blood levels of THC and dose-related mood effects (Azorlosa, Heishman, Stitzer, & Mahaffey, 1992).

ARE THE DOSES COMPARABLE TO STREET MARIJUANA?

Studying "typical" marijuana doses is much more difficult than studying the typical doses of other commonly used drugs such as alcohol, caffeine, or nicotine. First, THC levels are highly variable across different types of cannabis and even within marijuana. Second, the potency of marijuana continues to increase beyond levels in marijuana cigarettes prepared and supplied by the National Institute on Drug Abuse for research. THC content in seized marijuana has increased from a mean of 1.8% in 1981 to 3.1% in 1991 to 5.8% in 2001 (ElSohly et al., 2000; Research Institute of Pharmaceutical Sciences Eradication, 2004). Consequently, empirical data may underestimate the effects of more potent "street" marijuana. Third, the inconsistency of dose units across studies makes interpretation difficult. THC has been quantified by weight (e.g., 20 mg), weight relative to participant weight (e.g., 300 µg/kg), and by potency (e.g., 2.6%). These doses are all equivalent in a person of average weight (Ramaekers et al., 2004). Nonetheless, the existing literature has benefited from study of multiple active doses

and placebo-controlled designs. Despite the risk of titration with timed procedures, some differential dose effects have been reported. Thus, while impairments from 2.6–4.0% THC have been compared to blood alcohol concentrations of 0.05 g/dl (Liguori et al., 1998; Ramaekers et al., 2004), these studies do not answer the question of whether currently higher potencies endanger drivers.

IS ANOTHER DRUG STUDIED IN CONJUNCTION WITH MARIJUANA?

Many marijuana users simultaneously use other drugs, with alcohol most frequently paired (Earleywine & Newcomb, 1997). Consequently, nearly every study of marijuana and driving has included one or more alcohol dosing conditions, including one or more marijuana-alcohol combinations. Often the alcohol doses are selected with the goal of producing breath alcohol concentrations at or near the legal limits in Europe (0.05 g/dl) and the United States (0.08 g/dl). The selection of alcohol for interaction studies is logical not only because alcohol is the drug most commonly used with marijuana, but also because THC levels are less easily determined at a crash site than alcohol levels. Unlike alcohol, THC levels cannot be estimated from breath analyses. Easier and more sensitive testing methods for identifying THC levels in saliva are being developed (Teixeira et al., 2004). Nonetheless, the need to clarify the unique and combined contributions of THC and alcohol to collisions remains strong.

HOW REALISTIC IS THE SIMULATOR OR ROAD TEST?

Simulators and on-road testing have improved over time in parallel fashion, with realism varying but generally increasing across studies. From the late 1960s through the mid-1970s, studies used driving simulators that had realistic parts but simply required participants to watch a test film on a screen. In the earliest study (Crancer, Dille, Delay, Wallace, & Haken, 1969), steering, accelerating, and braking in response to events in the film did not alter the film presentation. In a later, more interactive study (Rafaelsen et al., 1973), speed and steering changes altered the movement of the landscape on the film, and occasional red lights appeared to indicate that stopping was required. However, these stop lights were located above and the landscape projected directly on the windshield, as opposed to some perceived distance from the vehicle.

Later studies increased realism of the simulated driving experience not only with improved verisimilitude of the road conditions and car dynamics,

but also with additional tasks to increase the information processing loads on the driver. The earliest (Moskowitz et al., 1976) synchronized a film of 31 miles of travel, projected on a 20-foot-wide cylindrical screen, to the steering, acceleration, and braking of the driver. In addition, the driver completed a "visual subsidiary task" in which lever responses were required in response to light signals near the sun visor of the car. Similar distracting tasks were used in other studies (Smiley, Moskowitz, & Zeidman, 1981; Stein, Allen, Cook, & Karl, 1983). For example, red and green lights on either side of the driver were turned off with foot pedals (Smiley et al., 1981) or signs randomly placed on the road were identified (Stein et al., 1983; see Smiley, 1998 for review).

The subsidiary tasks in these studies both help and hinder the realism of the driving experience. While they succeed in increasing demands upon a driver, they do so in unrealistic ways that would never be used in an actual on-road situation. Consequently, more recent simulator studies have required no additional distracting tasks but have attempted to increase further the realism of the driving experience in other respects. For example, speakers in some simulators under the driver's seat produced vibrations that could be felt by the driver when the vehicle left the road (Liguori et al., 1998, 2002, 2003). These vibrations simulated the rattling that a driver senses when driving on gravel. In addition, the simulated road is presented on multiple computer monitors providing a 180-degree field of vision for the driver.

Early on-road driving studies focused primarily on controlling the vehicle through twisting roads, with some study of speed. In one, a 1.1-mile closed-course driving track (maximum speed 30 miles per hour) was used with brief funnel, serpentine, zig-zag, s-bend, and straightaway components (Hansteen, Miller, Longero, Reid, & Jones, 1976). Participants drove this course for six laps within 10 minutes of smoking. A similarly conceived closed driving course with a tunnel, a U-shaped curve, serpentine components, and 90-degree turns was used in another laboratory (Sutton, 1983). The duration and average required speed within this course were not presented. Another driving course incorporated not only a closed course with cone-defined slalom, tunnel, and funnel components, but also driving on city streets (Klonoff, 1974). That course was approximately 16 miles and included two intersections and variable traffic and weather conditions that were usually moderate and dry.

Later on-road studies incorporated additional measures and tasks in their closed-course settings, typically with a licensed driving instructor either present (Lamers & Ramaekers, 2001; Ramaekers et al., 2000; Robbe, 1998) or following (Peck, Biasotti, Boland, Mallory, & Reeve, 1986). Among the unique aspects of these later studies were estimation of speed without viewing the speedometer (Peck et al., 1986), quantification of headway in a car-following task (Smiley, Noy, & Tostowaryk, 1986), and driving in both

business and residential areas with 2- and 4-lane roads (Lamers & Ramaekers, 2001).

WHAT ASPECTS OF DRIVING ARE BEING MEASURED?

Driving impairment has been operationally defined in many respects, but the most thorough studies have incorporated on-road testing with a plethora of dependent measures. Early simulator studies were limited by relatively primitive realism but did quantify braking, steering, and acceleration in terms of errors or reaction time. For example, Crancer et al. (1969) counted the total number of times the steering wheel was inappropriately placed, the total number of times braking, signaling, or acceleration (or the absence of these driving aspects) was unexpected, and the total number of times speedometer readings were outside a 20-mph range of speeds. Rafaelsen et al. (1973) measured reaction time (with the brake and gas pedals) to randomly appearing red and green lights. The simulator in other recent studies (Liguori et al., 1998, 2002, 2003) provided additional situational variability by quantifying brake latency in response to a yellow fence that appeared before the driver at random distances. However, these studies quantified no other driving measures. A greater combination of breadth and depth of data was provided by Moskowitz et al. (1976), who compiled means and standard deviations for measures of 25 aspects of driving across the areas of speed, steering, tracking, braking, and acceleration.

Early on-road studies quantified driving performance in both subjective and objective terms. In one study, driving was measured in terms of cones struck (on a closed obstacle course) and based on observer ratings of the driver's skills and emotions (e.g., tension, confidence) on city streets (Klonoff, 1974). Other closed-course studies opted for similarly simple measures of driving performance or reliance on observer ratings. For example, one study only quantified car handling (in terms of cones hit) and time to complete the course (Hansteen et al., 1976) but reported no other driving data. Another used subjective observer ratings of traffic violations, speed, atypical acceleration/braking, and centering within the lane but no objective quantification of actual driving performance (Sutton, 1983).

Perhaps the most thorough set of studies is from Maastricht University (Lamers & Ramaekers, 2001; Ramaekers et al., 2000; Robbe, 1998). These studies used road-tracking and car-following tests on a closed segment of highway, followed by a city driving test. The dependent measures included lateral position variability, distance variability, and reaction time to speed changes of a leading vehicle. Another asset of this approach was the inclusion of an eye

tracking system that monitored the extent to which participants observed other vehicles. While this system has filled a need for data on search frequency at intersections, it sacrifices realism because it requires cumbersome head-mounted gear including helmet, visor, and miniature cameras (Lamers & Ramaekers, 2001).

The benefit of the dichotomous "pass/fail" approach, similar to some earlier research (Sutton, 1983), is its breadth of data; other studies limited driving quantification to relatively fewer aspects of driving, such as brake latency, hit obstacles, speed, and/or handling errors (Hansteen et al., 1976; Liguori et al., 1998; Rafaelsen et al., 1973; Sutton, 1983). However, the "checklist" approach inherent in the Maastricht studies provided only general scores related to handling, turning, and observation. Some of the Maastricht studies incorporated objective driving measures such as standard deviation from lane position (Ramaekers et al., 2000; Robbe, 1998), reaction time to speed changes in the car being followed (Robbe, 1998), or frequency of visual search (Lamers & Ramaekers, 2001), but none incorporated all of these approaches.

WHAT ARE THE PREDOMINANT RESULTS?

Several meta-analyses (Laberge & Ward, 2004; Moskowitz, 1985; Ramaekers et al., 2004; Smiley, 1998) have reached similar conclusions. In general, marijuana slows driver performance, particularly in complex driving situations. Marijuana impairment was usually in the areas of speed, perception, and car control. Impairments are most likely to occur within the first few hours after use (Walsh, De Gier, Christopherson, & Verstraete, 2004). Reaction time data were somewhat less consistent than perceptual and handling data. In an early simulator study, brake reaction time was slowed by two doses of delta-1-tetrahydrocannabiniol (12 or 16 mg). However, across several other studies of simulated driving, any slowing of brake latency by delta-9-THC failed to achieve statistical significance (Crancer et al., 1969; Liguori et al., 1998, 2002, 2003; Moskowitz et al., 1976). This is consistent with several psychomotor studies showing that reaction time is among the least likely cognitive components to be impaired by marijuana (Chait & Pierri, 1992).

Marijuana appears to make drivers more aware of being intoxicated (Laberge & Ward, 2004) and consequently more cautious. Klonoff (1974) reported that both dose and the participant's ability to compensate for perceived impairment influenced the likelihood of decrements in driving ability. The ability to compensate is revealed in decisions not to pass a vehicle, to slow down, or to increase attention (Smiley, 1998), and increased headway when following a vehicle has been reported (Robbe, 1998). The extent to

which increased caution would be manifested differently in high-speed driving situations is less certain, as on-road studies have generally focused on closed-course and city street driving.

Across several studies that directly compared alcohol and marijuana impairment on simulated or real driving, alcohol doses produced breath alcohol concentrations in the 0.06–0.10% range. In early studies, marijuana and alcohol were not combined, and results were mixed. In the earliest simulator study (Crancer et al., 1969), signaling, braking, and acceleration in coordination with a filmed presentation were significantly impaired by alcohol (0.10% breath alcohol concentration) but not by marijuana (2 cigarettes with 1.3% THC) in periodic (at least twice monthly) smokers. In contrast, Rafaelson et al. (1973) reported that the same breath alcohol concentration produced brake latency slowing comparable to that seen with 12 or 16 mg delta-1-tetrahydrocannabinol. In a study of actual driving on a cone-defined obstacle course, 88 μg/kg (comparable to 5.9 mg) THC and alcohol (0.07 breath alcohol concentration) resulted in similarly increased numbers of hit cones and "rough" (i.e., awkward or superfluous) handling incidents (Hansteen et al., 1976).

Marijuana may be relatively more impairing than alcohol when the administered alcohol dose is low. For example, when participants' breath alcohol concentration averaged 0.04%, performance deficits were moderate after THC (up to 200 μg/kg) but only minor after alcohol (Ramaekers et al., 2000). In contrast, the combined effects of low-dose THC (100 μg/kg) and moderate dose alcohol (0.05 g/kg) on higher-level driving skills were minimal (Lamers & Ramaekers, 2001). The extent to which a history of chronic marijuana use—rather than acute marijuana dosing—augments the impairing effects of alcohol on driving has not yet been examined. However, the effects of alcohol on reaction times and tracking accuracy, two psychomotor skills needed for driving, did not significantly differ in daily versus once-monthly marijuana users (Wright & Terry, 2002). Others have reported that past use of marijuana does not increase the risk of collisions, suggesting that only recent marijuana use—proven by increased blood concentrations of THC—is likely to affect a driver (Ramaekers et al., 2004).

Marijuana did not significantly impair simulated driving performance at all in two interaction studies, both in recreational users. In a placebo-controlled double-dummy study that examined the effects of all possible combinations of alcohol (0.25 and 0.5 g/kg ethanol) and marijuana (1.75 or 3.33% THC) on brake latency and body sway (Liguori et al., 2002), the highest THC potency increased body sway but not brake latency, and no interactions with alcohol were found. The second study compared the direct effects of marijuana (placebo, 2, or 3.5% THC) and partial sleep deprivation (typically 2–3 hours of sleep instead of the usual 8). Although ratings of "high" were increased after partial sleep deprivation, neither partial sleep deprivation nor

marijuana impaired brake reaction time (Liguori et al., 2003). It should be noted, however, that perception and attention—components of driving very sensitive to THC—were not quantified in these two studies.

Several studies of actual driving have suggested that the combined impairments of alcohol and marijuana are more severe than those of either drug taken alone. In the first study, on-road obstacle course driving was measured in the presence of alcohol (0.06% breath alcohol concentration), marijuana (2% THC), or both (Sutton, 1983). Administered separately, neither marijuana nor alcohol differed from placebo, but the combination of the two drugs produced significantly greater impairment than placebo. In another study of actual driving, alcohol (0.04% breath alcohol concentration) combined with THC (100 or 200 µg/kg) resulted in lane position impairments comparable to breath alcohol concentrations greater than the U.S. legal limit of 0.08% (Ramaekers et al., 2000; Robbe, 1998).

Unlike alcohol, marijuana is typically not associated with dose-dependent driving impairments. The specific THC dose or general level of marijuana use that reliably impairs driving is uncertain. Doses up to 250 µg/kg by themselves have typically produced minor effects on driving performance in laboratory and on-road studies (Lamers & Ramaekers, 2001). The threshold may be 300 µg/kg or greater. Unique and significant effects of both low and high doses on performance have been reported wherein the degree of impairment increased from small to moderate as the THC dose increased from 100 to 300 µg/kg (Robbe, 1998). However, the dose-response curve of higher doses, including those comparable to breath alcohol levels of 0.08% and higher, remains unknown.

RECOMMENDATIONS

The following is a 7-step plan for improving research on marijuana and driving and clarifying the likelihood and nature of marijuana-induced impairments:

1. *Increase realism.* There is a need for more realistic road conditions in simulators. Besides increasing face validity, more realistic conditions would also augment the complexity inherent in routine driving performance. Such complexity appears to be a key variable in determining when marijuana produces impairments. Other cars on the road, maintaining traffic flow, and unexpected changes in road conditions are among the validity-increasing aspects that could be incorporated into future studies.

2. *Study women, minorities, and children.* Both risk-taking and attention problems (e.g., attention-deficit/hyperactivity disorder) are more prevalent among men than women. Although women are now being

included more frequently in studies of marijuana and driving, gender differences are generally not quantified in these studies. Such quantification is ultimately necessary to answer the question of whether women are less likely to be subject to the impairing effects of THC. Minority differences among women are also worthy of study, as the prevalence of marijuana use has recently increased among young black and Hispanic women (Compton, Grant, Colliver, Glantz, & Stinson, 2004). Another understudied population is marijuana-abusing teenagers. The percentage of American high school seniors who reported that they crashed while driving under the influence was comparable when marijuana (0.94%) or alcohol (1.14%) was used (O'Malley & Johnston, 2003). While ethical concerns preclude the study of acute marijuana doses in this population, controlled comparisons of marijuana abusers and non-abusing teenagers would help clarify the unique risks of marijuana use among this relatively inexperienced population of drivers.

3. *Study chronic users.* Chronic marijuana users are an understudied population that should be compared to the recreational users that are typically recruited. While acute dosing appears most likely to impair driving, the question of whether chronic users develop tolerance and thus perform less poorly behind the wheel than less experienced users has not yet been addressed in a controlled study.

4. *Clarify compensation for impairment.* Is the cautious driving observed in intoxicated drivers an attempt to compensate for feeling high? Time estimation is significantly slowed by THC (McDonald, Schleifer, Richards, & de Wit, 2003), and slowed brake reaction times (e.g., Klonoff, 1974), underestimation of speed (Peck et al., 1986), or increased headway (Robbe, 1998) may indicate a distortion of distance judgment. Whether the slower speed and risk avoidance associated with recent marijuana use is related to recognition of impairment or distortion of time and distance judgment remains in need of further study (Ogden & Moskowitz, 2004).

5. *Address the risk-taking paradox.* Several studies have shown that acute marijuana dosing reduces risk taking. However, self-report analyses suggest that risk-takers who use marijuana are likely to be involved in accidents. One retrospective survey of marijuana abusers before and after treatment found that treatment was associated with decreases in marijuana use, driving, and driving infractions while impulsivity and risk-taking remained stable (Macdonald, DeSouza, Mann, & Chipman, 2004). In contrast, another survey suggested that marijuana, alcohol, and cocaine all increased propensity to take risks (Chipman, Macdonald, & Mann, 2003).

6. *Clarify the relationship between sobriety testing and driving impairment.* Several recent simulator studies have revealed impairment of body sway by THC doses that did not concurrently impair brake reaction time (Liguori et al., 2002, 2003). Such findings raise concerns

that sobriety testing may incorrectly identify impaired drivers. Further studies incorporating more dependent measures should incorporate sobriety testing to address this question.

7. *Embrace the ratio scale.* The dichotomous checklist approach to driving quantification has provided a wider scope but limited depth of driving data. Accidents, especially the avoidance of accidents, are not a yes-no proposition. Braking 10 milliseconds sooner, or turning 30 milliseconds sooner, or changing lanes 100 feet farther away from the nearest vehicle are all relative, potentially life-saving decisions. The degree to which these decisions are made is not addressed in a dichotomous approach. Consequently, in addition to more realistic measures, more of these measures should be quantified with ratio scales.

CONCLUSIONS

Our understanding of what marijuana does and does not impair in a driver is improving. Existing results suggest that marijuana is most likely to impair driving when used immediately before or during driving and in situations requiring divided attention. Marijuana effects include unusually cautious behaviors such as increased following distance. When marijuana is associated with risk-taking behaviors, the extent to which personality characteristics or the drug itself influence those behaviors is unclear. Any impairing effects of marijuana are likely to be less severe than those of alcohol, although the impairing effects of commonly used THC doses have not been extensively studied. However, procedural limitations in many experiments illustrate that additional, more carefully controlled studies are needed. In particular, further direct comparisons of the unique effects of marijuana versus alcohol are of importance for clarifying policy needs. Further epidemiological studies clarifying the extent to which marijuana users actually use the drug immediately before driving (when impairments are likely to be greatest) are also needed.

Ideally, any policy related to drug use and driving must be based on known impairment rather than on whether or not the drug is in the bloodstream. The presence of a given substance in a driver implies but does not confirm causation of an accident, especially when other drugs or personality characteristics (such as risk taking or sensation seeking) are simultaneously involved. THC in particular represents an unusually risky substance to blame for collisions because it remains in the bloodstream for days after the impairing effects or desired high have subsided. Enough controlled studies have identified driving impairments following acute marijuana doses to justify recommendations to avoid driving while under the influence of marijuana. However, the extent to which marijuana-related impairments will likely cause or contribute to accidents remains uncertain. Attempts to connect marijuana use directly to collision responsibility have produced mixed results.

Several important questions related to marijuana use and driving have not yet been empirically addressed. The above recommendations will clarify the nature of marijuana impairment, particularly under several conditions that have not been well studied to this point (e.g., with additional distractions, sleep deprivation, etc.). Several alcohol interaction studies have suggested that marijuana may not always be an "at-fault" substance when THC is found in injured drivers who have been using multiple drugs. The extent to which marijuana causes accidents needs to be investigated in a variety of other controlled situations in which marijuana use is just one of multiple potentially damaging factors.

The assistance of Christopher Nave and comments from Dr. Linda Porrino are acknowledged with gratitude. Portions of this chapter were presented at the 2005 meeting of the College on Problems of Drug Dependence, Orlando, FL.

REFERENCES

Azorlosa, J. L., Heishman, S. J., Stitzer, M. L., & Mahaffey, J. M. (1992). Marijuana smoking: Effect of varying delta-9-tetrahydrocannabinol content and number of puffs. *Journal of Pharmacology and Experimental Therapeutics, 261*, 114–122.

Begg, D. J., Langley, J. D., & Stephenson, S. (2003). Identifying factors that predict persistent driving after drinking, unsafe driving after drinking, and driving after using cannabis among young adults. *Accident Analysis & Prevention, 35*, 669–675.

Blows, S., Ivers, R. Q., Connor, J., Ameratunga, S., Woodward, M., & Norton, R. (2005). Marijuana use and car crash injury. *Addiction, 100*, 605–611.

Brookoff, D., Cook, C. S., Williams, C., & Mann, C. S. (1994). Testing reckless drivers for cocaine and marijuana. *New England Journal of Medicine, 331*, 518–522.

Chait, L. D., & Pierri, J. (1992). Effects of smoked marijuana on human performance: A critical review. In L. Murphy & A. Bartke (Eds.), *Marijuana/Cannabinoids: Neurobiology and Neurophysiology* (pp. 387–423). Boca Raton, FL: CRC Press.

Chipman, M. L., Macdonald, S., & Mann, R. E. (2003). Being "at fault" in traffic crashes: Does alcohol, cannabis, cocaine, or polydrug abuse make a difference? *Injury Prevention, 9*, 343–348.

Compton, W. M., Grant, B. F., Colliver, J. D., Glantz, M. D., & Stinson, F. S. (2004). Prevalence of marijuana use disorders in the United States. *JAMA, 291*, 2114–2121.

Crancer, A. J., Dille, J. M., Delay, J. C., Wallace, J. E., & Haken, M. (1969). Comparison of the effects of marijuana and alcohol on simulated driving performance. *Science, 164*, 851–854.

Earleywine, M., & Newcomb, M. D. (1997). Concurrent versus simultaneous polydrug use: Prevalence, correlates, discriminant validity, and prospective effects on health outcomes. *Experimental and Clinical Psychopharmacology, 5*, 353–364.

ElSohly, M. A., Ross, S. A., Mehmedic, Z., Arafat, R., Yi, B., & Banahan, B. F. (2000). Potency trends of Delta(9)-THC and other cannabinoids in confiscated marijuana from 1980–1987. *Journal of Forensic Sciences, 45*, 24–30.

Fergusson, D. M., & Horwood, L. J. (2001). Cannabis use and traffic accidents in a birth cohort of young adults. *Accident Analysis & Prevention, 33*, 703–711.

Gerberich, S. G., Sidney, S., Braun, B. L., Tekawa, I. S., Tolan, K. K., & Quesenberry, C. P. (2003). Marijuana use and injury events resulting in hospitalization. *Annals of Epidemiology, 13*, 230–237.

Hansteen, R. W., Miller, R. D., Longero, L., Reid, L. D., & Jones, B. (1976). Effects of cannabis and alcohol on automobile driving and psychomotor tracking. *Annals New York Academy of Sciences, 282*, 240–256.

Higgins, S. T., & Stitzer, M. L. (1986). Acute marijuana effects on social conversation. *Psychopharmacology, 89*, 234–238.

Johnson, V., & White, H. R. (1989). An investigation of factors related to intoxicated driving behaviors among youth. *Journal of Studies on Alcohol, 50*, 320–330.

Jones, R. K., Shinar, D., & Walsh, J. M. (2003). State of knowledge of drug-impaired driving, DOT Report #809 642. *National Highway Traffic Safety Administration.*

Kalant, H. (2004). Adverse effects of cannabis on health: an update of the literature since 1996. *Progress in Neuro-Psychopharmacology & Biological Psychiatry, 28*, 849–863.

Klonoff, H. (1974). Marijuana and driving in real-life situations. *Science, 186*, 317–324.

Laberge, J. C., & Ward, N. J. (2004). Research note: Cannabis and driving: Research needs and issues for transportation policy. *Journal of Drug Issues, 34*, 971–989.

Lamers, C. T. J., & Ramaekers, J. G. (2001). Visual search and urban city driving under the influence of marijuana and alcohol. *Human Psychopharmacology–Clinical and Experimental, 16*, 393–401.

Liguori, A., Gatto, C. P., & Jarrett, D. B. (2002). Separate and combined effects of marijuana and alcohol on mood equilibrium and simulated driving. *Psychopharmacology, 163*, 399–405.

Liguori, A., Gatto, C. P., Jarrett, D. B., McCall, W. V., & Brown, T. W. (2003). Behavioral and subjective effects of marijuana following partial sleep deprivation. *Drug and Alcohol Dependence, 70*, 233–240.

Liguori, A., Gatto, C. P., & Robinson, J. H. (1998). Effects of marijuana on equilibrium, psychomotor performance, and simulated driving. *Behavioural Pharmacology, 9*, 599–609.

Lowenstein, S. R., & Koziol-McLain, J. (2001). Drugs and traffic crash responsibility: A study of injured motorists in Colorado. *Trauma, 50*, 313–320.

Macdonald, S., Anglin-Bodrug, K., Mann, R. E., Erickson, P., Hathaway, A., Chipman, M., et al. (2003). Injury risk associated with cannabis and cocaine use. *Drug and Alcohol Dependence, 72*, 99–115.

Macdonald, S., DeSouza, A., Mann, R., & Chipman, M. (2004). Driving behavior of alcohol, cannabis, and cocaine abuse treatment clients and population controls. *The American Journal of Drug and Alcohol Abuse, 30*, 429–444.

McDonald, J., Schleifer, L., Richards, J. B., & de Wit, H. (2003). Effects of THC on behavioral measures of impulsivity in humans. *Neuropsychopharmacology, 28*, 1356–1365.

Moskowitz, H. (1985). Marihuana and driving. *Accident Analysis & Prevention, 17*(323–345).

Moskowitz, H., Hulbert, S., & McGlothlin, W. H. (1976). Marihuana: Effects on simulated driving performance. *Accident Analysis & Prevention, 8*, 45–50.

Neale, J. (2001). Driving on recreational drugs: A qualitative investigation of experiences from behind the wheel. *Drugs: Education, Prevention, and Policy, 8*, 315–325.

O'Malley, P. M., & Johnston, L. D. (2003). Unsafe driving by high school seniors: National trends from 1976 to 2001 in tickets and accidents after use of alcohol, marijuana and other illegal drugs. *Journal of Studies on Alcohol, 64*, 305–312.

Office of Applied Studies. (2004). *Results from the 2003 National Survey on Drug Use and Health: National findings* (DHHS Publication No. SMA 04–3964, NSDUH Series H-25). Rockville, MD: Substance Abuse and Mental Health Service Administration.

Ogden, E. J., & Moskowitz, H. (2004). Effects of alcohol and other drugs on driver performance. *Traffic Injury Prevention, 5*, 185–198.

Peck, R. C., Biasotti, A., Boland, P. N., Mallory, C., & Reeve, V. (1986). The effects of marijuana and alcohol on actual driving performance. *Alcohol, Drugs, and Driving: Abstracts and Reviews, 2*, 135–154.

Rafaelsen, O. J., Bech, P., Christiansen, J., Christrup, H., Nyboe, J., & Rafaelsen, L. (1973). Cannabis and alcohol: Effects on stimulated car driving. *Science, 179*, 920–923.

Ramaekers, J. G., Berghaus, G., van Laar, M., & Drummer, O. H. (2004). Dose related risk of motor vehicle crashes after cannabis use. *Drug and Alcohol Dependence, 73*, 109–119.

Ramaekers, J. G., Robbe, H. W., & O'Hanlon, J. F. (2000). Marijuana, alcohol, and actual driving performance. *Human Psychopharmacology, 15*, 551–558.

Research Institute of Pharmaceutical Sciences Eradication. (2004). *Potency Monitoring Project, Quarterly Report #85; National Center for the Development of Natural Products*. School of Pharmacy, University of Mississippi.

Robbe, H. (1998). Marijuana's impairing effects on driving are moderate when taken alone but severe when combined with alcohol. *Human Psychopharmacology–Clinical and Experimental, 13*, S70–S78.

Smiley, A. (1998). Marijuana: On-road and driving simulator studies. In H. Kalant, W. Corrigall, W. Hall, & R. Smart (Eds.), *The health effects of cannabis* (pp. 173–191). Toronto, Ontario, Canada: Addiction Research Foundation.

Smiley, A., Moskowitz, H. M., & Zeidman, K. (1981). *Driving simulator studies of marijuana alone and in combination with alcohol.* Paper presented at the Proceedings of the 25th Conference of the American Association of Automotive Medicine.

Smiley, A. M., Noy, Y. I., & Tostowaryk, W. (1986). *The effects of marijuana, alone and in combination with alcohol, on driving an instrumented car.* Paper presented at the Proceedings of the 10th International Conference on Alcohol, Drugs, and Traffic Safety, Amsterdam.

Soderstrom, C. A., Dischinger, P. C., Kerns, T. J., & Trifillis, A. L. (1995). Marijuana and other drug use among automobile and motorcycle drivers treated at a trauma center. *Accident Analysis & Prevention, 27,* 131–135.

Stein, A. C., Allen, R. W., Cook, M. L., & Karl, R. L. (1983). *A simulator study of the combined effects of alcohol and marijuana on driving behaviour.* Hawthorne, CA: Systems Technology Inc. (National Highway Traffic Safety Administration Report No. DOT-HS-806405.)

Sutton, L. R. (1983). The effects of alcohol, marihuana and their combination on driving ability. *Journal of Studies on Alcohol, 44,* 438–445.

Teixeira, H., Proenca, P., Castanheira, A., Santos, S., Lopez-Rivadulla, M., Corte-Real, F., et al. (2004). Cannabis and driving: The use of LC-MS to detect delta9-tetrahydrocannabinol (delta9-THC) in oral fluid samples. *Forensic Science International, 146S,* S61–S63.

Walsh, J. M., De Gier, J. J., Christopherson, A. S., & Verstraete, A. G. (2004). Drugs and driving. *Traffic Injury Prevention, 5,* 241–253.

Wright, K. A., & Terry, P. (2002). Modulation of the effects of alcohol on driving-related psychomotor skills by chronic exposure to cannabis. *Psychopharmacology, 160,* 213–219.

SECTION II

Views From Abroad

Quite a few Americans will assert, with great fervor, that there's no place like America. Citizens worldwide undoubtedly feel the same way about their own country. No one expects policy formed in one country to create identical results in another. Nevertheless, the experiments of other lands can inform our considerations of our own laws. Two areas that have employed marijuana laws different from our own, Australia and the Netherlands, have generated enough data over sufficient time to draw some interesting conclusions.

Australia contains territories with statutes replacing criminal penalties for marijuana possession with civil penalties. First offenders in all territories receive counseling and education. In a reasoned and nuanced look at the literature, Wayne Hall analyzes the arguments for and against changes in Australian laws. He reviews all the harms that marijuana creates and details all the negative consequences that arise from prohibition. He emphasizes that a strong rationale for marijuana prohibition requires more than evidence that marijuana creates problems. Prohibition is justified only if criminal penalties decrease the troubles that marijuana creates. Even then, the decrease must be large enough to justify the associated costs of enforcing these policies. He weighs the pros and cons of different approaches in a way that will give everyone, from the staunchest proponent to the staunchest opponent of prohibition, considerable pause.

Dutch marijuana policy has become infamous, notoriously misunderstood, and incredibly influential. Switzerland, Germany, Spain, Austria,

Belgium, Luxembourg, Italy, Portugal, and England have all altered their laws in ways that seem influenced by the Netherlands, while other countries have stiffened penalties and criticized the approach. Craig Reinarman and Peter Cohen offer a detailed comparison of marijuana users in two comparable cities, San Francisco and Amsterdam. The cities differ dramatically in their approach to marijuana prohibition, and these researchers reveal that the laws may have dramatically less effect than more informal social controls within communities and cultures. Prohibition's effect on the use of hard drugs may also prove quite surprising.

Keen looks at other countries certainly have their limitations, but any informed discussion of marijuana policy undoubtedly turns to the experiences of those who have laws different from our own. As more countries experiment with new approaches to controlling access to marijuana, new data will help answer pressing questions on the balance between prohibition and problems.

5   A Cautious Case for
Cannabis Depenalization

Wayne Hall

Cannabis possession, use, cultivation, and sale are prohibited in Australia on the assumption that cannabis use presents a serious risk to the health of users and the community (Commonwealth Department of Health, 1984; Walters, 1993). Cannabis is, nonetheless, very widely used, with 59% of young adults between 20 and 29 reporting in 2001 that they had used the drug at some time in their lives (Australian Institute of Health and Welfare [AIHW], 2002; Donnelly & Hall, 1994). It is, in fact, the most widely used illicit drug in Australia (Donnelly & Hall, 1994).

The widespread use of cannabis has led to proposals over the past several decades to remove or relax the prohibition on cannabis use (Ali & Christie, 1994; Senate Standing Committee on Social Welfare, 1977). The response of various state governments (which are responsible for drug policy in Australia) has been to adopt some form of "depenalization," that is, to remove penal sanctions for cannabis possession (and sometimes cultivation) for personal use. Although it remains a criminal offense to use and possess cannabis in most Australian states, the penalties for possession and use have been reduced to civil penalties in South Australia (1987), the Australian Capital Territory (1992), the Northern Territory (1995), and Western Australia (2004; Lenton, 2004; MacDonald & Atkinson, 1995). The remaining states agreed to divert first offenders to counseling and education as part of an initiative funded by the federal government in 2001 (Vaughan, 2003a, 2003b; Wooldridge, 2001). In this chapter I evaluate the arguments that have featured prominently in the cannabis policy debate in Australia over the past several decades.

ARGUMENTS FOR RETAINING CANNABIS PROHIBITION

In Australia the main arguments for continuing to prohibit cannabis use have been that it prevents the adverse effects of cannabis use by deterring young people from using the drug. The following is a précis of the adverse health effects that have been most prominent in the Australia policy debate.

Cannabis and Motor Vehicle Crashes

The acute effect of cannabis that has been of greatest policy relevance in the Australian policy debate has been its effects on driving. This is for good reason: Cannabis intoxication produces dose-related impairments in a wide range of cognitive and behavioral performances that may affect driving, such as reaction time and information processing, perceptual-motor coordination and motor performance, attention, signal detection, tracking behavior, and time perception (Hall, Solowij, & Lemon, 1994; Ramaekers, Berghaus, van Laar, & Drummer, 2004; Solowij, 1998).

It has not been clear until recently whether these impairments increase the risk of motor vehicle accidents in cannabis users (Hall, Degenhardt, & Lynskey, 2001). Studies of the effects of cannabis upon on-road driving performance report modest impairments because cannabis-intoxicated drivers slow down and take fewer risks than alcohol-intoxicated drivers (Smiley, 1999). Epidemiological studies of cannabis in fatal motor vehicle accidents had also been equivocal (see Hall, Degenhardt, & Lynskey, 2001, for a review). A convergence of recent evidence from experimental and epidemiological studies suggests that cannabis does modestly increase the risk of motor vehicle crashes (Ramaekers et al., 2004). The most relevant evidence comes from studies that have measured THC, marijuana's primary intoxicant, in blood (rather than inactive metabolites that reflect past cannabis use), which have found a dose-response relationship between THC and accident risk (Ramaekers et al., 2004). (See Ligouri's chapter 4 in this volume for a more thorough review of this research.)

The Respiratory Risks of Cannabis Smoking

Over the past two decades, cross-sectional and longitudinal studies have shown that regular smokers of cannabis who do not smoke tobacco have more symptoms of chronic bronchitis than people who do not smoke either cannabis or tobacco (see Tashkin, 1999, for a review). The immunological competence of the respiratory system in people who only smoke cannabis is

also impaired, increasing their susceptibility to infectious diseases such as pneumonia (Tashkin, 1999). A large prospective study in New Zealand (Taylor, Fergusson, et al., 2002; Taylor, Poulton, Moffitt, Ramankutty, & Sears, 2000) of respiratory function in 1,037 New Zealand youths followed until age 21 found that cannabis-dependent subjects had higher rates of wheezing, shortness of breath, chest tightness, and morning sputum production than non-smokers, after adjusting for the effects of tobacco use. The effects of cannabis dependence on respiratory symptoms were "generally similar to and occasionally greater than for tobacco smokers of 1–10 cigarettes/day" (Taylor, Poulton, et al., 2000, p. 1673). A significantly higher proportion of cannabis-dependent subjects also showed evidence of impaired respiratory function; the adverse effects of tobacco and cannabis smoking were additive.

Respiratory Cancers

Cannabis *smoke* is potentially carcinogenic (MacPhee, 1999; Marselos & Karamanakos, 1999), so cannabis smoking is a potential cause of cancers in the lung and the aerodigestive tract (mouth, tongue, esophagus; Hall & MacPhee, 2002). Cancers of the aerodigestive tracts have been reported in young adults who have been chronic cannabis smokers (Donald, 1991; Taylor, 1988), including cases in young adults who did not smoke tobacco or drink alcohol and whose only shared risk factor was long-term daily cannabis use (Hall & MacPhee, 2002).

The results of the few epidemiological studies to date have conflicted. Sidney et al. (1997), who studied cancer incidence during an 8.6-year follow-up of 64,855 members of the Kaiser Permanente Medical Care Program, did not find more cases of cancer among those who had ever used cannabis or who were current cannabis users. Zhang et al. (1999) compared rates of cannabis use among 173 persons with primary squamous cell carcinoma of the head and neck and 176 controls matched on age and sex. Cases were more likely to have used cannabis than controls, with a 2.6 odds ratio for cannabis smoking after adjusting for cigarette smoking, alcohol use, and other known risk factors. Two other case control studies failed to find an association between cannabis use and oral squamous cell carcinomas (Llewellyn, Linklater, Bell, Johnson, & Warnakulasuriya, 2004; Rosenblatt, Daling, Chen, Sherman, & Schwartz, 2004).

There have not been any studies of any association between cannabis smoking and lung cancer. The seriousness of this risk should become clearer as the baby boomer birth cohorts (who were the first to smoke cannabis in large numbers) enter their sixties and seventies, when lung cancer incidence begins to rise steeply (Hall & MacPhee, 2002; Rosenblatt et al., 2004).

Cannabis Dependence

A cannabis dependence syndrome (American Psychiatric Association, 1994) occurs in some heavy, chronic users of cannabis who report problems in controlling their cannabis use (Roffman, Stephens, Simpson, & Whitaker, 1988; Stephens, Roffman, & Simpson, 1993). These users report withdrawal symptoms when abstaining; loss of control over their cannabis use; cognitive and motivational impairments that interfere with work performance; lowered self-esteem and depression; and complaints by spouses and partners about the effects of their cannabis use on their behavior (e.g., Hall & Pacula, 2003; Stephens et al., 1993).

Cannabis dependence was the most common form of illicit drug dependence in the United States in the early 1980s (Anthony & Helzer, 1991) and in Australia in the late 1990s (Hall, Teesson, Lynskey, & Degenhardt, 1999). The risk of developing cannabis dependence is similar to that for alcohol but lower than that for nicotine and opioids (Anthony, Warner, & Kessler, 1994) with around 10% of those who ever use cannabis estimated to meet criteria for dependence at some time in their lives (Anthony et al., 1994; Hall et al., 1994). Persons who initiate use early and who use cannabis daily are at greatest risk of becoming dependent (Hall et al., 1994).

Psychosis and Schizophrenia

A 15-year prospective study of cannabis use and schizophrenia in 50,465 Swedish conscripts (Andreasson, Engstrom, Allebeck, & Rydberg, 1987) found that the risk of schizophrenia increased with the number of times cannabis had been used by age 18. Compared to those who had not used cannabis, the risk of developing schizophrenia was 1.3 times higher for those who had used cannabis 1–10 times, 3 times higher for those who had used cannabis 1–50 times, and 6 times higher for those who had used cannabis more than 50 times. These relationships were reduced but remained statistically significant after adjustment for confounders.

The results of this study have been recently supported in a 27-year follow up of the same cohort study (Zammit, Allebeck, Andreasson, Lundberg, & Lewis, 2002). This study also found a dose-response relationship between frequency of cannabis use at baseline and risk of schizophrenia during the follow-up; the relationship also persisted when the authors statistically controlled for the effects of other drug use and other confounding factors, including a history of psychiatric symptoms at baseline. They estimated that 13% of cases of schizophrenia could be averted if all cannabis use were prevented.

The Swedish findings have been supported by several longitudinal studies. Van Os et al. (2002) reported a three-year study of the relationship between cannabis use and psychosis in a community sample of 4,848 people in the Netherlands. They found that the frequency of cannabis use at baseline predicted rates of psychotic symptoms during the 3-year follow-up in individuals who had not reported symptoms at baseline; these relationships persisted when they statistically controlled for the effects of other drug use; and the relationship between cannabis use and psychotic symptoms was stronger for cases with more severe psychotic symptoms. Those who reported psychotic symptoms at baseline were more likely to develop schizophrenia if they used cannabis than were individuals who had not. These results were confirmed in a study by Henquet et al. (2004) which found that cannabis use predicted an increased risk of psychotic symptoms over a four-year follow-up of 2,437 young Germans. As in the Dutch study, the risk of cannabis use was larger for persons who had a history of psychotic symptoms prior to using the drug.

These findings have also been replicated in two small New Zealand cohort studies. Arseneault et al. (2002) reported a relationship between cannabis use by age 15 and an increased risk of psychotic symptoms by age 26 in a prospective study of a New Zealand birth cohort (N=759). So too did Fergusson, Horwood, and Swain-Campbell (2003), who found that cannabis dependence at age 18 predicted an increased risk of psychotic symptoms at age 21 years (RR of 2.3) that remained significant after adjustment for potential confounders (RR of 1.8).

Cognitive Effects

Controlled studies have not found that long-term heavy use of cannabis produces severe impairment of cognitive function like that produced by chronic heavy alcohol use (Solowij, 1998). There is, nonetheless, evidence that long-term or heavy cannabis users show more subtle types of cognitive impairment (Solowij, 1998, 1999). A major concern with earlier studies was that the cannabis users may have poorer cognitive functioning than controls *before* they use cannabis (Solowij, 1998). Recent studies that have matched users and nonusers on premorbid intellectual functioning (Solowij, 1998) or on test performance before using cannabis (Block & Ghoneim, 1993; Block et al., 2002; Pope & Yurgelun-Todd, 1996) have found cognitive impairments in frequent and/or long-term cannabis users. Debate continues about whether these deficits can be attributed to lingering acute effects, residual drug effects, abstinence effects, or gradual changes occurring in the brain as a result of cumulative exposure to THC (Pope, Gruber, & Yurgelun-Todd, 1995; Solowij, 1998, 2002; Solowij et al., 2002).

The Effects of Adolescent Cannabis Use

The effects of cannabis on adolescents has been a focus in the Australian policy debate because many young Australians use cannabis and there is evidence that those who initiate cannabis use in their early teens are more likely to discontinue high school education and use other illicit drugs (Hall & Pacula, 2003; Lynskey & Hall, 2000). The difficulty in interpreting the association between cannabis use and school leaving is that adolescent cannabis users have lower academic aspirations and perform more poorly at school than their peers *before* they use cannabis (Hall & Pacula, 2003; Lynskey & Hall, 2000). A causal interpretation of the link has been supported by recent studies that have statistically controlled for variables on which cannabis users and non-users differ prior to their cannabis use (e.g. Fergusson & Horwood, 1997, 2000; Macleod et al., 2004). In these studies, early cannabis use predicts early school leaving after controlling for factors on which early users differ from their peers (Hall, Degenhardt, & Lynskey, 2001; Hall & Pacula, 2003; Lynskey & Hall, 2000).

The relationship between adolescent cannabis use and the use of other illicit drugs—the gateway hypothesis—has been central to arguments made for retaining prohibition. There is no doubt that among Australian adolescents cannabis use typically follows alcohol and tobacco use and precedes the use of stimulants and opioids (Hall, Degenhardt, & Lynskey, 2001; Hall & Lynskey, in press). The underlying reasons for this sequence of involvement remains controversial (Hall & Lynskey, in press). Some argue that the sequence arises because the pharmacological effects of cannabis increase the likelihood of using heroin and cocaine (Hall & Lynskey, in press). Others suggest that the sequence is better explained by two other hypotheses: (a) nonconforming adolescents who have a propensity to use a range of intoxicating substances are selectively recruited into cannabis use; and (b) once recruited and dependent upon cannabis, these adolescents engage in regular social interaction with drug-using peers and the illicit drug market, which increases the likelihood of their using other illicit drugs (Hall, Degenhardt, & Lynskey, 2001).

The latter hypotheses are supported by findings that adolescents who start cannabis use early are also at higher risk than their nonusing peers of using other illicit drugs *before* they begin to use cannabis (Fergusson & Horwood, 1997, 2000; Fergusson, Horword, & Swain-Campbell, 2002). They are also more likely to keep company with drug-using peers (Fergusson & Horwood, 2000). Nonetheless, well-controlled longitudinal studies show that the relationship between heavy cannabis use in adolescence and an increased risk of using "harder" drugs persists after controlling for preexisting differences between adolescents who do and do not use cannabis (Fergusson & Horwood, 2000; Fergusson et al., 2002; Hall & Lynskey, in press). Skeptics argue that the unexplained association is ascribable to un-

controlled factors, such as a genetic vulnerability to become dependent on a variety of different drugs (Macleod et al., 2004). The issue remains contentious but can potentially be resolved by further research (Hall & Lynskey, in press).

Health Effects and Cannabis Policy

Australian opponents of cannabis liberalization have argued that the decriminalization or legalization of cannabis use will increase the rate of occurrence of these adverse health effects (Criminal Justice Commission, 1994; Walters, 1993). They claim that these changes would remove the deterrent effect of criminal sanctions, implicitly condone cannabis use and increase the availability of cannabis to young people. These changes in turn, they argue, will increase the proportion of adolescents and young adults who regularly use cannabis and lead to increases in motor vehicle accidents, and higher rates of cannabis dependence, respiratory problems, psychoses, and the use of more dangerous illicit drugs (Criminal Justice Commission, 1994; Walters, 1993).

In Australia, as in most developed countries, the debate about cannabis policy has been simplified by the popular media to a choice of two options: (a) we should legalize cannabis, or at the very least decriminalize its use, because its use is harmless (or at least much less harmful than alcohol); or (b) we should continue to prohibit cannabis use because it is harmful to users (Hall, 1997). Given this simplification, an honest appraisal of the adverse health effects of cannabis use complicates the cannabis policy debate. Supporters of cannabis prohibition are troubled by the fact that the adverse health consequences are not manifestly more serious than those of alcohol and tobacco, and proponents of reform are often reluctant to concede that cannabis use has any adverse effects (e.g., Zimmer & Morgan, 1997) because to do so is to give up the most compelling argument for reform, namely, that cannabis use is harmless.

We should reject this simplification of the debate. It does not follow that cannabis use should be prohibited simply because it harms some users or even that these harms might increase if prohibition was repealed. Those who advocate for cannabis prohibition need to argue that criminal penalties are the best way to discourage cannabis use and decrease the harms that it causes. We need to consider the social costs of using the criminal law to deter people from using cannabis and decide whether we as a society are prepared to bear these costs in order to discourage young people from using cannabis. I therefore now consider the costs of enforcing cannabis prohibition that are central to the arguments used by proponents of cannabis law liberalization.

ARGUMENTS FOR CANNABIS LIBERALIZATION

Libertarian Arguments

Cannabis prohibition deprives adults of the liberty to enjoy the pleasurable effects of using cannabis, such as euphoria, relaxation, and sociability. According to libertarians, prohibiting the recreational use of any drug to protect users from harming themselves is an unwarranted infringement of individual liberty (Szasz, 1997) because it conflicts with John Stuart Mill's "harm principle," which states that "the sole end for which mankind are warranted, individually or collectively, in interfering with the liberty of action of any of their number, is self-protection . . . [i.e.] to prevent harm to others. His own good, either physical or moral, is not a sufficient warrant" (Mill, 1998).

Libertarian arguments for liberalizing cannabis law (Criminal Justice Commission, 1994; Ellard, 1992) have not received widespread political or public support in Australia. This is probably because their logical consequence is that cannabis should be made a fully legal commodity like alcohol or tobacco. In Australia, as in the United States, there has been strong bipartisan support for a continuation of paternalistic policies toward cannabis and other illicit drugs (Manderson, 1993). For libertarians, the fact that cannabis prohibition infringes individual liberty trumps all other arguments, but for the nonlibertarian majority, the loss of liberty is one cost that has to be weighed in the scale against whatever benefits are produced by prohibition.

Alcohol and Cannabis: The Argument From Hypocrisy

Australian opponents of cannabis prohibition have often argued that cannabis is no more harmful than alcohol, and since our society tolerates alcohol use, then we should on the grounds of consistency allow the use of cannabis (Ellard, 1992; Select Committee on HIV Illegal Drugs and Prostitution, 1991). Proponents of changing cannabis law also assert that cannabis prohibition, like alcohol prohibition, has failed (Wodak, Reinarman, & Cohen, 2002), with the failure of alcohol prohibition regarded as a fact that does not stand in need of supporting evidence.

Historians suggest that the American experience with alcohol prohibition was more complex than this (Kyvig, 1979; Tyrrell, 1997). Alcohol consumption was substantially reduced during Prohibition (Kyvig, 1979; Tyrrell, 1997), as indicated by marked and sustained reductions in liver cirrhosis deaths, hospitalizations for alcoholic psychosis, and arrests for drunkenness (Miron & Zweibel, 1991). Consumption began to recover levels by the late 1920s (Miron & Zweibel, 1991), and it gradually increased after Repeal in 1933, but it did not return to pre-Prohibition levels for another decade (Miron &

Zweibel, 1991; MacCoun & Reuter, 2001). Alcohol prohibition did produce a large black market in Chicago and New York, where it contributed to widespread corruption of public officials (Kyvig, 1979; Tyrrell, 1997). It is unclear how widespread lawlessness was elsewhere in the United States; the perception that lawlessness was widespread may have been created by Hollywood gangster movies (Kyvig, 1979) in much the same way that the media manufactured a national crack cocaine epidemic in the United States in the mid-1980s (Reinarman & Levine, 1989).

The complexities of the evidence on the costs and benefits of alcohol prohibition suggest that a more critical attitude is required toward similar claims made in the absence of evidence about the failures of cannabis prohibition. Nonetheless, those who defend cannabis prohibition face a major challenge in providing a rational justification for the apparently inconsistent policies adopted toward alcohol and cannabis use.

Consequentialist Arguments for Liberalization

The most common arguments in the Australian cannabis policy debate have been that the social and economic costs of cannabis prohibition outweigh any benefits that arise from reducing cannabis use (Select Committee on HIV Illegal Drugs and Prostitution, 1991), if it is conceded that prohibition reduces use at all. These arguments have two premises: (a) that prohibition has failed to deter cannabis use by young adults in Australia, and (b) that the social consequences of enforcing prohibition outweigh any benefits that it brings.

The Deterrent Effects of Prohibition

Those who argue that prohibition has failed to deter cannabis use point to the fact that most young Australians have used cannabis at some time in their lives (Donnelly & Hall, 1994). Those who defend it argue that rates of cannabis use would be much higher if use was legal (e.g. Nahas & Latour, 1992). Counterfactual claims are inherently difficult to test, but there is some support for the latter claim in that under prohibition most cannabis use is intermittent and most users discontinue cannabis during their mid to late twenties, whereas they continue to use alcohol and tobacco much later in adult life (Bachman, Wadsworth, O'Malley, Johnston, & Schulenberg, 1997; Chen & Kandel, 1995). According to this modified argument, prohibition has not eliminated cannabis use, but its illegality has moderated use and encouraged young adults to stop using it at an earlier age than they would if its use were legal.

Proponents of depenalization counter this argument by appealing to studies of the effect of small changes in legal penalties on rates of cannabis use. These studies have typically found that small reductions in penalties for cannabis use have little effect on rates of cannabis use (e.g., Donnelly, Hall & Christie, 1995, 1999; Single, 1989). More recent studies using large nationally representative samples and more sophisticated statistical methods (Cameron & Williams, 2001; Pacula, Chriqui, & King, 2003; Williams, 2004) suggest that changes in legal penalties produce small changes in rates of cannabis use, when account is taken of individual differences in propensities to use, the price of cannabis, enforcement patterns, and other factors (Cameron & Williams, 2001; Saffer & Chaloupka, 1999). All of these studies have examined the effects of small changes in legal penalties for *possession* of cannabis. One cannot therefore use their results to predict the effects of larger policy changes on rates of cannabis use, such as, the elimination of all penalties or the creation of a legal cannabis market.

The Social Costs of Prohibition

THE MONETARY COST OF ENFORCEMENT   The enforcement of cannabis prohibition imposes opportunity costs: Law enforcement resources devoted to enforcing cannabis prohibition are not available for enforcement of other criminal laws. One Australian study estimated that 13% of all criminal justice and police resources were devoted to detecting, arresting, and prosecuting Australian cannabis users (McDonald & Atkinson, 1995). It is not clear, however, that cannabis depenalization would eliminate these costs. In South Australia, for example, the number of minor cannabis offenses *rose* substantially after decriminalization, from 6,000 in 1987–1988 to approximately 17,000 in 1993–1994 (Christie, 1999). The anticipated declines in court costs were less than expected because only 50% of persons paid fines, but the total cost to the court system was reduced and the income from fines was greater than the costs of processing offenders (Ali et al., 1999).

THE COSTS OF THE CANNABIS BLACK MARKET   Cannabis is a much more expensive commodity under prohibition than it would be if it were sold in a legal market at a price that reflected the costs of its production and distribution. This is because the black market price reflects economic compensation for the risks of arrest and imprisonment incurred by those who illegally sell cannabis (Criminal Justice Commission, 1994; MacCoun & Reuter, 2001). Estimates of the size of the Australian black market for cannabis suggest that the annual turnover was $600 million in the Australian state of Queensland in the early 1990s, making it a crop second in value to sugar and many times more valuable than tobacco (Advisory Committee on Illicit Drugs, 1993).

A more conservative estimate, made in 1988, was that the turnover in the Australian cannabis market as a whole was $1.9 billion per annum (Parliamentary Joint Committee on the National Crime Authority, 1989).

CORRUPTION OF LAW ENFORCEMENT OFFICIALS   Significant profits are generated by the cannabis black market that could be used to corrupt law enforcement officials. However, the way in which cannabis is typically sold makes corruption of law enforcement officials less likely than is true in markets for heroin and cocaine. Because cannabis is easily grown indoors it is very difficult for police to prevent its cultivation and so there is less need for cannabis growers to corrupt law enforcement officials to evade detection. Moreover, cannabis supply is more decentralized, making it less likely that any seller commands sufficient resources to corrupt the large number of officials employed for protection (Hall & Pacula, 2003).

LACK OF REGULATION   There is no control on the quality of the cannabis sold on the black market. Cannabis may be cut with other, more harmful substances, and its THC content may vary in unpredictable ways. Minors are also able to purchase cannabis in the absence of any age restrictions, and the retail cannabis black market is not separated from that for cocaine and heroin (Cohen, 1976). Individuals seeking to buy cannabis may therefore be introduced to other illicit substances that they otherwise would not know how to obtain (Lenton, 2000).

FORGONE TAX REVENUE   The largest monetary cost of a cannabis black market is the potential tax revenue forgone. It is difficult to estimate what these revenues might be if cannabis were legal. We cannot assume that the tax revenue under a legal market would be a large percentage of the black market value because, as argued elsewhere (see Hall & Pacula, 2003, chap. 18), the price of cannabis will have to be much lower in a legal market to prevent any continuation of a black market. Consumption would also probably increase because individuals who were previously deterred by prohibition may no longer be so, producing a fall in price (Pacula et al., 2001). Without knowing how sensitive consumption is to changes in price, it is unclear what would happen to total revenue under a legal cannabis market, but it is unlikely to be nearly as large as the estimated revenue in the cannabis black market.

Other Social Costs of Cannabis Prohibition

A DISPROPORTIONATE PENALTY APPLIED IN A DISCRIMINATORY WAY   Critics of cannabis prohibition argue that a criminal penalty for usage is inappropriate, given that whatever harm the offense causes is largely restricted

to the user (Criminal Justice Commission, 1994; Kaplan, 1970). This argument has special force in Australian states in which the statutory penalty for cannabis use is a 15-year prison sentence. Since these states do not impose prison sentences for drunk driving, conduct that clearly endangers the health and safety of others, advocates of civil penalties argue that the same approach should be adopted toward cannabis use (McDonald, Moore, Norberry, Wardlaw, & Ballenden, 1994).

In Australia, fewer than 1 in 50 users are arrested in any year, a rate that probably explains the modest deterrent effects of prohibition. The rates were 2% in Queensland in 1990 (Advisory Committee on Illicit Drugs, 1993) and 1.5% in Western Australia in 1998 (Lenton, 2000), comparable to arrest rates in Canada in the early 1970s (Canadian Government Commission of Inquiry, 1970) and the United States in 1995 (MacCoun & Reuter, 2001). The low rate of detection and prosecution prompts another criticism: that the failure to enforce a widely broken criminal law brings the criminal law into disrepute among the majority of young Australians who break the law without being prosecuted. There is no research on the effect of disobedience to cannabis prohibition on public attitudes toward the rule of law, but this is a plausible hypothesis that deserves investigation.

The prohibition against cannabis is also applied in a discriminatory way. In Queensland in 1994, cannabis offenders appearing before the criminal courts were more likely to be unemployed and socially disadvantaged males than were the majority of people who reported cannabis use in community surveys of drug use in that state (Advisory Committee on Illicit Drugs, 1993). The same was true in the 1960s in the United States (Kaplan, 1970), and recent U.S. studies show disproportionately higher rates of arrests for cannabis offenses among Hispanics and blacks (Gettman, 2000; Human Rights Watch, 2000).

Critics also argue that having a criminal record for using cannabis harms the lives of otherwise law-abiding users (Lenton, 2000) in ways that are more serious than any harm that users may experience from using cannabis (Wodak et al., 2002). The limited research on the topic (Erickson, 1980; Lenton, Bennett, & Heale, 1999; Lenton, Christie, et al., 1999) suggests that a substantial proportion of persons convicted of these offenses have no other criminal records and that a criminal conviction hurts their employment opportunities and reputations while having a negligible effect on their rates of cannabis use (Lenton, Bennett, et al., 1999; Lenton, Christie, et al., 1999).

HEALTH EDUCATION ABOUT CANNABIS AND OTHER DRUGS   Critics argue that a major cost of cannabis prohibition is that users are given misleading information about the health effects of cannabis (Zimmer & Morgan, 1997). Like "the boy who cried wolf," the government makes exaggerated claims about the adverse health effects of cannabis, and as a result, young

people are made skeptical about *all* information on the adverse health effects of cannabis. There is some support for this claim (Hall & Nelson, 1995), so this too must be counted as a cost of prohibition.

A related concern is that exaggerated claims about the health effects of cannabis may reduce the perceived risks of using heroin and cocaine (Zimmer & Morgan, 1997). If we teach young people that the health risks of cannabis are similar to those of heroin and cocaine, these critics argue, then benign experiences with cannabis may make young people skeptical about the adverse health effects of heroin and cocaine (United Kingdom Police Foundation, 2000). This argument, which has been popular in the Australian debate, seems plausible, although the fact that most cannabis users do *not* try other drugs suggests otherwise. It clearly deserves to be researched.

THE LOSS OF MEDICAL USES OF CANNABIS   Critics in the United States argue that cannabis prohibition prevents patients with life-threatening and chronic illnesses, such as AIDS and cancer, from using cannabis for medical purposes (Grinspoon & Bakalar, 1993; Zimmer & Morgan, 1997). Similar arguments have been used in Australia (Hall, Degenhardt, & Currow, 2001). An estimate of the number of potential medical users of cannabis in the state of New South Wales suggested that there were 14,000 people who might alleviate symptoms in a population of approximately 5 million adults (Hall, Degenhardt, & Currow, 2001). This number was likely an overestimate because the symptoms of many of these patients would be relieved by existing treatments, and not all those whose symptoms were unrelieved would be interested in using cannabis. Thus, the number of medical users deprived of medicine remains difficult to estimate.

INCOMPLETE POLICY APPRAISALS   The contending parties in the Australian cannabis policy debate have provided incomplete views on the harms of cannabis use and cannabis prohibition. The defenders of current policy are arguably closer to the truth about two things. First, they recognize that cannabis use can harm some of those who use it, namely, younger and heavier users. Motor vehicle accidents may affect nonusers, but those who use the drug suffer the most common adverse effects, namely, cannabis dependence, respiratory problems, poor adolescent psychosocial outcomes, and psychosis (Hall, 1995). Second, they argue that although prohibition has failed to deter many people, it probably has reduced the frequency and duration of cannabis use. Their argument that depenalization will increase rates of use has not been well supported, but it is more plausible that legalization (under a regime like that for alcohol) would increase rates of cannabis use, the duration of regular use, and, as a consequence, rates of cannabis-related problems.

Defenders of prohibition err in ignoring the social costs of cannabis prohibition. These costs are better appreciated by advocates of cannabis

depenalization. They probably include: disrespect for a selectively enforced law; the economic and social costs of a large black market; forgone tax revenue; the restriction on the liberty of adults to use cannabis, including those who would use it for medical purposes; and more speculatively, adverse effects on health education of young people about the health effects of cannabis and other illicit drugs. We know a lot less about the extent and seriousness of the costs of prohibition than we do about the adverse effects of cannabis use. Better assessment of the costs and benefits of current policies should be a major policy research priority (Hall and Pacula, 2003; Manski, Pepper, & Petrie, 2001).

A Choice of Evils

The formulation of a cannabis policy requires some societal process for weighing the costs and benefits of cannabis use and the costs and benefits of prohibiting its use (Kleiman, 1992). In a democratic society this process is, and ought to be, undertaken by the political process. Ideally, this is a deliberative process that considers all the information and arguments that are relevant to the issue. On most plausible theories of democracy, my views on what decision the political process should come to deserve no more (nor less) weight than anyone else's. Here they are for what they are worth.

If cannabis use remains high among young Australians over the next few decades, I support Mark Kleiman's (1992) policy of "grudging toleration" that would allow a limited legal cannabis market. I would prefer cannabis to be supplied by a government monopoly on production and sale or by a restrictive licensing system that aimed to undercut the black market while adopting other policies that minimized the harms that would occur among adolescents and young adults who use cannabis regularly (see Hall and Pacula, 2003, for details).

Grudging toleration would reduce some of the social costs of prohibition: It would eliminate the injustice of using criminal laws to punish self-injurious behavior; it may reduce the size of the underground market that supplies more harmful illicit drugs; it would reduce disrespect for law enforcement; it would provide an opportunity for government to provide more credible information about the health risks of cannabis; and it may reduce the unregulated access that young people now have to the potent cannabis products that are produced by current enforcement policies.

Given the enthusiasm for free markets in most liberal democracies, cannabis is unlikely to be legalized in the restrictive way I have proposed. Indeed, if cannabis was legalized in the present regulatory environment, it is much more likely that it would be under a system like that which regulates (or fails to regulate) alcohol. This regime arguably maximizes the harms caused

by alcohol (Babor et al., 2003); it would probably do the same for the harms caused by cannabis use. I therefore am opposed to a free cannabis market.

In the absence of these more restrictive cannabis regimes, I would support cannabis depenalization as a lesser evil than prohibition for a number of reasons. First, it eliminates criminal penalties for a self-injurious behavior, and it brings the law into line with actual practice (which in Australia has been by and large not to enforce the criminal prohibition on cannabis use). Second, it may reduce pressure for more liberal cannabis policies, such as legalization (which is perhaps why a version of depenalization has been adopted by a conservative federal government in Australia). Third, it is a policy that is more easily reversed than a legal cannabis market if the community were to decide that it was mistaken.

Depenalization has two major weaknesses. First, it does not address the problems created by a cannabis black market. Second, it is not a long-term policy solution. Over the next decade or so, political pressure will build for further change which may involve either a return to criminal penalties or a move toward a fully legal cannabis market. Recriminalization is most likely to occur if depenalization is seen to produce large increases in cannabis use and cannabis-related harm; legalization will be the outcome if cannabis-related harms do not increase or come to be seen as of little consequence (as is currently the case with many alcohol-related harms).

The second weakness is its major attraction for me because it allows for a more considered cannabis policy to evolve over the next several decades (during which the current bipartisan political enthusiasm for free markets may well moderate). Ideally, the policy that emerges will be based upon (a) a more accurate evaluation of the health and other consequences of regular cannabis use (Hall & Babor, 2000), and (b) a better appreciation of the costs and benefits of enforcing prohibition. This will happen only if governments fund the necessary research on both of these important sets of policy issues (Hall & Pacula, 2003).

REFERENCES

Advisory Committee on Illicit Drugs. (1993). *Cannabis and the law in Queensland: A discussion paper.* Brisbane: Queensland Criminal Justice Commission.

Ali, R., & Christie, P. (1994). *Report of the National Task Force on Cannabis.* Canberra: Australian Government Printing Service.

Ali, R., Christie P., Lenton, S., Hawks, D., Sutton, A., Hall, W. D., et al. (1999). *The social impacts of the Cannabis Expiation Notice Scheme in South Australia. Summary report presented to the Ministerial Council on Drug Strategy.* (National Drug Strategy Monograph, Vol. 34). Canberra: Commonwealth Department of Health and Aged Care.

American Psychiatric Association (1994). *Diagnostic and statistical manual of mental disorders* (4th ed.). Washington, DC: American Psychiatric Association.

Andreasson, S., Engstrom, A., Allebeck, P., & Rydberg, U. (1987). Cannabis and schizophrenia: A longitudinal study of Swedish conscripts. *Lancet, 2,* 1483–1486.

Anthony, J. C., & Helzer, J. E. (1991). Syndromes of drug abuse and dependence. In L. N. Robins & D. A. Regier (Eds.), *Psychiatric disorders in America: The epidemiologic catchment area* (pp. 116–154). New York: Free Press.

Anthony, J. C., Warner, L., & Kessler, R. (1994). Comparative epidemiology of dependence on tobacco, alcohol, controlled substances, and inhalants: Basic findings from the National Comorbidity Survey. *Experimental and Clinical Psychopharmacology, 2,* 244–268.

Arseneault, L., Cannon, M., Poulton, R., Murray, R., Caspi, A., & Moffitt, T. E. (2002). Cannabis use in adolescence and risk for adult psychosis: Longitudinal prospective study. *British Medical Journal, 325,* 1212–1213.

Australian Institute of Health and Welfare. (2002). *National Drug Strategy Household Survey: Detailed findings.* (Drugs Statistics Series, Vol. 11). Canberra: Australian Institute of Health and Welfare.

Babor, T. (2003). *Alcohol: No ordinary commodity: Research and public policy.* Oxford: Oxford University Press.

Bachman, J. G., Wadsworth, K. N., O'Malley, P. M., Johnston, L. D., & Schulenberg, J. (1997). *Smoking, drinking, and drug use in young adulthood: The impacts of new freedoms and new responsibilities.* Mahwah, NJ: Lawrence Erlbaum.

Block, R. I., & Ghoneim, M. M. (1993). Effects of chronic marijuana use on human cognition. *Psychopharmacology (Berlin), 110,* 219–228.

Block, R. I., O'Leary, D. S., Hichwa, R. D., Augustinack, J. C., Ponto, L. L. B., Ghoneim, M. M., et al. (2002). Effects of frequent marijuana use on memory-related regional cerebral blood flow. *Pharmacology, Biochemistry and Behavior, 72,* 237–250.

Cameron, L., & Williams, J. (2001). Cannabis, alcohol, and cigarettes: Substitutes or complements? *Economic Record, 77,* 19–34.

Canadian Government Commission of Inquiry. (1970). *The non-medical use of drugs.* Ottawa: Information Canada.

Chen, K., & Kandel, D. B. (1995). The natural history of drug use from adolescence to the mid-thirties in a general population sample. *American Journal of Public Health, 85,* 41–47.

Christie, P. (1999). *Cannabis offenses under the Cannabis Expiation Notice Scheme in South Australia.* (National Drug Strategy Monograph, Vol. 35). Canberra: Commonwealth Department of Health and Aged Care.

Cohen, S. (1976). The 94-day cannabis study. *Annals of the New York Academy of Sciences, 282,* 211–220.

Commonwealth Department of Health. (1984). *Cannabis: A review of some important national inquiries and significant research reports.* Canberra: Australian Government Publishing Service.

Criminal Justice Commission. (1994). *Report on cannabis and the law in Queensland.* Brisbane: Criminal Justice Commission, Queensland.

Donald, P. (1991). Marijuana and upper aerodigestive tract malignancy in young patients. In G. Nahas & C. Latour (Eds.), *Physiopathology of illicit drugs: Cannabis, cocaine, opiates* (pp. 98–119). Oxford: Pergamon.

Donnelly, N., & Hall, W. D. (1994). *Patterns of cannabis use in Australia.* (National Drug Strategy Monograph, Vol. 27). Canberra: Australian Government Publishing Service.

Donnelly, N., Hall, W. D., & Christie, P. (1995). The effects of partial decriminalization on cannabis use in South Australia, 1985 to 1993. *Australian Journal of Public Health, 19,* 281–287.

Donnelly, N., Hall, W. D., & Christie, P. (1999). *Effects of the Cannabis Expiation Notice Scheme on levels and patterns of cannabis use in South Australia: Evidence from the National Drug Strategy Household Surveys 1985–1995.* (National Drug Strategy Monograph, Vol. 37). Canberra: Australian Government Publishing Service.

Ellard, J. (1992). The ninth crusade: The crusade against drugs. *Modern Medicine (Neutral Bay, NSW), 35,* 58–61, 64–68.

Erickson, P. G. (1980). *Cannabis criminals: The social effects of punishment on drug users.* Toronto: Addiction Research Foundation.

Fergusson, D. M., & Horwood, L. J. (1997). Early onset cannabis use and psychosocial adjustment in young adults. *Addiction, 92,* 279–296.

Fergusson, D. M., & Horwood, L. J. (2000). Does cannabis use encourage other forms of illicit drug use? *Addiction, 95,* 505–520.

Fergusson, D. M., Horwood, L. J., & Swain-Campbell, N. (2002). Cannabis use and psychosocial adjustment in adolescence and young adulthood. *Addiction, 97,* 1123–1135.

Fergusson, D. M., Horwood, J. L., & Swain-Campbell, N. R. (2003). Cannabis dependence and psychotic symptoms in young people. *Psychological Medicine, 33,* 15–21.

Gettman, J. (2000). *United States marijuana arrests, part two: Racial differences in drug arrests,* National Organization for the Reform of Marijuana Laws. Retrieved on April 4 from http://www.norml.org/index.cfm?Group_ID=5326.

Grinspoon, L., & Bakalar, J. (1993). *Marihuana, the forbidden medicine.* New Haven, CT: Yale University Press.

Hall, W. (1995). The public health significance of cannabis use in Australia. *Australian Journal of Public Health, 19,* 235–42.

Hall, W. D. (1997). The recent Australian debate about the prohibition on cannabis use. *Addiction, 92,* 1109–1115.

Hall, W. D., & Babor, T. F. (2000). Cannabis use and public health: assessing the burden. *Addiction, 95,* 485–490.

Hall, W. D., Degenhardt, L., & Currow, D. (2001). Allowing the medical use of cannabis. *Medical Journal of Australia, 175,* 39–40.

Hall, W. D., Degenhardt, L., & Lynskey, M. T. (2001). *The health and psychological effects of cannabis use.* (National Drug Strategy Monograph, Vol. 44). Canberra: Commonwealth Department of Health and Aged Care.

Hall, W. D., & Lynskey, M. (in press). Testing hypotheses about the relationship between the use of cannabis and the use of other illicit drugs. *Drug and Alcohol Review.*

Hall, W. D., & MacPhee, D. (2002). Cannabis use and cancer. *Addiction, 97,* 243–247.

Hall, W. D., & Nelson, J. (1995). *Public perceptions of health and psychological consequences of cannabis use.* Canberra: Australian Government Publishing Service.

Hall, W. D., & Pacula, R. L. (2003). *Cannabis use and dependence: Public health and public policy.* Cambridge: Cambridge University Press.

Hall, W. D., Solowij, N., & Lemon, J. (1994). *The health and psychological consequences of cannabis use.* (National Drug Strategy Monograph, Vol. 25). Canberra: Australian Government Publishing Service.

Hall, W. D., Teesson, M., Lynskey, M. T., & Degenhardt, L. (1999). The 12-month prevalence of substance use and ICD-10 substance use disorders in Australian adults: findings from the National Survey of Mental Health and Well-being. *Addiction, 94,* 1541–1550.

Henquet, C., Krabbendam, L., Spauwen, J., Kaplan, C., Lieb, R., Wittchen, H. U., et al. (2004). Prospective cohort study of cannabis use, predisposition for psychosis, and psychotic symptoms in young people. *Bmj Online First,* 1 December.

Human Rights Watch (2000). *Punishment and prejudice: Racial disparities in the war on drugs (Human Rights Watch Report vol. 12 no. 2).* Retrieved on November 17, 2004, from http://www.hrw.org/reports/2000/usa/.

Kaplan, J. (1970). *Marijuana: The new Prohibition.* New York: World Publishing Company.

Kleiman, M. A. R. (1992). Neither prohibition nor legalization: Grudging toleration in drug control policy. *Daedalus, 121,* 53–83.

Kyvig, D. E. (1979). *Repealing National Prohibition.* Chicago: University of Chicago Press.

Lenton, S. (2000). Cannabis policy and the burden of proof: Is it now beyond reasonable doubt that cannabis prohibition is not working? *Drug and Alcohol Review, 19,* 95–100.

Lenton, S. (2004). Pot, politics, and the press—Reflections on cannabis law reform in Western Australia. *Drug and Alcohol Review, 23,* 223–233.

Lenton, S., Bennett, M., & Heale, P. (1999). *The social impact of a minor cannabis offense under strict prohibition: The case of Western Australia.* Perth: National Centre for Research into the Prevention of Drug Abuse.

Lenton, S., Christie, P., Humeniuk, R., Brooks, A., Bennet, M., & Heale, P. (1999). *Infringement versus conviction: The social impact of a minor cannabis offense under a civil penalties system and strict prohibition in two Australian states.* (National Drug Strategy Monograph, Vol. 36). Canberra: Commonwealth Department of Health and Aged Care.

Llewellyn, C. D., Linklater, K., Bell, J., Johnson, N. W., & Warnakulasuriya, S. (2004). An analysis of risk factors for oral cancer in young people: A case-control study. *Oral Oncol, 40,* 304–313.

Lynskey, M., & Hall, W. (2000). *Educational outcomes and adolescent cannabis use.* Sydney: New South Wales Department of Education and Training.

MacCoun, R., & Reuter, P. (2001). *Drugwar heresies: Learning from other vices, times, and places.* Cambridge: Cambridge University Press.

MacDonald, D., & Atkinson, L. (1995). *Social impacts of the legislative options for cannabis in Australia. Phase I Research.* Canberra: Australian Institute of Criminology.

Macleod, J., Oakes, R., Copello, A., Crome, I., Egger, M., Hickman, M., et al. (2004). Psychological and social sequelae of cannabis and other illicit drug use by young people: A systematic review of longitudinal, general population studies. *Lancet, 363,* 1579–1588.

MacPhee, D. (1999). Effects of marijuana on cell nuclei: A review of the literature relating to the genotoxicity of cannabis. In H. Kalant, W. Corrigall, W. D. Hall, & R. Smart (Eds.), *The health effects of cannabis* (pp. 435–458). Toronto: Centre for Addiction and Mental Health.

Manderson, D. (1993). *From Mr Sin to Mr Big: A history of Australian drug laws.* Melbourne: Oxford University Press.

Manski, C. F., Pepper, J. V., & Petrie, C. V. (Eds.) (2001). *Informing America's policy on illegal drugs: What we don't know keeps hurting us.* Washington, DC: National Academy Press.

Marselos, M., & Karamanakos, P. (1999). Mutagenicity, developmental toxicity, and carcinogeneity of cannabis. *Addiction Biology, 4,* 5–12.

McDonald, D., & Atkinson, L. (1995). *Social impacts of the legislative options for cannabis in Australia. Phase 1 research.* Canberra: Australian Institute of Criminology.

McDonald, D., Moore, R., Norberry, J., Wardlaw, G., & Ballenden, N. (1994). *Legislative options for cannabis in Australia.* (National Drug Strategy Monograph, Vol. 26). Canberra: Australian Government Publishing Service.

Mill, J. S. (1998). *On liberty and other essays, edited with an introduction and notes by John Gray.* Oxford: Oxford University Press.

Miron, J. A., & Zweibel, J. (1991). Alcohol consumption during Prohibition. *American Economic Review, 81,* 242–246.

Nahas, G., & Latour, C. (1992). The human toxicity of marijuana. *Medical Journal of Australia, 156,* 495–497.

Pacula, R. L., Chriqui, J. F., & King, J. (2003). *Marijuana decriminalization: What does it mean in the United States?* (NBER Working Paper, Vol. 9690). Cambridge, MA: National Bureau of Economic Research.

Pacula, R. L., Grossman, M., Chaloupka, F. J., O'Malley, P. M., Johnston, L., & Farrelly, M. C. (2001). Marijuana and youth. In J. Gruber (Ed.), *An economic analysis of risky behavior among youths.* Chicago: University of Chicago Press.

Parliamentary Joint Committee on the National Crime Authority (1989). *Drugs, crime, and society.* Canberra: Australian Government Publishing Service.

Pope, H. G., Gruber, A. J., & Yurgelun-Todd, D. (1995). The residual neuropsychological effects of cannabis: The current status of research. *Drug
and Alcohol Dependence, 38,* 25–34.

Pope, H. G., & Yurgelun-Todd, D. (1996). The residual cognitive effects of
heavy marijuana use in college students. *Journal of the American Medical Association, 275,* 521–527.

Ramaekers, J. G., Berghaus, G., van Laar, M., & Drummer, O. H. (2004).
Dose related risk of motor vehicle crashes after cannabis use. *Drug and
Alcohol Dependence, 73,* 109–119.

Reinarman, C., & Levine, H. G. (1989). The crack attack: Politics and media
in America's latest drug scare. In J. Best (Ed.), *Images of issues: Typifying
contemporary social problems* (pp. 115–137). Hawthorn, NY: Aldine de
Gruyter.

Roffman, R. A., Stephens, R. S., Simpson, E. E., & Whitaker, D. L. (1988).
Treatment of marijuana dependence: Preliminary results. *Journal of Psychoactive Drugs, 20,* 129–137.

Rosenblatt, K. A., Daling, J. R., Chen, C., Sherman, K. J., & Schwartz, S. M.
(2004). Marijuana use and risk of oral squamous cell carcinoma. *Cancer
Research, 64,* 4049–4054.

Saffer, H., & Chaloupka, F. J. (1999). The demand for illicit drugs: Effects of
decriminalization. *Economic Inquiry, 37,* 401–418.

Select Committee on HIV Illegal Drugs and Prostitution (1991). *Third interim report: Marijuana and other illegal drugs.* Canberra: Legislative Assembly of the Australian Capital Territory.

Senate Standing Committee on Social Welfare (1977). *Drug problems in Australia: An intoxicated society?* Canberra: Australian Government Printing
Office.

Sidney, S., Quesenberry, C. P., Jr., Friedman, G. D., & Tekawa, I. S. (1997).
Marijuana use and cancer incidence (California, United States). *Cancer
Causes and Control, 8,* 722–728.

Single, E. W. (1989). The impact of marijuana decriminalization: An update.
Journal of Public Health Policy, 9, 456–466.

Smiley, A. (1999). Marijuana: On road and driving simulator studies. In
H. Kalant, W. Corrigall, W. D. Hall, & R. Smart (Eds.), *The health effects
of cannabis.* Toronto: Centre for Addiction and Mental Health.

Solowij, N. (1998). *Cannabis and cognitive functioning.* Cambridge, UK:
Cambridge University Press.

Solowij, N. (1999). Long-term effects of cannabis on the central nervous system. I. Brain function and neurotoxicity. II. Cognitive functioning. In H.
Kalant, W. Corrigal, W. Hall, & R. Smart (Eds.), *The health effects of
cannabis* (pp. 195–265). Toronto: Centre for Addiction and Mental
Health.

Solowij, N. (2002). Cannabis and cognitive functioning. In E. S. Onaivi
(Ed.), *Biology of marijuana: From gene to behavior.* London: Taylor &
Francis.

Solowij, N., Stephens, R. S., Roffman, R. A., Babor, T., Kadden, R., Miller, M.,
et al. (2002). Cognitive functioning of long-term heavy cannabis users

seeking treatment. *Journal of the American Medical Association, 287,* 1123–1131.

Stephens, R. S., Roffman, R. A., & Simpson, E. E. (1993). Adult marijuana users seeking treatment. *Journal of Consulting and Clinical Psychology, 61,* 1100–1104.

Szasz, T. (1997). *Ceremonial chemistry: The ritual persecution of drugs, addicts, and pushers* (Rev. ed.). Holmes Beach, FL: Learning Publications.

Tashkin, D. P. (1999). Effects of cannabis on the respiratory system. In H. Kalant, W. Corrigall, W. D. Hall, & R. Smart (Eds.), *The health effects of cannabis.* Toronto: Centre for Addiction and Mental Health.

Taylor, D. R., Fergusson, D. M., Milne, B. J., Horwood, L. J., Moffitt, T. E., Sears, M. R., et al. (2002). A longitudinal study of the effects of tobacco and cannabis exposure on lung function in young adults. *Addiction, 97,* 1055–1061.

Taylor, D. R., Poulton, R., Moffitt, T., Ramankutty, P., & Sears, M. (2000). The respiratory effects of cannabis dependence in young adults. *Addiction, 95,* 1669–1677.

Taylor, I. F. (1988). Marijuana as a potential respiratory tract carcinogen: A retrospective analysis of a community hospital population. *Southern Medical Journal, 81,* 1213–1216.

Tyrrell, I. (1997). The U.S. Prohibition experiment: Myths, history, and implications. *Addiction, 92,* 1405–1409.

United Kingdom Police Foundation. (2000). *Drugs and the law: Report of the Independent Inquiry into the Misuse of Drugs Act 1971.* London: The United Kingdom Police Foundation.

Van Os, J., Bak, M., Hanssen, M., Bijl, R. V., de Graaf, R., & Verdous, H. (2002). Cannabis use and psychosis: A longitudinal population-based study. *American Journal of Epidemiology, 156,* 319–327.

Vaughan, S. (2003a). Australian diversionary programmes: An alternative to imprisonment for drug and alcohol offenders. In *UNAFEI annual report for 2002* (pp. 143–165). Tokyo: United Nations Asia and Far East Institute for the Prevention of Crime and the Treatment of Offenders.

Vaughan, S. (2003b). A setting for Australian drug diversion programmes: The Australian Drug Strategic framework. In *UNAFEI Annual report for 2002* (pp. 123–142). Tokyo: United Nations Asia and Far East Institute for the Prevention of Crime and the Treatment of Offenders.

Walters, E. (1993). *Marijuana: An Australian crisis.* Malvern, VIC: E. Walters.

Williams, J. (2004). The effects of price and policy on marijuana use: What can be learned from the Australian experience? *Health Economics, 13,* 123–137.

Wodak, A., Reinarman, C., & Cohen, P. (2002). Cannabis control: Costs outweigh benefits. *British Journal of Medicine, 324,* 105–106.

Wooldridge, M. (2001). *Media release: Drug offenders in Queensland offered new hope in diversion initiative.* Australian Government Department of Health and Ageing, March 20. Available at http://www.health.gov.au/internet/wcms/publishing.nsf/Content/health-mediarel-yr2001-mw-mw01017.htm.

Zammit, S., Allebeck, P., Andreasson, S., Lundberg, I., & Lewis, G. (2002). Self reported cannabis use as a risk factor for schizophrenia in Swedish conscripts of 1969: Historical cohort study. *British Medical Journal, 325,* 1199–1201.

Zhang, Z. F., Morgenstern, H., Spitz, M. R., Tashkin, D. P., Yu, G. P., Marshall, J. R., et al. (1999). Marijuana use and increased risk of squamous cell carcinoma of the head and neck. *Cancer Epidemiology Biomarkers and Prevention, 8,* 1071–1978.

Zimmer, L., & Morgan, J. P. (1997). *Marijuana myths, marijuana facts: A review of the scientific evidence.* New York: Lindesmith Center.

6 Law, Culture, and Cannabis: Comparing Use Patterns in Amsterdam and San Francisco

Craig Reinarman
Peter Cohen

Where customs are strong, law is unnecessary. Where customs are weak, law is useless.

—Professor Edwin H. Sutherland,
"father" of American criminology

Humans have ingested cannabis for about 10,000 years, since the beginning of agriculture in the Old World (Schultes, 1978). For some of those millennia, this use has been controversial. The ancient Chinese referred to cannabis as both the "Liberator of Sin" and "The Delight Giver" (Goode, 1969a). When cannabis (or marijuana)[1] use slowly spread in the 20th century, particularly as North American and European youth adopted it as a cultural practice in the 1960s, it became a crucible in a kind of culture war that continues to this day. American public discourse has rarely lacked for heated debate about cannabis's effects, villainous or virtuous depending upon one's point of view.

One way of approaching this minefield is to see it as a contest between two competing hypotheses or interpretive frameworks about the consequences of cannabis use. On one side, there is what we will call the *life disruption hypothesis*, which holds that once people taste the pleasures of cannabis intoxication, they will tend to increase their use to the extent that it results in significant social dysfunction. According to this view, cannabis use tends to become so central in the lives of users that they can no long perform their roles adequately or fully meet their responsibilities. When pushed, most scientists in the drug field who lean toward this view acknowledge that there

are many intervening variables that increase or decrease the likelihood of any of the effects attributed to cannabis use, and that life disruption is not inevitable but is rather contingent on many factors other than cannabis consumption.

On the other side of the debate are those who claim that these very same pleasures of cannabis typically enhance the lives of users without leading to increased use or dependency. In this view, when otherwise ordinary humans ingest cannabis, the vast majority learn to integrate it into their lives so that it does not disrupt their social functioning. We will call this view the *life integration hypothesis*. When pushed, most scientists who lean toward this hypothesis acknowledge that a small minority of cannabis users use it very intensively and seem to develop one or more problems related to this use. And like their counterparts in the opposing camp, these scientists note that numerous intervening variables related to intensive users' characteristics and the contexts in which they use better account for apparent cannabis-related problems than consumption of the drug alone.

Neither the research we report here nor any other study can decisively adjudicate between these competing views. And even if they could, that would not settle the matter, for ultimately the debate is about the morality of pleasure seeking, a political issue about which scientific data are mostly mute (e.g., Goode, 1969b). The data we present in what follows do, however, provide a rare glimpse into patterns of cannabis use over time, which can provide valuable clues as to the degree to which cannabis use takes the form predicted by the life disruption hypothesis or the form predicted by the life integration hypothesis.

These data on career patterns of use also bear upon drug policy issues. Across the globe, cannabis laws and policies are predicated on the life disruption hypothesis. But by the end of the 20th century, the governments of numerous countries had become openly skeptical about its validity. Since the end of the 1960s, the trend in Western democracies has been toward liberalization of cannabis laws. In 1972, after exhaustive study by top experts, U.S. President Richard Nixon's handpicked National Commission on Marijuana and Drug Abuse recommended decriminalization of cannabis because they found arrest, imprisonment, and stigma more harmful than the drug itself. Drug control officials, however, argued strenuously that Congress should ignore the commission's recommendations, which it did.

At about the same moment in history, however, the Dutch government formed its own national commission, and its study of the evidence on cannabis arrived at a similar conclusion: that there was greater risk of harm to users and society from criminalization of cannabis use than from the use itself. In 1976, the Netherlands adopted de facto decriminalization. We say "de facto" because in Dutch law (*wet*), cannabis remains criminalized, but since 1976 the Ministry of Justice has made it national policy (*beleid*) to not

enforce that law.[2] After 1980, a system of "coffee shops" evolved in which the purchase of small quantities of cannabis by adults was first informally tolerated and then formally permitted under licensing regulations (Cohen, 1997; Engelsman, 1989; Leuw and Marshall, 1994; Scheerer, 1978).

Drug-control officials in the United States have regularly denounced Dutch drug policy as the devil's work. One former U.S. drug czar asserted that Dutch youth in Amsterdam's Vondel Park were "stoned zombies." Although only cannabis, not heroin, had been decriminalized, a subsequent czar alleged that "you can't walk down the street in Amsterdam without tripping over dead junkies." In 1998, the Clinton administration drug czar, Barry McCaffrey, announced, prior to a "fact-finding tour" of the Netherlands, that the Dutch approach to drug policy was "an unmitigated disaster" (CNN, July 9, 1998; Reinarman, 1998, 2000).

Despite overt and covert pressure from U.S. officials, other countries moved their drug policies in the Dutch direction. During the 1990s, the governments of Switzerland, Germany, Spain, Austria, Belgium, Luxembourg, and Italy shifted their cannabis laws toward Dutch-style decriminalization. Since 1996, all jurisdictions in Australia have liberalized their cannabis laws, with half moving to a system of expiation notices or parking ticket–style fines. Portugal decriminalized cannabis in 2001. England similarly reclassified cannabis possession and use as minor offenses in 2004. Canada has partially decriminalized cannabis, and New Zealand is currently considering it. These shifts constitute the first steps away from the dominant drug policy paradigm long advocated by the United States, punishment-based prohibition (Bewley-Taylor, 2001; Bruun, Pan, & Rexed, 1975; Musto, 1973).

As this trend toward decriminalization was developing, the U.S. government moved in the opposite direction, stiffening criminal penalties for drug offenses and increasing arrests for cannabis offenses. Since 1996, voters in eight states and Washington, D.C., have passed ballot initiatives allowing the use of cannabis for medicinal purposes,[3] but the federal government has fought vigorously to prevent their implementation. In 2002, the Drug Enforcement Administration began raiding medical cannabis organizations (Murphy, 2002), and the White House Office of National Drug Control Policy launched a campaign against cannabis (Office of National Drug Control Policy [ONDCP], 2002b, 2002c). In 2003, a new high of more than 725,000 U.S. citizens were arrested for cannabis offenses, about 85% of which were for possession (FBI, 2004).

Prohibitionist drug policies like these are based on criminal punishment and are explicitly designed to deter use. The core empirical claim of criminalization proponents is that absent the threat of punishment, the prevalence, frequency of use, and quantity of cannabis use will increase and threaten public health.[4] The question of whether deterring use enhances public health was

beyond the scope of our study, but in what follows we do examine the relationship between drug policies and use patterns. This relationship has been explored by those critical of criminalization in the United States (e.g., Nadelmann, 1989) and by those at least skeptical of Dutch decriminalization (e.g., MacCoun & Reuter, 1997). But there have been no rigorously comparative studies of user behavior designed to assess whether criminalization constrains use or decriminalization increases it. In this chapter we compare the career use patterns of representative samples of experienced cannabis users in two cities with many similarities but with different drug-control regimes—Amsterdam (decriminalization) and San Francisco (criminalization).

We selected San Francisco *not* because it is representative of the United States, of course, but because it is the U.S. city most closely *comparable* to Amsterdam. Both are large, highly urbanized port cities with diverse populations of more than 700,000. Both are financial and entertainment hubs for larger regional conurbations. Both have long been seen within their home countries as cosmopolitan, politically liberal, and culturally tolerant.

Law enforcement in San Francisco is not as zealous in its enforcement of cannabis laws as law enforcement in most U.S. cities. Nonetheless, San Francisco is embedded in the drug policy context of criminalization that holds in the state and nation in which it is situated, a markedly different drug policy context than in Amsterdam. Purchase and sale of small amounts of cannabis for personal use are permitted in Amsterdam in 288 licensed coffee shops (Bieleman & Goeree, 2000), while in San Francisco possession and use remain criminal offenses. In Amsterdam, there is neither proactive nor reactive policing of use or low-level sales (although police do enforce regulations against coffee shops' advertising, selling to minors, distributing any other drug, and creating public nuisances). In San Francisco, there is strong proactive and reactive policing of sales, and moderate reactive policing of use. Most important, these drug policy differences are palpable to users. San Francisco students are suspended from schools and placed in treatment for cannabis use. San Francisco users face at least some risk of arrest, citations, and fines if detected buying, possessing, or using cannabis. Amsterdam users do not face any of these risks.

A BRIEF NOTE ON METHODS

We wanted to study use patterns as they evolved over time, so we needed to survey representative samples of cannabis users who had enough experience to be able to answer questions about use over a "career." We defined as "experienced" those who had used cannabis on at least 25 occasions in their lives. We recruited the Amsterdam respondents from those who took part in a drug-use prevalence survey in the general population. This survey was

administered to a random sample drawn from Amsterdam's Municipal Population Registry. The overall response rate was 50.2%, yielding a sample of 4,364 (Sandwijk, Cohen, Musterd, & Langemeijer, 1995). We compared responders with nonresponders and with city demographic data and found no significant differences requiring weighting.

All respondents who reported having used cannabis at least 25 times (n=535; 12.3% of the population sample) were asked to participate in an in-depth interview about their cannabis use. Of the 535 experienced users identified in the general population sample, 216 (40.5%) were ultimately interviewed in 1996 (Cohen & Sas, 1997). This modest response rate necessitated a check on representativeness. We compared the 216 who responded to the 319 who did not on 12 demographic and drug-use prevalence variables. Respondents had slightly higher levels of formal education and slightly higher last-year cannabis use (Cohen & Sas, 1997; Cohen & Kaal, 2001), but otherwise showed no differences with nonrespondents and thus were reasonably representative of experienced cannabis users in the general population.

We replicated the Amsterdam survey of experienced users in San Francisco beginning in 1997. San Francisco does not maintain a population registry, so to remain consistent with Amsterdam we first drew an area probability sample by randomly selecting census tracts, blocks, buildings, households, and adults within households. We then administered a brief prevalence survey consisting of demographic and drug-use prevalence questions. Unlike the Amsterdam prevalence survey, which was an extensive study in its own right, this brief prevalence survey in San Francisco was principally a means for generating a random representative sample of experienced cannabis users. Homeless and institutionalized inhabitants were not interviewed in either city.

The overall response rate in the San Francisco prevalence survey was 52.7%, yielding a sample of 891 (Piazza & Cheng, 1999). Of these, 349 (39.2%) reported using cannabis 25 or more times—three times the prevalence found in the Amsterdam sample. We asked these experienced users to participate in the longer interview. Of these 349 experienced users, 266 (76.2%) were ultimately interviewed in depth about their career use patterns. As a check on their representativeness, we compared respondents and nonrespondents on 10 demographic and drug-use prevalence variables and found no statistically significant differences.[5]

Age of Onset, First Regular Use, and Maximum Use

Despite the difference in drug policy context, the average age of first use of cannabis was nearly identical in both cities: 16.95 years in Amsterdam and 16.43 years in San Francisco (see Figure 6.1). The mean age at which respondents commenced regular use, which we defined as once per month or more,

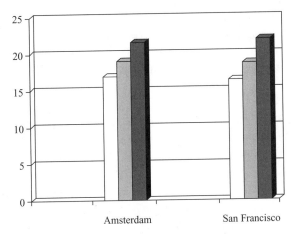

Figure 6.1. Age at First Use, First Regular Use, and Start of Heavy Use Among Experienced Cannabis Users

also was nearly identical: 19.11 years in Amsterdam, 18.81 years in San Francisco. Respondents in both cities began their periods of maximum use about two years after they began regular use, at a mean age of 21.46 years in Amsterdam and 21.98 years in San Francisco. The majority of experienced users in both cities reported periods of maximum use of three years or less.

Use Patterns Over Time

To assess how cannabis use patterns change over time, we asked our respondents about the typical frequency and quantity of their use and the intensity and duration of intoxication in each of four time periods. Figure 6.2 depicts the frequency of cannabis use reported for these four periods. Respondents in both cities reported similar frequency of use. During the first year of regular use, strong majorities reported using cannabis once a week or less, and small percentages used it daily. Frequency increased in the period of top or maximum use, but declined sharply thereafter. Amsterdam respondents reported somewhat more frequent use than San Francisco respondents during their first year of regular use (t=4.019, 479 df; p=.000) and their maximum use period (t=2.979, 479 df; p=.003). Comparing the maximum-use period with the last year, daily use declined from 49% to 10% in Amsterdam and 39% to 7% in San Francisco. In both cities, this decline was greater still in the last 3 months.

The basic trajectory of use frequency across careers is parallel in both cities. Most users reported a period of maximum use of 2–3 years, after which they sharply reduced their frequency of use or stopped using. In both

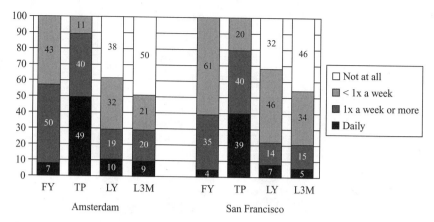

Figure 6.2. Frequency of Cannabis Use in 4 Periods, by City (% of All Respondents)

FY = First Year of Regular use (=>once/month)
TP = Top Period (period of maximum use)
LY = Last Year (12 months prior to interview)
L3M = Last 3 Months (3 months prior to interview)

cities, about three in four reported using less than once a week or not at all in the year prior to interview.

Quantity of Use

In the first year of regular use, few respondents in either city consumed large quantities of cannabis (Figure 6.3). Only 3% in Amsterdam and 5% in San Francisco reported using 28 grams (about 1 ounce) in an average month. Amsterdam respondents reported using significantly smaller quantities than did San Francisco respondents in this period. Combining the two smallest categories, two thirds in Amsterdam (66%) and about three fifths (59%) in San Francisco consumed 4 grams per month or less in their first year of regular use. More than one in three in each city used less than 2 grams per month during their first year of regular use.

Naturally, the quantities used during periods of top or maximum use were larger, although they remained very similar across cities. About two thirds consumed an average of 14 grams per month (half an ounce) or less—69% in Amsterdam, 64% in San Francisco. Less than one in five in each city (18%) consumed an average of 28 grams per month or more during their maximum use periods.

In the year prior to interview, those still using reported sharply lower quantities of use. Clear majorities reported using 4 grams or less per month,

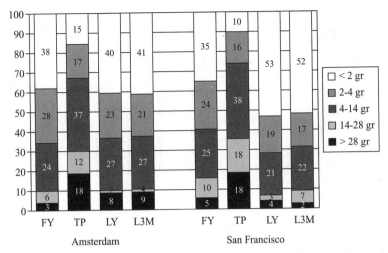

Figure 6.3. Average Quantity of Cannabis Used Per Month (for Last-Year and Last-3-Months Periods, Percentages Are of Respondents Still Using)

although less so in Amsterdam (63%) than in San Francisco (72%; t=2.207, 297 df; p=.028). Roughly one third of respondents in each city reported no use in the year prior to interview (last-year and last-month figures exclude those who had quit). Overall, the patterns were parallel in both cities: Quantities used increased from first regular use to a period of maximum use, but then declined steadily or ceased altogether over the course of their careers.

Intensity of Intoxication

To tap another dimension of use, we asked our respondents to estimate "how high or how stoned you generally got" when consuming cannabis. Some recalled this with greater consistency than others, but they were able to make basic ordinal distinctions between more and less intense highs. To increase the reliability of their estimates, we displayed a simple 6-point scale ranging from "light buzz" (1) to "very high" (6) and asked them to select the number that best summarized their highs in each period.

As Figure 6.4 indicates, respondents in both cities tended to increase the intensity of their highs in periods of maximum use but moderated them thereafter (last-year and last-month figures exclude those who had quit). In the first year of regular use and in maximum use periods, Amsterdam respondents were significantly more likely to report *milder* intoxication; mean scores were 3.5 in Amsterdam and 3.9 in San Francisco (t=−3.180, 476 df; p=.002), rising in maximum use periods to 3.9 and 4.4, respectively (t=−4.932, 413df; p=.000).

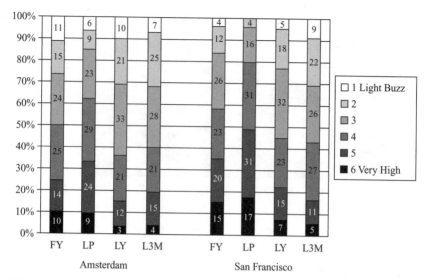

Figure 6.4. Intensity of Intoxication at Typical Occasion of Cannabis Use (for Last-Year and Last-3-Months Periods, Percentages Are of Respondents Still Using)

We found the same pattern for the more recent periods, although the mean scores declined (last-year and last-month figures exclude those who had quit). The proportion of respondents who chose 6, "very high," remained small, between 3% and 7% in both cities, although slightly larger in San Francisco. In the last year, Amsterdam respondents were again significantly more likely to report milder intoxication ($t=-2.233$, 310df; $p=.026$). During the three months prior to interview, majorities in both cities reported milder highs. In short, regardless of drug policy, respondents reported getting *less* intoxicated over the course of their careers.

Duration of Intoxication

We also asked our respondents "about how long" they had been high during a typical occasion of use in each of the four periods. Reported durations were correlated with frequency and quantity, although they were not a function of frequency and quantity alone. Here, too, we found a tendency toward moderation over the course of users' careers in both cities, regardless of drug policy.

As Figure 6.5 shows, Amsterdam respondents reported highs of somewhat longer duration in the first year of regular use ($t=2.329$, 476 df; $p=.020$).[6] In the other 3 time periods, however, there were no significant differences; clear majorities in each city regulated their ingestion so as to be high 2–3

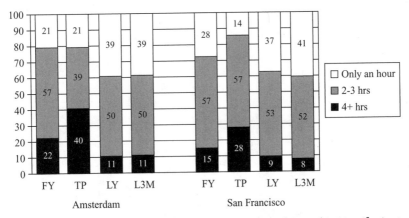

Figure 6.5. Duration of Intoxication, Typical Occasion of Cannabis Use (for Last-Year and Last-3-Months Periods, Percentages Are of Respondents Still Using)

hours or less. Substantial minorities in each city reported being high for four or more hours during maximum use periods, but these proportions dropped sharply thereafter. Of those still using in the 3 months prior to interview, 89% in Amsterdam and 93% in San Francisco reported being high for 2–3 hours or less in a typical occasion of use.

Overall Career Use Patterns

Beyond the specifics of frequency, quantity, intensity, and duration, we asked respondents to characterize their *overall* career use patterns. We showed them the typology of trajectories depicted in Figure 6.6 (Morningstar & Chitwood, 1983), and asked them to select the one that "best describes" their cannabis use over time.

We found that two career patterns were the most common in both cities (Table 6.1). Pattern 4, gradually increasing use followed by sustained decline, was the most common (about half in each city). The second most common was Pattern 6, wide variation over time (about one fourth in each city). Patterns 1, 2, 3, and 5 were each selected by only 6–8% of the combined sample. Pattern 3, stable use from the start onward, was selected significantly more often by Amsterdam respondents (11.1%) than by San Francisco respondents (1.9%), and Pattern 5, intermittent use (many starts and stops over time) was selected significantly more often by San Francisco respondents (9.5%) than by Amsterdam respondents (3.2%).

These findings on overall career use patterns are consistent with those on frequency and quantity of use, and on intensity and duration of intoxication, and may have important implications. Claims that cannabis produces addiction

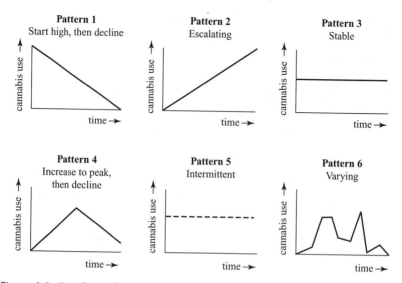

Figure 6.6. Typology of Career Use Trajectories

or dependence[7] would lead one to expect that many experienced users would report Pattern 2, increased use over time. But this pattern was reported by only 6% in both cities, which means that regardless of drug policy, 94% reported overall career use patterns that did *not* entail a trajectory of increased use.

Other Illicit Drug Use

How do cannabis policies affect the use of other illicit drugs? One objective of U.S. criminalization is to reduce cannabis use and thereby reduce the extent to which it would serve as a gateway or stepping-stone to "harder" drugs.[8] By this logic, one might expect the ready availability of cannabis in

Table 6.1. Career Use Trajectories

	Amsterdam		San Francisco	
	n	%	n	%
Pattern 1 - declining	17	8	18	7
Pattern 2 - escalating	13	6	17	6
Pattern 3 - stable	24	11	5	2
Pattern 4 - increase/decline	104	48	133	50
Pattern 5 - intermittent	7	3	25	9
Pattern 6 - variable	51	24	66	25
Total	216	100	264	100

$\chi^2 = 32.31$; df = 10; p = .000

Amsterdam to lead to higher prevalence of other illicit drug use there than in San Francisco. On the other hand, the architects of Dutch decriminalization took as one of their objectives the "separation of markets," meaning that they hoped lawfully regulated cannabis distribution would reduce the likelihood that people seeking cannabis would be drawn into deviant subcultures where drugs thought to pose greater risks were also sold (Cohen, 1997; Engelsman, 1989; Leuw & Marshall, 1994). In this view, one might expect lower prevalence of other illicit drug use in Amsterdam than in San Francisco. Our data can neither prove nor disprove either proposition because so many factors besides the differing drug policies can affect other illicit drug use, but the comparative data are still interesting.

We noted earlier that people who had ingested cannabis 25 times or more were far more prevalent in San Francisco than in Amsterdam, and this also turned out to be the case with other illicit drugs. As Table 6.2 indicates, Amsterdam respondents reported significantly *lower* lifetime prevalence of the use of other illicit drugs than did respondents in San Francisco. Among those who had tried these drugs, last-3-months prevalence of crack and opiate use also were significantly higher in San Francisco, although rates of cocaine, amphetamine, and ecstasy use were not significantly different. (Note, too, that this table shows high rates of *discontinuation*—the decline from lifetime to last-3-months prevalence—ranging from 64% to 98% for all drugs in both cities.)

THE LIMITED RELEVANCE OF DRUG POLICY: SUMMARY OF FINDINGS

Overall, our findings do not support claims that decriminalization leads to earlier, greater, or more intense use, or, conversely, that criminalization deters or reduces use. Despite widespread lawful availability of cannabis in Ams-

Table 6.2. Lifetime and Last-3-Months Prevalence of Other Illicit Drug Use

	Amsterdam n = 216		San Francisco n = 264		Significance Chi-Square	
	LTP	L3MP	LTP	L3MP	LTP	L3MP
cocaine	48.1	9.3	73.2	7.5	***	n.s.
crack	3.7	0.5	18.1	1.1	***	&
amphetamine	37.5	1.9	60.4	4.5	***	n.s.
ecstasy	25.5	9.3	40.0	6.4	***	n.s.
opiates	21.8	0.5	35.5	2.7	***	&

*** = p < .001; & = too few cases in cells to compute test of statistical significance

terdam, users there did not differ from users in San Francisco in terms of age of first use, age of first regular use, or age at the start of maximum use. Either criminalization has had no effect on availability in San Francisco, making it roughly equivalent to that in Amsterdam, or availability per se does not influence age of onset or of other career phases.

We also found consistent similarities across the different policy contexts in career use patterns over time. Although there were a few statistically significant differences in either direction on a few dimensions of use in some career phases, the basic trajectory was the same in both cities on all dimensions of use: *increasing into a limited period of maximum use, then sustained decrease over time or cessation.* Even during their periods of maximum use, clear majorities of experienced users in both cities never used daily or large amounts, and use levels generally declined after that. Further, clear majorities in both samples reported similarly steady declines in how high they got and for how long.

Proponents of criminalization claim that it decreases availability of supply, discourages demand, and provides incentives to quit, whereas decriminalization increases availability, encourages use, and provides disincentives to quit. This would lead one to expect increased use, longer careers, and fewer quitters under the Dutch system, but again, the data did not support these expectations. Only 6% in each city reported a career trajectory of increased use over time. Cannabis careers ranged in length from 1 to 38 years, with 95% in both cities reporting careers of three years or longer. The mean career length was slightly greater in San Francisco (15 years) than in Amsterdam (12 years), although this was ascribable mostly to the somewhat higher mean age in the San Francisco sample (34 vs. 31). Similarly, nearly identical proportions in each city had quit using entirely at interview—33.8% in Amsterdam, 34.3% in San Francisco.

If drug policy was a potent influence on user behavior, it is very unlikely there would be such consistent similarities across such different drug control regimes. Dutch decriminalization does not appear to be associated with greater use of other illicit drugs relative to San Francisco, nor does criminalization in San Francisco appear to be associated with less use of other illicit drugs relative to Amsterdam. Indeed, if the strikingly higher lifetime prevalence of other illicit drug use in San Francisco is any indication, the reverse may be the case.

Of course, this study has limitations,[9] and until it is replicated in other cities over longer periods, we must remain cautious about what inferences we draw from it. The comparability of our samples and measures does *help* isolate the effects of drug laws and policies, but there are a range of other, nonpolicy factors that may influence cannabis use. Culture and social conditions are different in Amsterdam and San Francisco. It is conceivable that if the Dutch had not decriminalized cannabis use, their prevalence rates might

be even lower than they are. And even if decriminalization has not led to increased drug use and drug problems in the Netherlands, such increases remain a possibility in the United States if it were to adopt a Dutch approach. That said, such increases are by no means certain, for studies of the effects of cannabis decriminalization in 11 U.S. states in the 1970s found no evidence that this led to increased use or misuse relative to comparable states that did not decriminalize.[10] Nonetheless, further research on use patterns before and after such policy shifts would be illuminating.

IF NOT LAW, WHAT? TOWARD A CULTURAL INTERPRETATION

If our comparative analysis of experienced users finds no evidence that differences in drug law are related to differences in drug use, then how are we to understand our findings? How can we make sense of the consistent similarities in use patterns we found across the two different drug policy contexts of Amsterdam and San Francisco? After further data analysis, we came to the following explanation: Most experienced users come to value the effects of cannabis because these serve certain purposes or functions for them; they therefore tend to develop informal rules with which they regulate use so that it serves those functions or purposes—regardless of drug law.

We asked our respondents about effects because we felt this would help us understand what they were getting out of the experience and thus shed additional light on their use patterns. We asked whether they had experienced a long list of effects after consuming cannabis, about the feeling states and changes in the self that they attributed to cannabis, about various advantages and disadvantages they found in cannabis, and about their reasons for using it.

The most frequently reported effects were "laughter" and "cotton mouth," noted by over four in five respondents in both cities. Majorities in both cities also reported effects such as a sense of "well-being" or "euphoria" and "having no cares." The next most frequently reported feelings were "relaxed," "slow," "lazy," "merry," and "talkative." The most common changes in the self they attributed to cannabis were greater "self-knowledge," increased "appreciation of beautiful things," "having more fun in life," "being more open to others," "feeling happier with oneself," "taking oneself less seriously," becoming "more balanced," and becoming "less ambitious."

We also asked our respondents about the advantages and disadvantages they saw in cannabis. Two to one, they identified relaxation as the drug's primary benefit. This was followed by a variety of responses having to do with sociability, amplification of the senses, general euphoria, and cognitive enhancement like "thinking more deeply" or creatively. The most common

disadvantages reported seemed to be the flip side of relaxation—feeling "sluggish," "slow," or "sleepy." When we asked our respondents their reasons for using cannabis, the same themes emerged. "Relaxation" again dominated, followed by feelings of euphoria, enhanced enjoyment, sociability, and "seeing the world with fresh eyes."

What might these responses tell us? Though there were several recurring themes, "relaxation" and related effects and feelings stand out.[11] There has been much clinical speculation about an "amotivational syndrome" among cannabis users. The gist of the claim is that cannabis makes users passive, unambitious, and unproductive.[12] Most studies that examine this question in representative samples of users outside of treatment do not find evidence supporting a causal link between cannabis consumption and aspirations, school achievement, employment status, or earnings.[13] But our respondents led us to suspect that this issue has been miscast. The authors who assert the existence of an amotivational syndrome, and even some of the authors who refute it, tend to assume that "it" is an *undesirable* and *unintended* effect of cannabis use, and that it extends beyond the period of intoxication to somehow infect the character structure of the user.

Our data suggest that this is a misinterpretation. We found no reason to believe that experienced users who reported feeling "less ambitious" or who felt they took themselves "less seriously" after using were lamenting this as a disadvantage. Those who reported feeling "slow" or "lazy" as effects generally were not listing negative side effects they sought to avoid. Rather, most appeared to value such effects as a means of giving themselves *episodic time-outs* from the stresses and demands of daily life.[14]

Historically, Western societies such as the United States and the Netherlands have been famous for and proud of their work ethic, according to which impulses toward gratification, pleasure, leisure, or consumption are to be renounced in favor of ambition, hard work, and production. For many, perhaps most of our respondents, cannabis use is a ritual means of stepping outside that ethic for a couple of hours—to take a break from it, to seek changes in consciousness that momentarily reduce its sway. That this cuts against the grain of the dominant work ethic is likely an important reason why cannabis has been regarded as threatening and thus readily stigmatized and criminalized. But regardless of any moral or political assessment, our experienced users seemed to be employing the effects of cannabis periodically as what Foucault calls a *technology of the self*[15]—a tool with which they can achieve, as many said, "less stress" or "more balance" in their lives.

Many nonusers of cannabis decide to forgo some increment of fortune or fame in order to spend more time with their families or to fish, garden, or play golf. Some put aside ambition, pass up a promotion, or retire early for the same purposes. Such people calculate that what they might gain from remaining within the work ethic would not be worth the added effort, stress,

or reduction in leisure time. Cannabis users appear to be making a similar calculation, not unlike people who drink a martini, a beer, or some wine at the end of the workday to unwind, relax, and relieve stress, anxiety, and so on.[16] From this viewpoint, what has been called a chronic "amotivational syndrome" caused by cannabis use is more often a limited-duration, purposeful consequence of cannabis use which most respondents sought and valued as functional in their lives. And though we have focused on relaxation because it was the most common theme among respondents, we think that a variety of other constellations of effects, changes in the self, and advantages also can be understood in terms of the function they serve in users' lives.

Like any other drug, cannabis can have unwanted disadvantages as well as sought-after advantages. Our respondents reported a variety of negative effects, although only "cotton mouth" was experienced by a large number. The most often mentioned disadvantage is that cannabis tends to make one "inactive," which, as we suggested above, seems also to be bound up with the most important advantages and reasons for use. Though serious negative effects were very rare, most respondents in both cities had at some point experienced one or more negative effect.

We came to suspect, however, that the relative rarity of negative effects derived in some measure from users' skill in avoiding them. Because our samples consisted of experienced users, they might be expected to have reduced the incidence of negative effects by "listening" to sensory information during use (and also learning from what happened when they had not listened). Over time, their lived experience of the advantages and disadvantages, feeling states, changes in the self, and other effects of cannabis appear to have given them something like a set of sensory instruments by which to gauge whether the effects they want (and don't want) occur. In a sea of sensations, such instruments seem to serve as navigational tools with which to chart a course that maximizes advantages and desired effects while minimizing disadvantages and undesired effects (Cohen & Sas, 1998). The more experience one has with effects, the more developed such instruments tend to be. We think this is an important piece of the puzzle of how users in different drug policy contexts structure their use in quite similar ways.

Howard Becker and others have suggested that users develop "informal social controls" as part of a "user culture."[17] Following his lead, we asked our respondents detailed questions about when, where, and with whom they had used cannabis. Though there were minor variations across cities, overall we found a similarly patterned selectivity about the circumstances in which they used cannabis. In both cities, strong majorities said they had rules about their use—69% in Amsterdam and 73% in San Francisco—to which nearly all said they adhered "all" or "most of the time." Tellingly, the rule cited most often in both samples was "not during work (or study)," followed by the re-

lated rules "not during the day" and "not in the morning." This is consistent with our interpretation above that the relaxation or time-outs that users seek are time-limited, for these rules seem expressly designed to prevent cannabis use from interfering with social functioning. The same theme emerged in their responses to our question about the situations in which they most commonly used cannabis. They most frequently mentioned "with friends," "at parties," and "at home." When asked which situations they felt were *not* suitable for cannabis use, they most frequently mentioned "during work or study," followed by "with parents" and "in public spaces."

Other types of questions elicited more evidence of selectivity, discretion, and informal, regulatory rules. For example, when we asked if there were "people with whom you definitely would *not* use cannabis," 81% in Amsterdam and 90% in San Francisco said "yes." Parents, coworkers, and relatives topped the list, which suggests that users felt it was inappropriate to consume cannabis either around people they would not feel comfortable with or around people who might not feel comfortable with them while they used. Similarly, about one in five in each city reported that they had persuaded someone to *not* use cannabis, most often friends and family members. When we asked why they had done this, the most frequent reasons they gave were protective: The experience might have negative effects, or the person was "too young" or "not mentally mature enough." When we asked which emotional states were suitable for cannabis use, respondents in both cities most often mentioned positive states like "being relaxed," "feeling good," "happiness," and "cheerfulness, joy." Ironically, these are quite comparable to the effects of the plant. In both cities, 69% agreed that there were emotional states that were unsuitable for cannabis use; most often noted were "depression," "sadness," "upset," and feelings of "anxiety" or "paranoia" or "anger." When we asked an open-ended question on what advice they would give to a novice cannabis user, between 80% and 90% in each city had suggestions, the overwhelming majority of which had to do with the virtues of caution and moderation.

The strong similarities across drug policy contexts in terms of this selectivity, discretion, and rules suggest they were not shaped by drug law but were rather a kind of etiquette, or, in Becker's terms, part of a broader user culture. Our respondents' accounts of this were elicited by survey questions and are therefore somewhat fragmentary and partial. A full description of the systems of rules by which users organize and regulate their cannabis consumption would require ethnographic observations and depth interviews that were beyond the scope of our study. We can say, however, that their rules, etiquette, and culture helped limit use to appropriate circumstances, to keep it within the specific bounds of time and space that worked best in their everyday lives. In this sense, these elements of user culture seemed to be the

means by which the great majority of experienced users in both cities integrated cannabis use into their lives and kept it from disrupting them.

CONCLUSION

Anthropologists have always understood drug-taking rituals among exotic, faraway tribal peoples as part of their cultures. Yet when social scientists explore such rituals at home in their own modern industrial societies, they tend to avert their gaze from culture and to view drug-taking rituals through legal lenses, seeing deviance or crime as a result. But our data suggest that regardless of its legal status, cannabis use is in fact a *cultural practice* in modern societies. To be fully understood, it must be viewed as such.

Looked at this way, the informal social controls found in user culture hold potential significance for harm reduction and drug control in a broader sense. As Becker (1967) noted about the increase in LSD use and the decrease in frequency of "bad trips," learning what effects to expect from a drug and how to interpret and manage them are integral parts of user culture. As their culture develops, users enthusiastically teach each other how to reduce risks of harm and maximize the benefits they seek, so the incidence of unanticipated or unwanted effects declines. With legal or illegal drugs, most users are governed most of the time not so much by formal social controls like law as by the informal social controls that operate close up in their social worlds. Unlike their formal, statutory siblings, these informal social controls are widely adhered to by users precisely because they were invented by and for them, within their culture, rather than imposed upon them from outside it.[18]

Such social learning and the development of user culture are essential parts of a longer term process we will call the *cultural domestication of intoxicants*. In his masterly work of historical sociology, *The Civilizing Process*, Norbert Elias (1939/1978) showed how the most beastly behaviors of feudal warrior-knights and the quotidian crudities of the Middle Ages were slowly eliminated as the manners and internalized self-control found in royal courts diffused outward across Western societies (cf. van Ree, 2002).

We note the same sort of logic at work in the Netherlands, a center of European and world trade for 500 years, where all manner of intoxicants and other goodies flowed in and out of its busy ports. There is even a word in Dutch, *genotmiddelen*, which, roughly translated, means substances that give pleasure or enjoyment to the senses. It includes food delicacies and spices along with fermented cider, beer, wine, distilled spirits, coffee, opiates, tobacco, cannabis, and other drugs. In the space between capitalist material

abundance and Calvinist moral restraints,[19] this history has afforded the Dutch a rich lived experience of and a lexicon for talking about intoxicants in which controlled use is expected and normative. Such social learning about drugs and how to use them in ways that are functional seems to us part of the reason the Dutch have both liberal drug policies and low prevalence rates.

Cultural domestication of intoxicants can be a slow and fitful process. In 18th-century England, great masses of agrarian peasants were uprooted from the land, migrated into cities in search of work, and lived under the worst imaginable conditions. At this same historical moment, potent new forms of distilled spirits were introduced into what had been largely a beer culture. This lead to the difficult decades of what was called the "gin epidemic." But the destructive consequences unleashed by this conjuncture gradually abated as people learned more about these new forms of drink (Dillon, 2003; Warner, 2003). In the 19th century, the United States went through a similarly wrenching transformation from a small-town agrarian society to an urban industrial one. In this context, alcohol was scapegoated as the cause of virtually all social problems by a ferocious Temperance Crusade. But after the failure of Prohibition in the early 20th century, the "demon destroyer" of drink became gradually less menacing as drinking practices were normalized, and the consumption of alcoholic beverages settled into accepted cultural patterns (Levine, 1984).

The ingestion of chemicals for purposes of consciousness-alteration goes back at least to beer brewing in Samaria 10,000 years ago, probably longer. Notwithstanding slogans like "zero tolerance" and "drug-free America," there is no historical evidence to indicate that it can be stopped. There is, however, historical evidence of the cultural domestication of intoxicants. Our data suggest that the regulatory rules and other informal social controls invented within user culture are an important part of that process, and that they are likely to have greater power to reduce risk and harm than the formal social controls of government.

The research on which this chapter is based was supported by grants from the Dutch Ministry of Health and the U.S. National Institute of Drug Abuse (Grant #1 R01 DA10501-01A1). The views expressed herein do not necessarily reflect those of the funding agencies. The authors are grateful to Manja Abraham, Hendrien Kaal, and Arjan Sas for their assistance with tables and graphs. Portions of this chapter were previously published in the *American Journal of Public Health* (94/5, 2004), which has generously granted permission for their use here. Early versions of some of this material also were presented at the 97th Annual Meeting of the American Sociological Association, Chicago, 2002; the 15th Annual International Conference on the Reduction of Drug Related Harm, Sydney, 2004; the Second Perspectives on Cannabis

Conference, Liverpool, 2005; the International Conference on Drug Policy, Royal Institute of British Architects, London, 2005; and at the Center for Social Research on Alcohol and Drugs, University of Stockholm, 2005.

NOTES

1. We use the generic term "cannabis" because it includes hashish as well as marijuana, both of which are common in Europe, where nearly half our interviews took place.

2. The Dutch legal system has two tiers: legislation or formal law (*wet*) and national policy (*beleid*) on its enforcement. "The law merely indicates the bounds within which policy must operate" (Ruter, 1988, p. 154).

3. By 2004, the human and fiscal costs of prisons, swelled by the mandatory minimum sentences required by the harsh drug laws of the 1980s, had led nearly thirty states in the United States to consider additional changes in drug laws that would reduce severity of punishment for drug offenses.

4. See, e.g., Center on Addiction and Substance Abuse, 1995; Hall et al., 1994; Kandel, Yamaguchi, & Chen, et al.; National Institute on Drug Abuse [NIDA], 1995; ONDCP, 2002a; Swan, 1995.

5. For the San Francisco portion of the study, the Dutch questionnaire was translated into English and Spanish (bilingual interviewers used as needed). Non–English-speaking Asian Americans were excluded because of the prohibitive costs of training interviewers in the many Chinese and other Asian languages found in San Francisco and of translating their results. This was not consequential because national prevalence studies show that illicit drug use among Asian Americans is the lowest of any ethnic group (e.g., Substance Abuse and Mental Health Services Administration [SAMHSA], 1995), the non-English speakers being mostly elderly and thus least likely to be cannabis users. More details on sampling and methods may be found in Piazza and Cheng (1999); in the Dutch Final Report on the comparative study (Cohen & Kaal, 2001); on the website of the Centrum voor Drugsonderzoek at the Universiteit van Amsterdam: www.cedro-uva.org/lib/; and in Reinarman, Cohen, and Kaal (2004).

6. There is a divergence between San Francisco respondents, who report more intense highs in 3 of the 4 periods, and Amsterdam respondents, who report highs of longer duration in only one period. We found no reason to suspect that either sample played up or down their responses on any of the questions, so this divergence may indicate culturally specific consumption styles and/or cultural grammars of intoxication (see MacAndrew & Edgerton, 1969; Alasutari, 1992).

7. Cf. Hall, Solowij, & Lemon, 1994; NIDA, 1995; Swan, 1995.

8. See, for example, Kandel et al., 1992; Center on Addiction and Substance Abuse, 1995; NIDA, 1995; ONDCP, 2002a.

9. Our findings share the limitations of all self-report studies, including vague or selective memory, over- or understatements of fact, and so on. We

minimized these problems by means of careful question wording, extensive pretesting, and use of multiple measures. The questionnaire is available under "questionnaire" at http://www.cedro-uva.org/lib/cohen.canasd.html.

10. See Crusky, Berger, and Richardson, 1978; Johnston, Bachman, and O'Malley, 1981; Maloff, 1981; and Single, 1981.

11. This is consistent with findings from other societies, e.g., Kleiber and Soellner (1998, p. 168) found that relaxation ranked first as a reason for cannabis use among 1,458 German users; in a study of long-term and current users in Australia, Didcott, Reilly, Swift, and Hall (1997, p. 34) found relaxation and relief of stress "the most popular reasons" to use cannabis (61%); half of a Greek sample of 45 working-class, chronic cannabis users reported relaxation as the most common desired effect (Stefanis, Dornbush, & Fink, 1977, p. 40). Goode's study of 204 cannabis users in New York also found relaxation the most often mentioned reason for use (1970, p. 153).

12. See, e.g., Himmelstein, 1983; McGlothlin and West, 1968; Kolansky and Moore, 1971, 1972; Shalala, 1995; NIDA, n.d. An insightful critique of the procedures used to make empirically erroneous claims about the effects of cannabis may be found in Goode, 1974.

13. See Shedler and Block, 1990; Brill et al., 1971; Hochman & Brill, 1973; Miranne, 1979; Goode, 1971; Musty and Kaback, 1995; Kandel and Davies, 1990. For an excellent overview of the debate, see Zimmer & Morgan (1997).

14. The concept of "time-out" was developed by MacAndrew and Edgerton in their classic cross-cultural analysis of alcohol intoxication, *Drunken Comportment* (1969).

15. Foucault generally employed the term to mean a form of social control or "governmentality" which had been insinuated into or internalized by individuals. But his definition is broad enough to encompass our meaning, namely a tool for managing or regulating the self, moods, and consciousness: "technologies of the self . . . permit individuals to effect by their own means . . . a certain number of operations on their own bodies and souls, thoughts, conduct, and way of being, so as to transform themselves in order to attain a certain state of happiness, purity, wisdom, perfection, or immortality" (1994, p. 225).

16. This is different in degree although not in kind from the millions of people who are prescribed Valium or other tranquilizers for much the same purposes.

17. Becker, 1967. See also Alasutari, 1992; MacAndrew & Edgerton, 1969; Maloff, Becker, Fonaroff, and Rodin, 1982; Zinberg, 1984.

18. Becker, 1967; also Johnson, 1973; MacAndrew and Edgerton, 1969; Maloff et al., 1982; Zinberg, 1984.

19. This theme is developed in rich detail by Simon Schama (1988, p. vii) who opens his definitive book on Dutch culture with a quote from John Calvin: "Let those who have abundance remember that they are surrounded with thorns, and let them take great care not to be pricked by them."

REFERENCES

Alasutari, P. (1992). *Desire and craving: A cultural theory of alcoholism.* Albany: State University of New York Press.

Becker, H. S. (1963). *Outsiders: Studies in the sociology of deviance.* New York: Free Press.

Becker, H. S. (1967). History, culture, and subjective experience: An exploration of the social bases of drug-induced experiences. *Journal of Health and Social Behavior, 8,* 162–176.

Bewley-Taylor, D. (2001). *The United States and international drug control, 1909–1997.* London: Continuum.

Bieleman, B., & Goeree, P. (2000). *Coffeeshops geteld: Aantallen verkooppunten van cannabis in Nederland* [Coffee shops counted: Numbers of points of sale of cannabis in the Netherlands]. Groningen, Netherlands: Stichting Intraval.

Brill, N. Q., Crumpton, E., & Grayson, H. M. (1971). Personality factors in marihuana use. *Archives of General Psychiatry, 24,* 163–165.

Bruun, K., Pan, L., & Rexed, I. (1975). *The gentlemen's club: International control of drugs and alcohol.* Chicago: University of Chicago Press.

Center on Addiction and Substance Abuse. (1995). *Cigarettes, alcohol, and marijuana: Gateways to illicit drugs.* New York: Center on Addiction and Substance Abuse.

Cohen, P. (1997). The case of the two Dutch drug policy commissions: An exercise in harm reduction, 1968–1976. In P. G. Erickson, D. M. Riley, Y. W. Cheung, and P. A. G. O'Hare (Eds.), *Harm reduction: A new direction for drug policies and programs* (pp. 17–31). Toronto: University of Toronto Press. Available at http://www.cedro-uva.org/lib/cohen.case.html.

Cohen, P., & Sas, A. (1997). *Patterns of cannabis use in Amsterdam among experienced users.* Amsterdam: University of Amsterdam, Center for Drug Research. Available at http://www.cedro-uva.org/lib/cohen.canasd.html.

Cohen, P., & Kaal, H. (2001). *The irrelevance of drug policy: Patterns and careers of experienced cannabis use in the populations of Amsterdam, San Francisco, and Bremen.* Amsterdam: University of Amsterdam, Center for Drug Research. Available at http://www.cedro-uva.org/lib/cohen. 3cities.html.

Crusky, W. R., Berger, L. H., & Richardson, A. H. (1978). The effects of marijuana decriminalization on drug use patterns. *Contemporary Drug Problems, 7,* 491–532.

Didcott P., Reilly, D., Swift, W., & Hall, W. (1997). *Long term cannabis users in New South Wales North Coast* (Monograph #30). Sydney, Australia: National Drug and Alcohol Research Center.

Dillon, P. (2003). *Gin: The much-lamented death of Madam Geneva.* Boston: Justin Charles.

Elias, N. (1978). *The civilizing process: Sociogenic and psychogenic investigations* (E. Jephcott, Trans.). Oxford: Basil Blackwell. (Original work published 1939)

Engelsman, E. L. (1989). Dutch policy on the management of drug-related problems. *British Journal of Addiction 84,* 211–218.

Federal Bureau of Investigation. (2004). *Uniform crime report: Crime in the United States, 2003.* Washington, DC: U.S. Department of Justice.

Foucault, M. (1994). Technologies of the self. In P. Rabinow (Ed.), *Essential works of Foucault, 1954–1984: Vol. 4. Ethics: Subjectivity and truth* (pp. 223–251). New York: New Press.

Goode, E. (Ed.). (1969a). *Marijuana.* Chicago: Atherton Press.

Goode, E. (1969b). Marijuana and the politics of reality. *Journal of Health and Social Behavior 10,* 83–94.

Goode, E. (1970). *The marijuana smokers.* New York: Basic Books.

Goode, E. (1971). Drug use and grades in college." *Nature, 234,* 225–227.

Goode, E. (1974). The criminogenics of marijuana." *Addictive Diseases, 1,* 297–322.

Hall, W., Solowij, N., & Lemon, J. (1994). *The health and psychological consequences of cannabis use.* Canberra: Australian Government Publishing Service.

Himmelstein, J. L. (1983). *The strange career of marihuana: Politics and ideology of drug control in America.* Westport, CT: Greenwood Press.

Hochman, J. S., & Brill, N. Q. (1973). Chronic marihuana use and psychosocial adaptation. *American Journal of Psychiatry, 130,* 132–140.

Johnson, B. D. (1973). *Marihuana users and drug subcultures.* New York: Wiley.

Johnston, L. D., Bachman, J. G., & O'Malley, P. M. (1981). Marijuana decriminalization: The impact on youth, 1975–1980 (Monitoring the Future, Occasional Paper 13). Ann Arbor: University of Michigan, Institute for Social Research.

Kandel, D. B., & Davies, M. (1990). Labor force experiences of a national sample of young adult men. *Youth and Society 21,* 411–445.

Kandel, D. B., Yamaguchi, K., & Chen, K. (1992). Stages of progression in drug involvement from adolescence to adulthood: Further evidence for the gateway theory. *Journal of Studies on Alcohol, 53,* 447–457.

Kleiber, D., & Soellner, R. (1998). *Cannabiskonsum: Entwicklungstendenzen, Konsummer und Risiken.* Weinheim, Germany: Juventua Verlag.

Kolansky, H., & Moore, W. T. (1971). Effects of marihuana on adolescents and young adults. *Journal of the American Medical Association, 216,* 486–492.

Kolansky, H., & Moore, W. T. (1972). Toxic effects of chronic marihuana use. *Journal of the American Medical Association, 222,* 35–41.

Leuw, E., & Marshall, I. H. (Eds.). (1994). *Between prohibition and legalization: The Dutch experiment in drug policy.* Amsterdam, Netherlands: Kugler.

Levine, H. G. (1984). The alcohol problem in America: From temperance to alcoholism. *British Journal of Addiction, 79,* 109–119.

MacAndrew, C., & Edgerton, R. (1969). *Drunken comportment: A social explanation.* Chicago: Aldine.

MacCoun, R. J., & Reuter, P. (1997). Interpreting Dutch cannabis policy: Reasoning by analogy in the legalization debate. *Science 278,* 47–52.

Maloff, D. (1981). A review of the effects of the decriminalization of marijuana. *Contemporary Drug Problems, 10,* 307–322.

Maloff, D., Becker, H. S., Fonaroff, A., & Rodin, J. (1982). Informal social controls and their influence on substance use. In N. E. Zinberg & W. M. Harding (Eds.), *Control over intoxicant use: Pharmacological, psychological, and social considerations* (pp. 53–76). New York: Human Sciences Press.

McGlothlin, H. W., & West, L. J. (1968). The marihuana problem. *American Journal of Psychiatry, 125,* 1126–1134.

Miranne, A. C. (1979). Marijuana use and achievement orientations of college students. *Journal of Health and Social Behavior, 20,* 194–199.

Morningstar, P., & Chitwood, D. (1983). *The patterns of cocaine use.* Rockville, MD: National Institute on Drug Abuse.

Murphy, D. E. (2002, September 6). California: Medicinal marijuana raid. *New York Times,* p. A20.

Musto D. (1973). *The American disease: Origins of narcotics control.* New Haven, CT: Yale University Press.

Musty, R. E., & Kaback, L. (1995). Relationships between motivation and depression in chronic cannabis users. *Life Sciences 56,* 2151–2158.

Nadelmann, E. A. (1989). Drug prohibition in the U.S.: Costs, consequences, and alternatives. *Science, 245,* 939–947.

National Institute on Drug Abuse. (N.d.). *The facts about marijuana.* Rockville, MD: U.S. Dept. of Health and Human Services.

National Institute on Drug Abuse. (1995). *Marijuana: What parents need to know.* Rockville, MD: National Institute on Drug Abuse.

Office of National Drug Control Policy. (2002a). *Drug facts: Marijuana.* Available at www.whitehousedrugpolicy.gov

Office of National Drug Control Policy. (2002b, October 7). My child is not an honor student [advertisement]. *New York Times,* A5.

Office of National Drug Control Policy. (20002c, September 18). An open letter to parents about marijuana [advertisement]. *The New York Times,* A23.

Piazza, T., & Cheng, Y. (1999). *Sampling methods and field results of the San Francisco Drug Use Study* (Technical Report #44). Berkeley, University of California, Survey Research Center.

Reinarman, C. (1998, July 30). Morele Ideologie US Haaks op Drugsbeleid Nederlands. *Het Parool.*

Reinarman, C. (2000). The Dutch example shows that liberal drug laws can be beneficial. In S. Barbour (Ed.), *Drug legalization: Current controversies* (pp. 102–108). San Diego, CA: Greenhaven Press.

Reinarman, C., Cohen, P., & Kaal, H. (2004). The limited relevance of drug policy: Cannabis in Amsterdam and San Francisco. *American Journal of Public Health, 94,* 836–842.

Ruter, F. (1988). Drugs and the criminal law in the Netherlands. In J. van Dijk (Ed.), *Criminal law in action: An overview of current issues in Western societies* (pp. 147–165). Arnhem, Netherlands: Gouda Quint.

Sandwijk, P. J., Cohen, P., Musterd, S., & Langemeijer, M. (1995). *Licit and illicit drug use in Amsterdam II.* University of Amsterdam, Center for Drug Research. Available at http://www.cedro-uva.org/lib/sandwijk.prvasd94.html.

Schama, S. (1988). *The embarrassment of riches: An interpretation of Dutch culture in the golden age.* Berkeley: University of California Press.

Scheerer, S. (1978). The new Dutch and German drug laws: Social and political conditions for criminalization and decriminalization. *Law and Society Review, 12,* 585–606.

Schultes, R. E. (1978). Plants and plant constituents as mind-altering agents throughout history. In L. L. Iversen, S. D. Iversen, & S. H. Snyder (Eds.), *Handbook of psychopharmacology: Vol. 11. Stimulants* (pp. 219–241). New York: Plenum Press.

Shalala, D. (1995, August 18). Say "no" to legalization of cannabis. *Wall Street Journal,* p. A10.

Shedler, J., & Block, J. (1990). Adolescent drug use and psychosocial health. *American Psychologist, 45,* 612–630.

Single, E. W. (1981). The impact of marijuana decriminalization. *Research Advances in Alcohol and Drug Problems, 6,* 405–424.

Stefanis, C., Dornbush, R., & Fink, M. (1977). *Hashish: Studies of long term use.* New York: Raven Press.

Substance Abuse and Mental Health Services Administration. (1995). *Preliminary estimates from the 1994 National Household Survey on Drug Abuse* (Advance Report #10, pp. 77–79). Rockville, MD: U.S. Department of Health and Human Services, Substance Abuse and Mental Health Services Administration, Office of Applied Studies.

Swan, N. (1995). Marijuana antagonist reveals evidence of THC dependence in rats. *NIDA Notes, 10,* 1–2.

van Ree, E. (2002). Drugs, the democratic civilising process, and the consumer society. *International Journal of Drug Policy, 13,* 349–353.

Warner, J. (2003). *Craze: Gin and debauchery in an age of reason.* New York: Random House.

Zimmer, L., & Morgan, J. P. (1997). *Marijuana myths, marijuana facts.* New York: Lindesmith Center/Drug Policy Alliance.

Zinberg, N. H. (1984). *Drug, set, and setting: The basis for controlled intoxicant use.* New Haven, CT: Yale University Press.

SECTION III

Depictions of Addictions

The distance between our thoughts about reality and reality itself can grow quite vast. Policies about marijuana reflect our perceptions about the plant, its potential for harm and good, and the costs and benefits of different attempts to control it. The accuracy of these perceptions is almost always debatable. Subtle and not-so-subtle biases can creep into the reporting of facts from the marijuana literature. Some stem from simple choices of words; others arise from flagrant disregard of some data in favor of others.

The contentiousness of the marijuana debates has contributed to the way prohibitionists and reformers frame their arguments and present their data. One of the most accessible and persuasive sources of information is the media. Bruce Mirken reviews some salient examples of the way reporting can go awry. He questions the idea that alarming events are more newsworthy and therefore more likely to generate more consumers of media. In a sense, he argues that the lay public is more intelligent than many media sources think. Most readers are willing to appreciate nuanced arguments filled with complications and caveats, so there's no need to simplify any difficult literature. These oversimplifications have the potential to backfire if they contradict people's personal experience.

Roger Roffman and Anne Nicoll continue the theme. They emphasize that complete information on the potentially negative consequences of marijuana use is essential. They encourage anti-prohibitionists to take up this cause in an effort to increase their credibility. They argue that recreational users of marijuana show considerable interest in learning about the

drug's safety. These recreational users might be particularly open to opponents of prohibition when learning new ways to make their use safer.

The question of addictiveness of marijuana has resulted in loud arguments about the plant's potential to lead users to consume when they would rather not. Laboratory work with animals has required some highly artificial circumstances to generate marijuana dependence, but work with humans has established an identifiable withdrawal syndrome. In an attempt to assess professional opinions on the topic, Robert Gore and Mitch Earleywine survey hundreds of mental health professionals. These experts rate marijuana's addictiveness as comparable with caffeine's. More importantly, their ratings parallel their own experiences and backgrounds in ways that should make us all wonder about how individual lenses can cloud perceptions.

7   Marijuana and the Media: Science, Propaganda, and Sloppy Reporting in the U.S. News Media

Bruce Mirken

Science moves forward in fits and starts, sometimes in sudden leaps but more often in small, incremental accumulations of knowledge. These incremental advances typically leave unanswered questions and gray areas. Scientific articles tend to state their conclusions with numerous caveats, acknowledgments of uncertainty, and extended descriptions of possible sources of error because experienced researchers have a profound understanding of how little they really know.

The mass media live in a different universe altogether. The media world is one of dramatic developments, punchy headlines, and seven-second sound bites. Though subtlety and nuance are not unknown, they are not the norm—particularly in radio and television, but increasingly in print media as well. The old line "If it bleeds, it leads" carries a strong element of truth: If something is exciting and dramatic, it's news; if it isn't, it may well be ignored. Reporters and editors instinctively look for clear, involving story lines that can be summed up in just a few words. Such an approach almost inevitably does violence to the subtleties and uncertainties of science.

The problem is exacerbated by the ever-present constraints of time, space, and money. Even when journalists would like to do a thorough job of reporting a story, they too often lack the time or resources to do so. The need to get the story done quickly and cheaply only heightens the tendency toward oversimplification.

The problem is further aggravated by the usual approach to reporting taken by media outlets seeking to be "objective"—that is, most of the U.S.

mainstream news media. The standard template in U.S. news reporting is for the journalist not to inject his or her judgments or opinions into the story, but simply to quote the assertions made by the opposing sides. For example, rather than reporting, "Senator So-and-So announced today that the moon is made of green cheese, a statement that was clearly false," it is conventional practice for journalists to write, "Senator So-and-So announced today that the moon is made of green cheese, but his statement was immediately questioned by astronomers." This serves the purpose of taking the reporter's views out of the story, and often also saves time: It is generally simpler and faster to call the astronomy department at the nearest university for a quote than to pour through books on lunar geology in an attempt to verify or disprove the senator's statement. Unfortunately, such an approach can also create the impression that the two statements are of equal validity, which may or may not be the case.

These tendencies toward oversimplification and "he said/she said" reporting are problems for the reporting of scientific issues generally, but they become particularly apparent when the press is covering a scientific question that is also a subject of public and political controversy—whether that controversy involves global warming, partial-birth abortion, or drug policy. All sides in any such controversy know the habits of the news media and try their best to tailor their announcements and arguments to fit sound-bite-and-sensation-driven media practices. Supporters of prohibition are aided in this by the fact that arguments for drug prohibition are easily stated in simple terms: "Drugs like marijuana are dangerous! We must ban them to stop them from harming society and keep them out of the hands of children!" The arguments against prohibition—acknowledging that marijuana can cause harm but questioning whether arrests and jail cells are the most effective way to minimize that harm—are inherently more subtle and difficult to render in flashy headlines and short sound bites.

Faced with this predicament, the media, not meaning to misreport a significant issue but simply following their usual habits, may inadvertently become propagandists for one side or the other. In marijuana policy, it is the pro-prohibition side—backed by massive government budgets and armies of tax-funded officials, researchers, and PR people who vastly outnumber the human and dollar resources of those who question prohibition—that is most often able to frame the terms of the debate. Sometimes they do this so skillfully that the press doesn't even appear to know it is happening.

I experienced this phenomenon firsthand in early 2002, about three months after taking the position of communications director at the Marijuana Policy Project (MPP), a Washington, D.C.–based organization that opposes marijuana prohibition and seeks to bring marijuana into a regulated system much like alcohol. One night, flipping aimlessly from channel to

channel, I happened upon WBAL, the NBC affiliate in Baltimore, just as a promotional blurb for the 11 p.m. newscast came on.

"They used to call it the mellow drug," an announcer dramatically intoned. "But now—*marijuana turns violent!* An I-Team investigation, tonight at 11!" A similar teaser was repeated a little while later, as the newscast began.

I was concerned. I'd been boning up on the literature and was pretty sure the evidence showed that marijuana does not normally induce violent behavior in users, with the possible exception of a few individuals with preexisting mental disturbances. What, I wondered, was going on?

What was occurring, it turned out, was that Baltimore was experiencing a series of bloody turf battles between drug-dealing gangs. The people shooting at each other weren't using marijuana, at least as far as the story indicated, but were fighting over who controlled the marketing rights in particular sections of town. The violence being reported—certainly a legitimate news story, involving injuries and deaths in a crowded urban area—had nothing to do with the effects of marijuana and everything to do with the fact that the marijuana trade is illicit and thus unregulated. A more accurate teaser might have been, "But now—*prohibition turns violent!*"

What this TV station did was to mistake the effects of prohibition for the effects of marijuana. This is a common error, in part because it is actively encouraged by government agencies such as the White House Office of National Drug Control Policy (ONDCP). Statements from prohibition-supporting agencies and officials regularly blame drugs such as marijuana for the damaging effects of prohibition, and such statements are often reported uncritically.

For example, an April 18, 2003, ONDCP press release was headlined, "White House Drug Policy Office to Air Earth Day Ad Outlining the Negative Impact of the Drug Trade on the Environment." The statement sounded the alarm over "thousands of acres ruined on U.S. public lands due to marijuana cultivation" and quoted ONDCP Director John Walters as saying, "The billions of dollars worth of illegal drugs produced here and abroad are taking a horrific toll on some of the most fragile and diverse ecosystems on the planet." The release went on to explain, "In the United States, the illegal growth and cultivation of marijuana has destroyed and contaminated thousands of acres of public lands." It described in detail the environmental damage done by clandestine marijuana farms hidden in remote corners of national forests, parks, and wilderness areas (ONDCP, 2003).

U.S. Rep. Mark Souder (R-IN), a leading congressional advocate of tough-on-drugs policies, continued this theme with a subcommittee hearing held on October 10, 2003, in Sequoia National Park. Souder opened the hearing with a statement in which he decried how "marijuana cultivation has particularly ravaged public lands here in California." He noted with alarm

that "workers are often armed . . . and have engaged in shootouts with law enforcement (Souder, 2003).

Unmentioned in any of these statements was the fact that such clandestine marijuana farms—hidden in public lands and often protected by armed guards or booby traps—are an artifact of prohibition. Why, after all, does one never hear of clandestine vineyards hidden in parks and wilderness areas, surrounded by booby traps and thugs toting AK-47s? Because grapes are grown and turned into wine by legal, regulated farmers and vintners. The only reason that marijuana cannot be grown and processed in a similarly safe, regulated manner is that the law bars legitimate businesses from doing so.

Indeed, federal government statistics and independent research suggest that government "marijuana eradication" efforts not only completely fail to eliminate marijuana production, but in fact tend to drive marijuana growers toward more remote (and thus more ecologically sensitive) areas. The Department of Justice (2004) reported in April 2004 that, despite decades of "eradication" programs, "Marijuana is widely available throughout the United States, and this availability is relatively stable overall." Citing numerous examples of marijuana and opium growers outwitting law enforcement by moving to harder-to-find locations, a recent Florida State University analysis concluded, "A long history of drug enforcement efforts suggest that elimination of supplies coming from one area will soon lead to increased cultivation elsewhere" (Rasmussen & Benson, 2003, p. 699).

But such considerations are almost never acknowledged in media coverage of the issue, which often reports "eradication" efforts without stopping to consider the role of prohibition in creating the problem in the first place. For example, a lengthy story in the August 4, 2003, issue of *Time* followed a law enforcement team as it raided a clandestine marijuana farm in California's Tahoe National Forest, quoting one Forest Service investigator as saying: "We're good at jungle warfare. We're the ninjas of the woods" (Roosevelt, 2003). The story carefully catalogued the number of marijuana farms that police agencies claim to have destroyed in California and their reported value, lacing the account with alarming tales of Mexican drug cartels and growers toting automatic rifles. The piece failed to even consider that such farms might be a consequence of prohibition and did not quote a single source critical of current policies. Indeed, the *only* sources cited or quoted in the story were representatives of law enforcement agencies.

Stories about Souder's hearing in the *Modesto Bee* and *Fresno Bee* followed a similar pattern, failing to even acknowledge the existence of another side to the story.

Such a failure to include voices critical of the "war on drugs" appears to be the rule, not the exception. In 2003, MPP contracted with an independent media research firm, CARMA International, to analyze coverage of marijuana issues in the major U.S. news media, both print and broadcast. In

quarterly reports covering the period from October 2003 through September 2004, CARMA tallied the number of stories citing or quoting various organizations involved in drug policy, and the results are startlingly consistent. For the full year and in each individual quarter, the organizations that appeared most often in news coverage were the Drug Enforcement Administration and ONDCP. For the full year, the Drug Enforcement Administration appeared in 287 stories, and the ONDCP was cited in 168.

None of the pro-reform groups examined—MPP, the American Civil Liberties Union, the National Organization for the Reform of Marijuana Laws, and the Drug Policy Alliance—even came close. The American Civil Liberties Union appeared 99 times, and none of the other reform organizations appeared more than 75 times. In the latest quarter examined as of this writing, July-September 2004, the Drug Enforcement Administration appeared in 84 stories. The four drug reform groups *combined* appeared in a total of 51 (CARMA International, 2003; 2004). Clearly, in a great many news stories, the statements of professional drug warriors are going unanswered.

The result of this neglect to mention reformers is that dubious, and at times outright false, assertions made by prohibitionists go unrefuted, and the reader or viewer is left with no hint that such claims are even in dispute. For example, on October 9, 2003, the Reuters news service reported on a talk given by Drug Czar John Walters at the Center for Strategic International Studies, a Washington think tank. Walters, sounding a theme that recurs frequently in his public statements, condemned Canada for alleged lax enforcement of its marijuana laws, saying: "It's their domestic policy in a sovereign country, it's their business. Shipping poison to the United States is our business" ("Canada headed," 2003). The story cited no contrasting data or voices whatsoever, leaving uncontested the notion that marijuana is "poison."

Walters is fond of referring to marijuana as "poison," and such statements routinely appear in news stories unchallenged. A quick search turned up similar references to marijuana as poison in a widely reprinted May 2003 story by reporter Colin Nickerson (appearing in the *Boston Globe* and *San Jose Mercury News*, among other papers), as well as in several 2003 stories in the *Toronto Star*. Although the *Star* quoted Canadian government officials who defended their policies, none of these stories contained any information disputing the notion that marijuana is a "poison," or any suggestion that such an assertion might be open to question.

But marijuana is indisputably not a poison, defined as "a substance that through its chemical action usually kills, injures or impairs an organism" (Merriam-Webster, 2004). As one recent expert review noted, "The acute toxicity of cannabinoids is very low. There are no confirmed published cases worldwide of human deaths from cannabis poisoning, and the dose of THC required to produce a 50% mortality in rodents is extremely high compared with other commonly used drugs" (Hall & Solowij, 1998). Large cohort

studies have found no increase in mortality associated with marijuana use (Andreasson & Allebeck, 1990; Sidney, Beck, Tekawa, Quesenberry, & Friedman, 1997). This result contrasts with readily available data and anecdotal information documenting both acute and long-term toxicity of common legal drugs such as tobacco, alcohol, and many over-the-counter pain and cold remedies (including acetaminophen, the active ingredient in Tylenol). Nevertheless, readers and viewers of mass media news reports may be left with the impression that marijuana's status as a poison is not in any doubt.

Why do news media personnel—who regularly speak of their work using terms such as "balance" and "fairness"—leave patently false statements unchallenged? Why do they so often leave one side of the issue completely out of the discussion and fail to provide appropriate context for statements that are misleading or worse? Some of the problem surely stems from a lack of resources and deadline pressures. But there is good reason to suspect that other factors may be at work, and clues to these factors can be found in how marijuana and drug policy issues are typically framed in media reports.

Though there are exceptions, the media typically characterize the two sides of the marijuana policy debate in terms that echo the rhetoric of officials, which tends to marginalize or mischaracterize the positions of those who oppose prohibition. And the rhetoric chosen by these officials is no accident. Knowing that most Americans believe illicit drug use to be dangerous and harmful, they prefer to characterize their side in drug policy debates as "antidrug," while referring to those opposed to prohibition as "pro-drug," or some variation on that theme. Such references turn up routinely in the statements of drug warriors. For example, a 2002 ONDCP press release slammed campaigns for drug policy reform ballot initiatives as "pro-drug propaganda" (ONDCP, 2002). Souder opened an April 2004 House subcommittee hearing in a similar vein, railing against "a large and well-funded pro-drug movement" that, in his view, has misled voters into passing laws allowing medical use of marijuana (House of Representatives, 2004). Such characterizations seek to turn a debate about the best way to minimize the harms associated with drug use into a cartoon battle between pro-drug and antidrug forces.

These statements constitute a standard propaganda technique—advocates often seek to paint their opponents in the least flattering terms possible—but are also misleading. Just as opposing laws banning abortion does not mean one wants to encourage women to have more abortions, opposing marijuana prohibition does not mean one encourages or even approves of marijuana use. Though a few who seek to reform marijuana laws do celebrate and promote marijuana use, they are not the leading voices within the movement. Mainstream drug policy reform groups like MPP and Drug Policy Alliance state clearly that they do not encourage or promote marijuana use, but simply believe that prohibition causes more harm than

marijuana itself and seek approaches that recognize this reality. MPP's mission statement explains that the organization seeks to "minimize the harm associated with marijuana," whether that harm comes from drug itself or from laws criminalizing its use (Marijuana Policy Project, 2004). The Drug Policy Alliance's mission statement states that the organization seeks "to advance those policies and attitudes that best reduce the harms of both drug misuse and drug prohibition" (Drug Policy Alliance, 2004).

Nevertheless, mainstream news reports commonly ignore such statements, characterizing reformers in language nearly identical to that used by the opponents of reform. For example, a November 2002 *Time* cover story on efforts by MPP and others to change marijuana laws repeatedly referred to these groups and individuals as "pro-pot forces." Though the story did quote reformers explaining their views, it also referred to the movement to legalize medical use of marijuana as a "ruse" intended to further a broader legalization agenda, repeating an argument made by the drug warriors as if it was an undisputed fact (Stein, 2002).

Such characterizations occur relatively frequently in the U.S. news media, even when the context clearly indicates that such a characterization is inaccurate. A September 2003 *Boston Herald* story about a controversy over a marijuana reform billboard is illustrative. The billboard in question urged Massachusetts residents to "legalize and tax marijuana" to save tax money and thus preserve local government services. Although the sign made no statement at all about whether marijuana use is good or bad, the *Herald*'s headline called it a "pro-pot sign," and the body of the story characterized the billboard as "pot-promoting" (Rothstein, 2003).

Indeed, reformers can't even seem to get onto newspaper opinion pages without being erroneously tagged as "pro-drug." A column on a related billboard controversy, written by Bill Piper, the director of national affairs for the Drug Policy Alliance (2004, April 29), was headlined, "Move to penalize pro-drug views amounts to censorship," by the *Atlanta Journal-Constitution* despite the fact that no "pro-drug views" were expressed in either the billboards in question or the column. The author was left quietly furious at the mislabeling of his work (Piper, 2004, November 29).

Whether intentional or not, such references—repeated frequently in the American media—reinforce the impression that the two sides in the debate are antidrug and pro-drug or "anti-marijuana" and "pro-marijuana." The central core of reformers' view—that marijuana can indeed cause harm, but that those harms could be better mitigated by a policy of legal regulation similar to that used for alcoholic beverages—is either marginalized or ignored altogether.

This is not to say that reformers' views never get favorable play in the media. Sometimes journalists' habits work to the advantage of those seeking to change marijuana laws, particularly regarding medical use.

In particular, journalists love personality-based stories, and stories of medical marijuana patients—who often tell heartbreaking tales of illness and suffering, compounded by fears of arrest and imprisonment—are tailor-made for a personality-driven media culture. Those patients brave enough to come forward and the advocates who work with them have made use of this predilection, producing some of the most favorable coverage obtained by critics of the war on drugs.

For example, television talk show host Montel Williams, who uses marijuana to treat the pain caused by multiple sclerosis, has become an outspoken advocate for the cause. The combination of Williams's articulate, passionate delivery and his straight-arrow persona often seem to short-circuit interviewers' critical faculties. When MSNBC's Joe Scarborough—a hard-nosed Republican ex-congressman not generally shy about being tough on guests—interviewed Williams at length on June 15, 2005, he never asked a single difficult question. Williams blasted the federal ban on medical use of marijuana as "the most ridiculous thing on the planet," while his conservative host managed nothing rougher than, "Our thoughts and prayers are with you" (MSNBC, 2005).

Medical marijuana patients who aren't famous also tend to get gentle treatment. Angel Raich, whose challenge to federal prosecution of medical marijuana patients resulted in a June 2005 U.S. Supreme Court ruling permitting federal prosecutions to continue, received generally mild treatment from the press. Though other coverage of the case included rough-and-tumble debates, Raich and fellow plaintiff Diane Monson consistently seemed to receive the benefit of the doubt—for example, in a November 2004 *Los Angeles Times Magazine* profile in which the obligatory quotes from federal drug warriors were swamped by Raich's emotional story (Mithers, 2004).

Such personality-based feature stories contrast sharply with the day-to-day run of news, which tends to be dominated by the actions and statements of official sources. Often, it appears that journalists fail to consider the political dimension inherent in the statements of government officials, including researchers who work for government agencies. This failure is puzzling, as the national press corps gives every appearance of understanding this same principle in other contexts. By and large the media simply take it as a given that, for example, Justice Department statements about antiterrorism efforts will attempt to put the administration's policies in the best possible light, just as no one expects the Environmental Protection Agency to be a source of neutral, unbiased information regarding government antipollution efforts. It is standard operating procedure in reporting such stories to treat government statements as having such a political aspect and to include an opposing perspective for the sake of balance. But despite the fact that the U.S. government has a decades-long history of implementing, encouraging, and touting the benefits of prohibitionist drug policies, releases of data from

government antidrug agencies are rarely treated as statements from one side in a contested policy debate.

A wave of 2004 stories reporting the alleged dangers of "stronger pot" illustrates this phenomenon. In early May, newspapers and news broadcasts around the country carried alarming stories about a study of marijuana just published in the *Journal of the American Medical Association* (*JAMA;* Compton, Colliver, Glantz, & Stinson, 2004). "Stronger marijuana makes more addicted," proclaimed the *Los Angeles Daily News.* "Abuse and dependence rise as pot becomes more potent," headlined the *Seattle Post-Intelligencer.* "Stronger pot propels addiction rate higher," the *Atlanta Journal-Constitution* chimed in. Rising marijuana potency, the stories claimed, was getting more Americans hooked.

The government-funded study on which the stories were based was conducted by scientists from the National Institute on Drug Abuse and the National Institute on Alcohol Abuse and Alcoholism. It compared survey data from 1991–92 to 2001–02, indicating an increase in marijuana "abuse" or "dependence," as defined by the DSM-IV, the American Psychiatric Association's (1994) official diagnostic manual for mental disorders. The study's authors hypothesized that the most likely cause for this increase is "increased marijuana potency" (Compton et al., 2004, p. 2117).

Such an explanation jibes perfectly with official government rhetoric, which has emphasized the dangers of increased THC levels for years. In a 2002 *Washington Post* column, for example, ONDCP Director Walters wrote: "But marijuana is far from 'harmless'—it is pernicious. Parents are often unaware that today's marijuana is different than that of a generation ago, with potency levels 10 to 20 times stronger than the marijuana with which they were familiar" (Walters, 2002). Walters's statistics were dubious, but his point is an effective one that government officials have hammered home again and again in recent years: Parents should forget anything they remember from the marijuana they may have smoked in the 1960s or '70s, because the stuff kids are smoking now is far stronger, more dangerous and more addictive.

The fact that a study by government researchers tracks closely with government policies and rhetoric is not by itself sufficient cause to disbelieve the research, but it ought to lead responsible journalists to at least ask a few probing questions. And the *JAMA* study raised a number of red flags that should have caused reporters to doubt the conclusion that higher potency marijuana was leading to a surge in addiction. For one thing, despite listing increased potency as the most likely reason for the increase in abuse and dependence, the study cites no evidence that higher potency marijuana increases the likelihood of such outcomes, and for a good reason: No such evidence has been published (Earleywine, 2004). The hypothesis that "potent pot" is leading to more addiction is speculation.

Second, as the Compton article notes, under DSM-IV criteria, people can be classified as marijuana "abusers" if they experience recurrent "legal problems related to marijuana use." The FBI Uniform Crime Reports, which annually tabulate reported arrests in the United States, show that marijuana arrests skyrocketed from fewer than 300,000 in 1991 to more than 700,000 in 2001 (Federal Bureau of Investigation, 2002). Since most of the increase reported by Compton was in the category of abuse, not dependence (which has different criteria), it is striking that the article failed to identify which abuse/dependence criteria actually increased, and by how much. The reader is thus left with no way to know whether the supposed effects of "potent pot" might be simply the results of shifting law enforcement priorities.

All three wire stories that constituted most of the newspaper coverage, from the Associated Press, Cox, and Scripps Howard news services, failed to note any such reasons for doubt and failed to make clear that there was no actual evidence to back up the conclusion that higher potency marijuana must be to blame. Indeed, the Cox story, published in the *Journal-Constitution* and *Daily News*, completely tossed aside the qualifiers and disclaimers that appeared in *JAMA* and presented readers with what appeared to be a definitive conclusion: "Marijuana abuse and addiction have increased over the past decade, even though the percentage of people using pot has remained roughly the same, a new study says. The reason: It's not your parents' marijuana" (Wahlberg, 2004). Though the other stories were somewhat less absolute in their language, they all had one thing in common: None quoted even a single source who was not on the payroll of the U.S. government (Bowman, 2004; Tanner, 2004; Wahlberg, 2004).

The sort of critical voices that no one bothered to consult in reporting this story are important not for some abstract sense of "balance," but because those with different points of view might call attention to flaws that others fail to see—or choose to ignore. In this case, an obvious hole in Compton et al.'s (2004) logic (which arguably should have been caught by *JAMA*'s reviewers) went unnoticed: The increased "abuse" occurred almost entirely among young blacks and Hispanics, with no similar increase among whites in the same age group. This result fails to jibe with the "potent pot" hypothesis, since young blacks and Hispanics have no special access to high-THC marijuana (and arguably have less access, given the high cost of high-potency cannabis), and there is no evidence that THC affects black and Hispanic brains differently than those of whites. However, people of color are well documented to be at disproportionate risk for arrest for drug crimes. For example, although African Americans constitute only about one tenth of the U.S. population, blacks represented nearly one third of all people arrested on drug charges in 2003 (Federal Bureau of Investigation, 2003).

None of the major news services reporting this story interviewed anyone who might have had the knowledge and inclination to point out such discrepancies.

Including the opposing points of view on a controversial issue is essential, but it is not, in and of itself, sufficient to assure that reports will be fair and accurate. Indeed, as illustrated by a later permutation of the "potent pot" story, a token inclusion of opposing voices can actually serve to marginalize them and make the official viewpoint appear stronger than it is.

The widely circulated July 19, 2004, Reuters story, "Stronger Pot Raising Concerns in U.S.," by Washington, DC–based reporter Maggie Fox, painted a frightening view of increased marijuana potency. "Alarmed by reports that marijuana is becoming more potent than ever and that children are trying it at younger and younger ages, U.S. officials are changing their drug policies," the story's lead declared. The next sentence contained an even more unnerving and definitive declaration: "Pot is no longer the gentle weed of the 1960s and may pose a greater threat than cocaine or even heroin because so many more people use it" (Fox, 2004).

The piece then presents a series of alarming statistics, all of which came directly from either government sources or from government-funded or closely allied groups such as the national Center on Addiction and Substance Abuse (CASA). It notes that THC levels in marijuana have reportedly doubled from 1988 to 2003, to more than 7 percent. It further cites a 142 percent rise in the number of children and teens in treatment for marijuana dependence or abuse since 1992, noting with alarm that "children and teens are three times more likely to be in treatment for marijuana abuse than for alcohol, and six times likelier to be in treatment for marijuana than for all other illegal drugs combined." Walters is quoted at length about how marijuana is no longer "a soft drug," and Nora Volkow, the director of the National Institute on Drug Abuse, speculates in great detail about possible (though unproven) effects of high-THC marijuana on young brains and potential similarities between cannabinoids and opiates.

Unlike the reports of the *JAMA* article (Compton et al., 2004), this story did contain a brief quote from someone with a contrasting view. Here it is in its entirety:

Proponents of legalizing marijuana disagree with the official line. Krissy Oechslin of the Marijuana Policy Project disputes the finding that cannabis products are stronger.

"They make it sound like the THC levels in marijuana were almost nonexistent, but no one would have smoked it then if that was true," she said.

"And there's evidence that the stronger the THC, the less of it a person smokes. I don't want to say it's good for you, but I'll say [more potent marijuana] is less bad for you."

That's everything in the story that in any way casts doubt on the government line that high-potency marijuana is a serious public health menace—86 words out of an 813-word story. Let us now examine the relevant context that Fox failed to include and how the writer framed this bit of opposition.

Consider the opening sentence. The fact that government officials are "alarmed" by increased marijuana potency and have thus reconsidered their policies is presented as undisputed fact. But other writers have suggested a different possibility: that officials are cynically using exaggerated tales of increased potency to alarm parents and maintain support for prohibition. In one such analysis, investigative reporter Dan Forbes charted Walters's wildly inconsistent claims about potency levels and quoted UCLA professor Mark Kleiman's explanation that the evidence actually indicates that young marijuana smokers are not getting any more stoned, despite the alleged increase in THC content—meaning that if they are smoking stronger marijuana, they are smoking less of it (Forbes, 2002).

The second sentence, though stopping just short of stating that marijuana's direct effects are more dangerous than those of heroin and cocaine—a claim that most researchers would find laughable—strongly implies that they are at least close to those of the harder drugs. That is the only context in which the assertion that marijuana's more widespread use makes it more dangerous than the other drugs makes any sense. None of the data that follow—rising THC levels, more kids in treatment, and so on—directly prove that higher-THC marijuana has more pernicious effects. Rather, they build a circumstantial case. But that circumstantial case is plausible only because the relevant context is omitted.

For example, the claimed doubling of THC content from 3.5 percent to 7 percent sounds markedly less alarming when compared with Walters's previous claims that today's marijuana is 10 to 20 times stronger than marijuana available in the 1970s. It sounds less alarming still if one takes note of the European Union study of marijuana potency released less than three weeks before Fox's article, which described only "a slight upward trend" in the potency of U.S marijuana, adding pointedly that even with this increase, "the effective potency of the aggregated cannabis products [in the U.S.] has been low by European standards" (King, 2004, p. 53). And anxiety over a 7 percent THC level starts to look downright silly when one considers that the minimum THC level set by the government of the Netherlands for medical marijuana sold by prescription in Dutch pharmacies is 15 percent (Deutsch, 2003). None of these relevant facts was mentioned in the Reuters story.

The claim about skyrocketing numbers of teens in treatment for marijuana abuse or dependence also depends on the omission of relevant context. Not mentioned by Fox was that this frightening increase was driven almost entirely by arrests, with teen marijuana treatment admissions resulting from criminal justice referrals tripling from 1992 to 2001. In 1999, the number of teens forced into treatment after being arrested on marijuana charges exceeded for the first time the number referred to treatment from all other sources combined, a trend that has continued since then. Since 1996, adolescent treatment admissions for marijuana abuse/dependence unrelated to arrests have declined. In contrast, the number of arrest-related treatment admissions for teens whose favored drug was alcohol (which is, of course, equally illegal for teens to possess), without marijuana being involved, dropped by more than half, from more than 12,000 in 1992 to 5,525 in 2001 (Substance Abuse and Mental Health Services Administration, 2003). In other words, what occurred during this time period was most likely not an explosion in teen marijuana addiction, but rather a shift in either police practices or juvenile court sentencing procedures and preferences.

Present marijuana policies have created a self-perpetuating paradigm in which arrests are used to justify more arrests, particularly among adolescents: Authorities arrest kids for smoking marijuana, force them into treatment under threat of jail, and then the government uses those treatment admissions as "proof" that marijuana is so dangerously addictive that a further crackdown is required. But Reuters gave the public no clue as to the true nature of this Orwellian formulation.

Now let us return to the token opposition included by Fox (2004) and consider how it was presented. First, the only critic quoted is MPP's Krissy Oechslin, described as a "proponent of legalizing marijuana." No scientists who disagree with the government's hypothesis—indeed, no scientists not on the federal payroll—are quoted. Though organizations such as MPP are always happy to be included in such stories, the failure to quote or even mention any scientist who questions the official view—of which there is no shortage—creates an inherent imbalance in the story, an imbalance that is accentuated by labeling Oechslin as a legalization proponent. That characterization, while not entirely inaccurate, creates a different impression than other descriptions the reporter might have used, such as "proponent of harm reduction," or "proponent of marijuana regulation," either of which would have been at least as accurate.

Second, the story undercuts Oechslin by never directly citing the claim to which she was responding when she said, "They make it sound like the THC levels in marijuana were almost nonexistent." That statement is a reference to oft-repeated claims by federal officials that marijuana used in the 1960s and 1970s contained only 1% THC. Such assertions occur regularly in statements by officials such as Walters, and are the basis for his claim of a 10- to 20-fold

increase in marijuana potency, but because the specific statement is not cited in Fox's story, Oechslin's response seems like an overreaction.

Also left dangling, with insufficient context or explanation, is Oechslin's statement that "there's evidence that the stronger the THC, the less of it a person smokes. I don't want to say it's good for you, but I'll say [more potent marijuana] is less bad for you." Her comment is in fact solidly grounded in science, but readers of the article would never know it. Though the harms allegedly caused by high-potency marijuana are entirely speculative, the most well documented physical harm from marijuana is related to the irritants in smoke, which clearly can increase the risk of bronchitis and related ailments in heavy smokers (Hall & Solowij, 1998). Research done with relatively low-potency marijuana has indicated that when potency is increased, smokers smoke less, and thus take in smaller amounts of tar and other harmful components of smoke (Matthias, Tashkin, Marques-Magallanes, Wilkins, & Simmons, 1997). Readers were given no clue that, in terms of what could firmly be established with published, peer-reviewed data, Oechslin's statements were much more solidly grounded than Volkow's.

But even stories that make a more serious attempt at balance may end up misleading readers because claims made by partisans on one side or the other receive insufficient investigation or analysis. Consider, for example, the *Los Angeles Times* story about CASA's 2004 annual survey of teen substance use, which was also reprinted in a number of other papers. Unlike most others who covered this story, reporter Jia Lynn Yang seems to have made a real attempt to incorporate contrasting views, quoting both Keith Stoup (of the National Organization for the Reform of Marijuana Laws) and me. But even with this effort, the story had the effect of giving CASA's survey more credibility than it deserved (Yang, 2004).

In publicizing its survey, CASA heavily promoted a purported link between sexual activity and the use of alcohol and drugs. Yang, like nearly every reporter covering the story, made that connection the centerpiece of her report, emphasizing CASA's finding that teens with sexually active friends or who spent more than 25 hours per week with a boyfriend or girlfriend were more likely to use drugs or alcohol, and that girls with boyfriends two or more years older were "2.5 times more likely to drink and six times more likely to have tried marijuana."

The contrasting quotes that Yang used pointed out that CASA appeared to be sensationalizing common adolescent behavior and may have been trying to change the subject to avoid confronting the study's finding that teen drug use remains widespread despite decades of intensive antidrug efforts. In that sense, Yang did a far better job than most reporters, who failed to acknowledge any skeptical views at all. She followed the usual mass media template—using organizations with contrasting opinions to provide balance

and, presumably fairness. This approach, as noted above, is standard operating procedure in nondrug stories, and Yang deserves credit for doing what most other journalists did not.

And yet even Yang's story failed to look into CASA's report in any detail—for example, by examining the data that CASA chose not to highlight, or considering whether its conclusions made any sense. Unmentioned in Yang's story—or any other reports that turned up in an online search—was the fact that the percentage of kids reporting marijuana use rose this year, as did the number reporting having tried marijuana by age 13. Both of these facts were omitted from CASA's main report or the press release announcing it, but instead were tucked away in an appendix (CASA, 2004).

Press accounts, including Yang's (2004), also uniformly failed to note other omissions: Missing altogether, for example, was any indication of which, if any, of the results—including the touted correlations between drugs and sexual/dating behavior—were statistically significant. That's important, because some of the most sensational conclusions were based on breathtakingly small numbers. For example, that alarming figure about girls with boyfriends two or more years older being far more likely to drink or to smoke marijuana was based on a sample of 21 girls who said they had boyfriends two or more years older, half of whom smoked marijuana and 35 percent of whom got drunk.

That's 11 girls smoking marijuana and 7 getting drunk, out of a total sample of 1,000 kids. And the data an outside observer would need to run his or her own mathematical tests for statistical significance were left out of CASA's report.

So even Yang's admirable effort to include skeptical views—something virtually none of her mass media colleagues did—left readers uninformed about the survey's substantial gaps and weaknesses. The problem lies not so much in any one reporter's work as it does with the standard media template for news stories, which substitutes balance for the actual investigation and in-depth reporting it would take to get at the truth. Such reporting does happen occasionally, of course—most often in feature stories and magazine-type pieces (either print or broadcast), in which journalists may have more time to look under the surface of events and dig for little-known facts. But the mass media machine that cranks out day-to-day headlines takes that kind of time all too rarely.

The intersection between science and public policy—whatever the given subject—is a complicated area for journalists to cover. Reporting that truly informs the public must be free of prejudgments, include a healthy skepticism for all views—including official ones—and must take the time to examine what, if any, substance lies behind the breathless press releases churned out by all sides in such debates. In the area of marijuana policy, at least, mainstream U.S. news media frequently fail this test.

REFERENCES

Andreasson, S., & Allebeck, P. (1990). Cannabis and mortality among young men: A longitudinal study of Swedish conscripts. *Scandinavian Journal of Social Medicine, 18,* 9–15.

Bowman, L. (2004, May 5). Abuse and dependence rise as pot becomes more potent. *Seattle Post-Intelligencer.* Retrieved June 2, 2005, from http://seattlepi.nwsource.com/national/171890_pot05.html.

Canada headed "wrong way" on illegal drugs. (2003, October 9). *Reuters* news service. Retrieved June 2, 2005, from http://www.cisum.com/news/thread17520.shtml.

CARMA International. (2004). *MPP media analysis Oct.–Dec. 2003, Jan.–Mar. 2004, Apr.–June 2004, and July–Sept. 2004.* Washington, DC: Author.

Center on Addiction and Substance Abuse. (2004). *National survey of American attitudes on substance abuse IX: Teen dating practices and sexual activity.* Washington DC: Author.

Compton, W., Grant, B., Colliver, J., Glantz, M., & Stinson, F. (2004). Prevalence of marijuana use disorders in the United States, 1991–1992 and 2001–2002. *Journal of the American Medical Association, 291,* 2114–2121.

Department of Justice. (2004). National drug threat assessment. National Drug Intelligence Center. Retrieved April 28, 2004, from http://www.usdoj.gov/ndic/pubs8/8731/.

Deutsch, A. (2003, September 1). Medical marijuana sold in the Netherlands. *Associated Press.* Retrieved June 2, 2005, from http://www.newsday.com/news/health/ats-ap_health11sept01,0,3836793.story?coll=sns-health-headlines.

Drug Policy Alliance. (2004). *Mission and vision.* New York: Author.Earleywine, M. (2004). Marijuana arrests and increase in marijuana use disorders. *Journal of the American Medical Association, 292,* 802.

Earleywine, M. (2004). Marijuana arrests and increase in marijuana use disorders. *Journal of the American Medical Association, 292,* 802.

Federal Bureau of Investigation. (2002). *Crime in the United States, 2002.* Washington, DC: Author.

Federal Bureau of Investigation. (2003). *Crime in the United States, 2003.* Washington, DC: Author.

Federal Bureau of Investigation. (2004). *Crime in the United States, annually.* Washington, DC: Author.

Forbes, D. (2002, November 19). The myth of potent pot. Retrieved June 2, 2005, from http://www.slate.com/id/2074151/.

Fox, M. (2004, July 19). Stronger pot raising concerns in U.S. *Reuters* news service. Retrieved June 2, 2005, from http://www.ucsfhealth.org/childrens/health_library/reuters/.

Hall, W., & Solowij, N. (1998). Adverse effects of cannabis. *The Lancet, 352,* 1611–1616.

House of Representatives. (2004, April 1). Hearing on medical marijuana. Retrieved April 1, 2004, from www.mapinc.org.

King, L. (2004). *EMCDDA insights: An overview of cannabis potency in Europe.* Lisbon, Portugal: European Monitoring Center for Drugs and Drug Addiction.

Marijuana Policy Project. (2004). *MPP mission statement.* Washington, DC: Author.

Matthias, P., Tashkin, D. P., Marques-Magallanes, J. A., Wilkins, J. N., & Simmons, M. S. (1997). Effects of varying marijuana potency on deposition of tar and delta-9 THC in the lung during smoking. *Pharmacology Biochemistry and Behavior, 58,* 1145–1150.

Medline Plus Medical Dictionary. (2004). Retrieved December 1, 2004, from http://www.nlm.nih.gov/medlineplus/mplusdictionary.html.

Mithers, C. (2004, November 14). The plaintiff. *Los Angeles Times Magazine,* p. 20.

Merriam-Webster's collegiate dictionary (11th ed.). (2004). Springfield, MA: Merriam Webster.

MSNBC. (2005, June 15). Scarborough and Montel discuss medical marijuana, transcript of interview. Retrieved September 26, 2005, from http://msnbc.msn.com/id/8231829.

Office of National Drug Control Policy. (2002, November 6). *White House drug czar: Ballot initiative results a stunning victory of common sense over pro-drug propaganda.* Washington, DC: Author.

Office of National Drug Control Policy. (2003, April 13). *White House drug policy office to air Earth Day ad outlining the negative impact of the drug trade on the environment.* Washington, DC: Author.

Piper, B. (2004, April 29). Move to penalize pro-drug views amounts to censorship. *Atlanta Journal-Constitution.* Retrieved June 2, 2005, from http://nl.newsbank.com/sites/ajc/.

Piper, B. (2004, November 29). Personal communication.

Rasmussen, D., & Benson, B. L. (2003). Rationalizing drug policy under federalism. *Florida State University Law Review, 30,* 679–734.

Roosevelt, M. (2003, August 4). Busted! *Time.* Retrieved June 2, 2005, from http://www.time.com/time/archive/preview/0,10987,1005342,00.html.

Rothstein, K. (2003, September 11). State cops riled by photo of trooper on pro-pot sign. *The Boston Herald,* p. 24.

Sidney, S., Beck, J. E., Tekawa, I. S., Quesenberry, C. P., & Friedman, G. D. (1997). Marijuana use and mortality. *American Journal of Public Health, 87,* 585–590.

Souder, M. (2003, October 10). *Drug production on public lands—A growing problem.* Opening statement at joint hearing of the Subcommittee on Energy Policy, Natural Resources and the Regulatory Affairs and the Subcommittee on Criminal Justice, Drug Policy, and Human Resources. Retrieved June 2, 2005, from http://reform.house.gov/CJDPHR/Hearings/EventSingle.aspx?EventID=7225.

Stein, J. (2002, November 4). Is America going to pot? *Time*, pp. 56–61.

Substance Abuse and Mental Health Services Administration. (2003). *Treatment episode data set (TEDS) 1992–2001*. Washington, DC: Author.

Tanner, L. (2004, May 5). More adults using marijuana. *Associated Press*.

U.S. Department of Justice. (2004). Drug Threat Assessment 2004. Washington, DC: National Drug Intelligence Center.

Wahlberg, D. (2004, May 5). Stronger pot propels addiction rate higher. *Atlanta Journal-Constitution*, p. A1.

Walters, J. (2002, May 1). The myth of "harmless" marijuana. *Washington Post*, p. A25.

Yang, J. L. (2004, August 20). Report links teen sex to drug, alcohol use. *The Los Angeles Times*, p. A31.

8 Disseminating Accurate and Balanced Marijuana Education: An Opportunity for the Policy Reform Movement

Roger A. Roffman
Anne Nicoll

The central tenet of this chapter is that the anti-prohibition movement will enhance its effectiveness in promoting liberalized policy and better serve the public if the movement's mission is expanded to include the dissemination of accurate, thorough, and balanced marijuana educational information, tailored for each of its current and potential constituencies. A number of premises underlie this position, and they will be discussed as a prelude to approaching this chapter's central theme. We will also note that many people with varying personal interests in marijuana stand to benefit from an expanded mission of the policy reform movement such as that envisioned here, and we will identify each of these groups and briefly consider both their needs and the advantages they might subsequently enjoy if the movement does in fact make a greater investment in marijuana education.

Data from a 2004 survey of individuals who attended Seattle's annual two-day Hempfest festival will be presented to estimate the extent to which the reform movement's constituents would be receptive to the expanded function called for in this chapter. Then, with apologies to David Letterman, we will offer our "top 10 reasons" why devoting resources to the dissemination of accurate, thorough, and balanced marijuana education will be good both for the public and for the policy reform movement.

FOUR DECADES LATER

Roger Roffman's history with marijuana includes conducting the initial surveys focusing on the drug's use by U.S. Army enlisted personnel stationed in Vietnam in the late 1960s and serving as principal investigator of nine marijuana abuse/dependence treatment outcome trials funded by the National Institute on Drug Abuse and Center for Substance Abuse Treatment over a 20-year period. As a Washington State coordinator for the National Organization for the Reform of Marijuana Laws in the mid-1970s, Roffman lobbied for marijuana decriminalization and later for passage of that state's medical marijuana research law. He assisted with the design and implementation of medical marijuana research conducted by the Washington State Board of Pharmacy in the early 1980s, and he wrote a book (1983) for patients considering self-medicating with marijuana. He has counseled marijuana-dependent adults as a therapist in private practice, and has taught courses on alcohol and other drugs to undergraduate and graduate social work students for 32 years. A personal credential derives from the fact that his own casual use of marijuana evolved into a compulsion for a few years, leading him to decide to abstain. Along the way, he has gained a healthy respect for the validity of marijuana dependence, been sensitized to the difficulties faced by many in overcoming dependence, and become considerably discouraged about the half-truths and misrepresentations that too often accompany debate among various stakeholders when marijuana is the topic. Each of these impressions underlies the expanded mission of the marijuana policy reform movement called for in this chapter.

Over those four decades, the public's support for marijuana policy reform grew in the 1960s and 1970s when the movement was successful in promoting decriminalization in a number of states and municipalities. Support for liberalized laws eroded sharply in the early 1980s and then reemerged, but in a form largely limited to the medical use of the drug. With just a few exceptions in recent years such as passage of a Seattle initiative asking local law enforcement to place marijuana possession arrests at a low priority, calls for removing all criminal sanctions for nonmedical marijuana possession and sale have not been heeded in the United States. The policy reform movement's institutions (e.g., the Marijuana Policy Project, the Drug Policy Alliance, and the National Organization for the Reform of Marijuana Laws) are alive and kicking, and their arguments have contributed much to public discourse via newspaper editorials and radio and TV talk shows. However, the movement's legalization agenda—again with the exception of medical marijuana—has not been realized. Nonetheless, there are compelling reasons for continuing the dialogue about recreational

marijuana policy. The ideas presented in this chapter are offered in the interest of enhancing the reform movement's effectiveness in promoting continuing policy discussion.

FOUR PREMISES

Several premises that are highly relevant in any discussion of non-medical marijuana policy need to be acknowledged. The first is that despite the outcome alluded to in the title of the ubiquitous organization, "The Partnership for a Drug-Free America," it is difficult to envision circumstances in which a drug-free nation might come to exist. The epidemiology of marijuana use in recent history, a time in which much effort has been devoted to supply eradication and demand reduction, suggests a foreseeable future in which the drug will be used by a substantial part of the population.

A second premise is that along with marijuana's continuing popularity, it is virtually certain that a sizeable percentage of current and future users will experience related adverse consequences. Impairment of functioning, particularly among younger and heavier users, motor vehicle accidents, compulsive use, respiratory problems, and other related difficulties—not solely those that can be attributed to the drug's illegality—will warrant efforts devoted to prevention and treatment. Moreover, if alcohol regulation can be used to anticipate what might follow the liberalization of marijuana policy, prevention and treatment will remain important public health concerns even if punitive legal sanctions are entirely removed for possessing the drug.

If the past foretells the future, a third premise is that advocacy for and against marijuana policy reform will remain a constant in American politics for the foreseeable future. In discussing contributing factors in the history of alcohol policy, Joseph Gusfield (1963) concluded that public support for alcohol prohibition represented a convergence of negative reaction to the rapidly changing American economic and social landscapes and the threats they presented to a way of life. Some years later, the Shafer Commission, appointed by Nixon and charged with examining cannabis's effects, titled its report to the Congress, "Marihuana: A Signal of Misunderstanding," once again pointing to the symbolic role that marijuana played in broader cultural conflict, as well as the maelstrom of misinformation conveyed to the public by competing advocacies (United States, Commission on Marihuana and Drug Abuse, 1972). These lessons from history portend a future in which underlying cultural conflicts will be manifested in calls continuing to be made for marijuana policy reform, whether aimed at moving away from prohibition and toward decriminalization or regulation or vice versa. It appears inevitable that election campaigns for years to come will see candidates raising

the alarm of marijuana's threats, while others decry the fallout resulting from overzealous policies and infringements upon civil liberties.

A final premise is that the battle for hegemony as marijuana policy is debated will continue to see the dissemination of incomplete, one-sided, and distorted information about the drug by various stakeholders in the public and private sectors. Politicians and other government leaders, even those in the health professions, who are tempted to advocate for a more science-based and balanced approach will likely recall former Surgeon General Jocelyn Elders' fate and remain silent. (Dr. Elders was forced to resign by President Bill Clinton when she spoke in favor of more accurate and complete sex education for children.)

If, as we believe, a well-informed public is a necessary and desired foundation for good decision making, a number of population subgroups currently are not well served by being given an incomplete and often inaccurate picture as a consequence of marijuana politics. These circumstances offer a vitally important opportunity to those advocating changes in policy.

CURRENT AND POTENTIAL CONSTITUENCIES OF THE LIBERALIZATION MOVEMENT

An individual's needs for marijuana-specific knowledge will vary based on his or her specific circumstances. Liabilities incurred as a consequence of not having access to accurate and balanced information also will vary among subgroups.

Potential User

Children and adolescents constitute one subgroup of potential users. The educational needs of young people change dramatically with advancing stages of development. An approach to drug education that has the objective of shaping antidrug attitudes in the grade school years is less effective in high school when one-sided and biased information is likely to be challenged and/or disregarded. Drug-use prevention messages typically are constructed to highlight dangers (e.g., unwanted pregnancies, school failure) and omit mention of any benefits associated with a drug's use.

Might the marijuana policy reform movement fill a prevention gap for youth? A stereotyped notion of the reform movement's motivations might quickly dispatch such a possibility as unlikely. Yet, if adults who promote marijuana policy reform conveyed a credible message to young people about the reasons to delay a decision about use until adulthood, while also offering

accurate and balanced information about the drug, might their perspective be effective in preventing use by minors?

Another subgroup in this category includes adults who have not used marijuana and, in making informed decisions, would be well served by being educated about the potential risks for those with specific illnesses (e.g., cardiovascular disease, predisposition to psychotic illness) as well as the benefits. Once again, however, the innovation would be an approach to education that offers a complete, accurate, and balanced story to the consumer. Being presented with one-sided information in the expectation that it will fulfill an individual's needs for information when making decisions may be effective with some people, but at a cost with regard to the information's credibility with many others.

Current User

As is the case with alcohol, it is reasonable to believe that one can learn to consume marijuana moderately and responsibly. The drug's illegality, however, constrains publicly funded organizations from disseminating "safe use" guidelines. Research on marijuana use that would be the equivalent of drinking behavior studies could evaluate approaches to educating users in consumption technologies and skills to avoid such adverse consequences as lung functioning impairment or disease, marijuana dependence, or the precipitation of psychotic episodes in those who are vulnerable.

With few exceptions, the current marijuana user depends on folk wisdom or trial and error for ways to minimize risks to health or functioning. Although the movement's efforts to remove criminal penalties for marijuana possession are intended to benefit the user, their benefits from the movement might be considerably expanded if the potential risks and benefits of marijuana use were fully acknowledged and harm prevention strategies were identified in accurate and balanced marijuana educational materials tailored specifically for those who smoke marijuana.

User Who Is Beginning to Experience Related Problems

The concept of "stage of change," initially developed to describe the process of smoking cessation, has been useful in conceptualizing a continuum of readiness to acknowledge problems, committing to make changes, and taking action (Prochaska & DiClemente, 1983). One such stage, termed "contemplation," is characterized by concurrent competing motivations favoring and opposing change. At present, supportive resources are not available for

marijuana users who have concerns or questions about their use but have not made a decision to stop or cut back.

A counseling approach for addressing this need has been evaluated in controlled trials. Termed the "Marijuana Check-Up" (Doyle, Swan, Roffman, & Stephens, 2003; Stephens, Roffman, Fearer, et al., 2004), this brief intervention was adapted from a similar service (the "Drinker's Check-Up"; see Miller & Sovereign, 1989; Miller, Sovereign, & Krege, 1988) designed for concerned alcohol consumers. Participants are first assessed and then receive personalized feedback designed to aid them in an in-depth exploration of their marijuana use experiences, positive and negative consequences, attitudes favoring and opposing change, and confidence in their ability to make changes if these are desirable. Key elements of checkup interventions include acknowledgment that the individual will not be pressured to change, delivery in a nonconfrontational counseling style, protection of the individual's privacy, and provision of accurate and balanced educational materials. In-person, Web-based, and interactive computer versions of this intervention have been developed and are at varying stages of evaluation.

The user who is concerned about possible risks related to his or her marijuana use but is not committed to changing would be unlikely to approach a treatment agency for fear that the response would be pressure to make such a commitment right away. Friends, teachers, and family members similarly might be expected to try to influence the individual in one direction or another. Were the marijuana policy reform movement, through its websites, publications, conferences, and festivals, to offer supports akin to the Marijuana Check-Up, and if the delivery of these supports were based on an accurate, thorough, and balanced approach to marijuana education, it would be rendering an invaluable, sorely needed service to this subgroup.

Heavy User Who Is Marijuana Dependent

Counseling guidelines are available from controlled trials that have evaluated interventions with marijuana-dependent adults who wanted help in quitting or reducing use (Budney, Higgins, Radonovich, & Novy, 2000; Copeland, Swift, Roffman, & Stephens, 2001; Marijuana Treatment Project Research Group [MTPRG], 2004; Stephens, Roffman, & Curtin, 2000; Stephens, Roffman, & Simpson, 1994). The policy reform movement could support marijuana-dependent adults by featuring descriptions of these materials on their websites and at conferences and festivals, and by providing information on how interested individuals (and their therapists) can obtain counseling protocols from the researchers who conducted these studies.

The "Concerned Other" of a User Who
Is Experiencing Related Problems

A number of resources that could be made available by the marijuana policy reform movement would be helpful to individuals who are concerned about another individual's marijuana-related difficulties. Some examples are:

- Accurate, thorough, and balanced information about marijuana and its effects on health and behavior
- Behavioral signs of abuse and dependence
- Communication skills in expressing concern to another person
- How to find a counselor who can support the "concerned other"
- How to obtain counseling guidelines designed for marijuana disorders

The "Concerned Other" of a Potential User

The parent, teacher, or friend of an individual who is considering using marijuana may have questions about what to anticipate, whether or not to be concerned, and how to communicate what they are thinking in a manner that will be most effective. Once again, accurate and balanced information that is tailored for this individual's needs would fill an important gap.

The Service Provider

Unless they have read the journals in which controlled trials and their findings are reported, or learned about these studies while attending professional conferences, counselors and health professionals will not know that counseling protocols exist that offer guidance in working with clients who are using marijuana and want support in either quitting/cutting back or taking stock of their marijuana experiences. The marijuana policy reform movement would be addressing an unmet need if it were to devote resources to publicizing these materials, describing them on the movement's websites, and providing the addresses of researchers who have conducted the studies.

A SURVEY OF INDIVIDUALS ATTENDING
SEATTLE'S 2004 HEMPFEST

Since 1991, 13 summertime Hempfest political rallies have been held in Seattle. The rallies feature speakers advocating the reform of marijuana and commercial hemp policy, live band performances on multiple stages, and

booths where merchandise including hemp products and food are sold and where organizations distribute information. The first Hempfest drew about 500 people. In 2004, 70,000 to 90,000 individuals attended.

Hempfest leaders worked collaboratively with the authors to plan a survey to be conducted at the August 21–22, 2004, event. A questionnaire, intended to be completed anonymously by a convenience sample of adults who attended the festival, was designed to assess the extent to which respondents would support or oppose various marijuana education activities if they were included in the event the following year. Respondents were also asked questions concerning their demographics, their marijuana use experiences in the preceding three months, the number of years they had smoked marijuana, whether their use had ever been on a daily or near-daily basis, and, if it had, for how long. The final draft of the questionnaire and its method of administration were approved by the Hempfest Steering Committee and the University of Washington's research ethics Internal Review Board.

Eight individuals were hired to serve as survey staff and received three hours of training that included an explanation of the survey's purpose and the importance of respondent confidentiality, how to approach people to invite their participation, how to respond to queries or critical comments, and how to handle the questionnaires once they had been completed. To enhance the diversity of the study sample, two-person teams were assigned to give increased attention to collecting data from specific age groups (i.e., young, middle-age, and older adults), and all were asked to purposefully seek racially diverse participation.

Those who were not familiar with Hempfest were encouraged to visit its Web site (www.hempfest.org) to learn more about the event. Staff members wore T-shirts labeled "Hempfest Survey Crew," worked 8-hour shifts on the 2 festival days, and were stationed at various locations in the large municipal park where the event was held. Several staffed a project booth with a banner that read, "Fill Out the Hempfest Survey."

SAMPLE CHARACTERISTICS

Of the 952 questionnaires completed, 908 were available for analysis after 44 that had been given inadvertently to minors were destroyed. Table 8.1 presents demographic and marijuana use experience information for the sample.

Respondents were primarily male, white, and averaged 30 years of age (range = 18–78). The majority of participants were employed either full or part time. Most (86.2%) had smoked marijuana in the past 90 days, and users reported having smoked on an average of 54 days of the past 90. Respondents had smoked an average of over 12 years. They estimated being high almost five hours and smoking an average of over 3 times on a typical

Table 8.1. Demographics and Marijuana Use Experiences

Respondent	% of Total Sample
Age (in years)	30.1 (11.8)
Sex (male)	64.3%
Ethnicity (Hispanic)	6.3%
Race	
American Indian/Alaskan Native	4.7%
Asian	1.5%
Black or African American	4.0%
Native Hawaiian/Other Pacific Islander	1.7%
White	75.5%
Mixed race	10.0%
Other	2.5%
Employed (full or part time)	62.0%
Used marijuana in the past 90 days (yes)	86.2%
Days of marijuana use in the past 90 days	53.5 (37.9)
Amount of marijuana smoked per week in past 90 days	
None	15.2%
Less than ½ ounce	46.4%
Between ½ ounce and ⅞ of an ounce	13.6%
1 ounce or more	24.7%
Number of hours felt high on a typical day of use	4.8 (5.2)
Number of times marijuana was smoked per day	3.4 (4.8)
Number of years marijuana has been smoked	12.6 (10.4)
Used marijuana on a daily or near daily basis (yes)	82.8%
Number of years marijuana used on a daily or near-daily basis	9.0 (9.3)

N=908. All values are means followed by standard deviations in parentheses unless otherwise indicated.

day of use. Their volume of marijuana smoked in a typical week was less than half an ounce for over 40% of the sample, and 1 ounce or more for almost a quarter of the sample. Most respondents had smoked marijuana daily (or near daily) at some point in their lives. Those who had ever smoked at this rate reported having done so for an average of 9 years.

ATTITUDES CONCERNING MARIJUANA EDUCATION ACTIVITIES

In addition to being asked to rate three general educational activities (i.e., distributing brochures, presenting workshops, and inviting a speaker to address marijuana's effects on health), respondents also rated their attitudes toward six examples of specific brochures and four examples of workshops. Each type of activity was rated on a 5-point continuum (terrible idea, bad idea, no opinion, good idea, great idea).

These educational activities represent four categories of information: (a) *enjoying safe use* (accurate and science-based information about marijuana's effects on health); (b) *dealing with marijuana-related problems* (what to do if you think you're dependent or smoke too much, and how to find help); (c) *influencing young people* (how to talk with them about marijuana, and how they can make good decisions); and (d) *expressing concern about another person's marijuana use* (what to say/do if you perceive a problem).

As is evident in Table 8.2, the responses to all "general activity" items were quite favorable, all receiving positive ratings (combining good idea and great idea) of 85% or higher. With reference to "specific activities," none received a negative rating (when ratings for "bad idea" and "terrible idea" were combined) exceeding 18 percent. The two specific activities that received the most negative responses were brochures and workshops focusing on what to say or do if one thinks that a friend or relative smokes too much marijuana.

With reference to positive ratings for specific activities, none received less than 50% when "good idea" and "great idea" ratings were combined. Note that respondents had the option of rating an item "no opinion." In that context, the lower levels of enthusiasm were recorded for a brochure and a workshop on what to do/say if one thinks a friend or relative smokes too much marijuana and a workshop on what to do if you think you smoke too much marijuana. The higher levels of enthusiasm for specific activities were recorded for brochures on how to talk with kids about marijuana and how to enjoy marijuana while avoiding risks.

In summary, marijuana educational activities that would likely be highly supported at a future Hempfest event would address safe use and information for teenagers and their parents. Support at a more moderate level might be anticipated for activities focusing on what the user can do if he is concerned about his own use. Activities concerning how to respond to a friend or relative whose use is problematic would receive the lowest level of support.

Finally, the ratings of 312 respondents (34.3% of the sample) who were daily users (for the past 90 days) were examined separately. These users tended to smoke a relatively large amount of marijuana, with 42.3% consuming 1 ounce or more in an average week. The rationale for specifically looking at this group's ratings pertains to the greater likelihood of their experiencing adverse consequences. Learning how to meet their educational needs would be important.

Data concerning this subset of respondents will be found in Table 8.3. The ratings presented in this table indicate the percentages by age level of the daily users who perceived each activity to be either a good or great idea. One conclusion that can be drawn from these data is that daily marijuana smokers, when asked about "general activities," are very supportive of all

Table 8.2. Attitudes Concerning Education Activities

	Terrible Idea	Bad Idea	No Opinion	Good Idea	Great Idea
General Activities					
Brochures. Hempfest would distribute its own brochures with accurate and science-based information about marijuana's effects on health.	.4%	1.4%	6.7%	32.4%	59.2%
Workshops. Hempfest would present some brief (30-minute) workshops for people who have questions or concerns about marijuana.	.6%	3.0%	10.3%	39.9%	46.2%
Speaker. Hempfest would invite a speaker to talk about marijuana and health, including marijuana dependence.	.7%	2.0%	12.2%	36.7%	48.5%
Specific Activities					
Brochure: "How to enjoy marijuana while avoiding the risks."	2.1%	4.3%	13.1%	36.6%	43.9%
Brochure: "What to do if you think you're dependent on marijuana."	4.2%	5.9%	24.0%	34.4%	31.5%
Brochure: "If you're a teenager . . . making good decisions about marijuana."	1.5%	6.2%	16.4%	35.4%	40.4%
Brochure: "What to say if you think a friend or relative smokes marijuana too much."	7.3%	8.6%	30.7%	29.5%	24.0%
Brochure: "How to talk with kids about marijuana."	1.8%	3.7%	13.7%	35.5%	45.3%
Brochure: "How to find help if you're concerned about your use of marijuana."	4.0%	5.9%	21.6%	37.9%	30.6%
Workshop: "How to enjoy marijuana while avoiding the risks."	3.0%	6.2%	17.4%	38.9%	34.5%
Workshop: "What to do if you think a friend or relative is smoking too much marijuana."	6.7%	10.9%	31.9%	30.2%	20.3%
Workshop: "What to do if you think you smoke too much marijuana."	5.4%	10.1%	28.2%	33.0%	23.3%
Workshop: For parents: "How to talk with kids about marijuana."	2.5%	6.1%	15.5%	35.6%	40.2%

N = 908. The above percentages are based on those who rated each item. Between 39 and 58 respondents failed to indicate their ratings.

Table 8.3. Daily Marijuana Users Who Rated Each Activity as Either a Good or Great Idea

	Overall Sample* (n=312)	18–20 Years Old (n=74)	21–30 Years Old (n=142)	31–40 Years Old (n=37)	41–50 Years Old (n=43)	Over 50 Years Old (n=13)
General Activities						
Brochures. Hempfest would distribute its own brochures with accurate and science-based information about marijuana's effects on health.	88.1% (n=275)	83.8% (n=62)	90.1% (n=128)	94.6% (n=35)	88.4% (n=38)	76.9% (n=10)
Workshops. Hempfest would present some brief (30-minute) workshops for people who have questions or concerns about marijuana.	80.8% (n=252)	83.8% (n=62)	78.2% (n=111)	86.5% (n=32)	81.4% (n=35)	76.9% (n=10)
Speaker. Hempfest would invite a speaker to talk about marijuana and health, including marijuana dependence.	78.2% (n=244)	74.3% (n=55)	78.9% (n=112)	83.8% (n=31)	79.1% (n=34)	76.9% (n=10)
Specific Activities						
Brochure: "How to enjoy marijuana while avoiding the risks."	77.5% (n=242)	81.1% (n=60)	78.9% (n=112)	81.1% (n=30)	69.8% (n=30)	69.2% (n=9)
Brochure: "What to do if you think you're dependent on marijuana."	59.3% (n=185)	59.5% (n=44)	58.5% (n=83)	70.3% (n=26)	55.8% (n=24)	38.5% (n=5)
Brochure: "If you're a teenager . . . making good decisions about marijuana."	71.5% (n=223)	70.3% (n=52)	73.2% (n=104)	73.0% (n=27)	69.8% (n=30)	61.5% (n=8)

Table 8.3. (continued)

	Overall Sample* (n=312)	18–20 Years Old (n=74)	21–30 Years Old (n=142)	31–40 Years Old (n=37)	41–50 Years Old (n=43)	Over 50 Years Old (n=13)
Specific Activities						
Brochure: "What to say if you think a friend or relative smokes marijuana too much."	40.1% (n=125)	32.4% (n=24)	39.4% (n=56)	54.1% (n=20)	46.5% (n=20)	38.5% (n=5)
Brochure: "How to talk with kids about marijuana."	75.3% (n=235)	68.9% (n=51)	73.9% (n=105)	78.4% (n=29)	88.4% (n=38)	76.9% (n=10)
Brochure: "How to find help if you're concerned about your use of marijuana."	59.0% (n=184)	55.4% (n=41)	57.7% (n=82)	62.2% (n=23)	62.8% (n=27)	69.2% (n=9)
Workshop: "How to enjoy marijuana while avoiding the risks."	69.2% (n=216)	78.4% (n=58)	64.1% (n=91)	62.2% (n=23)	74.4% (n=32)	84.6% (n=11)
Workshop: "What to do if you think a friend or relative is smoking too much marijuana."	41.7% (n=130)	37.8% (n=28)	40.8% (n=58)	48.6% (n=18)	46.5% (n=20)	38.5% (n=5)
Workshop: "What to do if you think you smoke too much marijuana."	46.5% (n=145)	44.6% (n=33)	44.4% (n=63)	51.4% (n=19)	44.2% (n=19)	76.9% (n=10)
Workshop: For parents: "How to talk with kids about marijuana."	71.8% (n=224)	62.2% (n=46)	74.6% (n=106)	70.3% (n=26)	76.7% (n=33)	92.3% (n=12)

*Includes respondents whose age was unknown.

three categories (brochures, workshops, and speakers). Moreover, their enthusiasm does not appear to be reduced in any specific age groups.

A second conclusion is that daily marijuana smokers reflected the overall Hempfest sample in being quite positive about safe use education and materials directed toward teens. More moderate support was indicated for how to respond to personal concerns about marijuana use. Finally, as had been seen with the entire sample, daily users tended to give their

lowest levels of support to activities directed toward concerns for friends or relatives.

In summary, these data offer some important insights concerning the receptivity of regular marijuana smokers to a variety of marijuana educational activities as a component of a future Hempfest event. The data also offer some guidance concerning the tailoring of these activities to best meet the needs of various constituencies.

THE "TOP TEN REASONS" WHY DISSEMINATING ACCURATE, THOROUGH, AND BALANCED MARIJUANA EDUCATION WILL BE GOOD FOR THE POLICY REFORM MOVEMENT

As will be evident in what follows, a "road map" is offered in which devoting resources to marijuana education is both a route to success in stimulating meaningful dialogue about policy change and a service to the movement's current and potential constituents.

10. The movement is already perceived by many individuals, including current users, as having credibility in two aspects of education: challenging unsupported conclusions concerning marijuana-related risks and highlighting the costs of prohibition policies.

9. Data from a survey of individuals who attended Seattle's 2004 Hempfest indicate that marijuana users would be receptive to the reform movement's playing an active role in delivering accurate and balanced knowledge that is tailored to meet the educational needs of specific subgroups of users and of people in their social networks.

8. Publicly funded institutions would risk political reprisals if they disseminated accurate and balanced marijuana educational information, particularly if it offered strategies for harm reduction. The marijuana policy reform movement can and should fill this important unmet need.

7. The marijuana policy reform movement's credibility with growers, suppliers, and distributors puts it in a unique position to promote marketplace norms to protect minors and other vulnerable populations.

6. Producing and disseminating accurate, thorough, and balanced marijuana educational materials will raise the standard for drug education overall, putting the onus on publicly funded organizations to raise their standards.

5. Expanding the movement's mission as called for in this chapter (i.e., contributing to informed decision making, investing in harm

minimization, advocating the prevention of marijuana use by children and adolescents) will likely increase the movement's overall
credibility with the general public.

4. Enhanced credibility with the general public has the potential of
increasing the membership of marijuana policy reform organizations and enriching its funding base through annual dues, contributions, and foundation grants.

3. An increased funding base will enable the movement to invest in
harm minimization research (e.g., vaporization technology) and
studies of policy alternatives, neither of which are likely to receive
public funding at a time of marijuana prohibition.

2. Providing credible leadership in accurate and balanced education,
harm minimization, marijuana use prevention in children and adolescents, and research on policy alternatives will likely open doors
of access to the politically powerful, who will be able to justify
their receptivity to dialogue with reformers based on their good
work.

1. Increased credibility of the movement and alliances with the politically powerful will enhance the possibility for successfully achieving major policy change.

IMPLEMENTATION

Two key steps in the process of implementing these recommendations will
be: (1) developing educational materials and resources that clearly will be,
and will be perceived to be, science-based and balanced; and (2) evaluating
these materials and resources for their accessibility and effectiveness. The
first of these steps will require investing in the credibility of the effort.

Enhancing the credibility of these educational activities—overcoming
perceptions that information is being selectively presented in the service of
policy advocacy—will be an important factor. Though health professionals,
law enforcement specialists, educators, and members of other professions
are already involved as activists in the movement, the credibility of the marijuana education role called for in this chapter will require the involvement
of independent experts. The educational materials developed for dissemination should be reviewed and approved as accurate and balanced by a panel
of scientists. An advisory board should provide oversight, and its members
should be people whose impartiality will be recognized.

The evaluation process should address how best to promote awareness
of and access to the materials for the subgroups for which they have been
developed. It should identify the strengths and limitations of these resources
from the point of view of their target audiences and modify the materials
based on the findings of field tests.

SOME CLOSING COMMENTS

There are likely to be some opposing arguments to the positions taken in this chapter. We can anticipate a few of them: (a) because problems associated with marijuana use are caused by prohibition, when the policies are changed the most serious of marijuana's problems will no longer exist; (b) marijuana education is already within the scope of the movement's activities insofar as it works to dispel inaccurate information concerning marijuana's effects; and (c) marijuana education should be the responsibility of other institutions, not the policy reform movement.

There may be some truth to each of these points. However, just as the harmful outcomes of a criminal approach to marijuana prohibition are quite evident to those who work to reform policy, so has been the inability of the reform movement to garner sufficient political support to legalize nonmedical use. Taking the high road in disseminating accurate, thorough, and balanced marijuana education for the movement's current and potential constituencies offers a new direction for the movement, has the potential of serving important unmet needs for the public, and may open new options for politicians whose minds might be changed if they are in a position to refute charges that they are "soft on drugs" by being able to point to the effective prevention work of the reform movement.

REFERENCES

Budney, A. J., Higgins, S. T., Radonovich, K. J., & Novy, P. L. (2000). Adding voucher-based incentives to coping skills and motivational enhancement improves outcomes during treatment for marijuana dependence. *Journal of Consulting and Clinical Psychology, 8,* 1051–1061.

Copeland, J., Swift, W., Roffman, R., & Stephens, R. (2001). A randomized controlled trial of brief cognitive-behavioral interventions for cannabis use disorders. *Journal of Substance Abuse Treatment, 21,* 55–64.

Doyle, A., Swan, M., Roffman, R., & Stephens, R. (2003) The Marijuana Check-Up: A brief intervention tailored for individuals in the contemplation stage. *Journal of Social Work Practice in the Addictions, 3,* 53–71.

Gusfield, J. (1963). *Symbolic crusade.* Urbana: University of Illinois Press.

Roffman, R. (1983). *Marijuana as medicine.* Seattle: Madrona Press.

Marijuana Treatment Project Research Group (MTPRG). (2004). Brief treatments for cannabis dependence: Findings from a randomized multisite trial. *Journal of Consulting and Clinical Psychology, 72,* 455–466.

Miller, W. R., & Sovereign, R. G. (1989). The check-up: A model for early intervention in addictive behaviors. In T. Loberg, W. R. Miller, P. E. Nathan, & G. A. Marlatt (Eds.). *Addictive behaviors: Prevention and early intervention* (pp. 219–231). Amsterdam: Swets & Zeitlinger.

Miller, W. R., Sovereign, R. G., & Krege, B. (1988). Motivational interviewing with problem drinkers: II. The Drinker's Check-up as a preventive intervention. *Behavioral Psychotherapy, 16,* 251–268.

Prochaska, J. O., & DiClemente, C. C. (1983). Stages and processes of self-change of smoking: Toward an integrative model of change. *Journal of Consulting and Clinical Psychology, 5,* 390–395.

Stephens, R. S., Roffman, R. A., & Curtin, L. (2000). Comparison of extended versus brief treatments for marijuana use. *Journal of Consulting and Clinical Psychology, 68,* 898–908.

Stephens, R. S., Roffman, R. A., Fearer, S. A., Williams, C., Picciano, J. F., & Burke, R. S. (2004). The Marijuana Check-Up: Reaching users who are ambivalent about change. *Addiction, 99,* 1323–1332.

Stephens, R. S., Roffman, R. A., & Simpson, E. E. (1994). Treating adult marijuana dependence: A test of the relapse prevention model. *Journal of Consulting and Clinical Psychology, 62,* 92–99.

United States, Commission on Marihuana and Drug Abuse (1972). *Marihuana: A signal of misunderstanding.* Washington, DC: Superintendent of Documents, U.S. Government Printing Office.

9   Marijuana's Perceived Addictiveness: A Survey of Clinicians and Researchers

Robert Gore
Mitch Earleywine

Although experts influence public opinion regarding drug addictiveness, no previous research surveys the opinions of different groups of experts to compare their ratings of addictiveness. This chapter reports on a survey of addiction researchers, clinicians specializing in addiction, and generalist psychotherapists. Respondents rated the addiction, tolerance, and withdrawal potential of 12 drugs. They gave LSD, 3-4 methylenedioxymethamphetamine (MDMA), and cannabis the lowest ratings of addictiveness, and crack cocaine, nicotine, and heroin the highest. Addiction treatment specialists gave the highest average addictiveness ratings, followed by non-specialist clinicians and then by researchers. Respondents who had more formal education and had written more published articles gave lower ratings; those with more clinical contact gave higher ratings. Findings are explained in terms of the information each professional group routinely encounters and judgment and decision theory.

THE PROBLEM

Many drug policy arguments rely on addictiveness: People who seek to restrict the use of drugs argue that their high addictiveness requires legal restraints. Those who favor legalization argue that many legal intoxicants (such as alcohol and nicotine) have more potential to lead to addiction than do some illegal intoxicants (such as marijuana and LSD). Although many citizens assert

that addictiveness should have little to do with public policy because adults should be free to choose to ingest what they wish, both sides of the marijuana policy argument often rely heavily on presumed addictiveness in making their cases.

No approach to addictiveness measurement has universal acceptance (Earleywine, 2002), and basic science may not influence clinicians (Meehl, 1973). No systematic survey compares scientists, addiction specialists, and general mental health clinicians in terms of their opinions on drugs' addiction potential. This study addresses that gap.

Cannabis is particularly controversial. Recent debates on its addictiveness reveal that the issue has polarized pure researchers and treating clinicians. On one side, Voth (1997) wrote: "Marijuana is addictive. About time the public had that information. Of course, those of us who treat addicts have known that fact for years" (p. 34). In contradiction, neither of two scientific experts who independently rated six substances for their addictiveness rated any drug as less addictive than marijuana (Hilts, 1994). In his text on drug chemistry, Perrine (1997) also placed marijuana last in addictiveness. These opinions may be particularly important as more states and countries consider revising their cannabis laws.

We conducted this survey of researchers, drug professionals, and generalist clinicians (a) to ascertain overall professional opinion regarding drug addictiveness; (b) to determine what other factors (gender, ethnicity, clinical experience level, drug treatment experience level, publication history, and education level) correlate with expert opinion regarding addictiveness of drugs studied; and (c) to determine how cannabis compares with other drugs of abuse—especially those that are legal—in terms of professional opinion regarding addictiveness.

We predicted that addiction researchers (AR), as a group, would assign lower addictiveness ratings across the board than would substance abuse professionals (SAP). We also predicted that nonspecialist clinicians (NSC) would fall between those two groups. We made these hypotheses for three reasons. First, we believed that substance abuse professionals would be greatly influenced by the availability heuristic (Tversky & Kahneman, 1974)—their judgments would fall nearer to the high end of the addictiveness scale because of their frequent and recent contact with people reporting addiction to a variety of drugs. Second, we believed that scientific experts would be more likely to have advanced degrees and thus have more prior exposure to a greater diversity of opinions related to addiction. Third, by conducting research, addiction investigators are likely to encounter drug users who would not appear frequently in treatment settings. The NSC group, who likely saw some problem users and some nonproblem users, would rate addictiveness between the AR and SAP group for the same reason.

We began the study with three hypotheses.

Hypothesis 1. We hypothesized that AR participants would assign lower addictiveness ratings than SAP participants. We hypothesized that NSC participants would fall between those two groups.

Hypothesis 2. We further hypothesized that higher levels of education and greater numbers of publications would accompany lower addictiveness ratings. Conversely, we hypothesized that higher addictiveness ratings would accompany greater numbers of clinical hours—especially clinical hours with substance-abusing clients.

Hypothesis 3. We hypothesized that education would predict a significant increment of variance in addictiveness ratings after controlling for any significant demographic covariates, and we hypothesized that the direction of this relationship would be negative. We also hypothesized that clinical hours with substance-abusing clients would predict an additional increment of variance over and above the aforementioned variables and would be positively related to addictiveness ratings.

METHOD

Participants

Researchers were recruited via e-mail addresses from published articles in addictions journals. General mental health professionals were recruited from a purchased e-mail list. The National Association of Alcoholism and Drug Abuse Counselors (NAADAC), an association for addiction professionals, provided e-mail addresses for its members. Return rates for each group were 36.8% (AR), 39.5% (NSC), and 45.5% (SAP), which yielded group sizes of n=115, n=118, and n=513, respectively. Participants were 50% women and 49% men (1% did not indicate their sex). The sample was primarily Caucasian (83.5%), smaller numbers of African American (4.3%), Native American (2.9%), Latino (2.7%), Asian (0.8%), mixed race (0.8%), and race unspecified (5%). Mean age was 48.9 years. They averaged 13.8 years since getting their highest degree. The AR participants had the fewest clinical hours and the fewest clinical hours with substance abusing clients. The NSC participants had more hours, and SAP participants had the most ($F(2,725)=133.31$ and 152.24, $p<.05$).

Procedure

Participants completed an Internet survey requesting demographic information and their subjective ratings (from 1 to 7) of the tolerance, withdrawal, and addiction created by 12 drugs (alcohol, amphetamine, caffeine, cocaine,

crack cocaine, heroin, LSD, MDMA, methamphetamine, nicotine, and oxy-codone). Tolerance, withdrawal, and addictiveness ratings correlated r=.57 or higher, so for brevity we focus on addictiveness. Results were comparable for tolerance and withdrawal.

RESULTS

Average Ratings

Addictiveness ratings for all drugs appear in ascending order in Table 9.1. Of the 12 considered here, LSD and MDMA were rated significantly lower than cannabis. All other drugs were rated as more addictive than cannabis. Figure 9.1 puts in graphic form these same results for cannabis and the nine drugs perceived to be more addictive than cannabis.

A Multivariate Analysis of Variance (MANOVA) comparing the linear combination of ratings for all 12 drugs across the three groups revealed a significant multivariate effect $(F(12,733)=16.74, p<.001)$. This result means that a weighted combination of all ratings significantly separated the groups. In the long run, on the average, these groups tend to view the addictiveness of these drugs very differently. Rather than conduct all other analyses with 12 separate dependent variables and risk Type I errors (essentially concluding that two drugs differ in addictiveness when the results really arose by chance), we focused on mean addictiveness ratings for all drugs and separately analyzed ratings for cannabis.

Table 9.1. Mean Addictiveness Ratings Across All Groups (N = 746)

Drug	Addictiveness Rating (SD)	Effect Size Difference From Cannabis (Mean Difference Over Pooled SD)
LSD	3.26 (1.93)	−0.65**
MDMA	4.21 (1.91)	−0.14**
Cannabis	4.46 (1.78)	0
Caffeine	4.64 (1.74)	0.18*
Amphetamine	5.71 (1.45)	0.77**
Alcohol	5.84 (1.46)	0.85**
Cocaine	5.86 (1.37)	0.89**
Methamphetamine	6.05 (1.44)	0.99**
Oxycodone	6.25 (1.40)	1.13**
Crack Cocaine	6.48 (1.15)	1.38**
Nicotine	6.54 (1.05)	1.47**
Heroin	6.62 (1.05)	1.53**

*p < .01

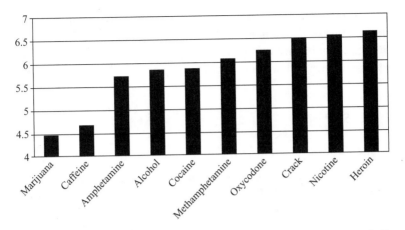

Figure 9.1. Addictiveness Ratings of 746 Drug Experts for Marijuana and All Drugs With Significantly Higher Ratings.

Demographic Effects

Women's ratings exceeded men's for average perceived addictiveness of all drugs $(t(736)=3.27$; mean difference$=.25$ (SE$=.077$) p$<.05$), and showed a trend for cannabis $(t(736)=1.87$; mean difference$=.25$ (SE$=.131$) p$=.06$). Ratings of participants without terminal degrees exceeded the ratings of those with terminal degrees. For mean addictiveness, $(t(320.21)=7.88$; mean difference$=.70$ (SE$=.089$) p$<.05$). For cannabis, $(t(744)=7.31$; mean difference$=1.03$ (SE$=.141$) p$<.05$).

Professional Experience Effects

Mean ratings of perceived addictiveness correlated inversely with the number of publications $(r=-.19)$, and positively with clinical hours $(r=.24)$, and clinical hours with substance-abusing clients $(r=.30$; all p$<.001)$. Addictiveness ratings for cannabis showed the same effects, correlating $r=-.14$ with publications, $r=.20$ with clinical hours, and $r=.27$ with clinical hours with substance abusing clients (all p$<.001$). As predicted, respondents who had produced more publications gave lower ratings of addictiveness, and those who had amassed more clinical hours, particularly with substance-abusing clients, gave higher ratings.

The AR, SAP, and NSC groups differed in sex and education. The AR group included a higher percentage of men (71% for the AR vs. 39% for the NSC group and 48% for the SAP group; $X^2(2)=26.25$, p$<.001$) and a higher percentage of participants with terminal degrees (M.D., Ph.D., or

Psy.D.$=92\%$ for the AR vs. 47% for NSC and 9% for the AR group; $X^2(2)=355.17$, p<.001).

A regression using dummy-coded sex and education variables as covariates and clinical hours with substance-abusing clients to predict mean addictiveness ratings revealed significant effects for both covariates (sex accounted for 0.7% of the variance, $F(1, 5.65)=7.7$, p<.05; education accounted for 2.8% additional variance, $F=22.98$, p<.001) but clinical hours with substance-abusing clients accounted for significant variance over and above the covariates (4%; $F=33.44$), as predicted. For cannabis ratings, sex was not significant. Education accounted for 2.4% of the variance ($F=19.04$, p<.001). Clinical hours with substance-abusing clients accounted for 2.9% more variance ($F=23.67$, p<.001), as predicted.

DISCUSSION

All hypotheses were supported. The SAP group gave the highest addictiveness ratings, the AR group gave the lowest, and the NSC group fell between them. Furthermore, participants with greater education tended to ascribe lower addictiveness ratings across drugs generally, and particularly ascribed lower addictiveness ratings to marijuana, compared to specialist and nonspecialist clinicians. Greater levels of contact with substance-abusing clients, on the other hand, were associated with significantly higher ascriptions of addictiveness to drugs in general and to marijuana in particular. Level of education was a significant predictor of mean addictiveness ratings, even after controlling for demographic variables, and clinical hours with substance-abusing clients made a significant contribution after all other variables were entered.

Although this study is a correlational survey of opinions—and therefore does not justify causal inference—findings are consistent with a model in which graduate education and scientific research influence people to ascribe less addictiveness to a variety of drugs, including cannabis. Clinical experience with drug-abusing populations, conversely, may motivate people to ascribe greater addictiveness to a variety of drugs. This study does not allow us to determine which experts are correct. Four explanations will be considered: (a) that clinicians and researchers respond to effects of the availability heuristic, leading them to different conclusions about addiction potential; (b) that clinicians have greater access to intimate information, and therefore a more accurate perspective; (c) that clinicians observe complex drug-drug interactions that are difficult to detect statistically, leading them to see the world more accurately than do researchers; and (d) that clinical work competes with time available to follow the scientific literature, impeding the ability to clinicians to keep up with developments in scientific knowledge about addiction potential.

Our findings are generally consistent with the effect of the availability heuristic—the tendency to derive inferences about base rates by considering how recently one has observed the phenomenon in question. Specialist clinicians more frequently observe addicted individuals (and rarely observe non-problem users), so their judgment of the prevalence of addiction is inflated. Generalist clinicians probably see addicted individuals less frequently and may fail to recognize many of those they see (Bryant, Rounsaville, Spitzer, & Williams, 1992; Grossman et al., 1997). Researchers—who are more likely to see non-problem users—ascribe lower addictiveness ratings.

In keeping with the availability hypothesis, the correlation between a respondent's number of publications and his or her addictiveness ratings was of a magnitude similar to that of the clinical experience–perceived addictiveness rating correlations, but in the opposite direction. Both these effect sizes were small (in the range of $r = .15$ to $r = .20$), however, accounting for at most 4% of the shared variance. It is possible that clinicians observe phenomena that are inherently difficult for researchers to study. Miller (1998) asserts that psychotherapists have access to information people ordinarily conceal from researchers. Furthermore, it is possible that clients in counseling or therapy develop an understanding of the role of drugs in their lives that can only come through the introspective process of therapy. People who have similar problems but are not in treatment may be unable to reach these conclusions, making it substantially less likely that their reports to researchers would fully reflect the problems drugs do cause in their lives. Addiction could operate in this fashion, with drug-dependent individuals recognizing their dependence only because they take part in a supportive process of introspection such as that afforded in psychotherapy.

However, this would not explain the observed difference between addiction specialists and nonspecialist clinicians in their ratings of addiction potential. Both groups have access to intimate information, and all therapists (specialist or not) see a notable proportion of clients with drug and alcohol problems (Regier et al., 1990). If psychotherapy affords a special view into the problems of addiction, both specialists and nonspecialist clinicians should show the effect to approximately the same degree.

The difference in addiction potential judgments between specialist and nonspecialist clinicians may result from the fact that nonspecialist clinicians are less likely to ask questions about drug use. Psychotherapists frequently underestimate or overlook drug problems (Bryant et al., 1992; Grossman et al., 1997). Perhaps mental health specialists ascribe higher addictiveness potential than do nonspecialist clinicians because the specialists do more consistent assessment for substance use problems and therefore detect a higher percentage of cases, which then affects their judgments of addictiveness. But if this were true, then the specialists with higher education should ascribe no lower addictiveness on average than would the less educated

addiction specialists. In fact, there is a significant (spearman r=.244, p=.008) spearman rank correlation between mean addictiveness rating and education level among the NAADAC group. More highly educated NAADAC members gave higher addictiveness ratings on average. This result tends to support the view that some of the difference between NAADAC and nonspecialists may be poor assessment and underdiagnosis among non-specialists. This did not happen for cannabis alone (spearman r=.129, p=.163).

One form of intimate information available to many specialist clinicians was not anticipated in our study design. Clinicians who specialize in substance abuse frequently report a history of addiction themselves. We believe that addiction researchers and nonspecialist clinicians may be less likely than addiction specialists to have substance-abuse histories or be in recovery. A survey of NAADAC members reports that 54% describe themselves as being "in recovery" (Lewin Group, 2003). Survey research suggests that around 2%–3% of the general population (of nonclinicians) is in some form of self-help group, including recovery-oriented groups (Borkman 1991, 1997), so specialist clinicians are more than 10 times as likely as members of the general public to be in recovery. People in recovery are likely to be privy to information that is not readily disclosed in paper-and-pencil or telephone surveys. Thus, researchers may have a hard time gaining the level of access to this form of information that observer-participants have by virtue of their own participation.

On the other hand, Hohman (1998) found that substance-abuse counseling students who identified themselves as alcoholics had less education yet were more likely to obtain a job in the addictions field than were students who did not self-identify as alcoholics. If people in recovery have less formal education, they have fewer opportunities to correct possible errors or biases developed through personal experience and contact with clinical populations. Clinical experience typically does not correct conceptual misunderstandings (Garb, 1989). Ongoing recovery activities may perpetuate the group differences observed here. Twelve-step programs, for example, emphasize as a matter of doctrine the addictiveness of drugs and the powerlessness of addicts to control their urges to use drugs. Our design does not allow us to determine whether NAADAC members in recovery are more or less accurate in their judgments of addictive potential than are clinicians and scientists who are not in recovery themselves. This does seem an obvious direction for future work.

Finally, drug interactions may influence specialist clinicians. In this case, scientists and specialist clinicians may both be correct: Marijuana may be relatively low in addiction potential when used alone, but it may have substantial addiction potential when combined with another drug, such as alcohol. Clinicians—especially addiction specialists—are likely to observe these real cases of polysubstance addiction and be influenced by them, while scientists

may fail to detect them because of the relatively low statistical power involved in attempting to detect interaction effects. Furthermore, clinicians may feel that it makes no meaningful difference whether someone is addicted to, for example, cannabis by itself or only in conjunction with alcohol. Clinically, it is very difficult to sort out causality in individual cases involving multiple factors, and clinicians are unlikely to feel comfortable encouraging a client who reports polysubstance addiction to try using each of several drugs individually and see if some of them are nonaddictive by themselves. As a practical matter, the individual client who is separately addicted to alcohol and cannabis is difficult to distinguish from the client who is addicted to cannabis only in conjunction with alcohol.

Recent data (Smucker, Earleywine, & Gordis, in press), in fact, suggest that concomitant alcohol use raises the addictive potential of cannabis. Clinicians may observe this phenomenon and conclude that cannabis is addictive, while researchers may see it as evidence only for the addictive potential of this combination, rather than as evidence for cannabis's addictive potential in itself.

A final explanation for our findings lies in inherent limitations on time available to professionals. It may be that clinicians have far less time than scientists to follow advances in the research literature on addiction. The correlation between mean addictiveness ratings and overall clinical hours was of a magnitude similar to that of the correlation between mean addictiveness ratings and clinical hours with substance-abusing clients ($r = .24$ versus $r = .30$; this difference is nonsignificant using a Fisher r-to-z test). The availability heuristic would predict a higher correlation between hours with substance-abusing clients and mean addictiveness ratings. This argues against the availability heuristic and in favor of competition for clinician time between the demands of practice and keeping up with the literature.

Further research should more carefully examine how researchers, nonspecialist clinicians, and addiction specialists are influenced by clinical and scientific data that are discrepant with their beliefs. This research should attempt to take into consideration professionals' prior and ongoing influences, such as a history of addiction, history of drug use without problems, and personal participation in recovery-oriented programs. An effort should also be made to measure and understand the influence complex drug-drug interaction cases have on clinicians and scientists. Furthermore, the reading habits of clinicians and specialist clinicians should be studied and taken into account by scientific experts to ensure the widest professional effect for drug research, especially given constraints on clinicians' reading time.

In summary, experts differ in their tendency to view a variety of drugs as addictive, with specialist clinicians giving the highest ratings on average and scientists the lowest ratings. All groups of experts, however, ascribe lower addictiveness ratings to cannabis, on average, than to most other drugs. Past research on the effects of clinical experience would lead us to expect

that substance abuse specialists are likely to overestimate the addictiveness of drugs in general, but it remains possible that scientists and nonspecialist clinicians underrate addictiveness because of reduced access to intimate information or an insensitivity to drug-drug interaction effects. Further research is warranted to better understand how clinicians and scientists make informed judgments of addictiveness. Nevertheless, cannabis appears to have little addictive potential in the opinion of most experts, particularly when compared to other common drugs, including caffeine.

REFERENCES

Borkman, T. J. (1991). Self-help groups. Introduction to the special issue. *American Journal of Community Psychology, 19,* 643–650.

Borkman, T. J. (1997). A selected look at self-help groups in the U.S. *Health and Social Care in the Community, 5,* 357–364.

Bryant, K. J., Rounsaville, B., Spitzer, R. L., & Williams, J. B. (1992). Reliability of dual diagnosis, substance dependence, and psychiatric disorders. *The Journal of Nervous and Mental Disease, 180,* 251–257.

Earleywine, M. (2002). *Understanding marijuana: A new look at the scientific evidence.* Oxford: Oxford University Press.

Garb, H. N. (1989). Clinical judgment, clinical training, and professional experience. *Psychological Bulletin, 105,* 387–396.

Garb, H. N. (1998). *Studying the clinician: Judgment research and psychological assessment.* Washington, DC: American Psychological Association.

Grossman, L. S., Willer, J., Stovall, J. G., McRae, S., Maxwell, S., & Nelson, R. (1997). Underdiagnosis of PTSD and substance use disorders in hospitalized female veterans. *Psychiatric Services, 48,* 393–395.

Hilts, P. J. (1994, August 2). Is nicotine addictive? It depends on whose criteria you use. *The New York Times,* p. C3.

Hohman, M. M. (1998). Comparison of alcoholic and non-alcoholic students in a community college addictions program. *Journal of Alcohol and Drug Education, 43*(2), 83–94.

Lewin Group. (2003). *Survey of NAADAC members: Years 1999 and 2001.* Alexandria, VA: NAADAC.

Meehl, P. E. (1973). *Psychodiagnosis: Selected papers.* Oxford, England: University of Minnesota Press.

Miller, R. B. (1998). Epistemology and psychotherapy data: The unspeakable, unbearable, horrible truth. *Clinical Psychology: Science and Practice, 5*(2), 242–250.

Perrine, D. M. (1997). *The chemistry of mind-altering drugs.* Washington, DC: American Chemical Society.

Regier, D. A., Farmer, M. E., Rae, D. S., Locke, B., Keith, S. J., Judd, L. L., et al. (1990). Comorbidity of mental disorders with alcohol and other drug abuse. *Journal of the American Medical Association, 264,* 2511–2518.

Smucker Barnwell, S., Earleywine, M., & Gordis, E. B. (in press). Alcohol consumption moderates the link between cannabis use and cannabis dependence in an Internet survey. *Psychology of Addictive Behaviors.*

Tversky, A., & Kahneman, D. (1974). Judgment under uncertainty: Heuristics and biases. *Science, 185*(4157), 1124–1131.

Voth, E. (1997, June 30). Marijuana is addictive. *Los Angeles Times,* p. 34.

SECTION IV

Ethical and Religious Perspectives

Morality, ethics, and religion generate enough controversy, rage, and misunderstanding without involving drugs. Nevertheless, the war on drugs has created a great deal of rhetoric about morals and values. Many remember former drug czar William Bennett's unfalsifiable moral argument: "The simple fact is that drug use is wrong. And the moral argument, in the end, is the most compelling argument" (Bennett, 1991).

Unlike other topics in this volume, these issues do not lend themselves to empirical research. Some recurring themes in temperance and prohibition messages involve individual responsibility, the importance of economic success, the value of resisting peer pressure, the inherent need for parents to assure that children do not use drugs, and the value of a deity or higher power in building a meaningful life. Arguments against prohibition have comparable themes. Even the expressions that appear in descriptions of drug problems have a certain biblical tone. Words like "demonized," "pestilence," "plague," "scourge," "evil," and even "epidemic" have an Old Testament feel. Sorting though all of these issues as they relate to marijuana prohibition remains a difficult task.

Merely asking the question of how morals or religion relates to drugs can create plenty of trouble. The idea that drugs are evil has considerable support. Stereotypes of religion or morality often accompany stereotypes of abstinence. Questioning current drug policies on moral or religious grounds can lead to quick accusations of immorality or heresy. But the tacit assumption, that drugs, particularly marijuana, are inherently evil, requires

examination. Some moral arguments, as presented, become circular or simplistic. Many reduce to the idea that drugs are wrong because they are immoral and immoral because they are wrong.

Most ethicists like general principles. A general principle—an overarching idea that can apply to almost any situation—has intuitive appeal and practical utility. The notion that drugs are evil has been adopted by some as a general principle. Once accepted, this principle makes decisions about drug laws easy. If drugs are evil enough, then we should take steps to eliminate them. Policing should be thorough, punishments should be swift and severe, and few other issues should take priority over eliminating drugs.

It is often with these ideas in mind that many citizens ask reformers why marijuana laws should change. Douglas Husak puts the shoe of the prohibition argument on the other foot, asking why drug possession requires state-initiated punishment. Given the general principle that the severity of a punishment should fit the severity of the crime, what is the most appropriate penalty for marijuana possession?

Many support moral arguments with references to sacred texts. These kinds of appeals to authority can turn some people away; others argue that empirical work is simply another form of appeal to authority. Distinguishing between the words of a sacred text and their meaning has filled many big books. Anyone who wants to understand the logic of these arguments will find a fine example here. Elliot Dorff proceeds through biblical passages and commentary in an effort to distinguish between drug use and associated negative consequences. This process could apply to any sacred text, or any text for that matter. Readers may be particularly surprised to learn that the Bible may not say exactly what they thought. In subsequent chapters, Charles Thomas explains how religious movements, even those opposed to drug use, can still support new laws on marijuana for the good of the people. He also documents the varied approaches that different religions adopt.

REFERENCES

Bennett, W. (1991). The plea to legalize drugs is a siren call to surrender. In M. Lyman & G. Potter (Eds.), *Drugs in society* (p. 339). Cincinnati: Anderson.

10   Do Marijuana Offenders Deserve Punishment?

Douglas Husak

In this chapter, I will attempt a somewhat novel defense of marijuana *decriminalization*. My argument will not rely upon the familiar complaint that marijuana prohibitions are counterproductive and ineffective. These criticisms, although undoubtedly correct, do not challenge the legitimacy of marijuana prohibitions *in principle*. I will begin by identifying some of the factors that may have prevented commentators from recognizing the principled objections to punishing users of marijuana. In the bulk of this chapter, I will argue that our best understanding of the normative foundations of punishment and sentencing theory supports my conclusion that marijuana use should be decriminalized. I am not so naïve as to suppose that the recommendations of academics have any immediate effect in the world outside academia. Criminal justice generally, and drug policy in particular, have been thoroughly politicized in the United States. Our rates of punishment are at unprecedented levels and dwarf those of other Western industrialized countries (see Whitman, 2003). Nonetheless, academic discussion is important to those who aspire to inform their views by reason and principle.

IMPEDIMENTS TO PROGRESS

Reasonable minds may differ about the substantive issue of whether and to what extent principles of justice allow users of marijuana to be punished. Unfortunately, debate about this difficult topic is obscured by confusion

about some basic conceptual issues that I believe can be resolved fairly easily. Any number of examples could be selected to illustrate these confusions. In this section, however, I will confine myself to a single example: the treatment of decriminalization in Robert J. MacCoun and Peter Reuter's (2001) influential *Drug War Heresies*. I focus on this book for two reasons. First, no one can doubt the expertise of the authors; their credentials as knowledgeable drug policy reformers are beyond dispute. Second, the tone of this book is overwhelmingly sympathetic to the general conclusion I defend here. I am not merely concerned to correct what I take to be errors in an otherwise excellent book. My point is that if astute commentators like MacCoun and Reuter needlessly cloud the basic conceptual issues to be decided, it is easy to understand how less sophisticated thinkers could do so as well.

MacCoun and Reuter make two important mistakes that obfuscate the very reforms they espouse. First, they unnecessarily muddy the meaning of decriminalization. The concept of decriminalization itself is straightforward. Anyone who proposes that the use of a given drug should be *criminalized* should be understood to hold that the use (and possession for use) of that drug should be a criminal offense.[1] Conversely, *decriminalization* means simply that the use (and possession for use) of that drug should *not* be a criminal offense. *Criminal* offenses, by definition, subject those who perpetrate them to state punishment. State punishment may be imposed only for conduct that has been criminalized. Thus someone who favors decriminalization of marijuana means that no one should be punished simply for using (or possessing for use) marijuana.

MacCoun and Reuter mention "two generic alternatives" to what they describe as the "contemporary American prohibition" (that is, the criminalization) of illicit drugs like marijuana. The first of these is of interest here. They write:

> For the purposes of this chapter, *depenalization* (often confusingly called decriminalization) refers to a substantial reduction of penalties for possession of modest quantities of prohibited psychotropic drugs (e.g., civil monetary fines). In this regime, the sale and manufacture of these drugs remains illegal and that prohibition is aggressively prosecuted at current levels. (p. 74)

This definition is misleading. If those who defend marijuana decriminalization (or depenalization) should be construed to favor "substantial reductions" in the "penalties" for possession of "modest quantities" of marijuana, it is almost impossible to find a responsible commentator who opposes it. Thinkers on all points along the political spectrum concur that punishments for marijuana offenses are far too severe and should be reduced dramatically. In reality, persons who defend marijuana decriminalization believe that criminal punishments should not merely be *reduced*, but *eliminated* altogether.

In fairness to MacCoun and Reuter, criminal law scholars are hardly unanimous in deciding which kinds of state sanctions are modes of punishment. No one denies that confinement to a jail or prison is a type of punishment. Clearly, however, persons can be punished without being imprisoned; incarceration is not the only mode of punishment known to the criminal law in the United States. The treatment regimes mandated by drug courts, for example, are best categorized as a type of punishment. Apparently, Mac-Coun and Reuter believe otherwise; how else might we explain their identification of decriminalization with depenalization? Admittedly, the status of many other kinds of state sanctions is unclear. Consider, for example, the tickets that are issued to drivers who commit moving violations. Typically, these tickets result in small monetary fines. Are these fines a mode of punishment? Criminal justice experts disagree. Suppose, then, that a reformer maintains that users of marijuana should be treated similarly, and issued tickets that are paid by modest fines. If he believes that these fines are a type of punishment, he should not be interpreted to endorse marijuana decriminalization as I have defined it here. But if he believes that these fines are not a type of punishment, he may be understood to support decriminalization. I make no attempt to resolve the debate about whether modest monetary fines should or should not be construed as a type of punishment.[2] I simply identify the implications of that debate for the meaning of marijuana decriminalization.

MacCoun and Reuter make a second mistake that is probably even more significant. We cannot hope to make progress in policy debates unless we begin by asking the right question. In the present context, that question is: Should the use of marijuana be criminalized? If I am correct to identify criminal offenses with conduct that subjects perpetrators to state punishment, a somewhat different version of this same question is: Should persons be punished simply for using marijuana? This is the fundamental question that must be addressed in any attempt to evaluate the justice or injustice of our marijuana policy. This fundamental question asks for a *rationale* for our policy. The search for a rationale involves an attempt to find moral reasons that *justify* our present policy of punishing marijuana users.

The question I have posed is fundamental for a simple reason. We should not punish people simply because we are unable to demonstrate the benefits of *not* punishing them. Any policy that resorts to punishment requires a justification. We should not assume that what we are doing is right unless someone can prove that it is wrong; we must always be prepared to show why what we are doing is right. If neither side in a debate produces good reasons, or if both provide reasons that are equally persuasive, victory should not be awarded to the side that supports the status quo—when that status quo involves criminalization. Punishment is the most terrible thing that a state can do to its citizens; it is the most powerful weapon in the government's arsenal.

The criminal sanction should not be invoked casually; it always requires a compelling defense. Those who favor punishments for marijuana users must explain why they think this policy is fair and just. The fundamental question, then, is not whether we have good reasons *not* to punish marijuana users—so that marijuana use should be *de*criminalized—but whether we have good reason to (continue to) *criminalize* the use of marijuana.

My point is not simply that the burden of proof on this issue has been placed on the wrong side—although that is certainly true. Nor is my point that we should not allow one side in the debate to gain an unfair rhetorical advantage over the other—although that is certainly true as well. My point is that the debate cannot proceed sensibly unless it begins with a reason in favor of punishing people who use marijuana. How can we possibly decide whether we should change our policy unless we know why we have that policy in the first place? Unless a reason to punish marijuana users has been put on the table, an opponent of the status quo has nothing to which he can respond. In other words, an effective argument for decriminalization must rebut an argument for criminalization. Without an argument for criminalization, there is nothing to rebut.

MacCoun and Reuter disagree with my formulation of the fundamental question that needs to be resolved in the decriminalization controversy. They discuss at length the standards by which alternative approaches to drug policy should be evaluated. Among the standards they reject is what they call the "philosophical standard." They write:

> If a society were starting from scratch, the burden might well be placed on those who would prohibit drug use. . . . If this standard were applied today, the current laws would be changed unless prohibiters could make a convincing case for the current laws. Though some reformers write as if this were the applicable standard, they are mostly talking to themselves, since it is [*sic*] seems unlikely that the American public is ready to accept this standard. (p. 324)

Since I endorse what they call the "philosophical standard," I believe that MacCoun and Reuter's grounds for rejecting it merit a reply. In the first place, I fail to see why these authors believe that the principles of justice that should be used to evaluate our drug policy should differ depending on whether or not we are starting our society "from scratch." In fact, no existing societies were begun from scratch. We can certainly imagine sailors shipwrecked on a desert island or astronauts colonizing the moon who might be said to create an entirely new social order. For the most part, however, these scenarios are the stuff of fiction. In the real world, we have no option but to evaluate policy options in the societies we already have. Why should those who support these policies be spared the need to defend them? MacCoun and Reuter seemingly suppose that the status quo needs no defense. But this

supposition cannot be correct—especially when the status quo involves punishment. Today, tomorrow, next week and next month, Americans will be punished simply for using marijuana. What could possibly justify their punishments? We should not answer, with MacCoun and Reuter, that those who ask such questions are "merely talking to themselves." Instead, those who ask such questions are talking to *each* of us—to each of us who cares about whether or not our social polices are just.

In the final sentence from the above quotation, MacCoun and Reuter (2001) suggest that the fundamental question I have posed is the wrong question to ask in evaluating our marijuana policy because "it seems unlikely that the American public is ready to accept [it]" (p. 324). I am skeptical that MacCoun and Reuter are correct about what "the American public" is ready to accept. I find it hard to believe that the American public really believes that justice allows our state to subject us to punishment without having good reasons to do so. But this is not my main objection to MacCoun and Reuters's grounds for rejecting (what they call) the philosophical standard. In deciding what criteria to apply in evaluating competing ideas about marijuana policy, the relevant test is not what the public *does* accept, but what the public *should* accept. In other words, the test is moral rather than empirical. The basic moral claim I make in this chapter is that no one should be punished in the absence of powerful reasons that explain why his punishment is deserved. I would not be persuaded to retract my basic claim because I was assured that the public did not accept it. Instead, I would redouble my efforts to convince those who disagree with me. If all proposals about how to reform our policies could be resolved by determining whether members of the public already accept them, there would be no point in trying to persuade anyone to change his mind.

Thus far, I have argued that the fundamental question that must be answered by those who favor criminalization is why the state is justified in punishing persons who use marijuana. Clearly, reasonable minds differ about how to answer this fundamental question. How, then, should we proceed? Progress requires a partial *theory of criminalization*: a set of principles to identify the conditions under which persons may be punished for what they do.[3] Obviously, I cannot hope to provide the details of such a theory here (see Husak, 2002). Still, I will try to say enough to defend my conclusion in favor of marijuana decriminalization.

A PRIMER ON DESERT THEORY

Sound principles of sentencing theory must justify whatever sanctions are ultimately imposed on marijuana offenders. Our criminal justice system should treat persons as they deserve, and not merely use them as a means to

serve the state's utilitarian ends. But what *do* marijuana users deserve? Attempts to answer this question require a principled application of desert theory to marijuana offenses. Producing such a theory requires the patience to wrestle with philosophical issues. In my experience, most drug law reformers are unwilling to explore these topics in sufficient depth. Remarkably, few of them understand much about the basic principles of criminal theory, and few criminal theorists know much about drug policy. The failure to integrate criminal theory with drug policy is monumental (See Husak, 1998). Marijuana reformers miss a golden opportunity by not recognizing that punishment and sentencing theory help to support decriminalization. In fact, their lack of attention to punishment and sentencing theory is barely excusable. We cannot possibly determine whether and to what extent users of marijuana deserve punishment without committing ourselves to some general propositions about whether and under what circumstances anyone deserves punishment for anything. This topic plunges us directly into the philosophy of punishment and sentencing.

Contrary to the beliefs and expectations of many scholars who do not specialize in punishment and sentencing theory, *retributivism*—or what is better called *just deserts theory*—is firmly ensconced as the rationale of whether and to what extent persons should be punished for what they do (see Dolinko, 1992). The centrality of desert theory is not confined to academic philosophers. The new *Sentencing Project Report* of the American Law Institute properly enshrines desert as the dominant rationale for punishment and sentencing (Model Penal Code, 2003). Admittedly, desert theory has its critics (see Christopher, 2002), although I make no effort to respond to them here. I will assume that the proper question to address in attempts to justify the sentencing of marijuana users is whether and to what extent their punishments are deserved. If we cannot show their punishments to be deserved, we should endorse the decriminalization of marijuana.

Drug offenses pose both theoretical and practical challenges to desert theory. Admittedly, a few other crimes—such as blackmail—raise comparable conceptual puzzles (see Symposium Blackmail, 1993). But a theory can survive as long as problems of application are relatively infrequent and unimportant. Drug offenses, however, pose a unique challenge to desert theory. Marijuana offenses are so ubiquitous that they might be said to be driving the entire criminal justice system. Hence any problems in applying desert theory to drug offenses cannot simply be dismissed as an insignificant anomaly. If these problems turn out to be sufficiently great, unbiased commentators should be urged to rethink the justifiability of drug offenses—or the viability of desert theory itself.

Desert theory, as explicated here, addresses both *whether* punishment is justified and *how much* punishment is justified. These two questions are intimately related because penal sanctions are stigmatizing and impose blame.

Punishment both expresses (as a matter of fact) and ought to express (as a normative matter) censure and disapprobation. If punishments convey blame, the quantum of punishment imposed should bear a reasonable relation to the degree to which conduct is blameworthy. Thus the cornerstone of desert theory is the *principle of proportionality*: The severity of punishment should be a function of the seriousness of the crime. The principle of proportionality is an almost inviolable requirement of justice that should not be overridden in the absence of a powerful rationale.[4]

Proportionality has two distinct dimensions. In what follows, I have almost nothing to say about the first dimension: *cardinal* proportionality. I assume that answers to the question of how much punishment a given offense—larceny, rape, or arson, for example—deserves cannot be given a meaningful answer in the abstract.[5] Any scale of penalties must be anchored, and the anchoring process depends on a variety of complex factors. I will have a bit more to say about the second dimension: *ordinal* proportionality, or how offenses should be scaled relative to one another. The expressive, censuring aspect of punishment provides the theoretical rationale for judgments about the *rank-ordering* of offenses. If one crime is more serious than another, it should be punished more severely. A less serious crime may not be punished with greater severity than a more serious crime without violating the principle of ordinal proportionality.

In order to decide whether one offense is more or less serious than another, criteria to gauge the relative seriousness of various crimes are required. Without these criteria, desert theory cannot be applied to specific cases. In other words, the severity of the punishment can be made proportionate to the seriousness of the crime only if degrees of seriousness can be distinguished. It is easy to sympathize with the vague and general proposition that the severity of punishment must be a function of the seriousness of the crime. It is much more difficult, of course, to apply this abstract proposition to particular cases in the real world. Most commentators agree that the seriousness of crime is a function of two variables: *harm* and *culpability*. Applications of the principle of proportionality to concrete cases thus necessitate *two* distinct inquiries: the first to measure the relative harmfulness of offenses, the second to assess the relative culpability of the persons who commit them.

Begin with the former variable: harm. Before the principle of proportionality can be applied to a given offense, one first must identify the harm this offense is designed to prevent. Usually, this determination is easy. No theorist is needed to tell us which harms are caused by most offenses. Theft violates our interests in economic security; battery violates our interests in physical well-being; false imprisonment violates our interests in liberty.[6] To be sure, theorists continue to debate the exact nature of the interests that are violated by a handful of crimes.[7] Typically, however, the more difficult issue is

not to identify the nature of the harm that an offense is designed to prevent, but to assess whether one such harm is greater or lesser than another. To rank-order different offenses, we need to decide whether a violation of our interest in economic security, for example, is greater or lesser than a violation of our interest in liberty.

In collaboration with Nils Jareborg, Andrew von Hirsch has adopted and refined a commonsense approach to this problem. They employ what they describe as a *living-standard* analysis to apply the principle of ordinal proportionality and gauge the relative harmfulness of particular crimes. Their basic insight is that "victimizing harms are to be ranked in gravity according to how much they typically would reduce a person's standard of living" (von Hirsch & Jareborg, 1991). The latter term is used broadly, to include both economic and noneconomic interests. Living-standard analysis does not focus on actual life quality or goal achievement, but on the means or capabilities for achieving a certain quality of life. The importance of the various interests violated by different crimes is placed on a common scale by assessing their typical effect on a person's living standard. Thus mayhem is more harmful than burglary, for example, because it causes more harm to the overall quality of the victim's life.

A few aspects of this analysis will prove especially important for present purposes. It is crucial to recognize that judgments about the seriousness of crime involve the harmfulness of act *types* rather than of particular acts (or act *tokens*). Some particular acts of larceny (for example) cause enormous amounts of harm; others cause little or none. How should our theories accommodate this obvious fact? Von Hirsch and Jareborg plausibly respond that crimes should be ranked according to their *typical* effect. The central idea is that each offense involves a *standard* (or paradigm) case. No problem arises if Smith's particular act of burglary is sufficiently similar to the standard case. But if his act deviates from the standard case to a significant degree, principles of aggravation or mitigation may be applied at sentencing to increase or decrease the severity of his punishment. I see little alternative but to construct these standard cases statistically; the harmfulness of a standard case of theft, for example, cannot be identified without some presuppositions about the extent of economic loss (and violations of other possible interests) caused by the statistically average theft. Since these standard cases are derived from statistical averages, theorists should be prepared to adjust their preconceptions about the harmfulness of given offenses as new empirical data become available.

What of culpability or *mens rea*, the second component in an analysis of the seriousness of crime? Until someone develops a better theory, the celebrated and influential culpability structure of the Model Penal Code should be employed here. The code assigns progressively greater culpability to persons who commit a given criminal act negligently, recklessly, knowingly, or

purposely (see Husak, 1996). Because persons who kill (for example) know-ingly are more culpable than persons who kill recklessly, the criminal law in all states distinguishes murder from manslaughter, and punishes the former crime more severely than the latter. Negligent killings—in which the defen-dant is not consciously aware that his act creates a substantial and unjustifi-able risk of death, even though a reasonable person in his circumstances would have been aware of the risk—is not even criminalized in many juris-dictions. No one holds that negligent acts are as culpable as acts perpetrated purposely or knowingly. And even though many commentators have come to resign themselves to the inevitability of *strict liability*—crimes that require no *mens rea* whatever—they are unwilling to regard these crimes as serious (see Simester, 2005).

How do these two variables combine to provide a coherent account of the seriousness of crime? Is an offense with a high degree of culpability but a small amount of harm more or less serious than an offense with a low de-gree of culpability but a large amount of harm? Perhaps there is no single continuum along which both of these variables can be placed. But this diffi-culty, however formidable for other purposes, need not detain us here. If a given crime should be regarded as serious, it must involve both a great deal of culpability *and* a large quantum of harm. The offense of possessing mari-juana, I will argue, contains almost no harm and little if any culpability, and thus should not be regarded as serious. In fact, its degree of seriousness is so minuscule that I will conclude that it should not be criminalized at all.

THE HARM OF MARIJUANA POSSESSION

Since the seriousness of crime is a function of harm and culpability, each must be examined separately in a systematic attempt to assess whether and to what extent marijuana offenders should be punished. In this section, I in-vestigate the harmfulness of marijuana possession; I turn to a consideration of culpability in the next section. It should be noted that possession is the most basic in the entire hierarchy of drug crimes. It is also the most fre-quently enforced; in an era of "zero tolerance" for drug users, marijuana ar-rests account for 45% of all drug arrests. Of those prosecuted for marijuana offenses, 88% are charged with simple possession (see Federal Bureau of In-vestigation, 2003). Possession generally, and marijuana possession in particu-lar, is still "the stuff of criminal justice work" (Collison, 1994). I see no prospects for gauging the seriousness of other drug offenses without under-standing the harm in marijuana possession.

Applications of the principle of proportionality require, first, that the harm of a given offense be identified. As I have indicated, this determina-tion is usually easy. In the vast majority of cases, the interests violated by a

particular offense are readily described. In the present context, however, specifying the harm to be prevented is not so straightforward. No consensus exists about the nature of the harm(s) the offense of marijuana possession is designed to prevent. Nor is there an authoritative source in which the "official" rationale for these prohibitions can be found. In order not to beg questions, I will refer to the harm(s) that the offense of marijuana possession is designed to prevent as *harm X*. Surprisingly, advances in gauging the harmfulness of marijuana possession are possible even though the exact nature of X remains unspecified. In what follows, I make no attempt to canvass the various opinions that commentators have offered about the identity of harm X.[8] Thus my inquiry is not empirical in the sense familiar to most social scientists. I do not present data to show, for example, how the memory capacity of marijuana users compares with that of abstainers. Instead, my analysis is philosophical. For purposes of applying the principle of proportionality, we can make considerable progress in assessing the harm of marijuana possession without depending on contested empirical findings.

Even without mentioning any of the possible candidates that might substitute for X, the analysis is immediately complicated by a factor that threatens to undermine the whole project. Recall that the harm of a given offense is constructed by identifying a standard case. Generalizations about the harm caused by marijuana possession should not be derived from extraordinary situations involving airline pilots, brain surgeons, 10-year-old children, pregnant women, or the like. The criminal law should enact (and, for the most part *has* enacted) narrower statutes to proscribe the harms caused by substances in these atypical situations. But what case is standard? The crux of the problem is that the *range* of harms caused by particular instances of marijuana possession is even broader than that for most other crimes. Recall that the harm caused by particular acts of theft spans from trivial to astronomical. But *all* thefts presumably cause *some* harm; each nonconsensual taking violates property rights and results in economic loss. By contrast, many (and certainly *most*) instances of marijuana possession cause no harm at all. In other words, a person can possess marijuana without violating the interests of anyone, including himself.

Thus it is crucial to recognize that the crime of marijuana possession is a special and fairly unusual type of offense—generally called an *inchoate* offense.[9] The most familiar examples of inchoate offenses known to the criminal law are attempt, solicitation, and conspiracy. These crimes are inchoate because not all of their instances result in harm; many (and perhaps most) attempts, acts of solicitation, or conspiracies actually cause no harm to anyone. Nonetheless, no responsible commentator demands that these offenses be repealed. These offenses are justifiable because they prevent culpable defendants from causing a substantial and unjustifiable *risk* of harm. The particular harm risked by these offenses is called the *completed harm*. In what

follows, I propose to construe the offense of marijuana possession as an instance of an inchoate offense—like the offenses of attempt, solicitation, and conspiracy. Given instances of marijuana possession may be (and typically are) harmless, but they are prohibited because they are alleged to create a substantial and unjustifiable risk of a complete harm.

A two-step process is required to measure the harmfulness of an inchoate offense. The first is to apply a living-standard analysis of the completed harm; the second is to make an appropriate discount for the degree of risk created by the inchoate offense (von Hirsch & Jareborg, 1991). Unfortunately, neither determination will prove straightforward. The first of these determinations has already been mentioned. What exactly is the completed harm of marijuana possession? For virtually any other inchoate offense, the answer is clear. A conspiracy to rob a bank, for example, is prohibited because it increases the probability of the completed harm of bank robbery. In the case of marijuana possession, however, a great deal of speculation and guesswork is needed to identify the interests that are violated when the risk materializes. It is crucial to recognize that the completed harm prevented by the inchoate offense of marijuana possession cannot be marijuana *use*. Even if it were criminalized (which it typically is not), marijuana *use* is no more a completed harm than is marijuana possession. That is, marijuana use *itself* is (or would be) an inchoate offense; it is proscribed because it increases the risk of some *further* harms. Again, we are left to puzzle about the nature of these further harms, that is, about the completed harm(s) X that the inchoate offense of marijuana possession is designed to prevent.

Additional problems plague our efforts to assess the harmfulness of inchoate offenses. Virtually all commentators agree in the need to *discount* the harm of these offenses. Without an appropriate discount, the seriousness of an inchoate offense (such as attempted murder) would be equivalent to the seriousness of the offense that causes the completed harm (murder). No one should equate the seriousness of those cases of attempted murder that do not result in death with the seriousness of murder itself. Similarly, no one should equate the seriousness of marijuana possession (or of marijuana use) with the seriousness of whatever offense causes the completed harm X. Thus the appropriate discount must be applied; but what discount is appropriate? Von Hirsch and Jareborg propose that the seriousness of crimes that "only create a threat or risk to a given interest" should be discounted to the "degree to which [the harm] is risked" (1991, p. 30). They do not propose a formula to calculate the extent of this discount, preferring to leave the matter to "further reflection" (p. 31). The simplest means—to multiply the seriousness of the harm by the probability of its occurrence—is likely to provide too low a measure of the seriousness of many inchoate offenses. Paul Robinson's (1987) suggestions are more promising. He proposes the following "general adjustment" of the penalty structure for offenses that risk harm.

Offenders who risk harm should be punished .3 to .5 times as severely as persons who cause the harm itself; if the risk is minor, offenders should be punished only .2 to .4 times as severely. When is a risk "minor"? According to Robinson, harm is *risked* when it is at least as likely as not to occur; minor risks are less likely than risks.

How would the harmfulness of marijuana possession be discounted if these proposals were implemented? Frankly, no one should pretend to know. In the first place, of course, no calculation can be performed in light of the foregoing difficulties in identifying the completed harm X. But the calculation is impossible for an additional reason. Possessory offenses cannot be enumerated or individuated; they are continuing.[10] It makes sense to inquire, for example, how many incidents of criminal solicitation occur each year. But how does one decide how many possessory offenses occur over a given period of time? To be sure, we can estimate how many persons commit possessory offenses annually. But that figure would be misleading for the purpose at hand; a person in possession of marijuana at all times throughout the year creates a greater risk of X than someone who possesses marijuana for only a few minutes. Perhaps the relevant figure is the number of instances of marijuana use. Although I have seen no respectable estimate of this figure, it almost certainly runs into the several billions. Only a tiny percentage of this astronomical number of offenses ever results in harm. Thus any reasonable device to discount the harm of the offense of marijuana possession by the probability of its occurrence yields the conclusion that these offenses are not serious to any measurable degree. Moreover, although the aggregate harm caused by millions of marijuana users committing billions of acts of marijuana consumption *may* be substantial, the harm that may be attributed to any particular user per incidence of consumption is so minuscule that one wonders why it does not fall under the legal principle of *de minimis* (too trivial to prosecute).[11]

Problems in solving the discounting problem have only begun. As I have indicated, commentators have long debated how the seriousness of an inchoate offense relates to the seriousness of the offense that causes the completed harm. However this debate is ultimately resolved, it is unlikely that anyone would ever contend that an inchoate crime could be *more* serious than the crime that causes the completed harm. In other words, the seriousness of the crime that causes the completed harm places an upper limit on the seriousness of the inchoate offense; it cannot be more serious to create a risk that a harm will materialize than to cause that very harm itself. I call this uncontroversial principle the *limits principle*.

Very curious results are produced when the limits principle is applied to the offense of marijuana possession. Perhaps the most plausible candidate for X is the harm to physical or psychological health risked by users of marijuana. Anyone who recommends that marijuana possession should be

decriminalized is bound to be informed of one or more empirical studies that purport to show that users cause various risks to their health. The evidence in favor of these allegations is generally weak (see Earleywine, 2002; Iversen, 2000; Zimmer & Morgan, 1997) but suppose, for the sake of argument, that some of these studies are correct and that marijuana poses risks to physical and/or psychological health. How would this supposition bear on the seriousness of the offense of marijuana possession? According to the limits principle, the upper boundary on the seriousness of this offense is established by the seriousness of the offense of actually causing the completed harm. The obvious problem in applying this principle is that there *is* no general offense of causing physical and/or psychological harm to oneself. Moreover, no one believes that such an offense should be enacted; it would make criminals of each and every living person. Thus applications of the limits principle, when conjoined with the most plausible candidate for harm X, support the conclusion that the offense of marijuana possession is exactly zero.

Unfortunately, attempts to gauge the harmfulness of the offense of marijuana possession stall almost before they begin. Insofar as any conclusions can be drawn from the above inquiry, a standard case of marijuana possession does not seem to be a serious offense at all.

THE CULPABILITY OF MARIJUANA POSSESSION

Whatever the difficulties in assessing the harmfulness of marijuana possession, an analysis of the culpability component seems much more straightforward. In virtually all state jurisdictions,[12] the offense of drug possession is defined to require the *mens rea* of knowledge (United States Code Service [USCS], 2005). The explicit requirement of knowledge for this offense is redundant, since possession itself (in the criminal law) is defined to involve knowledge.[13] As a consequence, the level of culpability of persons who possess marijuana is high relative to that of many other offenders; the majority of offenses can be committed with mere recklessness—a lesser amount of culpability on any hierarchy of culpable states. Thus, relative to most other offenses, marijuana possession involves a sufficient degree of culpability to qualify as serious.

Admittedly, not all drug offenses (including those involving marijuana) require knowledge. Remarkably, the particular drug offense regarded as the most serious under positive law—the strict liability for drug-related death statute—requires no culpability at all (New Jersey Statutes Annotated, 2004). In New Jersey, a defendant can be liable for a homicide of the first degree (comparable to murder) even though he was not even negligent with respect to the death that occurs. In other words, the defendant may be liable despite the fact that a reasonable person in his situation would not have

believed that the substance he distributed would cause death. How can an offense with such a severe punishment require no culpability whatever?[14] Perhaps this particular crime can be dismissed as an anomaly in an overall statutory scheme that otherwise requires a high degree of culpability for drug offenders. After all, this offense is rarely enforced. In any event, it is noteworthy that the drug offense punished *least* severely—simple marijuana possession—requires a high degree of culpability. The analysis seems simple.

Or is it? On closer inspection, the culpability of persons convicted of drug possession is less clear than appearances would suggest. In this section, I will describe a few fairly small reasons—and one very large reason—to be skeptical that persons who possess marijuana are especially culpable. Skepticism about the culpability of marijuana offenders emerges by examining the fate of persons charged with possession who *lack* the *mens rea* of knowledge. Most such cases involve *mistakes*. The practical significance of defining possessory offenses to require knowledge is to acquit defendants who are mistaken about the nature of what they possess. Of course, many such persons *are* acquitted. A defendant who is sent a package, wholly unaware of its contents, cannot be held liable for possession if the package contains an illicit drug. In fact, however, the substantive criminal law is far less generous to defendants who lack such knowledge than one might suppose.

In the first place, the very definition of knowledge is altered to allow persons who lack actual knowledge to be convicted of drug possession. Ordinarily, knowledge is defined to mean "practical certainty" (Model Penal Code, 1985a). Applications of this definition preclude conviction of a defendant who is not practically certain that he possesses an illicit drug. In many circumstances, however, practical certainty that the defendant possesses a drug is not needed. These circumstances are called "willful ignorance" (or "willful blindness"). Consider those defendants frequently called "mules." Suppose a person is paid to transport a container across a border and does not inquire about its contents. These individuals are not really *mistaken* about whether they are in illegal possession; more precisely, many have no belief one way or the other. Mules are routinely convicted of drug possession, despite their lack of actual knowledge. In such cases, the definition of knowledge is revised to mean "more likely than not" (Model Penal Code, 1985a). Many commentators have been critical of the use of this definition in cases of willful ignorance, alleging that it is virtually indistinguishable from recklessness, a lower culpable state (Husak & Callender, 1994). Moreover, much of the judicial resistance to harsh punishments for marijuana possession has been voiced in the context of sentencing mules.

Even *actual* mistakes are irrelevant for a number of crimes involving marijuana. Most states, for example, contain a separate and more serious offense for defendants who possess illicit drugs like marijuana in proximity to a school zone (New Jersey Statutes Annotated, 2004). Even a reasonable

mistake of fact about the existence of the school zone or its proximity to the place where the defendant is arrested is not a defense to the charge (see *State v. Ogar*, 1989). In addition, most states contain a separate and more serious offense for defendants who distribute drugs to minors or employ minors in a drug distribution scheme (New Jersey Statutes Annotated, 2004). The mere act of passing a joint may qualify as distribution (see *State v. Roach*, 1987). Even a reasonable mistake of fact about the age of the person to whom drugs are distributed, or the age of the person who is employed in the drug distribution scheme, is not a defense.

But my skepticism about the culpability of drug offenders is not derived solely from cases of mistake. The supposition that drug offenses require a high degree of culpability is misleading for a more fundamental reason. As I have indicated, the crime of marijuana possession is best construed as an inchoate offense.[15] That is, possession per se is not the completed harm this offense is designed to prevent. Instead, the offense of marijuana possession is designed to prevent some other harm: the elusive harm X. The basic problem is that a defendant may be liable for the inchoate offense of drug possession even though he has no culpability whatever with respect to this completed harm. Unlike the fairly unusual case in which a defendant is mistaken about what he possesses, a typical person probably *does* lack culpability with respect to harm X. That is, he need not have the slightest idea that his conduct will cause whatever completed harm the offense is designed to prevent. And neither would the hypothetical reasonable person.

Liability for most inchoate offenses typically requires purpose—the highest degree of *mens rea*—with respect to the completed harm X. This result is ensured by either of two devices. Sometimes this result is achieved by explicit legislative enactment: A statute requires doing one act with the intent (or purpose) to do another. Burglary, for example, is defined as a breaking and entering with the intent to commit a felony. As a result of this statutory definition, a very high degree of culpability—intention—is required with respect to the completed harm. Persons who lack this degree of culpability with respect to the completed harm X are not liable for the offense. On other occasions, this result is achieved by judicial interpretation. The most well known inchoate offenses—attempt, solicitation, and conspiracy—are all construed to require knowledge or purpose with respect to the completed harm. Thus a defendant is not guilty of an attempt to kill, for example, unless he performs an act with the intent (or perhaps with knowledge) to cause death (Model Penal Code, 1985b). Each of these devices ensures that defendants are not liable for an inchoate offense unless they act with a very high level of culpability with respect to the completed harm to be prevented.

The offense of marijuana possession, of course, is not interpreted in this way. A defendant is liable for this inchoate offense even though he has no culpability at all with respect to whatever harm X the offense is designed to

prevent. In other words, a defendant is *strictly liable* with respect to the completed harm X. By not identifying the completed harm X or including it in the offense, the state circumvents the two devices that ensure that defendants are highly culpable with respect to the completed harm X. The requirement that defendants knowingly possess marijuana is relatively unimportant, since no culpability for the harm this offense is *really* designed to prevent is needed.

In fact, a defendant may be liable for marijuana possession even though he deliberately tries to *prevent* X. This claim can be supported by reference to many of the plausible candidates that might be substituted for the X. Imagine, for example, that some commentators are correct to suppose that the offense of marijuana possession is designed partly to ensure that workers remain productive (see Wilson, 1990). Imagine that Smith smokes marijuana at night in order to help him sleep so he will be able to work harder the next day. To complete this story, suppose that Smith's strategy actually succeeds in increasing his productivity. Needless to say, he would be liable for marijuana possession, notwithstanding the fact that his criminal act was calculated to prevent, and succeeded in preventing, the occurrence of the completed harm X. A similar point could be made if other examples of possible harms were substituted for X. Smith may take effective steps to prevent his supply of marijuana from falling into the hands of children, for example.

The foregoing considerations reveal that culpability of persons who commit the offense of marijuana possession is not nearly as clear as appearances suggest. We may be impressed by the fact that this offense is defined to require the *mens rea* of knowledge. But this fact is superficial. Perpetrators need have no culpability at all with respect to the completed harm X that the offense of marijuana possession is designed to prevent. Since judgments about the seriousness of crime depend on both harm *and* culpability, I conclude that marijuana possession is not a serious crime.

CONCLUSION

I have described the overwhelming difficulties that arise in attempts to apply desert theory and the principle of proportionality to assess the seriousness of the offense of marijuana possession. These difficulties arise primarily (but not exclusively) because of the obscure nature of the harm that this offense is designed to prevent, and the absence of culpability of marijuana possessors with respect to that harm.

What conclusions should be drawn if the problems in applying the principle of proportionality to the offense of marijuana possession are as formidable as I have suggested? Three alternatives are available. When a general theory cannot be applied to a particular case, either the general theory

is defective, or something is suspicious about the particular case. A third possibility—to simply ignore the discrepancy and proceed as if no problem exists—is disingenuous in light of the sheer number of marijuana offenders punished within our criminal justice system. I will not disguise my own preference from the remaining two options. Like most legal philosophers, I am unwilling to compromise desert and the principle of proportionality in the hope of obtaining utilitarian gains. I will not *argue* for this alternative here. In any event, I do not believe that the difficulties I have identified in applying desert theory to the offense of marijuana possession provide good reasons to reject the theory. A desert theory of punishment and sentencing is far better confirmed than is the judgment that marijuana possession is a serious crime.

Perhaps some of the difficulties I have raised can be overcome. Until that time, however, we are entitled to conclude that the offense of marijuana possession is not at all serious. Its level of seriousness is so minuscule that it should not be a criminal offense at all. We seek a rationale for punishing persons who possess marijuana, and the most defensible position at this time is that no such rationale exists. Marijuana possession, in other words, should be decriminalized. I have supported this conclusion by applying our best theories of the normative foundations of punishment and sentencing. Although my route to this destination is somewhat novel, the conclusion itself is familiar. Many commentators have denounced marijuana prohibitions as ineffective and counterproductive. A few others have protested that drug prohibitions violate our moral rights. These arguments supplement my own, although it is important to note that I have not relied on them. Even if prohibition did not violate our rights and could be made to work without causing greater evils than marijuana possession itself, I conclude that these offenses would be unjustified.

NOTES

1. I take the fundamental question about marijuana criminalization and decriminalization to be about *use,* even though most jurisdictions proscribe *possession* rather than use.

2. Those who believe users of marijuana should be ticketed must explain the *point* of this sanction. Since most theorists (such as MacCoun and Reuter, 2001) concede that severe punishments fail to deter significant amounts of marijuana use, it is almost certain that modest fines would accomplish even less.

3. Even its critics concede the dominance of retributivism as the rationale for punishment and sentencing. See Dolinko (1992).

4. Of course, it is quite another matter to identify the branch of government that should be given the authority to decide whether the demands

of proportionality are satisfied. As a matter of constitutional law, courts have shown enormous deference to legislative judgments that one crime should be punished more severely than another. See *Rummel v. Estelle* (1980).

5. For a recent discussion of the difficulties of proportionality determinations, see Volokh (2004).

6. Here I presuppose that harm is the violation of an interest, so that identifying the interests that are violated by an offense is to identify the harm the offense is designed to prevent. See Feinberg (1984).

7. In particular, theorists remain divided about the harm of rape. See Wertheimer (2003).

8. For specific discussions, see Husak (2002).

9. Alternatively, these offenses are called *anticipatory* or *nonconsummate* (e.g. Husak, 1995)

10. For a discussion of some of the peculiarities of possessory offenses, see Dubber (2005).

11. American Law Institute: Model Penal Code §2.12 (1985).

12. The lone exception is Washington State, which allows an "affirmative defense" of "unwitting possession."

13. American Law Institute: Model Penal Code §2.01(4)(1985).

14. See *New Jersey v. Rodriguez* (1994), in which the constitutionality of the statute was upheld.

15. See the preceding section.

REFERENCES

Christopher, R. L. (2002). Deterring retributivism: The injustice of "just" punishment. *Northwestern University Law Review, 96*, 843–860.

Collison, M. (1994). Drug crime, drug problems, and criminal justice: Sentencing trends and enforcement targets. *Howard Journal of Criminal Justice, 33*, 25–40.

Dolinko, D. (1992) Three mistakes of retributivism *U.C.L.A. Law Review, 39*, 1623–1657.

Dubber, M. (2005). The possession paradigm: The special part and the police model of the criminal process. In R. A. Duff and Stuart Green (Eds.), *Defining crimes: Essays on the special part of the criminal law* (pp. 91–118). New York: Oxford University Press.

Earleywine, M. (2002). Understanding marijuana: A new look at the scientific evidence. Oxford: Oxford University Press.

Federal Bureau of Investigation. (2003). *Crime in the United States 2003*. Retrieved January 16, 2005, from www.fbi.gov/page2/oct04/ucr102504.htm.

Feinberg, J. (1984). *Harm to others*. New York: Oxford University Press.

Husak, D. (1992). *Drugs and rights*. Cambridge: Cambridge University Press.

Husak, D. (1995). The nature and justifiability of nonconsummate offenses. *Arizona Law Review, 37*, 151–195.

Husak, D. (1996). The sequential principle of relative culpability. *Legal Theory, 1*, 457–482.

Husak, D. (1998). Desert, proportionality, and the seriousness of drug offences. In A. Ashworth & M. Wasik (Eds.), *Fundamentals of sentencing theory* (pp. 187–219). Oxford: Clarendon Press.

Husak, D. (2002). *Legalize this!* London: Verso.

Husak, D. (2004). Criminal law theory. In W. A. Edmundson & M. P. Golding (Eds.), *Blackwell guide to the philosophy of law and legal theory* (pp. 107–121). Oxford: Blackwell.

Husak, D., & Callender, C. (1994). Willful ignorance and the equal culpability thesis: A study of the significance of the principle of legality. *Wisconsin Law Review, 29*, 701–754.

Iversen, L. (2000). *The science of marijuana.* New York: Oxford University Press.

MacCoun, R. J., & Reuter, P. (2001). *Drug war heresies: Learning from other vices, times, & places.* Cambridge: Cambridge University Press.

Model Penal Code, American Law Institute. Sentencing Report 129 §1.02(2)(a)(i)-(ii)(April 11, 2003).

Model Penal Code, American Law Institute. §2.12 (1985a).

Model Penal Code, American Law Institute. §2.02(7)(1985b).

Model Penal Code, American Law Institute. §5.01(1)(b) (2004).

New Jersey Statutes Annotated: 2C:35–37 (2004).

New Jersey Statutes Annotated: 2C:35–36 (2004).

New Jersey v. Rodriguez, 645 A.2d 1165 (1994).

Nolan, S. J. (2001). *Reinventing justice: The American drug court movement.* Princeton, NJ: Princeton University Press.

Robinson, P. H. (1987). A sentencing system for the 21st century? *Texas Law Review, 66*, 1–61.

Rummel v. Estelle, 445 U.S. 263 (1980).

Simester, A. (Ed.). (2005). *Appraising strict liability.* Oxford: Oxford University Press.

State v. Ogar, 551 A.2d 1037 (1989).

State v. Roach, 536 A.2d 282 (1987).

Symposium: Blackmail. (1993). *University of Pennsylvania Law Review, 141*, 1567.

United States Code Service. (2005). New York: LexisNexis.

Volokh, E. (2004). Crime severity and constitutional line-drawing. *Virginia Law Review, 90*, 1957–1983.

von Hirsch, A., & Jareborg, N. (1991). Gauging criminal harm: A living-standard analysis. *Oxford Journal of Legal Studies, 11*(1), 1–38.

Wertheimer, A. (2003). *Consent to sexual relations.* Cambridge: Cambridge University Press.

Whitman, J. Q. (2003). *Harsh justice.* Oxford: Oxford University Press.

Wilson, J. Q. (1990). Drugs and crime. In M. Tonry & J. Q. Wilson (Eds.), *Drugs and crime* (pp. 521–545). Chicago: University of Chicago Press.

Zimmer, L., & Morgan, J. P. (1997). *Marijuana myths, marijuana facts.* New York: Lindesmith Center.

11 Judaism and Marijuana

Elliot N. Dorff

This chapter will approach the issue of marijuana use from a religious ethical perspective. Though this chapter is written from a distinctly Jewish perspective, the approach taken here may be helpful to people from other religious backgrounds in thinking through this issue by clarifying the methods entailed when an ethical question is analyzed in light of a religious tradition.

A few questions help explore the import of this viewpoint. What is the role of an ethical perspective in approaching such an issue? Why is it important to be aware of varying religious and secular perspectives on moral matters in the first place? Why, in other words, do morals not come in one universal and eternal set of norms but rather in forms that vary among religions, societies, and times?

The answer is embedded in the very word "religion." The "lig" in that word comes from the Latin root meaning to tie together, the same root from which English derives the word "ligament," which is connective tissue. Religions describe human ties to family, community, the whole human species, the environment, and the transcendent (imaged in the Western religions as God). That is, religions give a broad picture of who human beings are and who they ought to be. Secular philosophies (Western liberalism, Marxism, existentialism, etc.) also provide such perspectives Indeed, what passes for secular ethics in Western countries is rooted in the particular viewpoint of Western liberalism, the product of such people as John Locke and Claude Montesquieu. But although secular theories generally are produced by one

person or a few people, attracting whoever becomes convinced of a particular philosophy, religions from their very origins are more likely to be tied to a *group* that endeavors to live out the religion's vision, using rituals, symbols, liturgy, and songs to remind adherents of that perspective and to induce continued loyalty to it. Furthermore, religious visions include attention to the transcendent element of human experience, whereas secular philosophies usually denigrate, ignore, or deny this element altogether.

The various religions of the world, then, articulate their own particular views of how people are and ought to be. They each suggest a particular pair of eyeglasses, as it were, through which one should look at life. No one can see the world without such lenses, for no one is omniscient. Humans instead must perforce look at the world from their own vantage point—Einstein's Theory of Relativity applied not just to knowledge of objects but also to knowledge of everything else. So, for example, the Jewish, Christian, and Western liberal lenses have much in common, but they also differ in significant ways.[1]

Specific moral norms are rooted in such big pictures. The differences in how the U.S. Supreme Court, Catholic doctrine, and Jewish law understand the status of the fetus, for example, leads to their differing positions on abortion and, in the case of Catholics and Jews, on embryonic stem cell research as well. Similarly, the differing ways in which those three systems of thought perceive the relationship between human beings and nature explain and motivate some of the ways in which they disagree with each other in understanding people's place in life and what they may and should do with modern technology in altering the world.

What are the methods at one's disposal in approaching the issue of marijuana use from an ethical and religious perspective? Every tradition, whether religious or secular, has its own way of addressing questions posed to it. Catholicism, for example, invokes the authority of the magisterium and, ultimately, the pope to decide moral issues, even though moral theology and past decisions of popes and church councils also play a role in shaping current Catholic doctrine. Protestants look to the Bible, personal conscience, and, to some extent, the traditions of their specific denomination to decide moral matters. American secular thought appeals to pragmatism and individual freedom to determine which moral issues should be addressed communally; then, if it is decided that a communal response is appropriate, majority vote is the primary and fundamental method of making decisions, although that is modified by representative government, appointed officials, and constitutional concerns. To address moral questions, Judaism uses a variety of materials together with the methods suitable to them. These include stories, proverbs, theology, and historical experience, but Judaism puts primary emphasis on case-based law.[2]

No matter what method a particular tradition uses, however, it must stretch to address many of the new questions posed by modern medical

technology and by modern medical health care. How traditions do that varies not only from one tradition to another, but even within a particular tradition. Thus some Americans think that legislative action is the best way to address new medical questions; others think that the courts should treat these cases by developing case law sensitive to the intricacies of particular situations; some think that the government should stay out of these affairs altogether, leaving as much as possible to individuals to decide; and still others think that the appropriate method depends on the issue. Even Catholics, who seemingly have a clear, regimented system to decide moral matters, differ among themselves as to the extent to which the Vatican should determine such issues, with some claiming that individual Catholic moral theologians and even the individual Catholic parishioner should have a greater role in formulating Catholic responses to modern issues.[3]

Without a central moral authority like the pope, Congress, or the Supreme Court, Jews differ among themselves even more markedly as to how to gain moral guidance from their tradition. Orthodox Jews look for precedents in established Judaic law, claiming that God provided the answers in that law to even the most contemporary issues if people would only be clever and persistent enough to interpret the law correctly. That does not prevent Orthodox Jewish writers from disagreeing with one another; on the contrary, some of the most vehement disputes occur within Orthodox circles. All of them, however, presume that the right answer, the one God wants people to reach, is contained wholly within the received tradition, if only people apply it rightly.

Conservative Jews also believe that Jewish law should be used to give authoritative directions to moral quandaries, but Conservative ideology asserts that from its very beginning Jewish law was the product of God and human beings, and it must be so today as well. Furthermore, the law appropriately changed over time to fit new circumstances, and it must be open to such changes in current times It is the rabbis of each generation, then, who must be entrusted with interpreting and applying the law to modern circumstances, but they cannot do that mechanically because Jewish law is simply silent about modern issues that did not exist in the past. In stretching Jewish precedents to apply to those issues, then, rabbis must keep in mind past as well as new Jewish understandings of God and what God wants of people as embedded in Jewish law, thought, stories, and proverbs; current historical and economic circumstances relevant to such decisions; and the needs and moral sensitivities of contemporary Jews.

Reform Jews focus on individual autonomy. Thus although rabbis, physicians, and others may and should help individual Jews in making their medical decisions, and although Jews need to know the Jewish tradition in order to make recognizably Jewish decisions, ultimately individuals may and should decide for themselves how they are going to respond to all issues in

their lives. Judaism may influence their decision, but each individual must decide whether it will and, if so, how.[4]

SOME FUNDAMENTAL PRINCIPLES EMBEDDED IN THE JEWISH LENS

To give readers a taste of both the content and the methodologies of Jewish medical ethics that are relevant to Judaism's understanding of marijuana, readers need to be familiar with several core Jewish beliefs that inform the Jewish discussion of all medical issues. In my book on Jewish medical ethics, I describe other central convictions relevant to other aspects of health care,[5] but the following core beliefs will suffice for the purposes in this article:

1. God owns a person's body. The Talmud maintains that there are three partners in the creation of each a human being—mother, father, and God. Unlike parents, however, God owns everything He created, including human bodies.[6] As a result, people have a fiduciary responsibility to God to safeguard their health and life[7] and, conversely, to avoid danger and injury.[8]

This appears to be in sharp contrast to the secular American point of view, which permits me to engage in downright dangerous behavior, refuse all medical treatment, or even commit suicide[9]—although not assist someone in committing suicide.[10] All of this stems from the American presumption that my body is, after all, mine.

This, though, overstates matters, for even on secular American grounds, I must take into account not only the direct, physical effects of my actions on others, but indirect consequences as well. So, for example, American law requires me to wear a seatbelt while driving or riding in a car, presumably because my failure to do so might raise other people's insurance premiums or threaten their physical or economic welfare if we were involved in an accident. For reasons that are less clear, American law also prohibits and punishes the use and, even more, the sale of marijuana, even if the user does not then engage in behavior that might endanger others, such as driving. Thus one cannot simply assert that American law permits me to do with my body anything I wish as long as I do not harm you. Still, people rightfully presume much more authority to determine what they may do with their bodies if they think that they are dealing with their own property rather than God's.

2. Each person is an integrated whole. Though people can certainly think and talk about their various faculties separately, the Jewish tradition insists that human beings are integrated wholes. That is, the body, mind, emotions, and will all interact and affect one another. Thus the Rabbis tell a story in which first the body and then the soul wants to deny responsibility for wrongdoing, but God "throws" the soul into the body and says, "This is how you were created, and this is how you will be judged" (B. *Sanhedrin*

91a–91b).[11] Conversely, the proper path for a person in life is to cultivate both the body and the soul, for focusing on one to the neglect of the other leads one to sin. Thus the Rabbis say: "Study of the Torah is beautiful (commendable) when combined with a gainful occupation, for when a person toils in both, sin is driven out of the mind. Study of Torah without work leads to idleness and ultimately to sin" (M. Avot [*Ethics of the Fathers*] 2:2). Thus health care in general and the effects of marijuana in particular must be considered on multidimensional levels, attending to the whole person and not to his or her body alone.[12]

On the theological level, the body is God's creation as much as the mind, emotions, will, and spirit are. Like all human faculties, the body should be used to live a life of holiness by obeying God's commandments. Thus Maimonides, a famous 12th-century rabbi, physician, and philosopher, says:

> He who regulates his life in accordance with the laws of medicine with the sole motive of maintaining a sound and vigorous physique and begetting children to do his work and labor for his benefit is not following the right course. A man should aim to maintain physical health and vigor in order that his soul may be upright, in a condition to know God . . . Whoever throughout his life follows this course will be continually serving God, even while engaged in business and even during cohabitation, because his purpose in all that he does will be to satisfy his needs so as to have a sound body with which to serve God. Even when he sleeps and seeks repose to calm his mind and rest his body so as not to fall sick and be incapacitated from serving God, his sleep is service to the Almighty. (M.T. *Laws of Ethics* [*Hilkhot De'ot*] 3:3)

3. Medicine is a good thing. Although some biblical passages assert that God governs illness and health,[13] the Rabbis found justification for human beings to engage in medical care based on other passages.[14] Rabbi Joseph Karo (1488–1575), author of the *Shulhan Arukh*, an authoritative code of Jewish law, goes further: He maintains that a physician who fails to try to heal when he can is effectively a murderer (S.A. *Yoreh De'ah* 336:1). Furthermore, Jews may not live in a city with no physician (J. *Kiddushin*; 66d; B. *Sanhedrin* 17b) for then they could not get the expert help they need to fulfill their fiduciary responsibility to God to take care of their bodies. Physicians, in fact, were very much honored in the tradition, and until the last century, when medical education began to take a decade or more of training, many rabbis also served as physicians and engaged in medical research.[15] God ultimately controls illness and health, but the physician is God's agent and partner in the ongoing act of healing: "Just as if one does not weed, fertilize, and plow, the trees will not produce fruit, and if fruit is produced but is not watered or fertilized, it will not live but die, so with regard to the body. Drugs and medicaments are the fertilizer, and the physician is the tiller of the soil."[16]

The talmudic image of human beings as God's partners in creation appears in B. *Shabbat* 10a and 119b. In the first of those passages, it is the judge who judges justly who is called God's partner; in the second, it is anyone who recites Genesis 2:1–3 (about God resting on the seventh day) on Friday night who thereby participates in God's ongoing act of creation. The Talmud in B. *Sanhedrin* 38a specifically wanted the Sadducees *not* to be able to say that angels or any being other than humans participate with God in creation.

4. Individuals are members of a thick, organic community. The Western liberal tradition is based on a strong sense of individual rights—indeed, as Thomas Jefferson said in the American Declaration of Independence, "inalienable rights." Governments are then "instituted among men to protect those rights." To be part of a nation and of smaller groups within their country, people may and do give up some of their rights—rights, for example, to keep all their money if the groups to which they want to belong demand taxes or dues. But on this view, all communities are voluntary. It may be hard to become an American citizen, for example, but as long as one has not committed a felony, an American can renounce his or her citizenship at will.

The Jewish tradition has a much thicker, organic sense of community. Once a person is born to a Jewish woman or converts to Judaism in accordance with Jewish law, he or she is a Jew for life. Jews who convert to another religion lose all their privileges as Jews—they may no longer be married or buried as a Jew, count for a prayer quorum, and so on—but they still have all the duties that Judaism imposes. That is because Judaism understands Jews to be knit together like the organs and tissues of a body, with none of them able to leave the body at will.

Positively, this indissoluble linkage between the individual and the group means that each individual is responsible for every other (M.T. *Laws of Repentance* 3:4. Cf. B. *Rosh Hashanah* 17a) without any specific assumption of that duty by the individual Jew and even against his or her will. Furthermore, virtually everything that one does is, in Judaism's view, everyone else's business. As the Talmud puts it:

> Whoever is able to protest against the wrongdoings of his family and fails to do so is punished for the family's wrongdoings. Whoever is able to protest against the wrongdoings of his fellow citizens and does not do so is punished for the wrongdoings of the people of his city. Whoever is able to protest against the wrongdoings of the world and does not do so is punished for the wrongdoings of the world. (B. *Shabbat* 54b)[17]

At the same time, the communal view of traditional Judaism does not swallow up the individual's identity; it actually enhances it by linking it to the larger reality of the group. Law professor and legal philosopher Milton Konvitz has expressed the resulting viewpoint well:

The traditional Jew is no detached, rugged individual. Nor is his reality, his essence, completely absorbed in some monstrous collectivity, which alone can claim rights and significance. He *is* an individual but one whose essence is determined by the fact that he is a brother, a *fellow Jew* His prayers are, therefore, communal and not private, integrative and not isolative, holistic and not separative. This consciousness does not reduce but rather enhances and accentuates the dignity and power of the individual. Although an integral part of an organic whole, from which he cannot be separated, except at the cost of his moral and spiritual life, let each man say, with Hillel, "If I am here, then everyone is here" (B. *Sukkah* 53a). (1980, pp. 143, 150)[18]

This organic sense of community has two important implications for the use of marijuana. First, the community as a whole has the duty to provide the requisite health care to those addicted to marijuana or other drugs to help them free themselves from their addiction and cope with its consequences. This obligation is part of the larger Jewish duty to provide health care for those who cannot otherwise afford it. It is based on the biblical passages "Do not stand idly by the blood of your brother" (Leviticus 19:16) and "Love your neighbor as yourself " (Leviticus 19:18). The Talmud uses the former verse to establish a positive duty to come to the aid of others: "On what basis do we know that if a man sees his fellow drowning, mauled by beasts, or attacked by robbers, he is bound to save him? From the verse, "Do not stand idly by the blood of your neighbor" (B. *Sanhedrin* 73a). Furthermore, the Talmud and Rabbi Moses ben Nahman (Nahmanides, 1194–1270) argue that "Love your neighbor as yourself " gives an express warrant to try to bring cure even when that involves the infliction of wounds through surgery or other risks to the patient, for everyone would (or should) prefer such risks to certain death. They also argue that the same verse also requires people to spend money to heal others if they lack the expertise.[19] (In the Jewish tradition the biblical command to "love your neighbor as yourself " is understood to require not only the feelings of caring for others but specific behaviors that manifest that attitude, of which the provision of health care is one.)[20] Note that, in contrast, in American law only Wisconsin and Vermont make helping others in distress a positive duty, with failure to do so a misdemeanor punishable by a fine of not more than $100; in fact, until many states recently passed "Good Samaritan laws," a person who unintentionally harmed someone in an attempt to save him or her could be sued.

Second, Judaism's strong sense of community requires that people avoid any behaviors that would impair their contributions to the welfare of the community. As I will discuss in greater detail below, Jewish law allows and even encourages people to take advantage of the joys of life, even if they involve some risk; but ultimately I must ensure that what I do with any part of my being does not preclude my acting responsibly as a member of the community.

5. Jews have a duty to God to fix the world. A Jew's duty to act responsibly is not limited to refraining from harming others; it includes also the obligation to work toward fulfilling the Jewish mission of *tikkun olam*, fixing the world. The Torah, according to the traditional count, includes 613 of God's commandments, and the rabbinic tradition expanded yet further on that long list of obligations. Some of these duties concern worship and rituals, and others require Jews to study and teach the Torah and other sacred texts of the Jewish tradition; but a large percentage of the commandments require Jews to take action to prevent or at least alleviate suffering, or, as the Mishnah puts it, to act "for the sake of fixing the world" (M. *Gittin* 4:2–7, 9; 5:3; 9:4. M. *Eduyot* 1:13). As the Mishnaic tractate *Ethics of the Fathers* asserts: "The world rests on three things—on Torah, on service of God, and on deeds of love (*gemilut hasadim*)" (M. *Avot* [*Ethics of the Fathers*] 1:2)—the last of which is the Hebrew term used in earlier times for what is now called also *tikkun olam*.

This emphasis of classical Judaism continues to this day and characterizes even Jews who are otherwise not very religious in their beliefs or practices. Modern Jews, in fact, often think of *tikkun olam* as *the* core commitment of Judaism. In fact, in a 1988 national poll of American Jews conducted by the *Los Angeles Times* (1988),[21] fully half listed a commitment to social equality as the most important factor in their Jewish identity.

One can only do that, however, if one's mind and body are fully functioning. Those who contract a disease or other disabling condition cannot contribute to this mission fully through no fault of their own, but those who consciously choose to do something they know will impede their ability to function thereby decrease their capacity to carry out their duties in this Jewish task I will discuss below how this affects the use of marijuana.

THE ANALOGIES TO ALCOHOL AND SMOKING

While Jewish discussions of marijuana are only recent, Jewish sources contain considerable material about the status of alcohol. Even though the first instances of the use of alcohol in the Bible—the cases of Noah (Genesis 9:18–29) and Lot (Genesis 19:31–38)—warn of the danger of becoming drunk and engaging in unwanted behavior while in that state, the Jewish tradition, unlike Islam and some forms of Protestant Christianity, permits the use of alcohol. In fact, some Jewish rituals, such as those beginning and ending the Sabbath and the wedding rites, actually require the use of wine (although grape juice may be substituted if legally or medically necessary).[22]

Jews did not restrict the use of wine to sacred occasions. The Rabbis actually recommend it for counteracting depression in line with the observation in the Book of Psalms asserts, "wine gladdens the human heart" (Psalms 104:15).[23] The Talmud suggests drinking wine to overcome mild depression

(B. *Bava Batra* 12b), and it records the custom of drinking wine at a house of mourning, imposing a limit of ten cups lest people get drunk and become unable to mourn the deceased (B. *Ketubbot* 8b, based on *Semahot* 14).[24] If the Rabbis had known of the health benefits that have been recently demonstrated of drinking a glass of wine each day, they would have recommended that practice for its health benefits as well.

Furthermore, the Rabbis did not regard the refusal to drink alcohol as an act of special merit. On the contrary, they saw it as a sin. They based this position on the Torah (Numbers 6:11), which requires a Nazirite, one who vowed for a period of time to abstain from drinking alcohol (among other things), to bring a sin offering after the period had elapsed. Thus the Rabbis even maintain that those who deny themselves the legitimate pleasures that God has provided actually sin, for they spurn and show ingratitude for the goodness of God.[25]

While the Rabbis thus approved and even endorsed drinking in moderation, drunkenness was another matter. They do maintain that on Purim one should get drunk to the point that one cannot distinguish between cursed Haman and blessed Mordecai. That, however, was in the specific context of that community celebration, and later rabbis do their best to soften that requirement (B. *Megillah* 7b).[26] The Rabbis also prescribed drunkenness for those about to be executed, requiring that they be given a potion of wine and a narcotic to induce unconsciousness to avoid a painful death (B. *Sanhedrin* 43a, citing Proverbs 31:6).[27]

In all other areas of life, however, one should avoid drunkenness because it prevents a person from acting responsibly. Isaiah castigates "the drunkards of Ephraim . . . who are overcome by wine" (Isaiah 28:1). Similarly, a midrash maintains that Aaron's sons, Nadav and Avihu, who "brought strange fire before the Lord" and died for that sin, were drunk when they did that, for shortly thereafter God tells Aaron that his remaining sons may not drink "wine and liquor" while in the sanctuary (*Leviticus Rabbah* 12:1 and 20:9, ed. Margoliot, pp. 255, 462–463).[28] The same passage also prohibits drunkenness when the priests were "to instruct authoritatively the people of Israel in all of the laws that the Lord your God has spoken through Moses," and the later tradition applied that to other teachers as well "unless he instructs on a point we can assume is obvious to everyone already" (M.T. *Laws of Coming to the Sanctuary* [*Hilkhot Bi'at ha-Mikdash*] 1:3).[29]

In law, the Rabbis make a distinction between two degrees of drunkenness: the lesser state, in which the drunk person retains some measure of self-awareness and control, and the "drunkenness of Lot," in which all self-control and awareness are lost. In the former state, the Rabbis make the drunk person fully responsible for any civil or criminal liability, but he is exempt from the requirements of formal prayer; in the latter state, the Rabbis exempt the person from all responsibility.[30] They thus recognized the distinction between

voluntary drunkenness, where one retains full culpability both for getting drunk and for what one does while drunk, and true alcoholism, where one has the duty to seek help to overcome the disease but cannot be held responsible for what one does under its influence. They describe Lot as a transgressor (e.g., B. *Horayot* 10b, citing Hosea 14:10) but only because he had failed to take the requisite steps to overcome his alcoholism so that he could function as a responsible member of society. In fact, the one context in which the Talmud seems to approve of total abstention from liquor is with regard to people who need to forswear alcohol in order to circumvent their addiction.[31]

Judaism's concern that drunk people will not be able to exercise responsibility is rooted in its larger concerns about family, community, and God. Drunk people distance themselves from all those parties. Drunkards are, to use the common parlance, "stoned"; they assert, in the famous words of Simon and Garfunkel, "I am a rock; I am an island. A rock feels no pain, and an island never cries." That, though, is self-deception, for all people feel pain and cry. Indeed, the drink is usually a way to soothe the pain that one is not connected to others. Thus the drinking man in Billy Joel's song "Piano Man" drinks "the drink called loneliness." Whether the alcohol is the cause or result of cutting oneself off from one's family, community, and God, the ultimate Jewish problem with drunkenness is that it severs connections with all those parties, whereas fundamental Jewish conviction, as described above, would have one create strong connections with them. Certainly this indicates that the community's approach to drunkenness must address not only the addictive qualities of alcohol for some people but also the underlying loneliness that leads people to drink uncontrollably—and, as I shall discuss, to use marijuana and other drugs.

Judaism's approach to smoking is the other analogy that can shed light on its understanding of the use of marijuana. Though imbibing alcohol has been part of human history for a very long time, mythologically since the days of Noah, Western people have been smoking tobacco only for the last four centuries or so. Originally, rabbis endorsed smoking as just another way that God provided for people to enjoy life. Unlike wine, no Jewish ritual requires smoking, and so Jews could choose not to smoke if they wanted to, just as they may choose among the other legitimate pleasures that life affords; but abstaining from smoking as a mark of piety would have been seen as not that at all but rather as a sin, along the lines of the biblical and rabbinic objections to the Nazirite's abstention from wine. Furthermore, through the beginning of the 20th century, Jews in both Europe and North America were heavily involved in the growing, manufacture, and sale of tobacco products.[32] When the surgeon general's report about the dangers of smoking came out in 1968, however, Jewish involvement in tobacco almost immediately ceased, largely fueled by Judaism's deeply rooted concern for preserving life and health. Conservative, Reform, and some Orthodox rabbis ruled in the 1970s that given the new information, Jews should not smoke.

Even those Orthodox rabbis who claimed that Jewish law could not be stretched to prohibit smoking nevertheless asserted that it was stupid to continue doing so.[33] The opposition to smoking grew even stronger when the evidence of secondhand smoke on bystanders became conclusive and well-known. This history has some important lessons for formulating a Jewish approach to the use of marijuana, to which I now turn.

APPLYING THESE JEWISH TENETS AND ANALOGIES TO THE RECREATIONAL USE OF MARIJUANA

A collection of papers titled *Judaism and Drugs*, published in 1973, reported that a group of Orthodox teenagers had asked three leading Orthodox rabbis at the time if the use of marijuana is permissible according to Jewish law (Landman, 1973). A third-century talmudic principle ordains that in civil matters "the law of the land is the law" (B. *Nedarim* 28a; B. *Gittin* 10b; B. *Bava Kamma* 113a; B. *Bava Batra* 54b–55a),[34] and their question specifically presumed that using marijuana was permissible in state law, for otherwise that principle would prohibit it in Jewish law as well on those extrinsic grounds. The three rabbis they asked—Rabbi Moshe Feinstein of New York, Rabbi Immanuel Jakobovits of London, and Rabbi Aaron Soloveitchik of Chicago—all said that it was prohibited for one or all of three reasons: (a) Marijuana use interferes with the study of the Torah and the performance of the commandments; (b) marijuana use leads to "slavish sensuousness," which is prohibited in Numbers 15:39 ("You shall not stray after your heart and after your eyes, following that for which you are lusting") and which destroys free will;[35] and (c) marijuana use is a violation of Deuteronomy 22:8 ("You shall not place anything dangerous in your house"), which, in rabbinic tradition, is interpreted to be a prohibition of anything likely to be harmful (e.g., B. *Ketubbot* 41b and parallels). "The fact that it is not now harmful to a person," one rabbi declared, "does not preclude the chance that it may one day be" (Landman, 1973, p. 205).

In that same volume, Rabbi Benny Kraut (also Orthodox) wrote, "The fundamental flaw [in these rulings] . . . is that no distinction is made between the 'pothead' and the occasional 'social user'" (pp. 210–211). Based on some evidence at the time, Kraut assumes that moderate use is neither physically nor mentally harmful, and he therefore compares marijuana use to alcohol use, which Judaism allows in moderation but not to the state of drunkenness. His argument, of course, depends on the truth of his assumption, which is a matter of empirical investigation.

In addition, Rabbi David Novak (originally Conservative but now affiliated with liberal Orthodoxy) later added yet a fourth reason to oppose

marijuana use. He specifically distinguishes it from imbibing alcohol on these grounds:

> Alcohol use has a long tradition going back to the very beginning of our history. During that history its use has been both socialized and sanctified. . . . In the case of marijuana, on the other hand, we have no such historical process of socialization and sanctification. There has not yet been the test of history. We do not yet know whether it enhances true community; perhaps it inhibits it. Furthermore, marijuana is more than a substance today. It has become *the symbol* of a whole drug culture, a culture based on the hedonistic imperative, "If it feels good, do it!" Can anything be more antithetical to Judaism, with all of its emphasis on sacrifice and discipline? (1986, p. 260)[36]

Novak thus suggests two arguments in addition to the three above: (d) Human beings do not have a long history of using marijuana, and so they cannot be sure, as they are with alcohol, that it can be used to strengthen and sanctify community even if it can also be abused through overuse; and (e) marijuana has come to symbolize a culture of license, which is antithetical to Judaism's insistence on living within rules designed for the public good and reinforcing piety.

What shall I say about these arguments? I'll begin in reverse order for reasons that will become apparent. Whether (e) marijuana has become a symbol of license over and above its intrinsic nature is, at best, a matter of judgment. Novak is clearly right in asserting that Judaism opposes total licentiousness and that it instead very strongly endorses a culture of commandments that define what a person may and may not do as well as what he or she must do. Why, though, is marijuana more a symbol of a culture of license in North America than are rampant and public sexuality, gross materialism, and overeating to the point of obesity, to name just three other obvious candidates? The use of marijuana for recreational purposes cannot, it seems to me, be evaluated intelligently merely on what Novak takes to be its symbolic value.

Novak is clearly right in asserting (d) that experience with socializing and sanctifying life through the use of marijuana is far shorter than the long history of doing so with alcohol. Still, the peyote decision of the U.S. Supreme Court reminds that Native American cultures have done just that with other drugs for centuries, and so it is not dreaming to imagine that Judaism might do the same thing with marijuana at some future time. In any case, a lack of historical experience with this cannot in and of itself be an argument against it, for if that line of argument is accepted, any and all features of modernity must be rejected.

The more serious arguments, it seems to me, are the first three. If indeed (c) marijuana proves to be dangerous, then it would definitely be prohibited

under Judaism's mandate to take care of one's body as the property of God. If that is the argument, however, one must remember that Judaism does not interdict all dangerous activities, for then it would be impossible to live life. After all, the most dangerous place to be is (statistically) at home and within a mile of it, for that is where you are most likely to be injured simply because you are there so often. But that would mean that you should never go home! Furthermore, Judaism permits even those activities that carry some risk as long as one takes reasonable precautions. Skiing, for example, certainly increases your risk of bodily injury, and yet no rabbinic authority that I know prohibits it. One certainly does need to take lessons, ski only on marked slopes, and follow the other guidelines for safe skiing, but within those bounds a Jew is universally permitted to ski. One may even, as is clear from the above, imbibe alcohol, not only to mark sacred occasions but even for sheer enjoyment, as long as one does so in moderation. Indeed, if Rabbi Bleich's arguments to permit smoking tobacco are to be taken as the basis, even it turns out to be unwise to use marijuana, Jewish law may not forbid it, for, as he quotes Psalms to make his legal point, Judaism legally permits a certain degree of risk and unwise behavior for "the Lord preserves the simple" (1977, p. 349–352).

The crucial aspects of this argument against using marijuana, then, are the degree to which one can use it without risking addiction or seriously compromising one's physical, mental, or emotional health. That is, the element of danger must be evaluated just as it is with alcohol. That is an empirical question that needs to be decided by scientists, not rabbis. It may be the case, as it is with alcohol, that some people may use marijuana safely and others cannot because of a variety of factors that make them especially susceptible to addiction. That is, Kraut is definitely right here: One needs to distinguish occasional use and "potheads" in scientifically determining the level of risk involved in using marijuana. Indeed, if alcohol is any indication, it may even turn out that, as in the case of red wine, science demonstrates that in moderation it is beneficial to use marijuana! My points here, in sum, are that (c1) Judaism does not prohibit any risk whatsoever, and that (c2) whether Jewish law should be interpreted as prohibiting marijuana should be determined by scientific analysis of the levels of risk to, on the one hand, occasional users and, on the others, to addicts.

Similar arguments relate to (b), the argument that using marijuana leads to "slavish sensuousness" that undermines free will and responsibility. If using marijuana does indeed do that, then it clearly violates the Jewish commitment to being people who not only take responsibility for their own behavior, but seriously contribute to fixing the world. These concerns, as described above, run very deep in the Jewish tradition, rooted as they are in the fundamental convictions about who Jews are as human beings and as a human community and who Jews should strive to be. The question, though, is

the factual one: Does recreational use of marijuana inevitably lead to becoming an addict so that one cannot exercise due responsibility for one's actions, let alone help to fix the world? If it does, then it must be prohibited on this ground. If, on the other hand, it is like alcohol, and most people can retain full responsibility for their actions even while imbibing and certainly during the rest of their lives, then marijuana use should be treated in the same way—permitted in moderation but not to excess. The Jewish criterion for judgment, then, is clear; what is necessary is that it be applied to the facts as determined by scientific evidence.

Finally, whether (a) the use of marijuana interferes with studying Torah and obeying its commandments also depends on the degree of use and scientific evidence about its effects. Certainly the same rabbis who make this argument have not prohibited alcohol on this basis, even though drinking alcohol may take time away from study or fulfilling other commandments. Life is simply not lived in a pressure cooker of performing one commandment after another, any more than it should be lived as slavishly committed to work. One needs "down time," including physical, social, aesthetic, and religious recreation, in order to live life fully—and even for the pragmatic purpose of being able to gear up again to take on the responsibilities of God's commandments and of one's own job. On the other hand, it is now known that even occasionally smoking tobacco has serious deleterious effects on the smoker and even on those who breathe in smoke secondhand, and so that, contrary to Rabbi Bleich, must be seen not only as unwise but as prohibited by Jewish law. After all, if smoking kills you and those around you, it clearly interferes with studying Torah and fulfilling the commandments! So again, this factor with regard to using marijuana must be judged by distinguishing moderate use from addiction and by taking seriously what science demonstrates about the effects of recreational use of marijuana on the user and those around the user.

It is important to restate that if government law forbids the use of marijuana, then Jews must abstain from it for that reason alone. The arguments above, however, should guide Jews in determining what they advocate as citizens in shaping, and possibly revising, the law.

APPLYING THESE JEWISH TENETS AND ANALOGIES TO THE MEDICAL USE OF MARIJUANA

The results are very different if one is instead talking about the medical use of marijuana to ease the pain of a dying person. Here the threat of addiction is unwarranted because it makes no difference if the person becomes addicted since he or she is dying of an untreatable disease anyway. A dying

person who is in pain cannot, with or without marijuana, do much toward the goals of studying Torah, fulfilling the other commandments, or fixing the world. At present, such people are given morphine and other drugs to quell their pain, but there is some evidence that marijuana does that at least as effectively and perhaps more so. The question, then, is whether Judaism would countenance such a use of marijuana.

The answer is clearly "yes." Unlike Christianity, in which pain is sometimes seen as a good thing and even theologically salvational, based on the model of Jesus' suffering on the cross, Judaism does not value pain. Retroactively, when trying to explain how God could be just and yet innocent people suffer, the rabbis suggested, among other approaches, that their pain may be "afflictions of love" (*yissurim shel ahavah*) designed by God either to teach the person virtues of patience and faith or to punish the person in this life for his or her small number of sins so as to make the reward in the next life pure and all the greater (e.g., M. *Avot* 2:16; B. *Berakhot* 4a; B. *Eruvin* 19a; B. *Ta'anit* 11a; B. *Kiddushin* 39b; *Genesis Rabbah* 33:1; *Yalkut Ecclesiastes* 978),[37] but that doctrine was never used before the fact to justify withholding pain medication from the suffering. On the contrary, the Talmud records that Rabbi Hiyya bar Abba, Rabbi Yohanon, and Rabbi Eleazar all say that neither their sufferings nor the reward promised in the world to come for enduring them are welcome—that is, they would rather live without both the suffering and the anticipated reward (B. *Berakhot* 5b). Moreover, from its earliest sources, Judaism has both permitted and required people to act as God's agents in bringing healing or, failing that, in reducing pain.

As a result, to the extent that marijuana proves effective as a narcotic that quells pain, Jews should advocate a change in government law to permit its use for this purpose. If science determines that recreational use is inherently dangerous because it inevitably or even usually leads to addiction, then Jews, along with citizens of other faiths, will need to help shape legislation that effectively prohibits recreational use but permits medical use. That may be difficult, but no more difficult, I would suppose, than what people now do with all controlled drugs. If, on the other hand, recreational use of marijuana proves to be no more harmful than occasional imbibing of alcohol, Jews should argue for adjusting secular law in both areas.

"A KINGDOM OF PRIESTS AND A HOLY NATION"

The Torah demands that Jews become "a kingdom of priests and a holy nation."[38] The Jewish tradition uses wine to sanctify holidays and marriages; it does not use marijuana for those purposes. Still, Judaism allows Jews to ingest many things that are not intrinsically holy as part of the effort to fulfill

the responsibility to maintain a healthy body, mind, and soul, and, furthermore, as part of enjoying God's bounty even when not directly related to matters of health. It further demands that one obey God's commandments, take responsibility for one's actions, and work to create a better world. Whether using marijuana recreationally fits into that Jewish description of the nature and purpose of life depends on what its effects turn out to be. If it decreases pain in dying patients, then one not only may, but must, work to make it legally available to them. Thus, in sum, marijuana in and of itself is not inherently bad or good; it must be judged in terms of its effects in creating a kingdom of priests and a holy nation.

NOTES

In the following notes,

M. = Mishnah (edited by Rabbi Judah, president of the Sanhedrin, c. 200 C.E.).
B. = Babylonian Talmud (edited by Ravina and Rav Ashi, c. 500 C.E.)
M.T. = Maimonides' *Mishneh Torah*, completed in 1177 C.E.
S.A. = Joseph Karo's *Shulhan Arukh*, completed in 1563 C.E., with glosses added by Rabbi Moses Isserles to describe when the practices of northern and eastern European (Ashkenazic) Jewry differed from those of Mediterranean (Sephardic) Jewry.

1. For a description of some of the major ways in which these three lenses agree and disagree with each other, see Dorff (2002), chap. 1.
2. For a description of how each of these factors plays a role in making Jewish moral decisions and the advantages and disadvantages of using law for that purpose, see the appendix of Dorff (2003).
3. See Drane (2004).
4. For some sample Jewish methodologies to address modern moral issues, see the articles by Borowitz, Israel, Ellenson, Newman, Dorff, Mackler, and Zoloth-Dorfman in Dorff and Newman (1995), chaps. 7–12, 15.
5. In my book on Jewish medical ethics, I identify and discuss seven such underlying principles; see Dorff (1998), chap 2.
6. See, for example, Deuteronomy 10:14; Psalms 24:1 (Revised Standard Version).
7. Thus, for example, bathing is a commandment, according to Hillel: *Leviticus Rabbah* 34:3. Maimonides includes rules requiring proper care of the body in his code of Jewish law as a positive obligation (not just advice for feeling good or living a long life), parallel to the positive duty to aid the poor: M.T. *Laws of Ethics (De'ot)*, chaps 3–5.
8. B. *Shabbat* 32a; B. *Bava Kamma* 15b, 80a, 91b; M.T. *Laws of Murder* 11:4–5; S.A. *Yoreh De'ah* 116:5 gloss; S.A. *Hoshen Mishpat* 427:8–10. Jewish law views endangering one's health as worse than violating a ritual

prohibition: B. *Hullin* 10a; S.A. *Orah Hayyim* 173:2; S.A. *Yoreh De'ah* 116:5 gloss.

9. One could ask, of course, what the state could do to you after you committed suicide? The truth is, though, that the state could prevent people who commit suicide from passing on their estate to their heirs, a serious consequence. States could even publicly shame you and your family by denying you a proper burial, as Jewish law officially does, although in Jewish law every suicide is ruled as temporarily insane, therefore not responsible for his or her actions, and consequently eligible to be buried according to the usual rites.

10. That suicide is legal in every state but assisting a person to do that legal act is illegal in all states except Oregon is, if I may say so, a rather curious development in American law. The Ninth and Second Circuits declared that assisting a suicide should be permitted as a constitutional right, based either on the liberty clause (the Ninth Circuit) or the equal protection clause (the Second Circuit) of the Fourteenth Amendment; see *Compassion in Dying v. State of Washington* 79. F.3d 790 (9th Cir. 1996) and *Quill v. Vacco* 80 F.3d 716 (2d Cir. 1996). I think that that well articulates the general American understanding of one's rights over one's body as declared by *Roe v. Wade* (1973, a woman's right to an abortion), *Nancy Cruzan* (1990, a person's right to refuse treatment), and other Supreme Court rulings. The U.S. Supreme Court, however, by a vote of 9–0, overruled those circuit court rulings, maintaining that this is not a matter covered by the Constitution but rather falls under the jurisdiction of state laws; *Washington v. Glucksberg* 117 S.Ct. 2258 (1997); *Quill v. Vacco* 117 S.Ct. 2293 (1997).

11. Also in *Mekhilta*, Beshalah, Shirah, chap 2 (Horowitz-Rabin version, 1960, p. 125); *Leviticus Rabbah* 4:5.

12. For an eloquent articulation of this point, see Heschel (1966).

13. God causes illness as punishment for sin: Leviticus 26:14–16; Deuteronomy 28:22, 27, 58–61. God is our healer: Exodus 15:26; Deuteronomy 32:39; Isaiah 19:22; 57:18–19; Jeremiah 30:17; 33:6; Hosea 6:1; Psalms 103:2–3; 107:20; Job 5:18.

14. B. *Bava Kamma* 85a bases the permission to heal on the Torah's requirement that assailants provide for the recovery of their victims in Exodus 21:19. B. *Bava Kamma* 81b maintains that we have not only permission to heal, but the duty to do so based on the duty to return lost objects to their owners in Deuteromony 22:2. B. *Sanhedrin* 73a uses Leviticus 19:16 as the ground for the duty to save lives and also to spend money to hire others to do so when one does not have the expertise.

15. According to Immanuel Jakobovits, quoting the historian Cecil Roth, no less than half of the best known rabbis in the Middle Ages—as well as poets and philosophers—were physicians by profession; see Jakobovits (1975), p. 205, and Roth (1943), p. 192. For more on this, see also Friedenwald (1944) and Nevins (1996).

16. *Midrash Temurrah* as cited in *Otzar Midrashim* (Eisenstein version, 1915). See also B. *Avodah Zarah* 40b, a story in which a rabbi expresses appreciation for foods that can cure. Although circumcision is not justified in the Jewish tradition in medical terms, it is instructive that the Rabbis maintained

that Jewish boys were not born circumcised specifically because God created the world such that it would need human fixing, an idea similar to the one articulated here on behalf of physicians' activity despite God's rule; see *Genesis Rabbah* 11:6; *Pesikta Rabbati* 22:4.

17. Along with Jeremiah (31:29–30) and Ezekiel (18:20–32), this offends the American sense of justice, but that is only because Americans are so used to thinking in individualistic terms.

18. See also Konvitz (1980), chap. 5 generally.

19. B. *Sanhedrin* 84b (on the permission to inflict pain in order to heal), 73a (on the requirement to spend money to heal when we lack the expertise); Nahmanides, *Torat Ha-Adam, Sha'ar Sakkanah*, quoted by Joseph Karo, *Bet Yosef*, Yoreh De'ah 336.

20. Though the tradition applies these verses only to fellow Jews, it nevertheless requires that Jews supply health care to non-Jews as well for the sake of good relations, even though historically non-Jews, far from providing health care for Jews, often persecuted, maimed, and killed them. That context makes this provision of Jewish law nothing less than remarkable. See B. *Gittin* 61a.

21. As reported in the *Los Angeles Times* (2003), a later poll conducted by the American Jewish Committee in 2003 asked 1,008 Jews to choose the quality most important to their Jewish identity; 41% said "being part of the Jewish people," 21% said "commitment to social justice," and only 13% chose "religious observance."

22. Wine required to mark the beginning of the Sabbath in *Kiddush*: B. *Pesahim* 106a. Wine required to end the Sabbath in *Havdallah*: M. *Berakhot* 8:5 and B. *Berakhot* 27b. Wine required at weddings: B. *Ketubbot* 7b. Grape juice permitted as a substitute for wine if necessary: Ginzberg, (1922), esp. pp. 7–12, 69–71.

23. See for the rabbis' recommendation to combat depression with wine.

24. See M.T. *Laws of Mourning* 13:8 and the commentary of Rabbi Joseph Karo to that in his *Kesef Mishnah* in the name of Nahmanides.

25. B. Ta'anit 11a, B. *Nedarim* 10a and parallels in other places in the Talmud.

26. Attempts to soften this requirement abound, however. See, for example, Maimonides, M.T. *Laws of Megillah* 2:15; Rabbi Joseph Karo, *Beit Yosef* on *Tur*, Orah Hayyim 695, end; Rabbi Moses Isserles, S.A. Orah Hayyim 695:2.

27. See also B. *Sanhedrin* 45a and parallels.

28. The relevant passages in the Torah are Leviticus 10:1 and 10:9.

29. See *Sifra*, Shemini, 46d; B. *Eruvin* 64a; B. *Sanhedrin* 42a; B. *Keritut* 13b; S.A. Hoshen Mishpat 7:5. The verse on which this prohibition is based is Leviticus 10:11.

30. B. *Eruvin* 65a. See T. *Terumot* 3:1; M.T. *Laws of Sale* 29:18 and *Laws of Nezirut* 1:12; *Responsa Tashbetz* by Rabbi Simon ben Zemah Duran (1361–1444; Amsterdam, 1739), #23.

31. B. *Nazir* 2a, B. *Sotah* 2a: "Rabbi Judah the President [of the Sanhedrin] said: Why is the section about the Nazarite [Numbers 6:1–21]

juxtaposed [in the Torah] to the section about the wayward wife (*sotah*) [Numbers 5:11–31]? To teach us that he who sees the adulteress in her disgrace will vow as a Nazarite to abstain from wine."

32. For a brief history of this, see Dorff (2004).

33. For the rulings on smoking of Rabbi Seymour Siegel (Conservative), Solomon Freehof (Reform), and J. David Bleich (Orthodox), see Dorff and Rosett (1988). Rabbi Bleich, who ultimately says that smoking is legal but unwise, nevertheless cites some Orthodox rabbis who had prohibited smoking by the time of his ruling (1977), including M. Aberbach. See Aberbach (1969), pp. 49ff.

34. For more on this principle, see Dorff and Rosett (1988), pp. 515–523.

35. See M.T. *Laws of Return (Teshuvah)* 6:3, where Maimonides states that habitual sin leads to the loss of free will.

36. I would like to acknowledge my indebtedness to Novak's article for calling my attention to the discussion of these issues in the Landman (1973) and for some of the thinking and sources that guided my own presentation above of the parallel with the use of alcohol.

37. Among later Jewish philosophers, Saadia is the first to affirm this doctrine (*Book of Opinions and Beliefs*, Books 4 and 5), while Maimonides rejects it (*Guide for the Perplexed*, Part III, chaps. 16–23).

38. Exodus 19:6.

REFERENCES

Aberbach, M. (1969). Smoking and the Halakhah. *Tradition, 10*(3), 49–58.

Bleich, D. J. (1977). Smoking. *Tradition, 16*, 130–133.

Compassion in Dying v. State of Washington, 79, F.3d 790 (9th Cir. 1996).

Cruzan v. Director, Missouri Department of Health, et al, 497 U.S. 261; 110 S. Ct. 2841; 111 L. Ed. 2d 224 (1990).

Dorff, E. N. (1998). *Matters of life and death: A Jewish approach to modern medical ethics*. Philadelphia: Jewish Publication Society.

Dorff, E. N. (2002). *To do the right and the good: A Jewish approach to modern social ethics*. Philadelphia: Jewish Publication Society.

Dorff, E. N. (2003). *Love your neighbor and yourself: A Jewish approach to personal ethics* Philadelphia: Jewish Publication Society.

Dorff, E. N. (2004). Judaism. In J. Goodman (Ed.), *Tobacco in history and culture: An encyclopedia* (pp. 281–285). New York: Charles Scribner's Sons.

Dorff, E. N., & Newman, L. E. (Eds.). (1995). *Contemporary Jewish ethics and morality: A reader*. New York: Oxford University Press.

Dorff, E. N., & Rosett, A. (1988). *A living tree: The roots and growth of Jewish law*. New York: State University of New York Press.

Drane, J. (2004). *More humane medicine: A liberal Catholic bioethics*. Edinboro, PA: Edinboro University Press.

Friedenwald, H. (1944). *The Jews and medicine.* Baltimore: Johns Hopkins University Press.

Ginzberg, L. (1922). *Teshuvah B'dvar Yanot.* New York: Jewish Theological Seminary.

Heschel, A. J. (1966). The patient as person. In A. J. Heschel (Ed.), *The insecurity of freedom: Essays on human existence* (pp. 24–38). Philadelphia: Jewish Publication Society.

Jakobovits, I. (1975). *Jewish medical ethics.* New York: Bloch.

Konvitz, M. R. (1980). *Judaism and the American idea.* New York: Schocken.

Landman, L. (1973). *Judaism and drugs.* New York: Federation of Jewish Philanthropies of New York, Commission on Synagogue Relations.

Nevins, M. (1996). *The Jewish doctor: A narrative history.* Northvale, NJ: Jason Aronson.

Novak, D. (1986). Alcohol and drug use in the perspective of Jewish tradition. In S. J. Levy & S. B. Blume (Eds.), *Addictions in the Jewish community* (pp. 245–263). New York: Commission on Synagogue Relations, Federation of Jewish Philanthropies of New York.

Quill v. Vacco, 80 F.3d 716 (2d Cir. 1996).

Quill v. Vacco, 117 S.Ct. 2293 (1997).

Religion; in brief; 51% of U.S. Jews claim synagogue membership (2003, February 1). *Los Angeles Times*, p. B23.

Roe v. Wade, 410 U.S. 113 (1973).

Roth, C. (1943). *The Jewish contribution to civilization.* Oxford: Oxford University Press.

Serious splits: Jews in U.S. committed to equality. (1988, April 13). *Los Angeles Times*, pp. A1, A14, A15.

Washington v. Glucksberg, 117 S.Ct. 2258 (1997).

12 How in God's Name Do We Reform Our Marijuana Laws?

Charles Thomas

The November 2004 national elections clearly demonstrated the power of religion in American politics. The voter turnout of the religious Right and the public's concerns about "moral values" are largely credited for President George W. Bush's reelection and the strengthening of the Republicans' hold on Congress. In discussing the role of religion in the 2004 elections, some pundits noted the role of religious leaders in the civil rights movement and other liberal causes in the past. The new book *God's Politics* explains that "history is most changed by social movements with a spiritual foundation" (Wallis, 2005, p. 24). Accordingly, it is unlikely that our nation's marijuana policies will be changed substantially without a critical mass of religious support. As executive director of the Interfaith Drug Policy Initiative (IDPI), I have a unique vantage point from which to survey some of the views of the religious wing of the marijuana-law reform movement. Even readers who disagree with IDPI's goals may enjoy the opportunity that this chapter provides to examine and challenge some commonly held assumptions about marijuana, morality, and the law. Those who still disagree are strongly encouraged to publish thoughtful, well-researched critiques.

Serious research into the views of religious individuals and denominations on this topic has been scant, and the breadth and depth of what does exist has been lacking. This chapter and the next are designed to change that by providing substantial polling data and quotes directly from the nation's most important religious bodies, on both sides of the issue and everywhere in between. These hard facts cannot be found in any other single source.

Why is this important? First, as previously mentioned, organized religion is extremely influential in modern American politics.

Second, whether or not people recognize it, the marijuana policy debate is at its core a morality debate. All sociopolitical debates are really about values; there are no issues on which policy makers simply plug all variables into a computer, give them equal weight, and print out an objective analysis of what the policies should be.

Where do people get their values? Clearly religion plays a major role. Accordingly, IDPI recently has embarked upon the arduous task of thoroughly researching the existing drug policy recommendations of more than 40 of the nation's largest and most influential religious denominations and other faith-based groups.

Thus far, this research has revealed that only two denominations, the Unitarian Universalist Association and the humanistic American Ethical Union, have official statements calling for the full legalization of marijuana. However, a few other denominations and religious groups have adopted official positions advocating the removal of criminal penalties for possession of marijuana for personal use. These include the United Methodist Church, Presbyterian Church (USA), Church of the Brethren, Central Conference of American Rabbis, and the National Council of Churches (which represents congregations from 36 Protestant denominations).

Other denominations and religious groups have a wide range of positions on the matter. Some do not oppose the laws prohibiting marijuana possession generally, but they specify an exception for medicinal use (e.g., the Episcopal Church, Progressive National Baptist Convention, and Union for Reform Judaism). Others oppose the use of marijuana but nonetheless are ambiguous or silent on what they believe the government's policies should be. Others explicitly support the total prohibition of marijuana, although some of these groups favor rehabilitation over harsh prison terms. Others do not seem to have any official positions on the topic.

This chapter briefly summarizes the marijuana-related positions that IDPI has located for the following: the 25 largest Christian denominations in the United States (for which information was available); the four major sects (known as "movements") of Judaism; Islam; Buddhism; and several other major Christian and other religious groups and coalitions with significant positions. In the next chapter I provide much more detail, quoting the most salient parts of each religious group's statements, elaborating on their background and rationale, and critiquing some of the positions. In this chapter, the "Views from the Pews" section features findings from several major public opinion polls about marijuana policy, delineated by religious affiliation, frequency of worship attendance, and other relevant variables.

The "Changing Hearts and Minds" section contains two subsections. The first details how current positions supporting some degree of policy reform

are being used to make changes in our nation's marijuana-related policies. The second subsection presents some arguments likely to be persuasive to religious people on the need for more substantial marijuana law reform, such as removing criminal penalties for personal-use possession and allowing legally regulated access.

Finally, the "Call for a Moral Response" section suggests what people of faith and goodwill, including marijuana consumers and policy-reform advocates, can do to change the current situation so that marijuana users and nonusers can ultimately live in peaceful coexistence.

SUMMARY OF RELIGIOUS GROUPS' POSITIONS

Table 12.1 lists the nation's most prominent religions in order of size (Linder, 2004) and identifies each group's positions on several possible policy options, including the following:

> "Legal" means legal access or "legalization," that is, allowing some legal means through which users may obtain marijuana. The specific options vary greatly, from allowing users to grow their own marijuana or allowing regulated sales similar to those for alcohol or tobacco to allowing special clinics to distribute the drug to undercut and dry up the criminal market.
> "Decrim" means decriminalization, that is, removing criminal penalties for possession and use, without necessarily allowing a legal means of access. Although people could no longer be arrested solely for personal-use possession, policy options may include imposing civil fines (similar to traffic tickets) and seizing the marijuana. Of course, it would remain a crime to do something while under the influence that is hurtful or dangerous to others.
> "Med" means medical marijuana, that is, allowing people to obtain and use marijuana to treat a medical condition if advised to do so by a health care professional. Options range from regulating marijuana like any other prescription drug to simply removing criminal penalties for bona fide patients who possess or grow their own medical marijuana.
> "Other" means that the group supports some degree of reform, such as restoring discretion to judges by repealing mandatory minimum sentencing laws, restoring college aid to drug offenders, or advocating treatment instead of incarceration for nonviolent drug-related offenses.

A list of religious groups supporting some of these other options appears in Table 12.2. (See the next chapter for more details on all of these denominations' and other religious groups' marijuana-related positions.)

Table 12.1.

Religion	Policy Recommendation			
	Legal	Decrim	Med	Other

25 Largest Christian Denominations, in Descending Order of Size

Religion	Legal	Decrim	Med	Other
Catholic Church	O	O	P	S
Southern Baptist Convention	O*	?*	N	S*
United Methodist Church	O	S	S	S
Church of God in Christ	N?	N?	N?	N?
Church of Jesus Christ of Latter-day Saints	N*	N*	N	N
Evangelical Lutheran Church in America	*	*	*	S
National Baptist Convention, USA	N?	N?	N?	S
National Baptist Convention of America	N?	N?	N?	S
Presbyterian Church (USA)	O*	S	N*	S
Assemblies of God	N*	N*	P*	N
Lutheran Church—Missouri Synod	N	N	N	N
African Methodist Episcopal Church	?	?	?	?
National Missionary Baptist Convention of America	N?	N?	N?	S
Progressive National Baptist Convention	N	N	S	S
Episcopal Church	N*	P	S	S
Churches of Christ	N	N	N	N
Greek Orthodox Archdiocese of America	O?	O?	?	?
Pentecostal Assemblies of the World	N	N	N	N
American Baptist Churches in the USA	N*	P	N	S
African Methodist Episcopal Zion Church	?	?	?	?
United Church of Christ	*	P	S	S
Baptist Bible Fellowship International	N	N	N	N
Christian Churches and Churches of Christ	?	?	?	?
Jehovah's Witnesses	N	N	N	N
Church of God (Cleveland, TN)	?	?	?	?

Other Christian Groups

Religion	Legal	Decrim	Med	Other
National Council of Churches	N*	S	N	S
National Association of Evangelicals	O	*	N	S
Quaker:				
Friends Committee on National Legislation	N	P*	N	S
American Friends Service Committee	N	S*	N	S
Philadelphia Yearly Meeting	P	S	N	S
Church of the Brethren	?	S*	?	S
Mennonite	?	?	?	S

Judaism

Religion	Legal	Decrim	Med	Other
Union for Reform Judaism	O*	P	S	S
Central Conference of American Rabbis	P	S	S	S
Religious Action Center of Reform Judaism	N?	S	S	S

(*continued*)

Table 12.1. (continued)

Religion	Policy Recommendation			
	Legal	Decrim	Med	Other
United Synagogue of Conservative Judaism	N	N	N	N
Union of Orthodox Jewish Congregations of America	N	N	N	N
Jewish Reconstructionist Federation	N	N	N	N
Islam	O*	?	?	?
Buddhism	N	N	N	*
Other Religious Denominations and Groups				
Unitarian Universalist Association	S	S	S	S
American Ethical Union	S	S	*	*
Progressive Jewish Alliance	S	S	S	S
Episcopal Diocese of New York	S	S	S	S

S = Support
O = Oppose
P = Possible support inferred
N = Neutral/does not specify
? = Don't know or not sure; either the policy could not be located or it is ambiguous
* = Policy does not quite fit this assessment for some reason; see subsequent chapter for elaboration

Though the denominations and other groups listed in Table 12.1 represent the vast majority of faith-community members in the United States, there are hundreds of other religions, denominations, sects, and nondenominational churches, some of which might also have official positions on marijuana policy.

VIEWS FROM THE PEWS

Several major public opinion polls have examined Americans' views about marijuana policy. Some of the polls shed light on the moral underpinnings of these opinions and the differences in beliefs about marijuana use and policy among people with different religious affiliations and frequencies of attendance at organized worship services. The most salient findings are presented in this section, along with some comments on the opportunities and challenges that they present to the marijuana law reform movement.

Long-term trends in beliefs about marijuana policy are best revealed by the National Opinion Research Center's General Social Survey, which asks a random sampling of Americans their opinions on a wide variety of issues

Table 12.2.

The listed denominations and other religious groups have adopted official policy statements on the topics listed below or endorsed IDPI's quoted sign-on statements. (Those with asterisks (*) have adopted their own statements but have not yet signed IDPI's statement.)

Repealing Mandatory Sentencing Laws

"To ensure that an individual's punishment fits the crime, judicial discretion should be restored. Accordingly, we advocate the repeal of mandatory minimum prison sentences."

U.S. Conference of Catholic Bishops*
National Council of Churches
United Methodist Church
Evangelical Lutheran Church in America
National Baptist Convention USA, Inc.*
National Baptist Convention of America, Inc.*
Presbyterian Church (USA)
National Missionary Baptist Convention*
Progressive National Baptist Convention
Episcopal Church
Union for Reform Judaism
American Baptist Churches in the USA*
United Church of Christ
Unitarian Universalist Association
Church of the Brethren Witness
Mennonite Central Committee U.S., Washington Office*
American Friends Service Committee*
Prison Fellowship Ministries*
Church Women United

Restoring College Aid to Drug Offenders

"Because education is a powerful antidote to drug abuse and crime, we advocate the repeal of the amendment to the Higher Education Act denying college aid to students convicted of drug offenses."

National Council of Churches
United Methodist Church (General Board of Church and Society)
Evangelical Lutheran Church in America
Presbyterian Church (USA)
Progressive National Baptist Convention
United Church of Christ
Unitarian Universalist Association
Church of the Brethren Witness
Friends Committee on National Legislation*
Religious Society of Friends (Philadelphia Yearly Meeting)*
Association of Jesuit Colleges and Universities*
Rainbow/PUSH Coalition*
Church Women United
Progressive Jewish Alliance

(*continued*)

Table 12.2. *(continued)*

"Eight Steps"

As of March 1, 2002, the executive offices of several denominations and other religious groups signed a statement by the National Coalition for Effective Drug Strategies, called "Eight Steps to Effectively Controlling Drug Abuse and the Drug Market" (NCEDS, 2002). This statement, subsequently published by IDPI, contains a variety of moderate policy recommendations, such as shifting the federal drug control budget to emphasize treatment rather than law enforcement, allowing access to clean needles, and so on. Most relevant to marijuana policy, the statement urges the federal government to "respect states' rights" on issues such as "medical use of marijuana" and "marijuana decriminalization." Signatories include:

National Council of Churches
Evangelical Lutheran Church in America
Presbyterian Church (USA)
United Church of Christ
Unitarian Universalist Association
Rainbow/PUSH Coalition
Progressive Jewish Alliance
Religious Society of Friends (Philadelphia Yearly Meeting)

roughly every two years. Since 1973, the survey has asked, "Do you think the use of marijuana should be made legal or not?" (NORC, 2002)

In the total sample population, the percentage of "yes" responses increased from 19% in 1973 to a peak of 31% in 1978, then decreased throughout the 1980s to an all-time low of 17% in 1990, then increased again throughout the past 15 years to an all-time high of 36% in 2002 (the last year for which data are available).

The NORC survey further analyzes these responses according to religious affiliation. In 2002, 27% of Protestant respondents said "yes," followed by 33% of Catholics, 50% of Jews, and 66% of those whose religious affiliation is "none." This pattern has been consistent throughout the years, with nonreligious people being the most supportive, followed by Jews, Catholics, and Protestants. Nevertheless, within each religion, "yes" responses in 2002 were higher than the cumulative averages from 1973–2003 (19% of Protestants, 24% of Catholics, 43% of Jews, and 52% of those with no religious affiliation). In short, support is increasing across the board.

The survey also analyzed the responses for a few other specified religions, although in any given year the number of respondents is too low to establish statistical significance. The cumulative averages over the 30-year period reveal that only Buddhists, with 67% responding "yes," exceed those with no religion. (No data are available for Unitarian Universalists.)

The NORC survey, although good at showing trends over time, has several shortcomings. First, in most years it did not distinguish between

fundamentalist/evangelical Protestants and mainline Protestants. Second, the question itself is not as clear as in other surveys: The word "legal" typically implies a legal market. Even though the survey specified "use," not sales, it is possible that favorable responses were lower than they would have been if not for the connotations of the word "legal." Other surveys more explicitly described various policy options.

A 2002 Time/CNN poll found that the percentages of people who "favor the legalization of marijuana" are as follows: total sample = 34%; Protestants = 20%; Catholics = 34%; Jews = 53%; "other" = 38%; and "no religion" = 54%. These responses were similar to the NORC survey, although even lower for Protestants. However, when asked, "Assuming marijuana is not legalized, do you think people arrested for small amounts of marijuana should be put in jail, or just have to pay a fine without serving any time in jail?" the percentage who oppose jail time amounted to 72% of the total sample, 67% of Protestants, 76% of Catholics, 80% of Jews, 70% of "other," and 82% of those with no religion. Although the favorable responses jumped considerably, notice that the ranking by religious affiliation followed the same pattern.

The Time/CNN survey also asked whether "adults should be allowed to legally use marijuana for medical purposes if their doctor prescribes it," and found 80% support in the total sample population, 78% among Protestants, 84% among Catholics, 94% among Jews, and 81% among "other." Oddly, on this question the "no religion" respondents ranked lowest in their support, with just 74%. It seems that religious people are more punitive of perceived wrongdoers but have more compassion for sick people, or those without a religious affiliation somehow see this question differently. Finally, the Time/CNN survey asked if respondents have "tried marijuana at least once." "Yes" responses were at follows: 47% of the total sample; 34% of Protestants; 47% of Catholics; 54% of Jews; 54% of "other"; and 61% of those with no religion (Harris Interactive, 2002).

A survey conducted in 2001 for the Pew Research Center analyzed responses according to religious affiliation but went further than the aforementioned surveys by distinguishing between "evangelical" and "nonevangelical" Protestants. (Jews were not included in the breakdown.) On the very precise question, "Do you think the possession of small amounts of marijuana should or should not be treated as a criminal offense?" the breakdown for those who agree that it should *not* be a criminal offense is as follows: total = 46%; Evangelicals = 29%; Catholics = 45%; nonevangelical Protestants = 54%; and "seculars" = 65%. Notice that with the more detailed breakdown, Catholics fall in between the two types of Protestants. This same pattern appeared on most of the relevant questions in that survey. For example, on the question about repealing "mandatory minimum prison sentences for nonviolent drug offenders," the favorable responses were: total = 46%; Evangelical = 33%; Catholic = 46%; nonevangelical = 60%; and secular = 67%.

Interestingly, when asked if "people should be allowed to take any drug they want so long as they don't hurt someone else," the rate of agreement for all religions was less than 12%. Only the seculars had 25% agreement (Princeton Survey Research Associates [PSRA], 2001).

Ellison Research conducted another useful survey in 2000. Protestant ministers were asked whether they support "legalizing marijuana for adult use." Support was disturbingly low—probably because of the connotations of the word "legalizing." Among mainline ministers, support was 16%; among evangelical ministers, support was 3%! When asked about "legalizing marijuana only for medical use, when prescribed by a doctor," support was 66% among mainline ministers but only 31% among evangelicals (Ellison Research, 2000).

Why is support for marijuana-law reform higher among parishioners than among their ministers? Actually, it may not be. The NORC survey found that the more frequently someone attends religious services, the less likely they are to support legal marijuana use. Looking at the cumulative averages from 1973–2002, legal use is supported by 34% of respondents who attend services less than once a year, 24% of those who attend once a month, and 12% of those who attend every week. This trend is similar within each Christian religious affiliation—even in mainline denominations (NORC, 2002). More research is needed to assess what messages people are hearing in church that might lead them to support punishment for marijuana users.

A 1999 survey found that 55% of the total sample population agreed that "using marijuana is morally wrong" (Beldon, Russonello, & Stewart [BRS], 1999). This is somewhat lower than the 64% who agreed that "using marihuana is morally offensive," as reported in 1972 by the National Commission on Marihuana and Drug Abuse (p. 133)—but there is still a long way to go. This so-called morality streak not only underlies marijuana prohibition, but may be generating support for another attempt at alcohol prohibition: A 1995 survey found that 26% of the total sample population "support making alcoholic beverages illegal." This level of support is 40% among "born-again" Christians (Belden & Russonello [BR], 1995).

Despite a common misconception that marijuana prohibition is the result of a culture war between drinkers and marijuana users, polling data show otherwise. The 1999 survey found that when asked whether alcohol or marijuana is "worse for a person's health," 65% of the total sample population said alcohol, and 28% said marijuana. However, 68% considered the following argument "convincing" for keeping marijuana illegal: "We have enough substances like alcohol and tobacco in society already; we should not encourage any more" (BRS, 1999). In addition, the NORC survey found that the frequency at which someone goes to a "bar or tavern" positively influences their support for legal marijuana use: Support is 40% among those who go to bars several times a week, 26% among those who go once a year,

and 14% among those who never go to bars (NORC, 2002). In short, the culture war against marijuana users seems mainly driven by people most opposed to using any substance, even alcohol, to alter consciousness.

CHANGING HEARTS AND MINDS

One way to start making progress toward marijuana-law reform is by utilizing the religious support that already exists for changing the most extreme laws, such as mandatory minimum sentencing and laws against medical marijuana. The most cost-effective tactic is to work with the leaders of supportive denominations, encouraging them to lobby members of Congress and state legislators on current bills.

IDPI sends these denominations' supportive positions to all appropriate public officials and arranges for denominations' spokespersons to testify before legislative committees and call key legislators. The organization also testifies before legislative committees, arranges for meetings with legislators, and organizes media events to draw public attention to supportive denominations' positions. This work builds momentum for reform on a variety of drug policy issues.

Through the process of building relationships with the leaders of these denominations, IDPI has the opportunity to educate them about the need for more substantial changes in marijuana law. Simultaneously, IDPI members attend religious conferences, use direct-mail outreach, and otherwise work to build a broad base of support from clergy, congregations, and individual people of faith and goodwill. These activists not only lobby their legislators on the issues currently under consideration, but they help IDPI to push the envelope—in the general public and within their denominations—in support of decriminalization and legally regulated access.

Mobilizing congregations and individual members of denominations is much more challenging than obtaining help from the denominations' leadership on issues. As the director of the Vanderbilt Program in Faith and Criminal Justice wrote: "[The] 'mainline' denominations . . . pass enlightened and progressive—sometimes prophetic—resolutions on criminal justice issues . . . which largely go unpreached and untaught at the local church level, either because many clergy disagree with them or because they are very controversial or unpopular among the laity in the pews" (Wray, 2003, p. 1).

Building a critical mass of active support among denominations, congregations, and individual people of faith will take years of sustained effort; but considering the aforementioned polling data, it is not possible to end marijuana prohibition without enough religious support. How much is "enough"? All, or even a majority, of denominations and religious individuals are not necessarily needed; however, there must be enough to change the perceptions

of the public and politicians that prohibition is the only moral way to address the marijuana situation. That myth of consensus must be broken. At a minimum, the movement would likely need at least a few more denominations (especially the most influential) to adopt official positions advocating the removal of criminal penalties for personal-use possession and, ideally, the establishment of a legally regulated system of access. In addition, enough individuals within most other influential denominations would speak out in support of these policy changes (analogous to how substantial numbers of Catholics advocate the use of contraception despite the church's opposition). Marijuana-law reform advocates must inspire dialogue and debate within seminaries, congregations, denominational meetings, and the religious and general media. The movement will not succeed until the public and politicians recognize that ending prohibition is a morally valid position.

Different arguments will work for different religious segments of the population. These arguments would need to be shaped by theologians, clergy, and other religious leaders. This chapter is an attempt to start that ball rolling.

Marijuana policy positions are generally based on an individual's or group's beliefs about marijuana and their beliefs about the role of the criminal justice system in the nation's response to the marijuana situation.

Possible beliefs about marijuana use include: (a) All marijuana use is sinful/bad/wrong, because it is inherently immoral and/or because it can have negative consequences; (b) There is a difference between marijuana use, abuse, and addiction: (b1) There is nothing inherently wrong with moderate, responsible use; and/or (b2) Abuse and addiction are problematic, but not necessarily immoral (i.e., they are health problems, although there may be significant spiritual health implications); or (c) Responsible marijuana use is not just morally neutral, but it may even be virtuous, at least for some people under some circumstances.

Possible beliefs about the criminal justice system's role include: (a) The criminal justice system should try to control marijuana use, abuse, or addiction by whatever means it deems appropriate, no matter how aggressive (provided that certain universally recognized human rights are not violated); (b) We must ensure that the policies responding to the marijuana situation do not cause more harm to individuals or society than does the use of the substance itself. Therefore, many different factors should be considered; or (c) It is inherently wrong or immoral to criminalize marijuana users, abusers, and addicts.

Beliefs about marijuana use and the criminal justice system's role interact to shape a religious entity's marijuana policy positions. For example, even if people believe that marijuana use is always immoral, it is still possible for them to support decriminalization if they believe that the laws cause more harm than good or that it is inherently wrong to use the criminal justice

system to enforce personal morality decisions. Denominations that take into consideration the harmful effects of the laws are more likely to support substantial reform than are those denominations that limit their assessment to the effects of marijuana.

One way to influence denominations and religious individuals is to present them with the favorable positions from other denominations, especially those that are similar to them in their theological and sociopolitical beliefs. Other potentially persuasive arguments appear below. (This section does not elaborate on the mechanisms for reaching denominational decision makers or the processes behind each religion's official positions. Individuals interested in learning more about that level are encouraged to contact the Interfaith Drug Policy Initiative [IDPI].) Rather, this section presents various moral arguments supporting decriminalization and legal access.

Father John Clifton Marquis, a Catholic priest, wrote an article, "Drug Laws Are Immoral," in 1990, which includes the following:

> Drug laws are a moral issue. Fifty years of drug legislation have produced the exact opposite effect of what those laws intended: the laws have created a tantalizingly profitable economic structure for marketing drugs. (p. 14)
>
> These laws are false gods promising a salvation they cannot produce. (p. 14)
>
> Moral leaders have no alternative but to choose between authentic morality, which produces good, and cosmetic morality, which merely looks good. . . . Authentic morality knows its limitations in the human condition and does all it can for the common good. (p. 15)
>
> There is no doubt that some people will abuse legal drugs; this happens with legal alcohol. . . . Human nature is, after all, wounded by the reality of sin. But lawmaking is not now, and never has been, the magic formula for goodness. (p. 15)

Walter Wink, a professor of biblical interpretation at Auburn Theological Seminary, wrote an article, "Getting Off Drugs: The Legalization Option," in 1996, which includes the following:

> The drug war is over, and we lost. . . . The harder we tried to stamp out this evil, the more lucrative we made it, and the more it spread. Our forcible resistance to evil simply augments it. An evil cannot be eradicated by making it more profitable. (p. 13)
>
> Drug laws have fostered drug-related murders and an estimated 40 percent of all property crime. . . . There are the ones killed in fights over turf; innocents caught in crossfire; citizens terrified of city streets; escalating robberies; . . . (p. 13)
>
> We cannot stop drug violence with state violence. Addicts will be healed by care and compassion, not condemnation. Dealers will be

curbed by a ruined world drug market, not by enforcement that simply escalates the profitability of drugs. A nonviolent, nonreactive, creative approach is needed that lets the drug empire collapse of its own deadly weight. (p. 16)

The articles by Marquis and Wink may be persuasive, especially to Catholics and mainline Protestants, respectively. Both articles focus primarily on the counterproductive consequences of drug prohibition. In making these kinds of arguments to religious audiences, one useful resource is the Marijuana Policy Project's "Marijuana Prohibition Facts: 2005" briefing paper, which references the most reputable government sources to make points including the following:

More than 700,000 people a year are arrested for marijuana-law violations year—and nearly 90 percent of those are for possession, not sale or manufacture. An estimated 77,000 people are in prison or jail right now for marijuana-law violations. Despite these aggressive and punitive policies, every year more than 85 percent of high school seniors consistently report that marijuana is already easy to obtain. At the same time, use is not higher in the 11 states that have removed criminal penalties for possession.

The fact that marijuana prohibition is harmful and ineffective may be persuasive to many people of faith, provided that they hear it from their clergy or others whom they trust. In addition, reform advocates must be sure to connect the dots as to how these laws violate various religions' core values.

Wray (2003, p. 10) writes, "While most Christian faith communities claim to believe in such values as fairness, peace, equality, justice, reconciliation, and forgiveness, too often their leaders and members tacitly or aggressively support a criminal justice system which routinely violates all these basic spiritual and ethical principles in massive and immensely damaging ways."

Christians (and other people of faith) must be reminded of these values and challenged to base their drug policy positions on them. Perhaps the simplest shared principle for marijuana policies is Christianity's Golden Rule: "Do unto others as you would have them do unto you." An article by Robinson (2004) that focuses on the Golden Rule notes that all of the world's major religions have some version of this "ethics of reciprocity."

People of all faiths should consider, "If you were a marijuana user, would you want criminal penalties for personal use?" Ethicists and religious leaders would be wise to encourage people to reflect on any potentially unhealthy behaviors of their own—drinking alcohol, eating too much junk food, failing to exercise, watching too much television, and so on. None of these activities are illegal. Why should marijuana users be treated any differently (unless they directly cause harm to others, which almost never happens)?

The basic argument that marijuana use is not necessarily sinful—and even if it is, that it should not be a crime—must be fleshed out using the

central religious texts of each religion. Because most Americans are Christian, the following is an example of how this can be done. (Anyone interested in persuading Jewish groups or individuals would benefit from reading the excellent resolutions passed by various Reform Jewish groups, cited in the next chapter, and Elliot Dorff 's chap. 11 in this volume.)

First, it should be stressed that the Bible does not mention marijuana or other currently illegal drugs. Some antidrug crusaders (e.g., Sanders, 1970) have written that the Greek root word for "sorcery," which is condemned in the *Holy Bible*, is "pharmakeia"—which is also the current root for words relating to drugs and medicine (e.g., pharmacy). They argue, therefore, that the use of marijuana and other drugs is forbidden. This argument is such a stretch that it is not even made in the official policy statements of the Southern Baptist Convention, Assemblies of God, National Association of Evangelicals, or any other fundamentalist or evangelical denomination or group. Nevertheless, the argument is sometimes used in evangelical recruiting materials, such as those distributed on college campuses. Miller (2000) lays this distortion to rest by explaining that the original Hebrew words for sorcery which the Greek interpreters mistranslated as pharmakeia include "kashaph" and "qacam," neither of which have any drug-related connotations. Ultimately, the English translators got it right: Sorcery means sorcery, not marijuana use.

Because the Bible does not mention marijuana, the most reasonable inferences about marijuana use and abuse can be drawn from the passages about alcohol—the only consciousness-altering substance specifically discussed. The Bible clearly distinguishes between use and abuse of alcohol, with moderate, responsible use not considered immoral. (For a more thorough analysis of this distinction, see Sullum, 2003, and Dorff, chap. 11.) Although the Assemblies of God and many other evangelical or fundamentalist Christian denominations oppose alcohol use for reasons discussed in the next chapter, most Christian denominations accept the responsible use of alcohol. (Indeed, Jesus' first miracle was turning water into wine at a wedding—see John 2:3–11.)

Moreover, no denominations opposing the use of alcohol take the position that people should be arrested simply for possessing alcohol for personal use. Therefore, even if marijuana use is a personal sin, it follows that the government should not arrest people for using it.

This point is the most important one: Jesus' words and deeds were all about mercy, not punishment or coercion. Quotations from Jesus include: "Blessed are the merciful" (Matthew 5:7); "Love your enemies" (Matt. 5:44); "[If] you do not forgive men their sins, your Father will not forgive your sins" (Matt. 6:15), and "Do not judge, or you too will be judged" (Matt. 7:1). Jesus reminds us that we are all sinners: When a mob was about to punish a woman for committing adultery, Jesus told them, "If any one of you is without sin, let him be the first to throw a stone at her" (John 8:7). Not one person could do

it. Some supporters of maintaining criminal penalties against sins point out that Jesus followed up by telling the woman, "Go now and leave your life of sin" (John 8:11). Some suggest that perhaps she should have been punished if she continued to sin—but that is not what Jesus said.

In fact, there is one example of someone disregarding Jesus' moral instructions and turning to walk away (Matt. 19:20–22). What did Jesus do? Did he order people to apprehend and incarcerate the person? Of course not. He let the person walk away, although he explained to his followers that the person would have a hard time entering the kingdom of heaven.

This distinction is a key one: God may punish sinners, but people must be kind to one another. We can use words to try to persuade people to refrain from sin, but ultimately this matter is between a person and God. Jesus very clearly explained that the role of government and the role of God are distinct: "Give to Caesar what is Caesar's, and to God what is God's" (Matt. 22:21). Though the government has a legitimate role in outlawing behaviors, such as murder or rape, that directly harm another person, personal sin is under God's purview.

Indeed, we must ensure that the government itself is not behaving in an immoral manner, since collectively we are the government and we are responsible for making sure that our own behavior is not sinful. Prohibition is immoral. Punishing people for what they put into their own bodies is immoral. Jesus said, "What goes into a man's mouth does not make him 'unclean,' but what comes out of his mouth, that is what makes him 'unclean'" (Matt 15:11).

That is, actions should be judged by their *consequences*. If someone uses marijuana and subsequently does something that hurts someone else, that is a problem for the government to address. But the vast majority of marijuana users who do not harm others should not be treated like criminals. In contrast, arresting marijuana users is always hurtful and does absolutely no good, as it does not even deter marijuana use. "No good tree bears bad fruit, nor does a bad tree bear good fruit," Jesus explained. "Each tree is recognized by its own fruit" (Luke 6:43–44). Marijuana prohibition, by any measure, is a bad tree. And what should become of a bad tree? According to Jesus, it should be "cut down and thrown into the fire" (Matt. 7:19). It's time to replace marijuana prohibition with reasonable regulations designed to reduce any potential harm associated with marijuana.

Good intentions cannot justify counterproductive laws. C. S. Lewis wrote, "Of all tyrannies, a tyranny sincerely exercised for the good of its victims may be the most oppressive. It may be better to live under robber barons than under omnipotent moral busybodies. The robber baron's cruelty may sometimes sleep . . . but those who torment us for our own good will torment us without end, for they do so with the approval of their own conscience" (1948/1970, p. 292). Because Lewis is very popular with evangelical Christians, this brilliant quote should be persuasive to them.

One argument sometimes made by marijuana enthusiasts is that one of the ingredients in the sacred anointing oil described in Exodus 30:22–30 is actually marijuana. The "fragrant cane" in the English translation was originally "Keneh bosem" in Hebrew. There are at least four possible translations, "cannabis" being one of them—based on cognate pronunciation (Kaplan, 1981). Nevertheless, this argument is unlikely to persuade any anti-marijuana Jews or Christians, who could believe that one of the other translations is more accurate. In fact, most Christians would likely consider that argument blasphemous.

Though I also doubt that the "cannabis" translation for "Keneh bosem" is accurate, I do believe that members of religions such as The Hawaii Cannabis (THC) Ministry that earnestly believe this translation should have the freedom to practice their religion. Other religions (e.g., Rastafarianism, Ethiopian Zion Coptic Church, some sects of Hinduism, and some counterculture churches) have made elaborate arguments as to why marijuana is an important component of their spiritual practice.

Federal law prohibits the government from burdening a person's sincere religious practice unless the burden furthers a compelling government interest and is the least restrictive means of furthering that compelling government interest. However, the courts have typically ruled against the use of marijuana for religious purposes, for a variety of reasons. For example, even if someone proves in court that his or her church requires the use of marijuana, the government can still argue that allowing that exception would open a can of worms and effectively undermine all of the laws against marijuana. These complex legal issues are beyond the scope of this chapter; however, readers interested in this topic may read Mazur (1991), Fuller (2000), and the information at http://www.thc-ministry.org.

CALL FOR A MORAL RESPONSE

It is time for religious leaders and other faith-based activists to devote substantial study, prayer, reflection, and action to this issue. This examination should include seeking to understand individuals who claim that marijuana has had a net neutral or positive effect on their lives. Many people of faith have never engaged in serious dialogue with individuals who are open about their nonproblematic marijuana use. As a result, their views are shaped by prohibitionist propaganda, media sensationalism, or personal knowledge about the small percentage of marijuana users who have developed problems with the substance.

There are several reasons why people who do not use marijuana, including many people of faith, know more about people with marijuana problems than they know about the vast majority of marijuana users who

experience positive or neutral effects from the plant. Those with marijuana problems may seek help from their families or faith community, whereas those without problems hide their use for fear of getting arrested or being ostracized. Relatives of those with problems may seek emotional support from clergy or fellow congregants. Marijuana abusers in recovery may talk openly about their past problems in a sincere attempt to help others avoid making the same mistakes.

This situation gives a skewed perspective: There are many kind, loving, productive marijuana users involved in faith communities, or in close relationships with people of faith, who hide their use so well that others in their faith communities do not know that these good people are living under the constant threat of having their lives devastated by a marijuana arrest.

A faith community should be a place where people are free to be open and honest about who they are without fear of being judged. Such genuine dialogue is necessary to understand the effects that these laws are having on real people. Until faith communities find a way to create "safe spaces" for such discussions, individual people of faith should at least read two books: *Understanding Marijuana* (Earleywine, 2002) and *Saying Yes: In Defense of Drug Use* (Sullum, 2003). The former is the most thorough, accurate, and balanced book examining the scientific evidence of marijuana's effects on people; the latter provides insights into the lives of real people who use marijuana and other drugs—it's the next best thing to actually looking people in the eye and talking with them.

Of course, some people of faith reading this chapter will flinch at the prospect of stretching to understand and accept people who use marijuana. Those who have the strongest reaction against this suggestion should especially try to read these books with an open heart and mind; indeed, it is what Jesus and all of the world's other great spiritual examples would do: put compassion ahead of prejudice.

Religious groups and people of faith and goodwill who already believe that marijuana users should not be punished must find the moral courage to speak out and get involved in the movement for more just and compassionate policies. Fear should never stand in the way of doing what is right.

It is also time for marijuana users to reflect on the ethics of their behavior. Is it morally wrong to use marijuana? If a marijuana user's religion says that it is wrong, then that position should be taken very seriously. The user should honor his or her religion enough to either stop using it, work to change that religion's position, or join another religion in harmony with his or her values.

Is marijuana use ever okay? At the very least, a current marijuana user should (a) make every effort possible to prevent any harm to others and to reduce any potential harm to one's self; (b) be honest about one's use, at least with a few close loved ones and respected members of one's faith community;

(c) make some effort to change the laws; and (d) make some effort to help others prevent or recover from marijuana-related problems.

Users should not be selfish, hiding from the law like common criminals and otherwise doing nothing to help others who use or abuse marijuana. Anyone interested enough in marijuana to actually use it, despite the laws against it, has a moral imperative to help liberate other users—not just from the harmful effects of the policies, but also from the potentially harmful effects of the substance itself. People who have problems with marijuana are human beings too, with innate worth and dignity. Those who use marijuana responsibly should not wash their hands of those with marijuana problems or those who may be especially vulnerable to developing marijuana problems, such as adolescents and the mentally ill. Everyone sinks or swims together.

REFERENCES

Belden & Russonello. (1995). *Poll regarding marijuana: Conducted for the American Civil Liberties Union.* Washington, DC: Author.

Belden, Russonello, & Stewart. (1999). *National survey on marijuana: Conducted for the American Civil Liberties Union.* Washington, DC: Author.

Earleywine, M. (2002). *Understanding marijuana: A new look at the scientific evidence.* New York: Oxford University Press.

Ellison Research. (2000). *Pastor study: Marijuana.* Phoenix: Author.

Fuller, R. C. (2000). *Stairways to heaven: Drugs in American religious history.* Boulder, CO: Westview Press.

Harris Interactive. (2002). *Time/CNN survey on gun control and marijuana.* New York: Time Public Affairs.

Kaplan, A. (1981). *The living Torah.* New York: Moznaim. Retrieved February 2002 from http://www.thc-ministry.org/thelivingtorah.jpg.

Lewis, C. S. (1970). The humanitarian theory of punishment. In W. Hooper (Ed.), *God in the dock: Essays on theology and ethics by C.S. Lewis* (pp. 287–294). Grand Rapids, MI: Eerdmans. (Reprinted from *Twentieth Century: An Australian Quarterly Review, 3,* 3 [1948])

Linder, E. W. (Ed.) (2004). *Yearbook of American and Canadian churches.* Nashville: Abingdon Press.

Marijuana Policy Project. (2005). *Marijuana prohibition facts.* Washington, DC: Author.

Marquis, J. C. (1990, May). Drug laws are immoral. *U.S. Catholic,* 14–15.

Mazur, C. S. (1991). Marijuana as a "holy sacrament": Is the use of peyote constitutionally distinguishable from that of marijuana in bona fide religious ceremonies? *Notre Dame Journal of Law, Ethics, and Public Policy, 5*(3), 693–725.

Miller, J. (2000, August 22). Witch [sic] way on drugs? *World Net Daily.* Retrieved February 2005 from http://www.cannabisnews.com/news/thread6788.shtml.

National Coalition for Effective Drug Strategies. (2002/2003). *Eight steps to effectively controlling drug abuse and the drug market.* Washington, DC: Interfaith Drug Policy Initiative.

National Commission on Marihuana and Drug Abuse. (1972). *Marihuana: A signal of misunderstanding.* Washington, DC: U.S. Government Printing Office.

National Opinion Research Center. (2002). *General social survey.* Chicago: NORC Data Archive. Retrieved February 2005, from http://www.icpsr .umich.edu/gss.

Princeton Survey Research Associates. (2001). *Pew Research Center for People and the Press: Drug war survey.* Washington, DC: Author.

Robinson, B. A. (2004). *Shared belief in the 'Golden Rule': Ethics of reciprocity.* Retrieved February 2005 from Ontario Consultants on Religious Tolerance at http://www.religioustolerance.org/reciproc.htm.

Sanders, J. (1970). Pharmakeia: The abuse of drugs. *Truth Magazine, 15*(6), 11–12.

Sullum, J. (2003). *Saying yes: In defense of drug use.* New York: Tarcher/ Penguin.

Wallis, J. (2005). *God's politics: Why the Right gets it wrong and the Left doesn't get it.* New York: Harper Collins.

Wink, W. (1996, February). Getting off drugs: The legalization option. *Friends Journal,* 13–16.

Wray, H. L. (2003). Models of criminal justice ministry and resistance: A southern Christian perspective. *Victim Offender Mediation Association Connections, 1*(1), 10–11.

13 Detailed Analyses of Religious Groups' Divergent Positions on Marijuana

Charles Thomas

This chapter is in some ways an elaboration of the previous chapter, in which I briefly summarized the marijuana-related positions of the nation's leading religious denominations and other groups. In this chapter I give detailed analyses of these religious groups' positions, including representative comments on their reasons for taking these positions. They are listed in the order that best illustrates the various faith-based perspectives on these issues. For a brief summary of these groups' positions, see Table 12.1 of the previous chapter.

There are essentially two ways in which a religious denomination or other group can take an official position on a sociopolitical issue: through its governing body or through its executive office. Religious denominations and other groups vary greatly in their governance. Some are governed exclusively or primarily by a council of bishops. Others are governed by a "general assembly" or "general conference" consisting of clergy and lay members of the denomination, who meet as often as every year or as infrequently as every four years. Positions taken by a group's governing body carry more weight than those taken by its executive office; in fact, the latter usually cannot take a position on an issue unless support can be logically inferred from positions adopted by the group's official policy-setting body on related matters.

UNITARIAN UNIVERSALIST ASSOCIATION

The Unitarian Universalist Association (UUA) is featured as having the most anti-prohibition position on marijuana policy. Despite being a relatively small denomination with just 220,000 members (including three members of the U.S. Congress), the UUA has been disproportionately influential in its advocacy on a wide range of cutting-edge sociopolitical issues.

The UUA was established in 1961 through a merger of the Unitarian and Universalist denominations, both of which began as Christian denominations more than 200 years ago. Today, the liberal denomination also draws from Eastern, humanist, and other religious traditions, and it encourages its members to seek religious truth out of their own reflection and experience. Instead of a creed, the UUA affirms and promotes seven guiding principles, such as "the inherent worth and dignity of every person," "acceptance of one another and encouragement to spiritual growth," "the right of conscience," and "peace, liberty and justice for all" (UUA, 2005).

The UUA's *Alternatives to the War on Drugs* statement of conscience (UUA, 2002) is grounded in these principles. The statement was passed by the UUA's General Assembly, which consists of delegates from most of the denomination's 1,000 congregations. It states: "Drug use, abuse and addiction are distinct from one another. Using a drug does not necessarily mean abusing the drug, much less becoming addicted to it." The statement also enumerates the many harmful effects of the drug war, such as "the increasing breakdown of families and neighborhoods, endangerment of children, widespread violations of civil liberties, escalating rates of incarceration, political corruption, and the imposition of United States policy abroad."

Accordingly, the statement recommends: "Establish a legal, regulated, and taxed market for marijuana. Treat marijuana as we treat alcohol." The statement also makes recommendations favoring the reform of laws regarding illegal drugs generally: "Remove criminal penalties for possession and use of currently illegal drugs, with drug abusers subject to arrest and imprisonment only if they commit an actual crime (e.g., assault, burglary, impaired driving)," and "Make all drugs legally available with a prescription by a licensed physician, subject to professional oversight."

The statement includes nearly a dozen more modest recommendations, such as: Make drug treatment more accessible; reduce spending on law enforcement and prisons; and reduce or eliminate racial profiling, civil liberties violations, mandatory minimum prison sentences, and property forfeiture.

This statement of conscience empowers the denomination's executive staff, congregations, and the affiliated Unitarian Universalists for Drug Policy Reform to advocate for any marijuana law reform options that could possibly be considered in the public square.

Though the 2002 statement broke new ground by calling for legally regulated access to other drugs, the UUA General Assembly had, in fact, passed a resolution in 1970 calling for the full legalization of marijuana. That resolution also enumerated several problems caused by the criminalization of marijuana users and noted that marijuana prohibition is "based largely on public hysteria and myth, rather than on any established data about the effects of marijuana on the user."

Of course, since 1970, scientists have established that inappropriate or excessive use of marijuana may be harmful (Earleywine, 2002). However, the resolution wisely staked out a principled position recommending that "any effects of the consumption of marijuana that may be found injurious to the user be handled by the proper psychological and medical care and not by criminal law."

Accordingly, it makes sense that the UUA recommends full legalization: Its beliefs about marijuana recognize that there is nothing inherently wrong with moderate, responsible use, and its beliefs about the role of the criminal justice system include that it is simply wrong to criminalize marijuana consumers, even if they do have a problem with it.

Note, however, that neither official position (2002 or 1970) declares that people *should* use marijuana, but instead that it should be a personal choice.

THE CATHOLIC CHURCH

The Catholic Church is the largest denomination in the United States, with more than 66 million members (including 154 members of Congress). The Vatican in Rome establishes the church's official positions on policy issues, although the U.S. Conference of Catholic Bishops may also issue additional policy statements, provided that it does not contradict those set by the Vatican.

The main Catholic resource on the drug issue is the pastoral handbook *Church: Drugs and Drug Addiction*, written by the Pontifical Council for Health Pastoral Care (Vatican, 2002). This 191-page handbook highlights and elaborates on many of the eighty statements about drugs and drug policy issued by Pope John Paul II, as well as statements of the cardinal secretary of state, the Pontifical Council for the Family, and the Pastoral Assistance to Health-Care Workers.

The handbook states that drugs should be addressed by "prevention, suppression, and rehabilitation" (p. 25). It does not establish any moral limits on the means of "suppression," other than to "question the fury with which certain 'small' distributors or more or less occasional consumers are pursued" (p. 68). Otherwise, the handbook defers to the world's governments,

noting that the fight against drugs is a "special duty of governments to face with courage" (p. 6).

In contrast, the handbook's moral assessment of drug use is unambiguous, proclaiming "from a moral point of view, there is need to totally reject the use of drugs" (p. 20). Drug use is purported to involve "an unjustified and irrational renunciation of thinking, willing and acting as free persons" (p. 20). Throughout the handbook, drugs are described as a "source of ruin and death" (p. 8), an "insidious social plague" (p. 18), "moral contagion," "disgusting epidemic," "vile market" (p. 15), "wicked trade" (p. 20), and "serious evil" (p. 16).

"Drugs encourage a way of behaving which borders on individualism and egocentrism, leading to withdrawal from meaningful communication with others" (p. 9), the handbook continues. It argues that "drugs testify to a kind of contempt for life and represent a personal attempt, which is certainly imaginary, of extricating oneself from reality and from the circumstances of human life" (p. 7). Drugs "frustrate the person precisely in his or her capacity for communion and self-giving" (p. 21).

These assessments about drugs explicitly include marijuana, as the handbook opposes making a "distinction between 'hard drugs' and 'soft drugs,'" asserting that "it is irresponsible to consider cannabis in a trivial way and to think of it as being 'a soft drug'" (p. 23, 43).

Regarding policy, the handbook explicitly rejects the possibility of legalizing any currently illegal drugs, including marijuana, claiming that doing so "would derive such a confusion that makes one believe that what is legal is normal and moral. This legalization would inevitably provoke high consumption, high criminality, a high number of road accidents, worsening of personal problems, an increase in the health problems at the expense of the general public, a State inclined to abdicate the duty to safeguard the common good, since it would give way to the destruction of youth, [etc.]" (p. 24).

The handbook also opposes removing criminal penalties for personal-use possession, stating, "Decriminalization opens the door to total liberalization, leading only to the perpetuation of drug addiction" (p. 69). It further proclaims "the necessity of taking action with regard to the consumers" (p. 68). Moreover, governments are urged to "continue to intensify their efforts in order to improve at all levels legislation against drug abuse and to *oppose all forms of drug culture* and trafficking" (p. 29, emphasis added).

It continues, "We cannot speak of the 'freedom to take drugs' or 'the right to drugs,' for the human being has no right to harm him/herself, nor the right to abdicate one's personal dignity, which comes from God!" (p. 21).

The handbook even maligns the drug policy reform movement, described as "certain pressure groups or activists favoring drug addiction, who deliberately parade their consumption and vindicate their right to use toxic products without being checked, especially regarding cannabis" (p. 68).

The handbook also enumerates many of the very serious problems that can be caused by alcohol abuse; however, the Catholic Church does not advocate the prohibition of alcohol. No explanation is provided as to why marijuana should be illegal while alcohol is not, except to note, "In many societies wine and alcohol form part of dining" (p. 59).

The church does not mandate that all Catholics should abstain from alcohol consumption. Interestingly, the handbook claims that "one 'joint' corresponds to the drinking of two glasses of whisky" (p. 59). No explanation is given as to why it is okay to drink two glasses of whisky but not to smoke one joint. Regardless, the church's views on marijuana will be difficult to change: "The basis of these values cannot be provisional and changeable 'majority' opinions, but only the acknowledgement of an objective moral law . . . is the obligatory point of reference for civil law itself" (p. 96).

Interestingly, the church's door might be open a crack for the eventual acceptance of the medicinal use of marijuana, as the handbook notes that its opposition to drugs applies "except on strictly therapeutic grounds" (p. 21). Although the Vatican's handbook is essentially silent on the immorality of various enforcement and sentencing practices, the U.S. Conference of Catholic Bishops (2000) issued a statement calling for various changes in the United States' criminal justice system.

Most noteworthy, the conference's statement recommends: "To the extent possible, we should support community-based solutions, especially for non-violent offenders, because a greater emphasis is placed in treatment and restoration for the criminal, and restitution and healing for the victim. We must renew our efforts to ensure that the punishment fits the crime. *Therefore, we do not support mandatory minimum sentencing that replaces judges' assessments with rigid formulations*" (emphasis added).

Accordingly, U.S. Catholics are crucial allies in one of the major legislative battles currently underway, in Congress and several states, that can help tens of thousands of nonviolent marijuana offenders to avoid excessive sentences.

UNITED METHODIST CHURCH

The United Methodist Church (UMC) is the third-largest denomination in the United States, with more than 8 million members (including 62 members of Congress and President George W. Bush). The UMC's official positions on sociopolitical issues are established through resolutions passed by its General Conference, a body of up to 1,000 delegates worldwide—half clergy, half lay—that meets every four years. These resolutions automatically expire after 12 years unless readopted.

The UMC's positions on marijuana (and other drugs) are a middle ground between those of the Unitarian Universalists and the Catholics. Though

opposing the use of marijuana in general, it recognizes the medical use of marijuana and calls for the removal of criminal penalties for all drug use.

Several current resolutions enumerate the various harms to individuals and society that can result from marijuana consumption and call for complete abstinence. These and other relevant resolutions are compiled in the *Book of Resolutions* (United Methodist Church, 2004a).

However, the UMC also recognizes that many harms result from the use of the criminal justice system to enforce abstinence. Accordingly, the *Equal Justice* resolution (amended and readopted in 2000) advocates "the repeal of some criminal laws against certain personal conditions or individual misconduct. Examples are criminal prohibitions of vagrancy, personal gambling, public drunkenness, drug use, and prostitution. Together, these charges alone account for more than half of all arrests in some jurisdictions. They result in little social good, but great evil in class discrimination, alienation, and waste of resources needed for other purposes." This position clearly supports decriminalization.

Nevertheless, the UMC does not support legal access, instead calling to "support strong, humane law-enforcement efforts against the illegal sale of all drugs" in its *Drug and Alcohol Concerns* resolution, amended and readopted in 2004.

That same resolution recognizes the medicinal use of marijuana: "Some countries permit the use of marijuana in medicines. Recently, some states in the United States have passed legislation permitting the medical use of marijuana. The medical use of any drug should not be seen as encouraging recreational use of the drug. We urge all persons to abstain from all use of marijuana, unless it has been legally prescribed in a form appropriate for treating a particular medical condition."

The *Equal Justice* resolution also opposes mandatory minimums, calling for "the provision for court-fixed sentences, rather than mandatory ones, in order to draw upon the skill and the training of qualified judges."

Interestingly, the UMC has finally modified its long-standing position that abstinence is the only acceptable option regarding alcohol. A 2004 amendment to the *Book of Discipline* reaffirms that abstinence is the preferred choice, but urges "with regard to those who choose to consume alcoholic beverages, judicious use with deliberate and intentional restraint, with Scripture as a guide" (UMC, 2005). Perhaps someday, although probably not until after the laws have been changed, this position will be expanded to include responsible marijuana use.

In addition to the policy statements made by the General Conference, the UMC's public advocacy arm, the General Board of Church and Society, also issues statements on various issues. These statements, though based on the church's official positions, do not have the same level of official status. They are nonetheless very useful in providing support for specific marijuana-

related proposals currently being considered in Congress and several state legislatures.

Accordingly, the General Board of Church and Society has endorsed the Interfaith Drug Policy Initiative's sign-on statements backing our three current legislative priorities: repealing mandatory minimum sentencing laws; repealing the federal law that denies financial aid to college students with drug convictions; and legalizing the medical use of marijuana (IDPI, 2004). See chapter 12 for these statements.

The UMC is a mainline Protestant denomination. Accordingly, the basis of its positions is not limited to biblical literalism, but to "a prayerful and thoughtful effort . . . to speak to the human issues in the contemporary world from a sound biblical and theological foundation as historically demonstrated in the United Methodist tradition" (UMC, 2005).

ASSEMBLIES OF GOD

The Assemblies of God (AG), an evangelical Protestant denomination, is the tenth-largest Christian denomination in the United States, with nearly 2.7 million members (including four members of Congress and former U.S. Attorney General John Ashcroft). Its official statements are passed by the General Presbytery. The AG positions are featured in great detail below because they contain more references to passages in the Holy Bible than do the positions of any other denomination.

Although the General Presbytery has not passed any statements specifically addressing marijuana or other illegal drugs, its *Abstinence* statement on alcohol, passed in 1985, is assumed to apply to all drugs. Indeed, the Alcohol, Tobacco, and Drugs section of the AG's *Matters of Christian Character* publication states, "Though drug use is not specifically mentioned in the Bible, its impact on the drug user and on society far exceeds the evil results of alcohol abuse" (AG, 2000). This publication has almost the same authoritative weight as something passed by the General Presbytery, having been reviewed by the Commission on Doctrinal Purity and approved for release by the General Council Board of Administration.

The AG's *Abstinence* statement, while recognizing "that some persons in the Old Testament drank fermented wine," nonetheless calls alcohol a "Satanic tool" that "insidiously afflicts and binds the bodies and minds of men and women" (AG, 1985). The statement cites several examples from the Holy Bible of people doing immoral deeds while under the influence of alcohol (e.g., Genesis 9:20–27, Genesis 19:30–38, Daniel 5).

The statement acknowledges that the Bible contains some favorable references to alcohol (e.g., "wine which cheers" in Judges 9:13 and "wine that makes glad" in Psalm 104:15). However, the statement notes that in

Leviticus 10:8–11, "priests were commanded to abstain from wine or intoxicating drink when they went into the presence of the Lord to minister." The statement explains that "all born-again Christians have been made priests to God," according to 1 Peter 2:9 and Revelation 1:6. Therefore, "We believe the standard of abstinence demanded of the Old Testament priest should be the standard of every Christian today."

But what about the vast majority of alcohol consumers who drink responsibly? "The Christian who advocates or condones 'drinking in moderation' is providing Satan an opening he would not have with an individual committed to total abstinence," the statement says, followed by a reference to Proverbs 23:29–35 which details many of the problems that alcohol abuse can cause. In short, the use of alcohol, and presumably therefore the use of marijuana, is just too risky. "Our bodies are the temples of the Holy Spirit," the statement says, referencing 1 Corinthians 6:19, and then adds, "We need to cleanse them from all profane habits, including alcohol."

In addition, the statement argues that even if a particular individual can drink responsibly, such use could tempt others who might not be able to maintain moderation: "The apostle Paul deals with the responsibility of the stronger brother toward the weaker brother in Romans 14:21. 'It is good neither to eat meat nor drink wine nor do anything by which your brother stumbles or is offended or is made weak.' . . . We must not set an example that will send others to hell and destruction."

The statement also quotes Jesus, in Luke 21:34, saying, "Take heed to yourselves, lest your hearts be weighed down with carousing, drunkenness, and cares of this life," and then elaborates, "As we watch and pray for the return of Jesus, our senses should be as sharp and clear as they can possibly be." The statement continues: "Many people who experience psychological problems (and some of them unfortunately are Christians) are tempted to seek an easy solution in 'a little bit' of alcohol. But what was used as a supposed cure has caused even greater problems. We are set free through Jesus Christ, not through a drug that dissipates and destroys us when we submit to its influence. In the final analysis, the use of alcohol is a spiritual problem. Alcoholism is sin, not sickness. Its shocking increase is another manifestation of the permissive, lawless spirit produced by the spiritual degeneration so much in evidence today."

To summarize the AG's *Abstinence* statement, the reasons that Christians should not use alcohol (or presumably marijuana) are: Intoxication can cause a person to sin; even moderate use opens the door to the possibility of problematic use or addiction, with numerous negative consequences; any use profanes our bodily temples; it sets a bad example for others; it can cloud the senses and distract someone from the prophesized Second Coming of Christ; and for people seeking an escape from psychological difficulties, it serves as a dangerous substitute for Jesus.

Interestingly, the statement does not call for a return to alcohol prohibition, but rather "to teach by word and example a life-style that abstains totally from the consumption of alcoholic beverages." Could this call to use "word and example," rather than criminal law, also apply to marijuana? Perhaps because Christians (according to the AG) are supposed to abstain no matter what, it doesn't matter what the laws are, especially pertaining to non-Christians.

Personal communication with the AG national headquarters (2005, February 16) confirmed that the denomination does not have a position one way or the other on the legalization or decriminalization of marijuana. However, AG congregations and individuals are free to advocate against such policy changes if they see fit. In addition, the aforementioned *Matters of Christian Character*'s section on drugs states, "We call upon all of society to fight these addictive substances used by Satan to keep individuals in bondage to his power over their lives" (AG, 2000). It doesn't explicitly advocate the use of the criminal justice system in this "fight"; perhaps the effort should be limited to education, treatment, prayer, and moral persuasion. Nor, however, does it explicitly oppose criminalization.

Moreover, the AG publication *Perspectives—Contemporary Social, Political, Medical, and Moral Issues* (AG, 2004) includes the following:

> If our society continues its trend toward greater secularization, Christians will face an increasing number of laws requiring actions or acceptance of behaviors the Bible tells us are sins against God. In light of this we as Christians may be called upon to resist such evil . . . [by] encouraging and promoting legislation that strengthens the nation morally, and speaking out both corporately and individually against any political issue that would have an adverse affect upon the kingdom of God or His moral absolutes.

This line of reasoning is probably sufficient backing for AG members and congregations, and perhaps even the denominational headquarters, to speak out against any legal changes that they believe would increase marijuana consumption.

Nevertheless, there appears to be an opening for persuading the AG to support medical marijuana. Its *Abstinence* statement includes: "Some well-meaning people have misused the instruction given by Paul to Timothy in 1 Timothy 5:23. When Paul suggested that Timothy 'Stop drinking only water, and use a little wine because of your stomach and your frequent illnesses,' he was not recommending wine as a social drink. The fact that Paul had to mention the medicinal use of wine indicates rather strongly that Timothy was committed to abstinence as a lifestyle." Could this apparent acceptance of the medicinal use of alcohol also apply to medical marijuana?

NATIONAL COUNCIL OF CHURCHES

The National Council of Churches of Christ in the USA (NCC) is a coalition comprising 36 denominations, which represent 45 million Americans from more than 100,000 local congregations. Its member denominations include the mainline Protestant denominations, most of the eastern Orthodox denominations, and many historically African-American churches.

The NCC's official statements are passed annually by its General Assembly, which consists of nearly 300 representatives from its member denominations. These positions do not supersede those of each member denomination; rather, the representatives do their best to base these positions on the shared values of their denominations. The NCC has its own advocacy personnel who give public witness to its positions.

The NCC member denominations include several that are further detailed in this chapter. Mainline Protestant denominations include the United Methodist Church, Evangelical Lutheran Church in America, Presbyterian Church (USA), Episcopal Church, American Baptist Churches in the USA, United Church of Christ, and Church of the Brethren. African-American denominations include the National Baptist Convention (USA), National Baptist Convention of America, African Methodist Episcopal Church, National Missionary Baptist Convention of America, Progressive National Baptist Convention, African Methodist Episcopal Zion Church, and Christian Methodist Episcopal Church. Others covered in this chapter include the Greek Orthodox Archdiocese of America and the Philadelphia Yearly Meeting of the Religious Society of Friends. More than 200 members of Congress belong to denominations that are members of NCC.

In 1973, the NCC Governing Board (now called the General Assembly) passed a motion supporting marijuana decriminalization. Specifically, the motion was to "support the basic recommendations in the first report of the National Commission on Marihuana and Drug Abuse for changes in federal and state law and urge our constituent church bodies to join in this action" (NCC, 1973).

That report, *Marihuana: A Signal of Misunderstanding*, was commissioned—and subsequently ignored—by the Nixon administration (National Commission, 1972). Its recommendations (endorsed by NCC) include: "Possession of marihuana for personal use would no longer be an offense, but marihuana possessed in public would remain contraband subject to summary seizure and forfeiture." In addition, "Casual distribution of small amounts of marihuana for no remuneration, or insignificant remuneration but not involving profit would no longer be an offense" (p. 152).

The NCC Governing Board added its support for "decriminalization of *cultivation*, importation, and exportation of marihuana on a scale which is obviously for personal use only" (emphasis added; NCC, 1973). A more detailed

NCC report accompanied the motion passed by the Governing Board, summarizing and analyzing the Marijuana Commission report. Excerpts from the NCC report, shedding light on the reasons for its endorsement, include:

> The current controversy over public policy concerning marihuana is draining human resources which could be focused on more significant challenges to our society." (p. 1)
>
> The inconsistencies of present public policy concerning marijuana are of such magnitude that many people, especially young adults, have become disillusioned with our criminal justice system and often with the democratic process as a whole. (p. 1)
>
> The commission lays the groundwork for thoughtful and active involvement by the religious community . . . by dealing with marihuana-related behavior as a human problem rather than a chemical one and by raising questions with theological and ethical implications. (p. 2)
>
> Marihuana is less dangerous than some other drugs which are widely used, for example, amphetamines and alcohol. . . . Therefore, when considering the danger posed by any drug to the public health, evaluations should be made comparatively. (p. 4)
>
> The fact that a very small percentage of sensitive or unstable individuals cannot use a substance without ill effects does not seem sufficient cause for use of that substance to be prohibited by public policy. (pp. 4–5)
>
> One of the gravest threats to our social order related to marihuana *is not caused by the drug itself, but by public policy which has criminalized marihuana use* [emphasis added]. The effect of incarceration in a jail or prison on the marihuana users is far more dangerous than marihuana use. (p. 5)
>
> Law enforcement officers may use marihuana laws to harass persons whom they regard as undesirable, when no other evidence of misconduct is available. (p. 6)

These concerns are even more on point today than when the NCC passed its motion and report in 1973.

The Marihuana Commission and the NCC explicitly rejected both "approval of use" and "elimination of use." Instead, the policy recommendations are part of an attempt at "discouragement of use" (p. 7).

Unfortunately, the NCC motion endorsing the Marihuana Commission report was not in the form of a policy statement, and therefore it is not still in effect as an official NCC position, although its reasoning is sound and should be seriously considered by all people of faith and goodwill today.

Fortunately, the NCC Governing Board did pass an official policy statement in 1979, *Challenges to the Injustice of the Criminal Justice System*, which includes the recommendation of "decriminalization (removal of criminal sanctions) of certain public and private acts where there is no intent to harm

or injury to another person or group of people" (p. 6). Though this statement does not give any examples of such acts, it stands to reason that marijuana possession is covered by this recommendation, especially considering the motion passed six years earlier. Because this text was an official policy statement, it remains in effect.

Although the NCC's executive office does not currently devote any efforts toward implementing its decriminalization recommendation, it has endorsed the Interfaith Drug Policy Initiative's sign-on statements backing two current legislative priorities: repealing mandatory minimum sentencing laws and repealing the federal law that denies financial aid to college students with drug convictions (IDPI, 2004). See the previous chapter for these statements.

NATIONAL ASSOCIATION OF EVANGELICALS

The National Association of Evangelicals (NAE) is a coalition comprising 50 evangelical Protestant denominations and several hundred independent churches; it represents 27 million Americans from more than 43,000 local congregations. Only two of NAE's member denominations are among the 25 largest Christian churches in the United States, and they are covered separately in this chapter: Assemblies of God and Church of God (based in Cleveland, Tennessee). Others include the Christian Reformed Church, Church of the Nazarene, Evangelical Methodist Church, and three Presbyterian denominations not affiliated with the mainline Presbyterian Church (USA).

About a dozen members of Congress belong to NAE's member denominations; one other congressional member identifies simply as "evangelical." In addition, at least a few of the 37 members of Congress who identify as simply "Protestants" or "Christians" are probably evangelicals. Regardless of whether their congregations are members of NAE, these members of Congress are likely to share NAE's beliefs on drug issues. Moreover, some members of mainline Protestant denominations are also evangelical in their beliefs; for example, President George W. Bush is a member of the mainline United Methodist Church, but he is personally evangelical.

Most important, the NAE and other members of the religious Right are very influential in the political process, so even mainline members of Congress must be concerned about the views of their evangelical and fundamentalist constituents. On "moral values" issues, they are often the squeaky wheels that get the grease. (Other fundamentalist and conservative denominations are covered later in this chapter.)

Before detailing NAE's positions, some definitions are in order. According to Wikipedia, the Web-based encyclopedia, Protestantism "generally refers to [Christian denominations] that separated from the Catholic Church

in the Reformation of the 16th century, their offshoots, and those that share similar doctrines or ideologies. It is commonly considered one of the three major branches of Christianity, along with Catholicism and Eastern Orthodoxy" (2005a).

Evangelical Protestantism commonly "refers to a more conservative version of Protestantism focused on witnessing and conversion, personal faith testimony, and a generally more conservative view of the Bible" (Wikipedia, 2005b). It is beyond the scope of this chapter to distinguish between evangelical and fundamentalist Protestantism, which "holds the Bible as infallible, historically accurate, and decisive in all issues of controversy that the Bible is believed to directly address" (Wikipedia, 2005c). For the sake of simplicity, consider both evangelical and fundamentalist denominations to be generally more conservative, theologically and politically, than the mainline Protestant denominations defined and discussed later in this chapter.

The NAE's official policy resolutions are passed by its National Convention. These positions do not supersede those of each member denomination or congregation; rather, they reflect the shared values of the denominations. The NAE has its own advocacy personnel that give public witness to these positions. Though these resolutions generally do not flesh out their reasoning with specific references to the Bible, it can be reasonably assumed that they are based on the same passages cited by the evangelical Assemblies of God, previously detailed in this chapter.

The NAE's 1970 *Traffic in Drugs* resolution declares that the "use of drugs is sweeping away the moral and spiritual foundations of our society. The whole future of our civilization is at stake at the point of moral integrity." Accordingly, the NAE "affirms adamant opposition to the illegal traffic in drugs and our strong insistence on adequate legislation and strict enforcement." The resolution adds, "We condemn contemporary arguments that marijuana is harmless and no worse than alcohol. We contend that marijuana and alcohol are both harmful, and are detrimental to the physical, emotional, moral and spiritual health of our society" (NAE, 1970).

The NAE's 1988 *Illegal Drugs* resolution states, "Because of biblical teaching regarding the body as a creation of God and because of the suffering, pain and death caused by drugs . . . NAE reaffirms its commitment to support all *appropriate* efforts to rid our society of this evil" (emphasis added).

Though it is clear that NAE opposes legal access to marijuana, it is unclear whether marijuana users should be subject to criminal penalties. What exactly does the NAE mean by "appropriate"? Furthermore, although NAE passed several resolutions opposing alcohol use and calling for increased restrictions on access and advertising (e.g., the *Alcohol Abuse* resolution, NAE, 1989), it is unclear whether the NAE advocates a return to alcohol prohibition. The 1961 *Beverage Alcohol* resolution states that "we encourage our

people to aid all governmental efforts to discourage by law the sale and use of alcoholic beverages"; however, it doesn't specify whether these laws would involve reasonable regulations or complete prohibition.

Regardless, there are some signs of hope. Many evangelicals are involved in prison ministry work, mainly working to rehabilitate offenders and convert them to evangelical Christianity. Through their work, they see firsthand how bad the prison situation is. Accordingly, NAE's 1983 *Sentencing Reform* resolution recognizes that "America's prisons now have far more inmates than they were designed to hold. A recent federal study revealed that this overcrowding results in discipline problems, increased violence, illness and suicides. . . . It is thus evident that the prison experience is more often than not destructive rather than rehabilitating." It adds that "half of those in prison have been convicted of non-violent offenses," and recommends that "non-dangerous offenders be punished through strictly enforced orders of restitution to the victims of crimes and through community service."

Therefore, it seems that NAE would support policy changes to keep marijuana users out of prison, short of removing the possibility of arrest and some form of community service (and probably coerced treatment). In addition, it is possible that NAE would support the repeal of mandatory minimum sentencing laws, thereby giving judges discretion to provide more appropriate sentences for non-violent marijuana distributors. The NAE has not taken a stand for or against allowing the medicinal use of marijuana.

SOUTHERN BAPTIST CONVENTION

The Southern Baptist Convention (SBC) is the second-largest denomination in the United States, with more than 16 million members (including 38 members of Congress). It is a fundamentalist Protestant denomination. Resolutions are passed during the annual convention meeting.

The SBC's 1997 *Resolution on Drug Abuse* says that the "nation's drug problem" is a "deadly enemy" that "continues to erode the physical, moral, and spiritual well-being of our nation." It recommends "total abstention from all alcoholic beverages and all illegal drugs" and "active involvement in the effort to rid our country of drug abuse."

It does not specify whether these efforts should involve the criminal justice system or should be limited to education, treatment, prayer, and moral persuasion. However, the SBC's 1970 Resolution called *Drugs and Alcohol* "opposes any legislation that causes increased use of drugs and alcohol," and recommends "appropriate new legislation that will result in enforceable and scientifically correct laws on narcotics, alcohol, and dangerous drugs."

This is probably understood by most Southern Baptists to mean opposing laws to allow legal access or the removal of criminal penalties for possession.

However, its precise wording indicates that the denomination would not oppose such policy changes as long as it can be proven that use would not increase.

The Southern Baptist Convention was an ardent advocate of alcohol prohibition, even passing a resolution in 1936, three years after the repeal of Prohibition, harshly condemning repeal and calling for the reenactment of "the prohibition of the manufacture, distribution and sale of all intoxicating beverages."

Note, however, that the convention did not call for criminal laws against possession of alcohol for personal use. Could this distinction also apply to marijuana policy?

It is also unclear whether the SBC even continues to support alcohol prohibition. The 1936 resolution says that "until we can secure the return and the firm re-establishment of prohibition, both State and National, which is our goal and for which we will constantly strive, we use all diligence to secure the enactment of much needed regulatory and restrictive measures." Indeed, the SBC passed numerous resolutions since that time (including as recently as 1991) calling for various strict regulations on alcohol advertising and access; however, none of these resolutions reaffirm its support for Prohibition. This adds further ambiguity to its position on marijuana policy, considering that abstinence is just as strongly recommended for both substances.

The SBC's position on mandatory minimum sentencing is also unclear. Its 1921 untitled resolution, issued during Prohibition, calls for a crackdown on "moonshining" and "bootlegging." It says, "We doubt whether this can be done unless the penalty is made more drastic and prison sentences made mandatory instead of being left optional with the judges." This is the only known resolution by a religious body expressing support for mandatory minimum sentencing.

Nevertheless, the SBC's 1971 *Resolution on Prison Reform* recommends "expanded parole alternatives necessary to make prisons more honestly correctional." This implicitly rescinds its support for mandatory minimums, as these sentencing laws do not allow parole.

The SBC has no official position on the medicinal use of marijuana. Interestingly, the SBC's 1991 *Resolution on Endangerment of Our Religious Liberties* criticizes a U.S. Supreme Court decision that curtailed the right of Native American Church members to use peyote (a psychedelic drug) in its religious rituals. The resolution states, "We emphatically do not condone the use of illegal drugs, while we strongly object to the court's reasoning in this case," as it "seriously threatens the protection of the free exercise of religion assured by the First Amendment to the United States Constitution." Perhaps this opinion would also apply to the religious use of marijuana (discussed in the previous chapter)?

In short, it seems that the nation's leading religious Right denomination, while strongly against the use of marijuana, is not necessarily (at least on paper) as clearly opposed to various marijuana law reform options as might have been assumed.

MAINLINE PROTESTANT DENOMINATIONS

In addition to the United Methodist Church (previously detailed), mainline denominations include the Evangelical Lutheran Church in America, Presbyterian Church (USA), Episcopal Church, American Baptist Churches in the USA, United Church of Christ, Disciples of Christ, and the Church of the Brethren.

They are among the most supportive denominations on marijuana law reform, as detailed individually below.

Although membership in most mainline denominations has been gradually declining for several years, six remain among the top 25 largest Christian denominations in the United States, and members are overrepresented in the U.S. Congress relative to their numbers in the general population. Most have Washington, D.C.-based public advocacy offices lobbying on behalf of their official positions.

Mainline Protestant denominations, according to Wikipedia, are those "with moderate theologies which attempt to be open to new ideas and societal changes without abandoning what they consider to be the historical basis of the Christian faith":

> They are neither ultra-liberal . . . nor fundamentalist in their beliefs. These groups have been more open to demands for the ordination of women. They have been far from uniform in their reaction to the gay rights movement, but have not rejected it out of hand in the way that it has been by the Catholic church and the more conservative Protestant churches. They take a moderate view with regards to military service . . . and none are historically peace churches except possibly the Church of the Brethren—but all express reservations about aggressive use of military force for any reason.
>
> The hallmark of the mainline churches would seemingly be moderation. Only a few members or ministers in them would condemn the use of alcohol in moderation. . . . Few would suggest that [the Bible] was . . . the result of God through the Holy Spirit directly dictating his revealed word to human authors, as more conservative groups generally maintain. . . . There is a general consensus that Scripture, while very important, must both be interpreted through the lens of the cultures in which it was originally written, and examined, like everything else, using God-given reason.

The Evangelical Lutheran Church in America (ELCA), despite its name, is actually a mainline, not evangelical, denomination. It is the sixth-largest Christian denomination in the United States, with more than 5 million members, including 17 members of Congress. Its most recent drug policy document, *Chemical Comforters and Drug Dependency*, is more than 30 years old and was passed by its predecessor church body (American Lutheran Church [ALC], 1972). Therefore, according to the disclaimer on ELCA's Web page, it is considered an "historical document" which may "act as policy when sufficient agreement exists and the ELCA has not adopted another statement on the same subject," but it is not in itself official policy.

Though recognizing various problems that drugs (including marijuana) can cause and discouraging "misuse," it states: "Much of the information circulated about drugs today is stereotyped, hysterical, and overly moralistic. . . . Drug users are often seen more as criminals than as victims or as persons with an illness, a disease, or a problem of living. Only recently have many persons discovered that drug misuse is more a problem of adjustment to life's demands than a crime" (p. 5).

Its recommendations include "Review present drug laws and work to change them where they are unjust," and "Work with other groups to establish fair and humane drug laws" (pp. 10, 11). In the context of the document's aforementioned criticism of treating drug users as criminals, the recommendations implicitly support decriminalization.

However, they stop short of supporting legal access, instead urging "efforts that focus on prosecuting illegal drug 'pushers' and those who traffic in illegal distribution of dangerous drugs" (p. 11).

Based on this document and other statements on matters such as racial justice, the ELCA's Office for Governmental Affairs endorsed the Interfaith Drug Policy Initiative's sign-on statements backing two current legislative priorities: repealing mandatory minimum sentencing laws and repealing the federal law that denies financial aid to college students with drug convictions (IDPI, 2004).

The same ELCA office also endorsed the 2002 sign-on statement *Eight Steps to Effectively Controlling Drug Abuse and the Drug Market*, which includes a variety of moderate drug policy reform recommendations (National Coalition for Effective Drug Stategies [NCEDS], 2002/2003; see also the previous chapter).

The Presbyterian Church (USA) is the ninth-largest Christian denomination in the United States, with more than 3.4 million members, including 43 members of Congress. Its General Assembly passed a *Freedom and Substance Abuse* resolution in 1993 urging "abstinence from the manufacture, sale, purchase, possession, or use of illicit drugs," but also "decriminalization of possession with judicial focus on drug manufacturers and suppliers."

This position builds upon five other drug-related positions the denomination has taken since 1948, all of which urge a compassionate response to drug use, abuse, and addiction. The 1993 resolution summarizes these positions, as well as its 1986 alcohol position, which recognizes "the choice to drink as a personal decision, and offered four guidelines: (1) Abstention in all situations should be supported and encouraged; (2) moderate drinking in low-risk situations should not be opposed; (3) heavy drinking in any situation should be vigorously discouraged; and (4) any drinking in high-risk situations . . . should be vigorously discouraged." In summarizing the principles guiding its past drug-related positions, the 1993 statement explains, "The use of mind-altering substances is to be judged by their effect on health, creativity, reason, conscience, and respect for self and others."

Accordingly, it seems that if marijuana were to be legalized or decriminalized—and demonstrated to be no more harmful than alcohol on these measures—then marijuana use would probably also be considered a personal decision subject to the same moderation guidelines.

Finally, the PCUSA also endorsed the Interfaith Drug Policy Initiative's aforementioned two current legislative priorities and the *Eight Steps* sign-on statement (see the previous chapter).

The Episcopal Church is the 15th-largest Christian denomination, with more than 2.3 million members, including 42 members of Congress.

The Episcopal General Convention passed a policy statement in 1985 noting that alcohol and drug abuse "are manifested by a three-fold impairment of the body, mind and spirit," which also affect the family and larger community. However, it does not actually recommend what the laws should be, except to point out that the church "has never endorsed prohibiting the use of beverages containing alcohol" and that "Scripture offers Jesus' example of the use and serving of wine in his first miracle at Cana and in the institution of the Holy Eucharist" (Episcopal Church, 1985). It is unclear as to whether this anti-prohibition sentiment also applies to marijuana, which isn't mentioned in the *Holy Bible*. Several subsequent resolutions on alcohol and other drugs also stress treatment and education, without specifying what the laws should be.

The Executive Council's 1970 *Drug Abuse* resolution expresses a "deep concern" about the "role of drugs in the enslavement of personality" and about drug-related crimes. However, it also recommends "more appropriate comparative legal penalties for the possession of specific drugs such as marijuana." It is unclear whether this would include removing criminal penalties. Interestingly, the resolution also urges the dissemination of information on drug effects, rehabilitation, legal aspects, and "criteria for responsible use of drugs" (Episcopal Church, 1970).

In 1982, the General Convention passed a resolution urging "that the therapeutic use of marijuana be permitted when deemed medically

appropriate by duly licensed medical practitioners" (Episcopal Church, 1982b). However, it quickly passed another resolution clarifying that its support for medical marijuana "in no way wishes to be understood as failing to recognize the serious problems of drug abuse in our society, especially among young people; and further, we do acknowledge and proclaim that there are harmful effects which can be permanently disabling with the use of marijuana, especially among young people who are physically, mentally, and spiritually in their developing years" (Episcopal Church, 1982a).

Finally, the General Convention passed a resolution in 2000 that opposes mandatory minimum sentencing for nonviolent crimes (Episcopal Church, 2000) and subsequently endorsed IDPI's mandatory minimum repeal statement.

In addition, the Episcopal Diocese of New York voted in 1975 to support "the immediate decriminalization of the possession in private of marijuana for personal use," as well as "a model of strict state-regulated control of marijuana sales to adults."

The American Baptist Churches in the USA (ABC) is the 19th-largest Christian denomination, with nearly 1.5 million members, including eight members of Congress.

The ABC's 1983 criminal justice policy statement, as modified in 2004, recommends, "Imprisonment should be imposed only when the continued freedom of the offender poses a direct threat to society and when no acceptable alternative exists." It recommends services such as "counseling, medical or social services" for "persons whose behavior is now termed illegal but does not violate the rights of others. Participants in such behavior reflect human needs which cannot be alleviated by the use of criminal sanctions" (ABC, 2004). Without specifically mentioning marijuana, personal-use possession would clearly meet these criteria.

The ABC's 1986 resolution on alcohol and other drugs enumerates the problems associated with drug abuse and addiction, but it does not specify what the laws should be; it says only that the government should "standardize" substance-related laws and "combat organized crime and its lucrative traffic in drugs." It also recommends more resources for treatment and education, including materials that "enable persons to make responsible decisions about alcohol and other chemical use." Might these "responsible decisions" include moderate, responsible marijuana use?

The 2004 statement also affirms the need for judges to be allowed some freedom in deciding on punishment in particular cases: "Mandatory sentences should be opposed. Sentences that best serve the needs of society and the offender require judicial discretion."

The United Church of Christ (UCC) is the 21st-largest Christian denomination, with 1.3 million members, including eight members of Congress.

The UCC's General Synod passed a dozen relevant resolutions between 1975 and 2002, discussing the problems associated with alcohol and other drug use, the need for more treatment and education, and the problems with our current criminal justice system. The strongest recommendations include: "Seek to reduce the punitive and harmful effects of various societal responses to substance abuse and abusers, including a reduction in the use of incarceration for minor offenses" (UCC, 1997); and "Shift its emphasis from a law enforcement paradigm in favor of a policy that treats drug use as a health problem with social and economic implications" (UCC, 2003).

This strongly implies support for decriminalization and leaves open the possibility of legal access alternatives to the current criminal market. In addition, the 2003 statement opposes mandatory minimum sentencing. The UCC's executive office also signed IDPI's statements on repealing mandatory minimums and restoring college aid to drug offenders, as well as a 2002 *Coalition for Compassionate Access* statement declaring, "We believe that seriously ill people should not be subject to arrest and imprisonment for using medical marijuana with their doctors' approval."

The Disciples of Christ is not one of the 25 largest Christian denominations, so research into their positions has not yet been completed. Finally, the public witness office of the Church of the Brethren (also not in the top 25) endorsed IDPI's sign-on statements on mandatory minimums and financial aid. In addition, the Brethren General Board's 1975 *Criminal Justice Reform* report recommends "that more appropriate and helpful means be found to deal with offenses such as vagrancy, drug use, drunkenness, gambling, and prostitution. (At present, half of those arrested and half of those in local jails are charged with these offenses)." This indicates support for marijuana decriminalization.

AFRICAN-AMERICAN DENOMINATIONS

Seven of the historically black churches are also among the 25 largest Christian denominations in the United States. More than 18 members of Congress belong to these denominations.

Unfortunately, most of these denominations do not seem to have any official policy statements on marijuana, alcohol, or other drugs—either on the use of the substances or on specific policies. (IDPI's research assistant spent three months trying to find any statements that might exist.)

The Progressive National Baptist Convention (PNBC)—the 12th-largest Christian denomination, with 2.5 million members—passed a resolution opposing mandatory minimum sentencing, which was promoted by IDPI at PNBC's 2004 annual conference. The PNBC also signed IDPI's statements supporting college aid for drug offenders and medical marijuana.

In addition, in January 2005, the PNBC, along with the National Baptist Convention USA (7th-largest), National Baptist Convention of America (8th-largest), National Missionary Baptist Convention of America (tied for 12th-largest), passed a joint resolution on several policy issues, including "an end to the prison-industrial complex," which includes this recommendation: "We call for elimination of mandatory minimum sentencing and oppose efforts to privatize prison operations and administration" (Joint Baptist Board Meeting, 2005).

Otherwise, these denominations don't seem to have any policy statements specific to drug policy. Moreover, the following denominations don't seem to have official positions on anything related to this topic: Church of God in Christ (4th-largest Christian denomination); African Methodist Episcopal Church (tied for 12th-largest); and African Methodist Episcopal Zion Church (20th-largest). The Christian Methodist Episcopal Church (not in the top 25) also did not have any relevant positions available.

QUAKERS

Quakers (officially known as Friends) are organized on the district level into what are known as "yearly meetings." Many of the 31 yearly meetings in the United States are members of Quaker denominational associations such as the Friends United Meeting and the Friends General Conference, although some are independent and some are members of smaller, more conservative associations.

Although a relatively small denomination (approximately 500,000, including one member of Congress), the Society of Friends has a long history of being disproportionately influential on issues such as peace, prison reform, and racial justice. It also has a long-standing position of advocating abstinence from the use of alcohol and other drugs that could cloud a person's direct experience of the "Inner Light" of God. However, the violence and other problems caused by the "War on Drugs" has led many Quakers to advocate various degrees of reform of these laws.

Three Quaker organizations, the Friends Committee on National Legislation (FCNL), American Friends Service Committee (AFSC), and the Philadelphia Yearly Meeting are featured here as having favorable marijuana-related policy positions.

The FCNL is governed by a General Committee of Friends representing 26 yearly meetings and seven national Friends organizations. Its 2003 *Statement of Legislative Policy* includes a criminal justice section, which recommends, "Violent acts that stem from using, selling, or transferring drugs, or obtaining money to use them, should be prosecuted through the criminal justice system. However, substance abuse itself is fundamentally a health

issue requiring prevention, education, treatment, and rehabilitation" (FCNL, 2003a). This implies some degree of support for decriminalization.

The FCNL also has a position supporting the rights of Native Americans to use peyote in its religious rituals (FCNL, 2003b). Perhaps this opinion would also apply to the religious use of marijuana?

The AFSC has been giving public witness to the Quaker values of peace and justice on a variety of issues in the United States and abroad for nearly 100 years. Its 2001 position on sentencing reform in Arizona includes a recommendation to "eliminate mandatory minimum sentences." The AFSC also has a statement on its Web page called, *Eight Myths About the War on Drugs*, one of which includes, "A good drug policy is a policy that outlaws the use of drugs" (AFSC, ca. 2000). By considering this a "myth," this indicates support for removing criminal penalties for personal-use possession. In fact, the refutation of this myth explains that "harm reduction" is a better approach, defined as "a set of practical strategies that reduce negative consequences of drug use, incorporating a spectrum of strategies from safer use to managed use to abstinence."

Most significant is the fact that the Philadelphia Yearly Meeting of the Religious Society of Friends (more than 300 years old) passed a statement in 1978 explicitly calling for the decriminalization of marijuana. Though noting that it did not "condone the use of marijuana," the meeting stated that it "strongly opposes the imposition of criminal sanctions by the state for an individual's refusal to heed this advice. We believe that imprisonment is an unjustifiably extreme response to the use and possession of small amounts of marijuana" (PYM, 1978).

In 2000, PYM passed a drug policy statement noting that the War on Drugs "bears all the hallmarks of war: displaced populations, disrupted economies, terrorism, abandonment of hope by those the war is supposedly being fought to help, the use of military force, the curtailment of civil liberties, and the demonizing of the 'enemies.'" The statement recommends "finding paths that lead us toward peace, reconciliation, and healing," such as "exploring ways in which the vast sums now being used in this war can be diverted towards treatment, research, and education." Although it does not specify whether a regulated system of legal access is a valid option, it opens the door to that possibility.

OTHER CHRISTIAN DENOMINATIONS

The Church of Jesus Christ of Latter-Day Saints (LDS) is the fifth-largest denomination in the United States, with nearly 5.5 million members, including 15 in Congress. The Mormons, as they are known, have one of the broadest abstinence positions of any denomination. In the Book of Mormon

(considered to be sacred scripture, along with the Bible), Mormon prophet Joseph Smith recorded the "Word of Wisdom" in 1833, which forbids the use of alcohol, tobacco, or "hot drinks" containing caffeine. The church considers this abstinence position to apply to all currently illegal drugs, as well.

However, the LDS Public Affairs Department wrote in a memo to IDPI that this position "is strictly doctrinal in nature and does not translate to public policy. Because of this it is very difficult for us to comment on specific legislation or recommendations which are intended to influence public policy" (Tuttle, 2005).

This makes sense, considering that if the church were to take a position supporting the illegality of marijuana, it would have to explain why this shouldn't apply also to alcohol, tobacco, and caffeine. It is interesting that when the church argued against relaxing some of Utah's alcohol regulations in 2001, it conceded, "Current laws already provide for the availability of alcoholic beverages for adults who wish to responsibly consume," and it urged the "continuation of existing sound practices and regulations" (LDS, 2001). This raises some key questions: Does the denomination really favor current regulations that allow legal access to alcohol, and would that opinion also apply to marijuana? Or does it simply want the policies for both substances to be as strict as currently possible, which would include continuing the prohibition of marijuana?

The Lutheran Church—Missouri Synod, a fundamentalist denomination, is the 11th-largest Christian denomination, with 2.5 million members, including three in Congress. It has passed two resolutions on alcohol and other drug abuse since 1973, neither of which addresses policy matters. It also has no statements on prison or other related issues.

The Churches of Christ, a fundamentalist denomination, is tied for the 16th-largest denomination, with 1.5 million members. It has no central offices, and therefore no official policy statements on anything. The Pentecostal Assemblies of the World, an evangelical denomination tied for 16th-largest, also has no official positions related to marijuana policy; nor does the evangelical Baptist Bible Fellowship International (22nd-largest).

Official marijuana-related policy positions could not be found, despite persistent attempts by IDPI's research assistant for three months, for the Christian Churches and Churches of Christ (23rd-largest) or the Church of God (Cleveland, Tennessee; 25th-largest). The Greek Orthodox Archdiocese of America (tied for 16th-largest) did not provide any useful information to IDPI's research assistant, although we found a publication stating that in 1970 the church "called for the retention and strengthening of existing laws" regarding marijuana (Harakas, 1983, p. 96). It is unclear whether this position still stands and whether any updates have been made regarding medical marijuana or mandatory sentencing.

The Jehovah's Witnesses (24th-largest) is explicitly neutral on all public policy issues as a matter of doctrine: "Following the examples set by Jesus and first-century Christians, Jehovah's Witnesses do not share in the politics or wars of any nation." However, the denomination instructs its members to "honor and respect governmental authority" and "be law-abiding" (JW, 2003). Accordingly, like most Christian denominations, members must obey the laws of the land except when such laws are in direct violation of God's laws. Even though the church does not require its members to abstain from alcohol, marijuana use is forbidden (at least as long as it remains illegal).

Finally, although the Mennonite Church USA is not among the 25-largest, because they are disproportionately influential on various peace and justice issues it is worth noting that the Mennonite Central Committee opposes mandatory minimum sentencing (Mennonite Central Committee, 2004).

JUDAISM

There are nearly 5 million Jews in the United States, including 37 members of the U.S. Congress. Although Judaism is technically considered one denomination, there are four different "movements" of Judaism analogous to distinct denominations: Reform, Conservative, Orthodox, and Reconstructionist. More than a million Jews self-identify as "just Jewish," and another million who identify with one of the four major movements are not members of a congregation (called a "synagogue"; Ament, 2005, pp. 35, 4). Unfortunately, no precise information is available for movement affiliations of Jewish members of Congress, so estimates are provided based on percentages of the total U.S. Jewish population.

The Union for Reform Judaism (URJ) represents nearly 1.5 million Reform Jews in the United States (including an estimated 18 members of Congress). The URJ passed several relevant resolutions since 1968. The most significant positions taken in these resolutions are detailed below.

The URJ's 1993 substance abuse resolution includes a recommendation that governments "reassess their priorities in combating drug abuse in the United States and Canada and in allocating resources emphasize prevention, education, and treatment rather than enforcement" (URJ, 1993). This raises the possibility of support for removing criminal penalties for marijuana possession.

Although Judaism advocates that individuals follow the laws of the land, provided that those laws do not violate God's laws (see chap. 11 of this volume), what if marijuana possession were no longer a crime? Some guidance may come from the URJ's position on alcohol, urging members to "exercise moderation in the consumption of alcoholic beverages,

demonstrating due regard for their personal well-being, the well-being of others, and an awareness of the example set for adolescents and children" (URJ, 1989).

Unfortunately, the URJ does not advocate regulated, legal access to marijuana; in fact, its 1989 resolution "[calls] upon the President and the Congress to provide adequate funding for the government's anti-drug programs to achieve its objective of cutting off the supply of cocaine and other illegal drugs" (URJ, 1989).

However, the URJ's long-standing position is that penalties should not be excessive. A 1999 resolution includes the recommendation, "Support legislation to repeal state and federal laws that require mandatory incarceration of first-time drug offenders, and to restore judicial discretion in sentencing first-time offenders" (URJ, 1999). Accordingly, the URJ endorsed IDPI's mandatory minimum sign-on statement.

The URJ also passed a detailed resolution in 2003 advocating legal access to medical marijuana, incorporating insights from Jewish theology as well as medical science and ethics. "According to our tradition, a physician is obligated to heal the sick," the resolution begins, and after thoroughly exploring all of the issues involved it concludes with several recommendations including, "Call upon congregations to advocate for the necessary changes in local, state and federal law to permit the medicinal use of marijuana and ensure its accessibility for that purpose" (URJ, 2003). This resolution is the culmination of several years of work, initiated by the Women of Reform Judaism, thanks to the diligent efforts of member Jane Marcus (who currently serves on IDPI's leadership council).

Two other Reform Jewish bodies also have relevant positions:

The Central Conference of American Rabbis (CCAR) represents the nation's Reform Jewish rabbis. The CCAR passed a resolution in 1972 urging the government to adopt the recommendations of the National Commission on Marijuana and Drug Abuse, including: "Possession in private of marijuana for personal use would no longer be an offense," and "Distribution in private of small amounts of marijuana for no remuneration or insignificant remuneration not involving a profit would no longer be an offense." The CCAR added that marijuana use "is essentially a matter of private behavior and individual conscience" (CCAR, 1972).

In 1993, the CCAR passed a resolution enumerating many of the harmful effects of the drug war and recommended "that our society must recognize drug use and abuse as the medical and social problems that they are and that they must be treated with medical and social solutions," and "that an objective commission be immediately empowered by Congress to recommend revision of the drug laws of the United States in order to reduce the harm our current policies are causing" (CCAR, 1993). This opens the possibility of regulated legal access.

In 2001, the CCAR passed a resolution recommending legal access to the medical use of marijuana (CCAR, 2001), which followed the Women of Reform Judaism's lead and helped build momentum toward the passage of the URJ medical marijuana resolution in 2003.

The Religious Action Center (RAC) of Reform Judaism is the URJ's public policy arm in Washington, D.C. Accordingly, it advocates the aforementioned positions of URJ and CCAR. The RAC elaborates on the Reform Jewish perspective on a variety of drug policy issues in its 2001 *Substance Abuse* issues report. For example, the RAC expressed its support for restoring college aid to drug offenders.

In addition, the RAC's report elaborates on substance abuse and Jewish values: "Our tradition teaches us that abusing substances is wrong. The introduction to Maimonides' Mishneh Torah states: 'Seeing that keeping the body healthy and whole is the way of God . . . therefore a person must distance himself from things that destroy the body. . . .' Drug abuse is therefore forbidden, but we are advised to learn to heal the body, not to punish it for things that already destroy it. Drug treatment is in keeping with Maimonides' injunction, while incarceration for personal use of harmful substances could be considered additional bodily punishment" (RAC, 2001).

Although this analysis fails to account for moderate, non-harmful use of marijuana, it wisely explains that even if someone's drug use is harmful, criminal penalties are not an appropriate response.

The United Synagogue of Conservative Judaism (USCJ) represents nearly 1.5 million Conservative Jews in the United States (including an estimated 13 members of Congress). Although the USCJ passed resolutions on substance abuse in 1987 and 1991, neither of these deals with policy issues. In addition, the USCJ has no relevant criminal justice or prison statements available.

Neither the Orthodox Union (representing nearly 600,000 Jews) nor the Jewish Reconstructionist Federation (representing approximately 50,000 Jews) has any relevant official policy positions.

Finally, the Progressive Jewish Alliance (a nondenominational social change organization) passed a *Drug Policy Reform Statement* in 2001 calling for a variety of very substantial drug policy changes, including "decriminalizing marijuana and reclassifying it as a legal, taxed, and regulated substance in the manner of alcohol" (PJA, 2001).

ISLAM

Estimates of the number of Muslims in the United States range from 1 million to 7 million, although the most likely estimate is approximately 2 million (Pluralism Project, 2005). Unfortunately, there are no distinct

denominational headquarters in the United States. The IDPI research assistant tried for three months to find any marijuana policy–related positions from a variety of Muslim associations, to no avail.

The World's Religions explains that the Koran (Islam's holy book) prohibits the use of alcohol. In addition, "Islam joins faith to politics, religion to society, inseparably" (Smith, 1991, p. 249). Accordingly, it is widely recognized that Islam's policy position on alcohol is that it should be eradicated through total prohibition.

Sullum (2003) provides a detailed analysis of this position with respect to marijuana and other drugs. First, there is the question of whether the term *khamr*, which the Koran forbids, refers only to alcohol or to any potential intoxicant. Muslims generally agree that it applies to anything that is potentially intoxicating. However, there is some disagreement among and within different sects of Islam as to which drugs produce intoxication akin to that which alcohol can produce. For example, coffee and tobacco are generally not considered to be *khamr*. What about marijuana (or hashish, made from marijuana resin)? Although hashish has been tolerated in many Muslim countries over the centuries, many Muslim authorities today also forbid the use of hashish. This view is most likely ubiquitous among Muslim leaders in the United States.

What about policy? Would the Islamic principles of justice and mercy be at odds with the excessively punitive approach in the United States? Could Muslims support the prohibition of marijuana but oppose criminal penalties for users or mandatory sentencing for nonviolent distributors? Would the Nation of Islam or other predominantly African-American Muslim groups in the United States be critical of the effect that drug sentencing laws are having on people of color? Do Muslims active in prison ministry consider these laws to be counterproductive? Further research is clearly needed.

BUDDHISM

Estimates of the number of Buddhists in the United States range from 1 million to 3 million (Moore, 1997). More precise estimates are difficult: In addition to Asian Americans, for whom Buddhism is their religion of origin, Buddhism is increasingly popular among Americans who were raised in other faiths but now incorporate Buddhist philosophy and practice into their lives instead of, or in addition to, their religions of origin. Although there are at least 1,500 Buddhist temples, retreat centers, and other groups throughout the United States, there are no central denominational entities. In fact, people can use Buddhist meditation techniques without being part of any group or even considering themselves Buddhists.

The Buddha provided many instructions to help people transcend greed, hatred, and delusion and become more wise, compassionate, and genuinely happy. One of these instructions is the precept to "refrain from the use of intoxicants causing heedlessness," as it is commonly translated. This is commonly understood to include marijuana.

The renowned Buddhist teacher Jack Kornfield argues that the aforementioned translation is not quite accurate; rather, the precept is to "refrain from using intoxicants *to the point of* heedlessness, loss of mindfulness, or loss of awareness" (emphasis added). His elaboration is as follows: "It does not say not to use them and it is very explicit. There is another translation of it which says not to use intoxicants which remove that sense of attention or awareness. Then it is left up to the individual, as are all of the precepts, to use as a guideline to become more genuinely conscious" (Forte, 1997, p. 120).

Regardless of the translation—whether or not the precept precludes moderate use of alcohol, marijuana, or other substances—an important point is that this is an instruction for those who choose to practice Buddhism, in order to foster their practice. Buddhism does not say that intoxication is a "sin" but that it is an impediment on the path to enlightenment. Punishment and coercion are not compassionate responses. Extensive research has revealed no Buddhist teachings that substance use should be a crime.

Unfortunately, because there are no Buddhist denominational entities in the United States akin to the Christian and Jewish groups that take positions on sociopolitical issues, there also do not seem to be any official Buddhist positions opposing the nation's current marijuana laws. Even the Buddhist Peace Fellowship has no relevant positions on drug policy or criminal justice matters.

Only one Buddhist group, the Engaged Zen Foundation, has taken a position on the matter: It opposes mandatory drug sentencing laws. The group's original mission was to teach prisoners how to meditate, but their observance of the "appalling conditions" in the prisons motivated them to call for a variety of criminal justice reforms (Engaged Zen, 2004).

OTHER RELIGIONS

The humanistic American Ethical Union, although a small denomination, is included in this chapter because its 1972 Annual Assembly passed a resolution criticizing the harmful effects of marijuana prohibition and calling for laws "permitting the use, possession, manufacture, sale and transfer of marijuana by adults similar to . . . tobacco and alcohol in American society" (AEU, 1972).

Religions not featured in this chapter because they comprise less than 1 percent of the U.S. population include Hinduism, Sikhism, Native American religions, and various pagan and Wiccan religions. Future research will attempt to find and analyze their positions, if any.

Special thanks to IDPI research assistants Troy Dayton, Lucia Cruz, Grant Smith, Rachel Flinn, and Ben Cooper, as well as the numerous archivists and public information personnel from dozens of denominations and other religious groups.

NOTE

If some of the policy positions are difficult to obtain from the religious groups, most of them can be accessed by visiting http://www.idpi.us/Earleywine_book_references or by calling the Interfaith Drug Policy Initiative Foundation at 301-938-1577.

REFERENCES

Ament, J. (2005). American Jewish religious denominations. *Report series on the National Jewish Population Survey 2000–01.* New York: United Jewish Communities.

American Baptist Churches in the USA. (1986). *Alcoholism and other chemical dependencies* [Resolution]. Valley Forge, PA: Author.

American Baptist Churches in the USA. (2004). *Criminal justice* [Policy statement]. Valley Forge, PA: Author.

American Ethical Union. (1972). *Legalization of marijuana* [Resolution]. New York: Author.

American Friends Service Committee. (ca. 2000). *Eight myths about the war on drugs.* Philadelphia: Author. Retrieved March 2005 from http://www.afsc.org/colombia/learn-about/myths-war-on-drugs.htm.

American Friends Service Committee. (2001). *Ten reasons why sentencing reform makes sense for Arizona.* Tucson: Author. Retrieved February 2005 from http://www.afsc.org/az/prisons/sentencing-reform.htm.

American Lutheran Church. (1972). *Chemical comforters and drug dependency.* Minneapolis: Author.

Assemblies of God. (1985). *Abstinence* [Position paper]. Springfield, MO: Author. Retrieved February 2005 from http://ag.org/top/beliefs/position_papers/4187_abstinence.cfm.

Assemblies of God. (2000). *Matters of Christian character: Alcohol, tobacco, and drugs.* Springfield, MO: Author. Retrieved February 2005 from http://ag.org/top/beliefs/christian_character/charctr_08_drugs.cfm.

Assemblies of God Perspectives. (2004). *Perspectives: Contemporary social, political, medical, and moral issues.* Springfield, MO: Author. Retrieved February 2005 from http://ag.org/top/beliefs/contemporary_issues/issues_07_law_crime.cfm.

Central Conference of American Rabbis. (1972). *Marijuana* [Resolution]. New York: Author.

Central Conference of American Rabbis. (1993). *Drug trade and drug legislation* [Resolution]. New York: Author.

Central Conference of American Rabbis. (2001). *Resolution on the medical use of marijuana.* New York: Author.

Church of the Brethren. (1975). *Criminal Justice Reform* [Statement]. Elgin, IL: Author.

Church of Jesus Christ of Latter-day Saints. (2001, October 10). *Written comments on alcohol advertising and alcohol policy.* Salt Lake City: LDS Newsroom. Retrieved March 2005 from http://www.lds.org/newsroom/showrelease/0,15503,4044-1-6496,00.html.

Coalition for Compassionate Access. (2002). *Medical marijuana sign-on statement.* Washington, DC: Marijuana Policy Project.

Earleywine, M. (2002). *Understanding marijuana: A new look at the scientific evidence.* New York: Oxford University Press.

Engaged Zen Foundation. (2004). *Our mission.* Sedgwick, ME: Author. Retrieved March 2005 from http://www.engaged-zen.org/mission.html.

Episcopal Church. (1970). *Drug abuse* [Resolution]. Austin: Author.

Episcopal Church. (1982a). *Recognize the distinction between the abuse and therapeutic use of marijuana* [Resolution]. Austin: Author.

Episcopal Church. (1982b). *Urge the adoption of laws permitting the medicinal use of marijuana* [Resolution]. Austin: Author.

Episcopal Church. (1985). *An Episcopal national policy on alcohol and drug abuse* [Policy statement]. Austin: Author.

Episcopal Church. (2000). *Reaffirm criminal justice system reform* [Resolution]. Austin: Author.

Episcopal Diocese of New York. (1975). *Marijuana* [Resolution]. New York: Author.

Forte, R. (Ed.) (1997). Psychedelic experience and spiritual practice: A Buddhist perspective. An interview with Jack Kornfield. In *Entheogens and the future of religion* (pp. 119–135). San Francisco: Council on Spiritual Practices.

Friends Committee on National Legislation. (2003a). *Statement of legislative policy.* Washington, DC: Author.

Friends Committee on National Legislation. (2003b). *Religious freedom for Native Americans* [Statement]. Washington, DC: Author.

Harakas, S. S. (1983). *Let mercy abound: Social concern in the Greek Orthodox Church.* Brookline, MA: Holy Cross Orthodox Press.

Interfaith Drug Policy Initiative. (2004). *Drug policy positions of religious groups* [Fact sheet]. Washington, DC: Author.

Jehovah's Witnesses. (2003). *Beliefs: Role in society.* Brooklyn: Watch Tower Bible and Tract Society. Retrieved February 2005 from http://www .jw-media.org/beliefs/society.htm.

Joint Baptist Board Meeting. (2005). *Points of agreed action* [Resolution]. Nashville: Author. Retrieved March 2005 from http://www.national baptist.com/Index.cfm?FuseAction=Page&PageID=1000098.

Mennonite Central Committee. (2004). *Issue: Criminal justice.* Washington, DC: Author. Retrieved February 2005 from http://www.mcc.org/us/ washington/issues/criminaljustice/index.html.

Moore, D. W. (1997). *The accidental Buddhist: Mindfulness, enlightenment, and sitting still.* Chapel Hill, NC: Algonquin Books.

National Association of Evangelicals. (1961). *Beverage alcohol.* Washington, DC: Author.

National Association of Evangelicals. (1970). *Traffic in drugs* [Resolution]. Washington, DC: Author.

National Association of Evangelicals. (1983). *Sentencing reform* [Resolution]. Washington, DC: Author.

National Association of Evangelicals. (1988). *Illegal drugs* [Resolution]. Washington, DC: Author.

National Association of Evangelicals. (1989). *Alcohol abuse* [Resolution]. Washington, DC: Author.

National Coalition for Effective Drug Strategies. (2002/2003). *Eight steps to effectively controlling drug abuse and the drug market* [Sign-on statement]. Washington, DC: Interfaith Drug Policy Initiative.

National Commission on Marihuana and Drug Abuse. (1972). *Marihuana: A signal of misunderstanding.* Washington, DC: U.S. Government Printing Office.

National Council of Churches. (1973). *Response to report of National Commission on Marihuana and Drug Abuse* [Motion and report]. New York: Author.

National Council of Churches. (1979). *Challenges to the injustice of the criminal justice system* [Policy statement]. New York: Author.

Philadelphia Yearly Meeting of the Religious Society of Friends. (1978). *Minute on decriminalization of marijuana* [Statement]. Philadelphia: Author.

Philadelphia Yearly Meeting of the Religious Society of Friends. (2000). *Minute on drug concerns* [Statement]. Philadelphia: Author.

Pluralism Project. (2005). New studies on number of Muslims in the U.S. *Religious Diversity News.* Cambridge, MA: Author.

Presbyterian Church USA. (1993). *Freedom and substance abuse* [Resolution]. Louisville, KY: Author.

Progressive Jewish Alliance. (2001). *Drug policy reform statement.* Los Angeles: Author.

Religious Action Center of Reform Judaism. (2001). *Substance abuse.* Washington, DC: Author.

Smith, H. (1991). *The world's religions.* New York: Harper Collins.

Southern Baptist Convention. (1921). *Untitled* [Resolution]. Nashville: Author.

Southern Baptist Convention. (1936). *Untitled* [Resolution]. Nashville: Author.

Southern Baptist Convention. (1970). *Resolution on drugs and alcohol.* Nashville: Author.

Southern Baptist Convention. (1971). *Resolution on prison reform.* Nashville: Author.

Southern Baptist Convention. (1991). *Resolution on endangerment of our religious liberties.* Nashville: Author.

Southern Baptist Convention. (1997). *Resolution on drug abuse.* Nashville: Author.

Sullum, J. (2003). *Saying yes: In defense of drug use.* New York: Tarcher/Penguin.

Tuttle, M. N. (2005, February 1). E-mail memo from Church of Jesus Christ of Latter-day Saints' public relations director to IDPI's research assistant.

Union for Reform Judaism. (1989). *Substance abuse* [Resolution]. New York: Author.

Union for Reform Judaism. (1993). *Dealing with substance abuse* [Resolution]. New York: Author.

Union for Reform Judaism. (1999). *Race and the U.S. criminal justice system* [Resolution]. New York: Author.

Union for Reform Judaism. (2003). *Resolution on the medicinal use of marijuana.* New York: Author.

Unitarian Universalist Association. (1970). *Legalization of marijuana* [Resolution]. Boston: Author.

Unitarian Universalist Association. (2002). *Alternatives to the war on drugs* [Statement of conscience]. Boston: Author.

Unitarian Universalist Association. (2005). *Principles and purposes.* Retrieved October 2005 from http://www.uua.org/aboutuua/principles.html.

United Church of Christ. (1997). *Compassionate response to substance abuse* [Resolution]. Cleveland, OH: Author.

United Church of Christ. (2003). *Confronting racism and militarism in U.S. drug policy* [Resolution]. Cleveland, OH: Author.

United Methodist Church. (2000). *Equal justice* [Resolution]. Nashville: Author.

United Methodist Church. (2004a). *Book of resolutions.* Nashville: Author.

United Methodist Church. (2004b). *Drug and alcohol concerns* [Resolution]. Nashville: Author.

United Methodist Church. (2005). *Book of discipline.* Nashville: Author. Retrieved October 2005 from http://www.umc-gbcs.org/site/pp.asp?c=fsJNK0PKJrH&b=845451.

U.S. Conference of Catholic Bishops. (2000). *Responsibility, rehabilitation, and restoration: A Catholic perspective on crime and criminal justice* [Statement of the Catholic Bishops of the United States]. Washington, DC: Author. Retrieved February 2004 from http://www.nccbuscc.org/sdwp/criminal.htm#policy.

Vatican: Pontifical Council for Health Pastoral Care. (2002). *Church: Drugs and drug addiction*. Rome: Libreria Editrice Vaticana.

Wikipedia: The free encyclopedia. (2005a). Protestantism. Retrieved March 2005 from http://en.wikipedia.org/wiki/Protestantism.

Wikipedia: The free encyclopedia. (2005b). Evangelicalism. Retrieved March 2005 from http://en.wikipedia.org/wiki/Evangelicalism.

Wikipedia: The free encyclopedia. (2005c). Christian fundamentalism. Retrieved March 2005 from http://en.wikipedia.org/wiki/Fundamentalist_Christianity.

Wikipedia: The free encyclopedia. (2005d). Mainline Protestantism. Retrieved March 2005 from http://en.wikipedia.org/wiki/Mainline_Protestant.

SECTION V

What About the Children?

Everyone on any side of the marijuana debate wants to see a bright future for the next generation, one that includes liberty and responsibility. Americans and most people worldwide are quite familiar with the idea that adults deserve freedoms and duties not granted to children. The fact that the word "minor" exists in our language reflects the idea. Current policies on ages for consent, trial as an adult, military service, driving, drinking, and a host of other behaviors reflect our repeated commitment to the idea that a certain level of development is required before enjoying certain privileges or taking on certain obligations. Critics of the notion that a specific chronological age will signify a set of appropriate abilities are numerous. Many find the different ages required for different rights and responsibilities ageist. Nevertheless, few would argue that everyone at every age has the skill to handle all the tasks stereotypically associated with adulthood. Resolving these issues would require, at the very least, an entire book in itself. Instead, these chapters focus on two key issues related to marijuana and considerations for policy.

The links between an early onset of use of most any drug and later troubles appears repeatedly in the research literature. Mary Ann Pentz and Steve Sussman provide a critical but optimistic view of current approaches to marijuana-abuse prevention. They note that a great many previous attempts to minimize the negative effects of drugs have met with unmitigated failure. Nevertheless, they describe key components of programs that can delay the onset of licit and illicit drug use. Prohibitionists

and anti-prohibitionists will likely find their words encouraging. Properly conducted drug-abuse prevention programs can be efficient, effective, relatively inexpensive, and respectful of the rights and intelligence of citizens who are too young to vote for alternatives.

Rodney Skager examines one of the most controversial issues in recent debates on medical marijuana. He takes a close look at data on teen attitudes and use in California after the passage of medical marijuana laws. Many have asserted that linking marijuana to medical illness could normalize the drug's use in teens' minds, thus suggesting to them that the drug must be harmless. He shows that empirical work does not support the idea, and tells an intriguing tale about how holding dearly to the idea of medical marijuana normalizing teen use, even in the face of contradictory evidence, has led to strange reactions to these data.

14   Marijuana Abuse Prevention

Mary Ann Pentz
Steve Sussman

The variety of possible types of marijuana-use policies has received virtually no attention as a potential drug-abuse prevention strategy. Marijuana policies for adults and debates related to those policies can alter adolescent perceptions. This chapter examines possibilities for changing policies to improve prevention of adolescent marijuana use, taking into account existing and perceived policies, and the potential for prevention programs and policies to interact in their effects on youths' marijuana use.

Marijuana is the most popularly used illegal drug in the world (Ministry of Public Health of Belgium, 2002; Sussman & Ames, 2001). Marijuana accounts for one sixth of all drug abuse among adults and teens (not including tobacco addiction), and is second only to alcohol in prevalence. Marijuana is also a source of controversy because several medical and economic benefits have been reported regarding the use of its constituents (e.g., THC, hemp; see Sussman, Stacy, Dent, Simon, & Johnson, 1996). There is general scientific and lay consensus that marijuana use impairs lung function, may cause cardiac problems in patients suffering from cardiovascular conditions, and may cause lung cancer (e.g., British Lung Foundation, 2004). Some people do become dependent on marijuana, and there are recognized withdrawal symptoms. Though THC probably does not produce any gross changes in cognitive or psychomotor functions that are permanent, some subtle enduring effects are reported by ex-chronic users long after termination of use, and decreased memory and executive cognitive function may be more pronounced and enduring for teen smokers (Joffe & Yancy, 2004). Marijuana

impairs skills related to driving (e.g., tracking and speed adjustment, reaction time and coordination), and recent use may increase the risk of auto accidents (Earleywine, 2002; Joffe & Yancy, 2004; Ministry of Public Health of Belgium, 2002; Sussman & Ames, 2001; Sussman et al., 1996).

Additional negative consequences have been associated with adolescent marijuana use. These include lower educational achievement, the increased risk of using other illicit drugs (Sussman & Dent, 2004; Sussman et al., 1996), a greater likelihood of dropping out of school (Bray et al., 2000), and the development of mental health problems in adolescence or adulthood (Newcomb & Bentler, 1988; Sussman et al., 1996). Withdrawal from marijuana use may also be associated with negative consequences, most notably increased anxiety and stress (Budney, Hughes, Moore, & Novy, 2001; Sussman et al., 1996).

MARIJUANA ADDICTION AND TEEN TREATMENT PREFERENCES

Once youths become regular marijuana users, they may experience withdrawal symptoms when they try to cut down consumption or quit. In fact, 9% of those who ever used marijuana report marijuana dependence at some time during their 4–5 year period of heaviest consumption (generally in the teen or emerging adulthood years; see Ministry of Public Health of Belgium, 2002), and about 20% of admissions to inpatient or outpatient treatment for drug-related problems are ascribed to marijuana use.

Some marijuana users do appear to quit without formalized support. Sussman and Dent (2004) reported the prediction of self-initiated marijuana use cessation among young adults who were regular users five years earlier (also see Sussman & Dent, 1999). Social, attitude, intrapersonal, violence-related, drug-use, and demographic baseline measures served as predictors of whether or not 339 teenage marijuana users reported having quit use five years later. Young adult social role variables were included as additional predictors. Quitting was defined as having not used marijuana in the last 30 days (42% of the sample at follow-up). After controlling for covariation among predictors, in a three-step analysis, only baseline level of marijuana use, male gender, young adult marital status, and friends' marijuana use (marginal) remained statistically direct predictors of quitting. These authors suggested that heavier smokers, who have more difficulty quitting, might be more likely to suffer withdrawal symptoms (e.g., appetite changes, sleep difficulties, irritability; see Budney et al., 2001). In addition, those youths who obtained a conventional adult life role, such as marriage, were relatively likely to quit marijuana use. This "settling-down" concept asserts that as young adults take

on responsibilities for others in their daily lives, they will tend to act in ways that will not interfere with their ability to perform these roles (also see Chen & Kandel, 1998). This concept can inadvertently imply that heavy marijuana use, addiction, and ensuing negative consequences are correctable simply through developmental passage into early adulthood. Such conclusions would not support the use of restrictive marijuana policies with youth.

Weiner, Sussman, McCuller, and Lichtman (1999) used open-ended and multiple-choice surveys and focus groups led by health educators to assess issues relating to marijuana use and cessation among high-risk youths. A total of 806 students participated and were assessed as two separate samples from 21 continuation high schools in southern California. Approximately 70% of the students were current marijuana users. More than half of the marijuana users surveyed had tried to quit and failed. Still, social images associated with marijuana smokers were predominantly positive, and subjects expressed a lack of confidence in the efficacy of marijuana cessation clinic programs. "Quit in private, on your own, without any policies" received the highest mean rating for effectiveness out of a list of 10 cessation strategies. Other methods of quitting marijuana use that received relatively high ratings for effectiveness were either restrictive or punitive. "Inpatient stay" received the second-highest mean effectiveness rating and "jail time" the third-highest effectiveness rating. "Fines" and "driver's license suspension" received the fourth- and fifth-highest effectiveness ratings, respectively. Thus, subjects believed that either self-help or punitive methods are the most effective means of effecting marijuana cessation. A limitation of this study was that perceptions of effectiveness could not be evaluated as predictors of actual quitting.

Studies do not give a clear picture of how best to protect adolescents from addiction to marijuana, other than offering suggestions about regulatory policies that might encourage them to quit using. First, however, researchers should consider policies that might decrease initiation of marijuana use during adolescence.

CURRENT PREVENTION EFFORTS AND IMPLICATIONS FOR POLICY

Marijuana generally is targeted along with several other drugs in prevention programs, most commonly cigarettes and alcohol (Ministry of Public Health of Belgium, 2002). Most marijuana-use prevention programs have been school-based. The more effective programs tend to address a comprehensive array of social influences that affect young adolescents, usually ages 11–13, and have also involved the family, media, or community (Ministry of Public

Health of Belgium, 2002; Palmgreen, Donohew, Lorch, Hoyle, & Stephenson, 2001; Pentz et al., 1989).

A meta-analysis of the one-year post-program effects of 207 drug-abuse prevention programs (Tobler et al., 2000) reveals that programs that target refusal assertion training are less effective than programs that target comprehensive life skills (social influences plus interpersonal skills and decision making) and that broad-based programs are more effective than school-only programs. Also, programs that are highly interactive appear to be a sine quo non of effective prevention. In interactive programs, structured discussions of participants with each other and with the teacher or facilitator are encouraged. Effects do not appear to differ much across different substances averaged across programs, although specific programs have found some differences in effects.

Skara and Sussman (2003) provided the first literature review of an exhaustive sample of 25 tobacco and other drug-use prevention studies that provided at least a 2-year follow-up and included at least a quasi-experimental design. The length of follow-up for the 25 studies was a mean of approximately 69 months (a range of 24 to 180 months). Of the 9 studies that provided long-term assessments of other drug use, such as alcohol and marijuana incidence and prevalence, two thirds (6 studies) reported positive program effects on follow-up periods ranging from two to five years. A small relative reduction of approximately 3–4% was reported for current (e.g., 30-day) marijuana use. The program contents of all 25 studies included prevention strategies that addressed social influences to smoke and the development of skills to resist such pressures, and it was conjectured that more comprehensive (multifaceted) social influence programs were relatively effective when measured initially and at follow-up.

COMPREHENSIVE SOCIAL INFLUENCES PROGRAMS

Social influences programs rely on the theory that teaching youths the skills to resist social pressures to use drugs will help prevent later use (Sussman, Dent, Burton, Stacy, & Flay, 1995). Social influence information and skills training may help counteract a high-risk social milieu that sees the use of drugs as common and desirable. This approach serves as the foundation for the entire curriculum of social influence prevention programs. Comprehensive social influences programs can be differentiated from more narrowly focused social influence programs. The latter focus on instruction of refusal assertion training and on combating direct social influences. Comprehensive social influences programs often contain other skills training (e.g., communication skills, assertiveness), provide instruction in decision

making, and include activism and public commitment components; these additional components permit youths to act on their environment to change it, make lower risk friends, or otherwise enter lower risk contexts. Not surprisingly, these programs are more effective than their narrower counterparts.

These curricula typically focus on 5 to 20 single-hour lessons, integrated into a semester-long health education class. The programs consist of three types of lessons. Basic information lessons encourage involvement in the curriculum and present information on the physical consequences of drug use. For example, youths learn long- and short- term consequences of marijuana use, such as lung damage, and the beginnings of addiction. Normative lessons counteract social pressure to achieve approval by using drugs. And informational lessons counteract social pressure to develop favorable opinions about drug use. Taking a class poll can be helpful (and has normative and informational aspects) because youths often learn that they overestimate the prevalence of marijuana use among their peers and that many of their peers in fact disapprove of marijuana use. The majority of these programs are universal prevention programs that reach whole populations of young adolescents who are not considered at special risk for marijuana (or other) drug use, in their naturally occurring groups in schools, classrooms, and/or extracurricular social settings.

TARGETED PREVENTION PROGRAMMING

A model of prevention that may have greater relevance for at-risk teens incorporates motivation, training in drug refusal, decision making, and other skills. High-risk adolescents have been shown to have low motivation to pursue prosocial behavior, in part because of multiple experiences of failure and others' expectations of failure (Sussman, 1996; Sussman et al., 2004). Relevant programs for these youths must attempt to enhance students' motivations, skills, and decisions to avoid drug abuse and anticipate or avoid problematic situations that may promote drug use. Ideally, youths learn that stereotypes about drug use are inaccurate, that their own attitudes about drugs may reflect their attitudes about themselves and their health, and that valuing health can help them to reach meaningful goals. In addition, students can learn skills for making changes, including effective listening, communication, and self-control. Finally, they learn to make decisions about their behavior by weighing accurate information about drug-use myths, the negative consequences of drugs, and the cognitive process of decision making. These three basic elements—motivation, skills, and decision making ("MSD" model)—appear in many prevention programs for high-risk youth. Nevertheless, of 29 targeted drug-abuse prevention programs located in a

recent review (Sussman et al., 2004), only 5 showed an effect specifically on marijuana use at a one-year follow-up.

WHERE SHOULD POLICIES PERTAINING TO MARIJUANA USE PREVENTION BE HEADED?

Marijuana-related policies and enforcement are sources of debate. Most studies find that relaxing marijuana possession laws does not increase the number of marijuana users. However, most of these studies do not control for differential enforcement of these laws. Adults may use less marijuana in locations where marijuana laws are strictly enforced; adolescents may or may not do the same (Ministry of Public Health of Belgium, 2002). In general, there are at least five types of policies one can consider pertaining to prevention and control of youths' marijuana use (Pentz, 2003a). One can (a) prohibit or regulate production and distribution of marijuana and related-products (e.g., pipes, papers, hemp products); (b) regulate the flow of information about marijuana use (e.g., restrict movies depicting marijuana use, control distribution of magazines such as *High Times*, create venues for printing consequences information); (c) regulate the consumption of marijuana (e.g., make arrests); (d) create campaigns to alter attitudes about marijuana (Pentz, Bonnie, & Shopland, 1996); and/or (e) institutionalize prevention programs that work.

The penalty for marijuana possession appears to have little relation to prevalence of regular use. Of course, law enforcement efforts generally are not taken into account in studies that have reviewed the relation of marijuana policies to its prevalence of use. (Arguably, anyone who wants to obtain marijuana can do it.) It appears that large social climate perceptions of the acceptability and safety of marijuana use appear more important determinants of the prevalence of use (Ministry of Public Health of Belgium, 2002).

HOW MIGHT MARIJUANA POLICIES SUPPORT OR DETRACT FROM PREVENTION EFFORTS?

The main goal of marijuana-use prevention efforts is to prevent harm to self or others. There are always unknown factors regarding whether there is a safe level of use or less harm to self. Certainly, ongoing regular use is likely to lead to numerous consequences, and use under certain conditions (e.g., before or during driving, using in wooded areas) is dangerous to self and others.

Rather than considering types of policies that require a standard for harm reduction, one way to approach consideration of policy is by gauging what "statement" a policy might make to a potential marijuana abuser. In

this case, the perception of policy, including the meaning of a policy, its enforcement, and its consequences, are considered more important a deterrent to use than the actual policy on record, if not more so.

The addictions have been referred to as a problem of perception. In this way of seeing addiction, vulnerable persons tend to distort information about themselves and others prior to even beginning to use drugs, and they continue to distort information in particular ways subsequent to beginning use, particularly during heavy use (Sussman et al., 2004). Information distortion is a function of many factors. A person's lifestyle could alter his or her physical and social environment, which in turn could alter perceptions of the prevalence of use and negative consequences. Cognitive distortions may be influenced, perhaps over a long period, by available policies or perceptions of policies.

Belief-behavior discrepancies can be brought to awareness to help youths not abuse drugs. One example is derived from Attitudinal Perspective Theory (Upshaw & Ostrom, 1984). The theory posits that there are two different aspects of one's attitudes about behaviors or events. First, one holds a general attitudinal perspective (e.g., as a moderate). Separately, one holds specific attitudes about behaviors or events (e.g., one believes that certain drugs should be legal). It is possible that one's general attitude about self may contradict one's specific attitude. If one is confronted with the discrepancy, one will tend to try to reduce it, which, in the present context, could lead to specific antidrug use statements. However, if one is confronted with recent widespread availability and liberalization of marijuana possession and use laws, one may shift one's perception of one's own marijuana-use behavior as being more moderate than one might have previously thought. One may continue to use marijuana, leading to problems among those who are regular users.

We like to live with certainty, based on the familiar. Representativeness or availability heuristics involve basing judgments on one's experiential schema of how representative a case appears to be, or how easily the case comes to mind, rather than relying on further evidence. Thus errors of frequency or importance occur for rare or vivid stimuli (Kahneman, 2003). If marijuana policy is a widely publicized event, it is possible that youths will overestimate the frequency of use among their peers, or the safety of use, leading to increasing prevalence.

CONSIDERATION OF TYPES OF POLICIES

The research summarized thus far suggests that there are many negative consequences of marijuana use. Thus any marijuana policy for adolescents should be focused on protection from harm, which arguably may eliminate

legalization as an option. There are at least three factors to consider before recommending the most protective marijuana policy for adolescents: (a) policies that exist and/or are under consideration for adults; (b) policies that exist and/or are implied for adolescents; and (c) policies that are perceived by adolescents.

Policies for Adults

Current marijuana policy classifies the sale and large-scale possession of marijuana as a felony and low-level possession for personal use as a misdemeanor (LeVay, 2003; Sussman et al., 1996). The severity of consequences for violation varies with the level of the crime (though possession of small amounts can still result in a $10,000 fine and 1 year in prison). However, enforcement varies widely from state to state, making assessment of policy effectiveness difficult (LeVay, 2003). Because sale and possession are the target behaviors of adult policy, the policy is focused on supply (rather than demand reduction) and on interdiction (Office of National Drug Control Policy, 2004). Interdiction is assumed to operate on both sellers and consumers: on sellers by increasing costs associated with lost revenue and prison or equivalent punishment, and on consumers by restricting the access to and availability of marijuana. There is little evidence to indicate that current adult policy has curbed the market for marijuana sales or use (Pentz et al., 1996).

Given the discouraging results of current policies, it seems to us that three policy changes are under consideration for adults, each of which would be expected to affect youths. These are legalization, decriminalization, and medical marijuana use.

Legalization would allow sales to adults with no repercussions but would attempt to curb sales to youths. Since there is to date no country that has completely legalized marijuana, the projected consequences of such a policy change can be considered only in terms of exemplars that have involved legalization of other substances, most notably tobacco and alcohol. There is substantial evidence to indicate that legalization of tobacco and alcohol has produced increases in marketing and advertising and decreases in prices, both of which have been associated with increased use by youths (Joffe & Yancy, 2004). However, whether the demand for marijuana would be equally price-sensitive under a legalization policy is not as clear (Grossman, Chaloupka & Shim, 2002). Another consideration is enforcement. For example, the Synar Amendment, which has attempted to restrict youth access to tobacco while still leaving it fully legal for adults, has largely failed, primarily because of a lack of funds and infrastructure for proper

enforcement (Pentz, Mares, Schinke, & Rohrbach, 2004). Overall, then, if marijuana were legalized for adults in the United States, a likely outcome would be increased use by adolescents.

Decriminalization, which decreases penalties for marijuana use and distribution while still considering the drug illegal, is already in operation in several states and countries, including Australia, New Zealand, and the Netherlands (Joffe & Yancy, 2004). Perhaps receiving the most international attention is the Netherlands, which despite proponents' claims to the contrary, has shown increases in use that are temporally associated with decriminalization (Joffe & Yancy, 2004). An analysis of the effects of decriminalization in the United States has been less clear, primarily because of the inconsistent treatment of offense (Pacula, Chriqui, & King, 2003). However, the same study showed that youths living in states that had lowered penalties for possession tended to report higher rates of marijuana use. There is also the possibility that decriminalization would decrease youths' perception of the perceived risk of consequences of use and subsequently increase use, just as decreased perceived risks of cocaine have increased its use in adolescents (Johnston, O'Malley, Bachman, & Schulenberg, 2004).

Finally, there is some evidence from Australia to suggest that decriminalization may decrease the street price of marijuana, which may increase the risk of use by youths (Williams, 2004). At the same time, in the same country, there is evidence to suggest that expiation of offenses through payment rather than criminal prosecution and incarceration is cost-effective (Hall, 2001). In the United States, the relationship of economic sanctions to marijuana use may be more complex. At least one study suggests that a combination of higher fines for marijuana possession, increased probability of arrest, and higher cigarette taxes are related to lower marijuana use (Farrelly, Bray, Zarkin, & Wendling, 2001). Since incarceration in the United States can cost more than $30,000 per drug offense, cost effectiveness would appear to be a key consideration in policy change (Consortium of Alcohol and Substance Abuse Services, n.d.). Nevertheless, the unintended increased risk of youths' marijuana use from decriminalization would appear to offset cost effectiveness considerations.

Medical marijuana use treats marijuana as a controlled substance, to be used in a small number of medical conditions under a physician's care or recommendation. Recent medical reports conclude that the medical use of marijuana should be restricted to the use of cannabinoids, not smoked marijuana, which has been associated with harmful effects, though there is still ongoing debate (Joffe & Yancy, 2004; LeVay, 2003; Sussman et al., 1996). There is already evidence that other medically controlled substances (e.g., oxycontin) reach adolescent populations and are used by adolescents (Johnston et al., 2004). Thus, available evidence suggests that a policy allowing

smoking marijuana for medical purposes is not likely to decrease marijuana consumption in either adults or youths.

Policies for Youths

Currently, there are two types of marijuana policy targeting youths: no/least harm and zero tolerance (Pentz, Sussman, & Newman, 1997). Both of these fall under the adult policy that marijuana use, possession, and sales are illegal and punishable (criminal). However, the youth populations to which these two variations of policy are directed vary, as does enforcement.

The no/least harm policy is primarily intended for high-risk youths who would likely suffer under a zero-tolerance policy. For example, if a zero-tolerance policy calls for suspension from school, a high-risk youth who is almost failing school is unlikely to benefit. For such youths, policy focuses on referrals to interventions that may improve overall functioning. Examples of least/no harm policies include referrals to drug treatment or counseling, close supervision at home, or diversion programs with community service. These policies focus more on reducing vulnerability to addiction and on removing access and environments conducive to marijuana use. Research on student assistance programs suggests that no/least harm policies that include supportive enforcement strategies such as counseling do help high-risk youths (Pentz et al., 1997).

Zero-tolerance policy is intended more for general (mainstream) youth populations, with the aim of preventing onset or progression of use. There is little evidence that zero-tolerance policies, when enforced with punishment, are effective (Pentz et al., 1989). However, such policies combined with supportive enforcement strategies, such as referral to prevention programs, are associated with less drug use (Pentz, 1999; Pentz et al., 1989).

Policies Perceived by Youths

Overall, youths are unaware of the actual drug policies to which they are subject in their communities and schools (Pentz, 2003a). However, they do form perceptions of policy. These perceptions can be measured in terms of perceived social norms for drug use, perceived consequences of getting caught, perceived personal risk of consequences, and perceived approval or disapproval of use by peers and adults. All of these variables have been evaluated and found to be significant risk factors (predictors) of drug use, including marijuana use (Pentz, 2003a; Sussman et al., 1996). As noted above, several of these perceptual risk factors are also successfully counteracted in evidence-based comprehensive social influence prevention programs; for

example, the perception that marijuana use is a social norm can be changed by informing youths about actual use rates. These risk-use relationships indicate that new youth drug policies should either build in an information dissemination component about enforcement and consequences and/or link policy to prevention programs that address these perceptual factors (Pentz, 2003b). Policies that deliberately use or counteract youths' perceptions may have the largest effect of all.

OPTIONS FOR YOUTH MARIJUANA POLICY

Thus far we have argued that the most effective policies for youths are those that: (a) combine with evidence-based prevention programs; (b) complement or at least are sensitive to the ripple effects of adult policy; (c) use support and prevention programs as enforcement strategies; and (d) address perceptions of policy. With these considerations in mind, options for policy change include which drug control strategy (demand vs. supply reduction), and which perspective (development, social, or market), to emphasize.

DEMAND VERSUS SUPPLY REDUCTION

Historically, demand and supply reduction have been considered separate strategies for drug control, each with separate targets of the seller, user/consumer, and service provider, although with differing degrees of emphasis (Pentz et al., 1996). Demand reduction strategies have relied primarily on programs, and supply reduction strategies have relied primarily on policies. In several independent studies, prevention programs that have attempted to reduce demand by counteracting risk factors have produced modest but significant and replicable effects on youths' marijuana use (Pentz, 1999, 2003a). Other studies on policy interventions have shown that use has been deterred by restricting youths' access and availability, increasing knowledge of and support for policy, and increasing taxation (Pentz, 1999, 2003a). Additionally, knowledge and regularity of enforcement appear to affect use, although indirectly through increasing perceived personal risk of consequences. Though these policies appear to be designed to reduce supply, they also try to reduce demand by affecting youths' perceptions of consequences and risks of consequences. Another type of policy, aimed directly at demand reduction, seeks to institutionalize effective prevention programs by legislating set-aside funds for prevention programs and training, for example through the various Drug Free Schools and Communities acts. Evaluation of this type of policy has been thus far limited to program implementation and sustainability; effects of this type of policy on youths' marijuana use must be

inferred (Pentz, 2000). Overall, since both demand and supply reduction appear to work with youths, it is suggested that an improved youth marijuana policy would address both, by targeting access, availability, price (indirectly through adult policies), and institutionalization of prevention programs. This dual emphasis on demand *and* supply targets primarily users/consumers.

POLICY PERSPECTIVE

Three novel policy options may be tailored to a perspective that appeals highly to legislators. The first, the most emotional and most humane, is policy from the perspective of preventing the development of adolescent addiction to marijuana. If this perspective takes priority in the U.S. Congress, youth policy could shift even more toward an emphasis on high-risk youths who have already experimented with drugs and are at risk for progression to addiction and related problem behaviors. Policy would aim to restrict youth access to and availability of drugs by removing youths from high-risk environments and disrupting any relationships with other users and pushers. This latter aim would necessarily involve a change in adult policy as well: Interdiction would shift slightly to remove pushers from environments affecting youths. At the same time, policy could institutionalize increased funding for supportive student assistance and counseling programs, and funding and training for parent and family management programs. Assuming no changes in funding for the national drug control effort, this type of policy change would probably result in a decrease in funding for universal (population-based) prevention programs and for enforcement of zero-tolerance violations.

The second perspective is social, and it calls for policies that are designed to decrease the social acceptability of marijuana use. This perspective requires that policy for adults stipulate that marijuana use remain illegal and criminally punishable, since a legalization or decriminalization policy for adults could inadvertently transmit a message of social acceptability of marijuana use. Policy for youths remains similar to that for adults, with the exception that consequences would be oriented toward support rather than incarceration, but enforcement and consequences would still be sufficiently important to heighten perceived risks of getting caught and prosecuted. Policy would be tied to social unacceptability and norms messages in prevention programs.

The third perspective is the market perspective (Pentz et al., 2004). From this perspective, policy for adults would remain the same, coverage of marijuana use in entertainment media would be discouraged (to drive down potential demand), and adult violations would carry heavy fines for minor

offenses. Increased monitoring and counseling and the provision of healthy alternatives such as job training could replace imprisonment and its associated costs. At the same time, policy for youths would involve a three-pronged approach to lowering demand through "institutionalizing" universal prevention programs for youths and their parents, increasing consumer demand for these programs, and enhancing the availability of program training and materials with subsidies to publishers and financial incentives to schools and communities. This policy is consistent with research and cost-effective.

The integration of demand and supply reduction approaches in youth policy is recent and thus far has not been evaluated for its effectiveness. In terms of perspectives to policy change, recent funding has already shifted somewhat to the addiction development perspective. However, the market perspective may be the most innovative approach to explore. Based on what is currently known about youth price sensitivity, community and school budgetary concerns, and incentive-driven consumerism in areas other than drug use, the market perspective also may hold the most potential for policy effectiveness.

REQUIREMENTS TO CHANGE YOUTH POLICY

Moving youth policy change forward requires a number of procedures and conditions for change. Ryder (1996) sees policy change as requiring eight stages, from setting the key issue on the public agenda through maintenance of policy change. In the area of youth marijuana policy, the United States is experiencing gaps in at least four of these stages: forecasting the likely consequences of various policy changes (stage 4), analysis of policy options to achieve optimal prevention (stage 5), monitoring policy enforcement (stage 7), and maintenance of policy change (stage 8; Pentz et al., 2004). However, it could be argued that even the first stage, agenda setting, is lacking as regards youth marijuana policy. Although the acute and chronic harm attributed to adult marijuana use has been widely publicized, including most recently the economic, social, and physical consequences of use applied to the medical marijuana policy issue, these negative effects have not achieved the same public attention for adolescents. Systematically documenting and publicizing these effects on youths could place improving youth marijuana policies on the public agenda.

Regardless of specific stages of the process that may be missing when considering how to change youth marijuana policy, the entire process can progress only under supportive conditions. In this case, evidence-based prevention programs that change social norms for drug use can have a reciprocally supportive effect on inducing policy change (Pentz, 2000; Pentz, 2003b). If the social norm shifts away from acceptance of marijuana use,

the public will be more likely to support policies that are geared toward nonuse.

The arguments put forth in this chapter encourage multifaceted policies that target adult and youths, or at least the coordination of adult policies and youth policies. At the local level, this coordination may require that communities generate special referenda that link adult and youth policies, enforcement, funding, and intervention. We are not aware of any studies that have evaluated such referenda or their outcomes.

Finally, policy change will require changes in personnel who may serve as the major link between adult and youth policies, and between youth policy and prevention programs. There are two logical candidates. Police or other local law enforcement personnel have the potential to link adult and youth policies in communities through enforcement strategies, pooled personnel and funding, and community education to increase knowledge of policy, enforcement, and consequences of policy violation. The other candidate(s) are local prevention coordinators, who are typically hired by school districts or local lead agencies at the regional level. The current role of these coordinators, which is primarily to select, train, and monitor implementation of prevention programs, could be expanded to link the prevention messages of policies and prevention programs. For example, prevention coordinators could increase their liaison with police, merchants, parents, and teachers regarding supportive referrals for youths caught violating policy, while at the same time including knowledge of policy and enforcement as part of prevention programs.

CONCLUSIONS

This chapter addressed possibilities for improving policy on youth marijuana use. Based on empirical and suggestive evidence from research and on archival reports of existing policy, seven recommendations are put forth. First, any change in youth policy should be considered in the context of (and with a grasp of the potential effects of) adult policy and of policy as perceived by youths. Second, youth policy should be coordinated or linked with evidence-based prevention programs in terms of making prevention messages consistent, targeting perceptual risk factors for use, and increasing knowledge and support of policy. Third, supply *and* demand should be incorporated into new policy. Fourth, zero-tolerance policy for the general population as well as no/least harm policy for high-risk populations should include supportive enforcement strategies. Supportive enforcement implies less harm and, by implication, less criminalization for offenses.

Fifth, policy change for youths requires an increase of public attention to youths' marijuana use. Sixth, community referenda for policy change may

need to integrate adult and youth policies. Finally, the role of law enforcement personnel and prevention coordinators should be expanded to link adult and youth policy enforcement, and policy and prevention program messages, respectively.

This research was supported by grants from the National Institute on Drug Abuse (DA07601, DA13814, and DA16094). Please send all correspondence to Steve Sussman, USC Institute for Prevention Research, 1000 S. Fremont, Box 8, Alhambra, CA 91803, ssussma@hsc.usc.edu. First authorship on this chapter is shared equally.

REFERENCES

Bray, J. W., Zarkin, G. A., Ringwalt, C., & Qi, J. (2000). The relationship between marijuana initiation and dropping out of high school. *Health Economics, 9*(1), 75–80.

British Lung Foundation. (2004). *A smoking gun? The impact of cannabis smoking on respiratory health.* London: British Lung Foundation.

Budney, A. J., Hughes, J. R., Moore, B. A., & Novy, P. L. (2001). Marijuana abstinence effects in marijuana smokers maintained in their home environment. *Archives of General Psychiatry, 58,* 917–924.

Chen, K., & Kandel, D. B. (1998). Predictors of cessation of marijuana use: An event history analysis. *Drug and Alcohol Dependence, 50,* 109–121.

Consortium of Alcohol and Substance Abuse Services. (2004). Monroe County/Greater Finger Lakes Region of New York State. Overview of the Reform of the NYS Drug Laws. Retrieved November 24, 2004, from http://www.flcasas.com/rockdrug.htm.

Earleywine, M. (2002). *Understanding marijuana: A new look at the scientific evidence.* New York: Oxford University Press.

Farrelly, M. C., Bray, J. W., Zarkin, G. A., & Wendling, B. W. (2001). The joint demand for cigarettes and marijuana: Evidence from the National Household Surveys on Drug Abuse. *Journal of Health Economics, 20*(1), 51–68.

Grossman, M., Chaloupka, F. J., & Shim, K. (2002). Illegal drug use and public policy. One can support the war on drugs' goal of reducing consumption without supporting the war itself. *Health Affairs, 21*(2), 134–145.

Hall, W. (2001). Reducing the harms caused by cannabis use: The policy debate in Australia. *Drug and Alcohol Dependence, 62*(3), 163–174.

Joffe, A., & Yancy, S. (2004). Legalization of marijuana: Potential impact on youth. *Pediatrics, 113*(6), 632–638.

Johnston, L. D., O'Malley, P. M., Bachman, J. G., & Schulenberg, J. E. (2004). *Monitoring the Future national survey results on drug use, 1975–2003. Volume I: Secondary school students* (NIH Publication No. 04–5507). Bethesda, MD: National Institute on Drug Abuse.

Kahneman, D. (2003). A perspective on judgment and choice: Mapping bounded rationality. *American Psychologist, 58,* 697–720.

LeVay, A. J. (2003). Urgent compassion: Medical marijuana, prosecutorial discretion, and the medical necessity defense. *Boston College Law Review, 43,* 699–753.

Ministry of Public Health of Belgium. (2002). *Cannabis 2002 Report. A joint international effort at the initiative of the Ministers of Public Health of Belgium, France, Germany, The Netherlands, Switzerland* (Technical Report of the International Scientific Conference). Brussels, Belgium: Author.

Newcomb, M. D., & Bentler, P. M. (1988). *Consequences of adolescent drug use: Impact on the lives of young adults.* Beverly Hills, CA: Sage.

Office of National Drug Control Policy. (2004). National drug control strategy. Washington, DC: Author.

Pacula, R. L., Chriqui, J. F., & King, J. (2003). *Marijuana decriminalization: What does it mean in the United States?* Retrieved November 24, 2004, from http://papers.ssrn.com/sol3/papers.cfm?abstract_id=406062.

Palmgreen, P., Donohew, L., Lorch, E. P., Hoyle, R. H., & Stephenson, M. (2001). Television campaigns and adolescent marijuana use: Tests of sensation seeking targeting. *American Journal of Public Health, 91,* 292–296.

Pentz, M. A. (1999). Effective prevention programs for tobacco use. *Nicotine and Tobacco Research, 1 Supp., 2,* 99–107.

Pentz, M. A. (2000). Institutionalizing community-based prevention through policy change. Special CSAP issue, *Journal of Community Psychology, 28*(3), 257–270.

Pentz, M. A. (2003a). Anti-drug abuse policies as prevention strategies. In Z. Sloboda & W. J. Bukoski (Eds.), *Handbook of drug abuse prevention: Theory, science, and practice* (217–237). New York: Plenum.

Pentz, M. A. (2003b). Evidence-based prevention: Characteristics, impact, and future direction. Special supplement, *Journal of Psychoactive Drugs, 35,* 143–152.

Pentz, M. A., Bonnie, R. J., & Shopland, D. S. (1996). Integrating supply and demand reduction strategies for drug abuse prevention. *American Behavioral Scientist, 39* (7), 897–910.

Pentz, M. A., Brannon, B. R., Charlin, V. L., Barrett, E. J., MacKinnon, D. P., & Flay, B. R. (1989). The power of policy: The relationship of smoking policy to adolescent smoking. *American Journal of Public Health 79*(7): 857–862.

Pentz, M. A., Mares, D., Schinke, S., & Rohrbach, L. A. (2004). Political science, public policy, and drug use prevention. *Substance Use and Misuse, 39*(10–12), 1821–1865.

Pentz, M. A., & Sussman, S., & Newman, T. (1997). The conflict between least harm and no-use tobacco policy for youth: Ethical and policy implications. *Addiction, 92*(9): 1165–1173.

Ryder (1996). The analysis of policy: Understanding the process of policy enactment. *Addiction, 91*(9), 1265–1270.

Skara, S. N., & Sussman, S. (2003). A review of 25 long-term adolescent tobacco and other drug use prevention program evaluations. *Preventive
Medicine, 37*, 451–474.

Sussman, S. (1996). Development of a school-based drug abuse prevention
curriculum for high-risk youths. *Journal of Psychoactive Drugs, 28*,
169–182.

Sussman, S., & Ames, S. L. (2001). *The social psychology of drug abuse.* Buck-
ingham, England: Open University Press.

Sussman, S., & Dent, C. W. (1999). One-year prospective prediction of marijuana use cessation among youth at continuation high schools. *Addictive
Behaviors, 24*, 411–417.

Sussman, S., & Dent, C. W. (2004). Five-year prospective prediction of marijuana use cessation among youth at continuation high schools. *Addictive
Behaviors, 29*, 1237–1243.

Sussman, S., Dent, C. W., Burton, D., Stacy, A. W., & Flay, B. R. (1995). *Developing school-based tobacco use prevention and cessation programs.* New-
bury Park, CA: Sage.

Sussman, S., Earleywine, M., Wills, T., Cody, C., Biglan, T., Dent, C. W., et al.
(2004). The motivation, skills, and decision-making model of "drug
abuse" prevention. *Substance Use and Misuse, 39*, 1971–2017.

Sussman, S., Stacy, A. W., Dent, C. W., Simon, T. R., & Johnson, C. A. (1996).
Marijuana use: Current issues and new research directions. *Journal of
Drug Issues, 26*, 693–726.

Tobler, N. S., Roona, M. R., Ochshorn, P., Marshall, D. G., Streke, A. V., &
Stackpole, K. M. (2000). School-based adolescent drug prevention programs: 1998 meta-analysis. *The Journal of Primary Prevention, 20*,
275–336.

Upshaw, H. S., & Ostrom, T. M. (1984). Psychological perspective in attitude
research. In J. R. Eiser (Ed.), *Attitudinal judgment* (pp. 23–42). New
York: Springer-Verlag.

Weiner, M. D., Sussman, S., McCuller, W. J., & Lichtman, K. (1999). Factors
in marijuana cessation among high-risk youth. *Journal of Drug Education, 29*, 337–357.

Williams, J. (2004). The effects of price and policy on marijuana use: What
can be learned from the Australian experience? *Health Economics, 13*,
123–137.

15 Revisioning Youth Policy on Marijuana and Other Drug Use: Alternatives to Zero Tolerance

Rodney Skager

For more than four decades, the United States has tried to eliminate alcohol, marijuana, and other drug use among teenagers. Ever since President Nixon declared war on drugs, *zero tolerance* has shaped all youth policy on substance use. Abstinence was, and still is, the single, overriding objective of federally approved drug education. However, zero tolerance is an ideological principle rather than a pragmatic guide to effective policy. A public health perspective would also address information and strategies that promote greater safety for those who choose to experiment. In contrast, zero tolerance rules out attempts to reduce harms often associated with the use of alcohol and other drugs. Moreover, young people who are caught in violation usually face deterrent punishment that is intended to frighten their peers rather than reform the offender.

Despite abstinence education and harsh punishments, a large majority of older teens still try alcohol, and half or more have used an illicit drug (mainly marijuana). The failure of strategies based on zero tolerance should raise questions not only about the value of current drug prevention education and disciplinary policies but also about the feasibility of the endeavor itself. Once marijuana joined alcohol as a part of normal social life for so many teenagers, was it really possible to return to prevalence levels of the 1950s or early 1960s? This is a subversive question in a nation committed to making war on drugs and drug users. Still, it is worth asking, since there is no sign that drug prevention education coupled with deterrent punishment policies in schools has, or ever will, achieve near universal abstinence among

Table 15.1. Lifetime Alcohol and Illicit Drug Use Among U.S. 12th-Grade Students Since 1975 on the Monitoring the Future Survey (MTF)

	1975	Lowest	Highest	2004
Any illicit drug	55.2	40.7 (92)	65.6 (81)	51.1
Marijuana/Hashish	43.7	32.6 (92)	60.4 (79)	45.7
Alcohol	90.4	76.6 (03)	93.1 (78)	76.8
Been drunk	Not assessed	60.3	65.4 (91)	60.3

young people. If there are doubts about this assertion, the numbers suggest otherwise. The national *Monitoring the Future Study* has tracked youth substance use annually since 1975 (Johnston, O'Malley, & Bachman, 2004). It tells a story of fluctuation from year to year in marijuana and other drug use, but reveals no trend in the direction of zero.

Table 15.1 reveals that lifetime use of any illicit drug (currently at 51% for 12th graders) is currently 4% lower than it was when the first *Monitoring the Future* survey was done in 1975. However, between these years this measure registered a low of 41% in 1992 and a high of 66% in 1979. This wide variation during the 28 years of the survey thus places current prevalence of any illicit drug in the midrange of the annual findings and puts into perspective the small (4%) difference between current and 1975 results. The same holds true for marijuana, the drug accounting for the lion's share of illicit drug use among youths. Lifetime marijuana use stood at 44% in 1975 and 46% in 2004. In the interim, it fluctuated between a low of 33% in 1992 and a high of 60% in 1979.[1]

The picture for alcohol, by far the drug most favored among youths, is different. The percent that drank at least once has shown a moderate trend downward in recent years, from 90% in 1975 to 77% in 2004. The current percentage is equal to the lowest registered in the 28-year period (in 2003), but still accounts for three quarters of high school seniors. In 2004, six out of 10 seniors reported being drunk at least once.

What are people to make of these findings? Proponents of current prevention could argue, although without supporting evidence, that more teens would have used drugs if it weren't for their programs. Yet the long-term perspective is that illicit drug use in general and marijuana use specifically—despite wide annual variation—remain approximately where they were in 1975 *before* drug prevention and highly punitive disciplinary policies became the norm in schools. This relative stability in marijuana use versus the moderate decline in drinking does not necessarily prove that current policy is "working" for alcohol but not marijuana. Current drug education, concentrated mainly in elementary schools, gives more emphasis to illicit drugs

than to alcohol. Television messages sponsored by the Office of National Drug Control Policy ignore alcohol. That most high school students will continue to experiment with alcohol, and in some instances recklessly, is tacitly accepted in current efforts to reduce binge drinking. Like sober driver programs, binge reduction strategies recognize that abstinence is an unrealistic goal for many teens and college-age youths and instead focus on dangerous drinking practices and situations. These programs take a pragmatic approach in accepting *harm reduction* as their goal. Yet proponents of current drug policies reject all attempts to develop such harm reduction strategies for marijuana or other illicit drugs. Their opposition has decimated even sober driver programs and youth-sponsored harm reduction efforts such as "Dance Safe," a service aimed at reducing dangers associated with "club" drugs. In doing so, they drive these activities underground to locations and situations that are less safe. In contrast to the United States, harm reduction (called "minimization" in Australia) is official policy in progressive countries such as Australia and in some Canadian provinces.[2] How is it that in the United States, policies that do not work, that may cause more harm than good, have persisted for so long?

PROPOSITION 215, THE CALIFORNIA MEDICAL MARIJUANA INITIATIVE

The November 1996 California ballot included a proposition legalizing medical uses of marijuana. This proposition was the target of doomsday predictions from proponents of the drug war. Prominent in the TV and other media spots opposing the proposition was the "wrong message" argument, which warned that passage would encourage more teenagers to try marijuana. Staff in a federal agency soon perceived the California referendum as the golden opportunity to test this prediction. Accordingly, the Substance Abuse and Mental Health Administration provided funds to the California Department of Alcohol and Drug Programs for a study of the effects of ads supporting the proposition and its possible approval by the voters should that occur. Staff in state and federal drug agencies seemed confident that marijuana use among California teenagers would increase should either or both occur, thus verifying the "wrong message" prediction.

The biennial California attorney general's survey of drug use among secondary school students (the *California Student Survey* or CSS), for which I serve as codirector, was the obvious vehicle on which such a study could be carried out.[3] The CSS has been administered biennially since 1985–86 in randomly selected California middle and high schools beginning in mid- or late November. The next survey would begin just after the 1996 election. The timing was perfect. The grant provided funding for a considerably larger

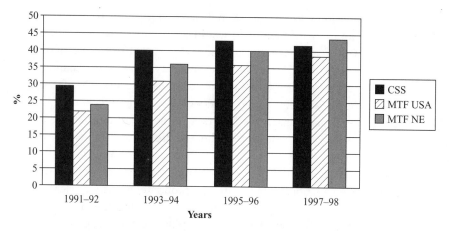

Figure 15.1. Percentage of California 11th-grade students reporting use of marijuana in the previous 6 months versus previous year for the national MTF survey of 12th-grade students. CSS=California students survey. MTF USA=National data. MTF NE=Data for Northeast.

sample for the 1996–97 survey and the addition of questions assessing reactions to the 215 initiative and its promotional messages. The pre– and post–Proposition 215 California data could then be contrasted with 12th-grader results for the *Monitoring the Future* national and eastern regional surveys, the latter being seen as more comparable to the California population than were surveys for the Midwest or South.

Figure 15.1 shows that the percentage reporting smoking marijuana at least once in a lifetime was on the increase for both the *Monitoring the Future* national and northeastern samples and for California through the 4-year period prior to the November 1996 election. In addition, for each of the three earlier intervals, marijuana use over the previous 6 months was *higher* among California 11th graders than for 12th graders over the entire year on the *Monitoring the Future* national and northeastern regional samples. That is, prevalence was higher in California even though the respondents were a year younger and reported for a shorter time period.

The post-election 1997–98 CSS survey sample showed a *lower* prevalence in California compared to the Northeast sample and reduced the difference between California and the national sample by more than half. In fact, marijuana use by California 11th graders had *leveled off*, even suggesting a slight reversal downward. In contrast, the national and northeastern samples continued on their moderate upward trends. California prevalence was below the northeastern region for the first time, though still a few points above percentages for the nation as a whole.

Responses to questions about Proposition 215 revealed that about two thirds of 9th and three quarters of 11th graders had read or heard something

about the proposition. Regardless of grade level, only one in 10 or fewer believed that "a lot more" of their peers would try marijuana as a result of passage. Only 30% of current users in grade 11 believed that more of their peers would try the drug. A much smaller minority of nonusers thought the same. On whether passage of Proposition 215 was a "good" or "bad" thing, 9th and 11th grade students varied considerably in their perceptions of the medical value of marijuana. Sixty-four percent of 9th graders and 58% of 11th graders were either "not sure" or thought Proposition 215 was a "bad" thing.

What implication could people draw from our findings? Causal statements from cross-sectional studies are inappropriate, but it was clear that the jump in marijuana use assumed under the "wrong message" mantra was not supported. So why is it that this main finding of our Proposition 215 study had no effect on state or national policy? The simple answer would be that it was ignored. This is not uncommon when research on social issues contradicts conventional wisdom. As it turned out, our findings were not ignored; they just weren't released.

BARRIERS TO CHANGE

Suppressing or ignoring information that would contradict a deliberately fostered climate of fear helps maintain support for current drug policy (Skager & Brown, 1998). So-called drug prevention education reflects this tactic. Information is restricted to possible negative aspects of substance use that are often portrayed as common rather than occasional or unusual. People who deliver balanced information on drugs or propose harm reduction strategies are accused of promoting drug use. The knee-jerk response is (once again), "You are giving the wrong message!" This accusation discredits the messenger without addressing the substantive issue. As a college debater, I learned to identify such ad hominem arguments as appeals to emotions or prejudice rather than being grounded on real evidence.

Nevertheless, attempts to indoctrinate older youth against marijuana are probably counterproductive. Widespread experience with drugs among both youth and adults ultimately discredits doomsday messages and could encourage drug experimentation out of curiosity or as oppositional behavior.

Research and development in controversial areas of public policy can be warped by political climate. Fully documenting this assertion in the case of research on marijuana and other drugs is beyond the scope of this chapter, but three telling examples can be cited, the first being our California Proposition 215 study. The second is the misinterpretation of correlation findings in order to demonize marijuana as the "gateway drug" to harder drugs and

eventual addiction. The third is the acceptance and application of questionable notions about conditions that promote marijuana initiation and use among young people. Such notions serve as the foundation for drug-use prevention curricula that incorporate so-called "normative" education and especially those curricula that train children to "resist" peer pressure.

FATE OF THE PROPOSITION 215 REPORT

We anticipated that our Proposition 215 findings would be newsworthy. Of course, public release of the results of the study was not our prerogative. Our job was to deliver a final report to the California Department of Alcohol and Drug Programs, which, as sponsor of the study, would be responsible for release. And we did produce the required report—in fact, three versions over a period of two years. Despite our diligence, those findings did not see the light of day until now, almost 10 years later.

The first report draft was dated September 10, 1998, reflecting the time it takes to finish data collection (in spring of 1997), process the results, write a detailed report, and wait though an internal review process before submission to the sponsoring agency. This report delivered about 40 pages of single-spaced text, tables, and figures. It focused not only on the results directly related to the proposition but on additional information on marijuana use among 7th-, 9th-, and 11th-grade students. Given the ostensible purpose of the grant, findings related to Proposition 215 were emphasized. These included the prevalence figures as well as student responses to the questions on awareness and perceived implications of the proposition.

This first report was rejected. The reasons were not clear, but my coauthor and I sensed that it might have something to do with results that conflicted with the dire predictions by zero-tolerance proponents. A longer report with less emphasis on results relating to Proposition 215 seemed strategic. This longer and admittedly padded report was delivered sometime after the date on the draft (April 1999). Its 89 pages offered voluminous data on all aspects of marijuana use and anything related to it. The title (*Marijuana Use and the Response to Proposition 215 Among California Youth: A Special Study from the 1997–98 California Student Survey*) did not reflect the main emphasis in content, in other words. The national comparisons reported in the figure above were given one page of text and a small line graph on pages 21–22. The results on student knowledge and attitudes about the proposition were delayed until Section VIII, pages 59–62. In other words, findings on what was supposed to be the main thrust of the report were now represented in about 6% of the text.

Eventually we were informed that this second report was not accepted. It was too long. (That was certainly true, as it had been our intention.)

Nothing was said about the apparently disturbing 215 results. Nevertheless, we dutifully developed and submitted a shorter report dated April 4, 2000. This 39-page document put the national comparisons in a numerical table in the appendix (buried among other tables on various aspects of marijuana prevalence). There was no supporting graph or figure to give a visual illustration of the results. The text on these findings was summarized in two paragraphs on page 36. However, we did not pull any punches in this text:

> There is no evidence supporting that the passage of Proposition 215 was associated with higher rates of marijuana use during this period, even though most students were well aware of the proposition and its meaning. (p. 36)

The department neither accepted nor rejected this document. There was no sign that the report was sent to the Substance Abuse and Mental Health Services Administration. Like Hamlet, the report was dead, and the rest was silence.

In frustration, I asked Bill Lockyer, the California attorney general and sponsor of the survey, to write a letter of protest to the Department of Alcohol and Drug Programs. This he kindly did. In his letter dated June 6, 2000, Lockyer posed the following question:

> The results of that study are relevant to current public policy surrounding the controversy which still exists regarding the use of medical marijuana. Does your department plan to publish this report in the near future?

As far as I know there was no response to Lockyer's letter. We eventually realized that the reports, if they still existed, would languish indefinitely in a file cabinet in the California Department of Alcohol and Drug Programs.[4] Such is the nature of the bureaucratic process. We will never know whether our results were buried deliberately or simply lost and forgotten in a miasma of indecision.

THE GATEWAY THEORY

Dan Baum's book *Smoke and Mirrors* (1996) provides a detailed history of how marijuana was singled out as the first step in progression to use of presumably harder drugs such as cocaine and heroin. Baum points out that by the early 1960s marijuana had become the "youth drug," even though teenagers usually try alcohol first and use it more widely. Indeed, by age 16 or 17, reported use of alcohol exceeds that of marijuana by 25% to 30%. Intense political pressure to do something about marijuana ignored this

discrepancy, perhaps because the idea that enjoyment of a beer or chardonnay might reflect the effects of a drug makes conventional people uncomfortable. Besides, the legacy of Harry Anslinger, the commissioner of the federal Bureau of Narcotics from 1930 to 1962 and assiduous promoter of antidrug hysteria, unwise legislation, and the idea that marijuana was the "lynchpin" of the drug problem, was implanted in the conservative psyche (Beck, 1998; Gray, 1998). This included zealots from organizations who got to President Carter's second drug czar, social worker Lee Dogoloff, and continued to dominate youth drug policy under his successors. The Parents Research Institute for Drug Education is still influential. This organization made sure that federal policy would establish the "youth drug" as the most dangerous of all. It was to become the gateway to addiction and eventual self-destruction.

The logical step was to sponsor research proving the validity of the gateway theory. It should be no surprise that most people graduating to heroin or cocaine had tried marijuana earlier (Kandel, Yamaguchi & Chen, 1992). However, they usually had tried alcohol or tobacco before that (and milk as well, as MacCoun and Reuter [2001] point out in one of their lighter moments). The correlational data reflecting the hardly surprising finding that most hard drug users had sampled marijuana earlier were widely assumed to prove that the latter had a *causal* role in a process of graduating to harder drugs. That correlation did not establish causation was ignored or not understood by policy makers or practitioners. Ultimately the gateway theory on marijuana was shown to be false empirically as well as logically (Golub & Johnson, 2001). The reality is that "the majority of cannabis triers never try harder drugs, and of those who do, few become regular users, much less addicts" (MacCoun & Reuter 2001, p. 347). This conclusion should be obvious to any thinking person. Given the spread of marijuana use into the youth and young adult population in the 1960s and later, millions of Americans would have been addicted to cocaine or heroin within a decade. By 1980 we would have been a nation of drugged-out zombies (although this may seem more plausible today).

The lesson of the gateway theory is that bad policy can be portrayed as supported by social science when research findings are not interpreted carefully or their interpretation warped by political climate. Besides, the warning that correlation does not prove causation runs against the grain for most of us. We see that problems in living are more common among youths who are heavy users of alcohol or other drugs. It seems obvious that drugs must cause those problems, and we ignore the other possibility: that heavy use and the personal problems that usually accompany such use may have the same underlying causes. For troubled youths and adults, drugs can seem to be a solution to their problems rather than their cause.

The legacy of the gateway theory is that generations of children have been assured in prevention classes that experimenting with marijuana is

likely to lead to addiction. When they enter the social world of teenagers, many perceive this threat as just another scare tactic delivered by adults who don't want kids to have fun. Earlier warnings are then ridiculed and disregarded.

QUESTIONABLE THEORIES ABOUT INITIATION OF USE BY YOUNG PEOPLE

Most current drug-use prevention curricula intended for the general population ("universal" curricula in the argot of the Center for Substance Abuse Prevention) apply two theories on why young people initiate drug use, and this usually means smoking marijuana. The first is the idea that peer pressure is a primary influence on kids who want to be accepted and belong, which of course means virtually every early teenager. This hypothesis must have great appeal to adults in view of its unquestioned acceptance. Yet it is another example of confusing correlation with causation. Teens who smoke marijuana usually have friends who do also. It is easy to jump from this observation to the conclusion that friends *cause* use by pressuring others to join in.

For most young people, use of alcohol and marijuana are social activities learned and practiced with their friends. We humans are the most adept imitators in the animal kingdom. Children attend to subtle social cues as early as their preschool years. A comprehensive review of social psychological research on this topic (Harris, 1995) concludes that social learning almost always involves voluntary imitation rather than forced compliance. Spontaneous modeling of the attitudes and behavior of others is the basic mode of human socialization.

But modeling and imitation is not the whole story when it comes to marijuana or alcohol. There is also attraction. Getting high can be fun. This possibility is ignored in approved prevention curricula. There is also curiosity about what it is like to get high. The CSS survey asks respondents why some of their peers try marijuana. Over many surveys the most frequently selected responses have been "to have fun" and "to find out what it is like." Drinking or smoking weed offers interesting and exciting entertainment in the social world most young people inhabit. Thus, a university student explained that as a high school student he tried marijuana because "I saw my friends having a blast, so I joined in." That this sort of experience might be common in contemporary youth culture demonstrates why training children to resist later peer pressure is usually a waste of time.

To discover the real motives for initiation, one has to ask young people instead of depending on the judgment of middle-aged Ph.D.s and self-

proclaimed experts on youth. The way to do this is to engage in nonjudg-mental dialog with teenagers in a situation where they feel safe and can talk freely (Cook-Sather, 2002). In a zero-tolerance atmosphere, talking with (rather than to) young people is not the way things are done.

I learned a great deal with the help of mainly 19- to 21-year-old students in my university class on adolescent development. We devised a project in which UCLA students conducted anonymous interviews of other youth approximately their own age. The subject was marijuana and other drug use in their high schools, but most of the responses referred to marijuana. There were questions on social acceptance of use; whether the interviewees knew members of social elites such as student body leaders, athletes, or honor students who smoked marijuana; whether they had ever experienced peer pressure; and what they thought about punishment policies for drug violations in their schools. It was clear in the results of more than 300 interviews conducted over a two-year period (2000–2001) that direct peer pressure was rarely the reason for initiation, and that social use of marijuana at parties was viewed as ordinary even by abstainers. Typical responses to the question on peer pressure included the following:

> Most people really want to try it, I think. They see how euphoric their friends are and they want to be in that same state of mind, so they try it. It's not peer pressure, it's curiosity. Parents like peer pressure because it makes their kids the "good" kids who have been influenced by the "bad kids." Ever think your kid was the "bad kid"?
>
> My friends offered marijuana because of courtesy . . . because they felt obligated since we were friends. However, they never teased me for not smoking.
>
> DARE (Drug Abuse Resistance Education) depicted people who offered drugs as being extremely domineering and won't take "no" for an answer. This is not the case. The people that usually offer it to you are your friends and they are nice and will take "no" for answer.

Though the large majority of interviewees clearly rejected the peer pressure hypothesis, there were a few responses that suggested the occasional possibility. The following could have been perceived as pressure, although it may have been friendly persuasion instead. There is a fine line here.

> My friends told me it was no big deal and to just try. When nothing happened to me after that first hit, they said it's better the second time and to try again. It led into a spiral pattern that was hard for me to escape from.

Given the general acceptance of peer pressure as self-evident, it is not surprising that there is little or no research proving that significant numbers of

teenagers start drinking or using drugs in response to it (Coggans & McKellar, 1994) or that teaching "resistance skills" has a long-term effect. Gorman (1995 and 1996) reported that resistance skills and other social skills training failed to reduce alcohol misuse. Flay (2000), Paglia and Room (1998), and Cuijpers (2002) concluded that resistance skills training were at best of limited effectiveness. A recent U.S. national survey found that only 8% of a national sample of 13–19 year olds cited "Pressure to do drugs or drink" as a major problem.[5]

The other common social skills approach in current prevention is usually referred to as "normative education." The idea is based on sound social science. We all, at least all of us that are sane, are sensitive to social norms. We have learned from experience the equivalent of that ancient adage, "When in Rome, do as the Romans do." My very English wife used to caution me with "It's not done!" whenever I was in danger of violating one of the unwritten rules of British social life. This happened rather often, especially at first.

Normative drug education demonstrates through an anonymous survey that most members of a group have not tried marijuana or some other drug. If the members of the group are young enough, drinking alcohol or smoking marijuana usually turns out to be relatively rare and thus will be perceived by participants as deviant rather than common or normal behavior as they might have thought before the demonstration. The idea that "everybody does it" turns out to be false.

Though this approach may reduce further the minuscule levels of use among preteen children, the social context is different in upper grades. A World Health Organization's review of research concluded that normative education is likely to be less effective in the higher grades (Hawks, Scott, McBride, Jones, & Stockwell, 2002). Other research found that the effects of this approach were not maintained through the 12th grade (Shope, Copeland, Kamp, & Lang 1998). Besides, older students may not be very far off in their predictions of use by peers. On a recent California Student Survey, two thirds of 16-year-olds estimated that half or more of their same-age peers had tried marijuana (Austin & Skager, 2003). This estimate was not far off when compared to self-reported use (historically between 40 and just under 50% on the California Student Survey for 11th graders). It is also possible that even on anonymous surveys, some respondents deny using because they do not trust the promise of anonymity or choose to conceal private, illegal activity. In other words, estimates of prevalence among peers may be reasonably accurate.

The assumption has been that drug-use prevention education can *inoculate* children against drug use later on when they are teenagers. In other words, drug education works just like vaccinating children against measles.

Accordingly, most prevention programs focus on the last years of elementary school. Some now have "booster" sessions for early teens, but this does not mean that new approaches are in order. This has not worked. One cannot vaccinate most human beings against the influence of new information and experiences in a social environment that contradicts earlier indoctrination.

The persistence of marijuana use among young people should not be surprising. Rejecting any goal other than abstinence as giving the wrong message, ignoring input from young people on what they think about prevention curricula they experienced, and building curricula around false hypotheses about why so many teenagers try alcohol and marijuana has been a prescription for failure.

SOCIAL BENEFITS OF CURRENT DRUG PREVENTION EDUCATION

A Carnegie Mellon/RAND econometric study of the social benefits of current drug-use prevention (reducing premature death, lost work time, medical costs, etc.) concludes that reductions in tobacco and alcohol use account for the lion's share of the gain and that only minimal benefits accrue from reductions in marijuana use (Caulkins, Liccardo Pacula, Paddock, & Chiesa, 2004). Part of the basis for this finding is that marijuana, when compared to alcohol and tobacco, "is less frequently the sole or even principal cause of specific harms (e.g., overdose deaths)" (p. 83). These authors concluded that public health would benefit more from reductions in alcohol and tobacco use than from any of the objectives of the war on illegal drugs.

STARTING AGAIN

It seems that we need to start all over again. Most drug education—honest and balanced education as distinguished from indoctrination—should be shifted to secondary schools and out of the upper elementary grades. Reasons for choosing abstinence would still be emphasized, but without exaggeration or scare tactics. Moreover, information on safety for students who do not abstain is essential for older youth. It should also be apparent that drug education is but one of three facets of a larger picture. The others are intervention and assistance for students whose lives are disrupted by problematic use or other problems plus disciplinary policies for students who violate rules on substance use. What do we need to change in each of these facets and how do we go about it?

CREATING MEANINGFUL INVOLVEMENT FOR YOUTH

Young people should be meaningfully involved in the development and test-ing of activities and programs that affect them (Cook-Sather, 2002). This includes drug education and school policies relating to drugs. Meaningful in-volvement means real rather than phony, symbolic consultation. Programs and policies that are supposed to influence the life choices of young people should be developed *with* them rather than designed *for* them and adminis-tered *to* them. Doing things *with* youth rather than *to* or *for* them extends to the entire educational process. Given this precondition, what should drug education be like for secondary and upper middle school students?

Full Implementation of an Interactive Learning Process

It has been understood that drug education should be *interactive* ever since Tobler and Stratton's (1997) analysis of a large number of drug-use preven-tion programs. Just what this means in practice has never been made clear. It is both easy and trivial to allow a token level of student interaction. Permit-ting kids to ask questions is token interaction. But what does it mean to go beyond tokenism? How about teenagers participating in agenda setting and sharing experience in an open discussion even to the point of risking the possibility that some will make positive statements about drinking or smok-ing dope? While such revelations are inconceivable when students do not trust the teacher, experience shows that genuinely interactive drug educa-tion elicits stories about negative as well as positive drug experiences. Teenagers discuss these experiences among themselves. Why do we fear dis-cussion in a drug education session where there is a knowledgeable adult to help put those experiences into perspective?

Fully interactive learning means leaving the door open to all relevant experience in a situation in which participants, including the adult facilita-tor, are not afraid to be honest. Teenagers are fully capable of understanding that they should not reveal something that may endanger them or harm someone else. Without this freedom to share their own observations and ex-periences, skeptical young people are likely to perceive the session as an-other attempt by adults to manipulate and deceive.

The mental capacities and behavioral potential of teenagers are much underrated in our society (Hine, 1999; Mailes, 1999). Even some educators think that all teens are risk takers or inherently irresponsible. In reality, teens are as diverse on these characteristics as adults are (Moshman, 1999). The important difference is that teenagers lack life experience, the kind that we all acquire over time by making mistakes and experiencing the consequences.

Yet despite deficits in experience, teenagers are intellectually adult in having the capacity to reason formally and hypothetically. This capacity underlies their ability to question the world around them plus an irritating tendency to detect inconsistencies when adults make assertions that conflict with their personal experience. Effective teachers are aware of this and show respect for the intelligence of their students.

Creating Connections and Trust

A second research-based principle is that positive relationships with adults and a sense of belonging to the school community are associated with positive health behaviors among teenagers, including lower levels of substance use (Resnick, et al., 1997). Schools that expel students for relatively minor infractions of discipline have been found lower on student connectedness that those that applied less severe consequences. Those that expelled permanently on the first occurrence were even lower on student connectedness (McNeely, Nonnemaker, & Blum, 2001)

Positive connections between youth and adults are grounded in mutual trust and respect. Young people must perceive adults to be genuinely interested in their welfare. What does this mean for drug education? First, adults who do this kind of work must be careful to accept the worth of the offender even when they deplore the behavior. A nonjudgmental attitude toward *people* as contrasted with their *actions* is a basic rule of all positive group practice and represents the best kind of teaching and mentoring when the topic is the choices we make in life.

Adult leaders begin this kind of interactive learning process by making their goals clear at the outset and establishing firm rules about disclosure. "What's said here stays here" is a fundamental rule of any group process than encourages involvement at a personal level. So is "No put-downs allowed!" Specific exceptions to confidentiality relating to threats of harm to self or others are made clear as well. These are first steps in building trust. Trustworthy adults are soon awarded that reputation schoolwide.

Addressing Safety for Young People
Who Choose to Experiment

Informing young people about principles of safety is the most controversial proposal offered here. It draws an emotional dividing line between supporters of zero tolerance and people who advocate rational and compassionate approaches to youth policy. Like the broader concept of harm reduction of which it is an example, giving information on safety or proposing strategies

that promote it such as sober driver programs provokes the "wrong message" backlash. Nevertheless, advice about specific dangers associated with use is the keystone of drug education that is truly concerned about the welfare of young people. It includes the advice that abstinence is the only sure way to be safe. When sources of harm cannot be eliminated, promoting safety is a basic principle of public health practice. It is analogous to reducing risks among people who are exposed to sources of infection or physical injury.

What do young people, not only those who choose to use, but also those who choose abstinence, need to learn about safety? Twenty years ago, Zinberg (1984) proposed *drug*, *set*, and *setting* as the three conditions that determine the effects of any mind-altering drug. These refer to the properties of the drug itself, the mind-set of the user at the time, and the setting in which a drug is used. That is, the effect of any drug depends not only on its pharmacological properties, but also on the psychological state of the user and the social or physical setting in which use occurs. Once I heard an elderly, recovering alcoholic reminiscing on his old resentments say, "I drank in order to remember not to forget!" In other words, he drank in order to dwell in his anger, even to enhance it. Nothing about setting here (which was probably a bar), but lots about his mental state, his reason for getting drunk, and the likely effect on his experience and behavior.

Young people need to understand these relationships. Negative emotional states may be enhanced rather than forgotten, sometimes leading to dangerous or even fatal behaviors. The wrong setting is associated with similar consequences—automobile accidents, rape and unprotected sex, violence and injury, and so on. Understanding the implications of Zinberg's principles, especially when communicated through concrete examples, is the foundation for safety education on drugs. In the case of older teenagers, concrete examples are likely to be available in the group and will be much more impressive than negative stories from an adult. This is how interactive learning works.

Binge drinking and how to prevent deaths caused by it is the most important single topic for both drinking and nondrinking youths. There are prevention programs aimed at binge drinking, but many don't go beyond avoidance messages. Unfortunately, bingeing is not likely to disappear. Among friends in the late high school and college years, it can be hilarious fun. It has long been a ritual in college fraternities and other social contexts. It may even moderate later drinking, since getting sick and harboring a hangover usually follows the fun. Nevertheless, bingeing leads to unconsciousness and death for some participants.

Young people should know that drunks sometimes die instead of "sleeping it off." They need to recognize specific signs that a peer is in danger and what to do about it. The danger signs are obvious: loss of consciousness and failure of vigorous attempts to restore it, such as dousing with cold water; or

shaking, accompanied by very slow breathing, pallor, and sweating. The response is straightforward. Turn the friend on his or her side to avoid aspiration of vomit (also fatal) and call for medical help. Teens often avoid calling for help, not only because they do not realize the true level of danger, but also because they are afraid their unconscious friend (and perhaps themselves) will get into trouble. Trouble goes away eventually, but death is permanent.

Marijuana is different. There is no lethal dosage for this drug. Unless combined with other drugs, it is rarely associated with visits to the emergency room or other catastrophic consequences associated with addiction to alcohol, opiates, or cocaine. Still, driving a car or doing things that require fast reaction time in a complex or dangerous situation is not advisable, especially for new or occasional users, including adolescents who are likely to drive fast anyway (Weil & Rosen, 2004). Young people who believe that marijuana enhances study are mistaken. While learning simple tasks is not affected, complex learning and problem solving can be severely disrupted (Earleywine, 2002). These are examples of basic information on safety.

The most important principle of safety for people who choose to use marijuana is that tolerance develops rapidly with frequent use. As tolerance increases, the pleasant effects many people experienced initially begin to wane. This calls for increasing the dosage, which further enhances tolerance. This is the path to dependency and addiction experienced by some marijuana smokers. Weil & Rosen (2004) warn that this progressive process is enhanced because marijuana is so easy to integrate with most leisure activities, from watching television to sports. In other words, "safest" use, in its broadest sense, is occasional use. These authors' 14 suggestions on marijuana use (pp. 146–147) would be an essential component of drug education for teenagers if public health rather than zero tolerance were the model. Their first point is that use of this drug is illegal and thus associated with real dangers current and future. Other suggestions include setting limits on using, using less rather than more if the desired effects are disappearing, not engaging in hazardous activities, and so on.

As to the "wrong message" complaint, we do not need research to prove that very few if any teenagers ask adults for permission to try weed. We can take that for granted. Giving them honest information about reasons for not using as well as for maximizing safety if they do use carries an underlying message that choosing to use a mind-altering drug is not a casual decision. As reported earlier in this chapter, the majority of teenagers believe that their peers try marijuana because they want to have fun or are curious about its effects. Weil and Rosen's suggestions counterbalance these simple and unqualified expectations with accurate warnings and qualifications. How does this make things worse, especially when use of marijuana in the youth population has persisted at the same average level since 1975 or before?

Student Assistance

Most middle and high schools are not equipped to identify and assist students who need help because of problematic substance use. Relatively few California high school students report on the CSS that peers who need help because of problematic drug use can find it at their schools (Austin & Skager, 2003). The approach to interactive drug education proposed here helps to identify problematic users and guide them to assistance instead of punishment. Adult facilitators in such programs often identify during group discussion the students who need help. They indicate at the outset that they are available for private consultation with students who self-identify as having a problem as a result of the group experience.

High school student assistance programs are a long-established tool for identification, assistance, and, where appropriate, referral.[6] Pennsylvania requires these programs in all of its high schools, but is probably the only state that does so. Research has shown that participants in student assistance programs show improved attendance and higher rates of promotion and graduation. Disruptive behaviors are also reduced in schools offering such programs (Fertman, Tarasevich, & Hepler, 2003). However, most student assistance programs do not offer the kind of drug education recommended here. Still, staff in these programs are good candidates for doing this kind of education because, unlike regular teachers, they usually possess relevant knowledge about drugs and may already be skilled in counseling and interactive group processes.[7]

Replacing Deterrence with Restorative Practices

The third and last facet of the larger policy picture is disciplinary policy for students who break rules on substance use. Deterrent punishment is the common reaction in American high schools to virtually all drug violations. Deterrent policies include exclusion from extracurricular activities for less serious first offences, transfer to another school, or suspension and permanent expulsion for serious or repeated offenses. As a strategy for eliminating drug use, deterrence makes examples out of offenders in the assumption that it will discourage their peers from engaging in the same behaviors. Yet such punishments neither reduce widespread experimentation and use, nor are they compatible with positive youth development, the basic mission of schooling.

Punishments that scapegoat and banish instead of offering support and rehabilitation are shortsighted. What are young people who are suspended and expelled for drug offences likely to do with their free time? Excluding students from extracurricular activities means that time has to be filled, but

with what? Is transfer to another school where the student is without friends likely to promote abstinence? Free time and loneliness on top of resentment and what Wachtel (1997) calls "stigmatizing shame" is likely to promote continued and even more intense substance use. And since few students who violate the rules are caught, others disregard the threat of punishment.

In the UCLA interviews, respondents were asked whether expelling students caught coming to school high discouraged peers from doing the same thing. The responses were overwhelmingly disdainful of this practice.

> If the school expels the student, he or she is just going to be transferred to another school to repeat the same behaviors. The rest of the students truly don't give a fuck if a student got suspended for coming to school high, because they think that they won't get caught and they're right, most students don't get caught.

Many of the respondents expressed concern about the welfare of peers who were caught and punished. If what they had to say on this issue seems obvious, why do we continue punishing instead of assisting?

> Expelling a student is getting rid of the problem kids and not getting rid of the problem in those kids.

> You are continuing the problem by expulsion. A kid who comes to school high is obviously in need of some attention and guidance and by kicking him or her our of school you may eliminate the only stability or direction that he or she has in their lives. Expulsion just encourages the negative behavior, and it leaves no alternative avenue open to the kid.

> Kicking a kid out of school is the dumbest thing ever. Then what are they going to do? Just sit at home and smoke pot all of the time.

For most offenders, deterrent punishment should be replaced with restorative practices designed to promote reform and reintegration into the life of the school. There is nothing new about restorative practice. It has a long history as an approach to justice in many tribal or clan societies and is even represented in the 12 steps of Alcoholics Anonymous, whose members make amends to people they have harmed.

Restorative practices in schools devolve from a criminal justice approach that substitutes punishment with structured interchange between victims and perpetrators, a result of which is that the latter makes amends that have been worked out collectively by both sides (Braithwaite, 1989). Substance use in school by students has a negative effect on school climate in general and other students and teachers personally. In schools, this approach reduces the number of suspensions and expulsions and keeps in school young people who would

otherwise be on the streets. Restorative practices have been shown to be effective for teenagers on probation from the courts or referred by child youth services and school districts (McCold, 2002). Restorative practices stress both high accountability (limit setting) and at the same time support for offenders (Wachtel, 1999). Wachtel cites six principles of a restorative procedure:

1. It fosters awareness on the part of the offending student of the effect his or her behavior has on others.
2. It promotes empathy for others by avoiding scolding or lecturing that leads offenders to react defensively.
3. It involves offenders actively by asking them to speak as well as listen to the victims and others they have affected and take part in deciding how to repair the harm they have caused.
4. It acknowledges ambiguity in recognizing that there is often some degree of fault on both sides.
5. It separates the deed from the doer and emphasizes that disapproval applies to the deed rather than the person.
6. It views every instance of wrongdoing as an opportunity for learning.

Restorative practice extends to the whole school when it includes the adults who work there. They also experience conflict and develop resentments toward colleagues and about policies. Morrison (in press) provides a comprehensive summary of restorative approaches that have been used successfully in schools, especially in reducing bullying and other conflicts. Putting drug education, intervention, and assistance plus restorative consequences for most drug violators together under coherent, compassionate and rational school and community policies is another way to begin anew.[8]

NOTES

1. The percentages also vary depending on the survey consulted. The *Youth Behavior Risk Survey* administered by the Center for Disease Control reports higher prevalence for 2003—83% for lifetime alcohol use among 12th graders and 48.5% for marijuana.

2. National Drug Strategic Framework, 1998–99 to 2002–03. Ministerial Council on Drug Strategy, Commonwealth of Australia. (See www.national drugstrategy.gov.au.)

3. Greg Austin of WestEd is the other codirector.

4. After a new director was appointed, a California Department of Alcohol and Drug Programs staff member informed me informally that we could now announce the results. There was no offer to print or distribute the study. The issue by then was off the front burner of news media. A publicist friend sent out a press release, but the only response was a press release from California NORML (a local chapter of the National Organization for the

Reform of Marijuana Laws), an organization promoting changes in marijuana laws.

5. *The State of Our Nation's Youth* (2003) by Peter D. Hart Associates for the Horatio Alger Association of Distinguished Americans, Inc.

6. See the National Student Assistance Association website (www.nsaa. us or info@nsaa.us).

7. One program that combines drug education and assistance/intervention is *UpFront: A Reality-Based Drug Education Program for High Schools* at cries4life@prodigy.net.

8. For information, materials and training workshops on restorative practices in schools, criminal justice, and other settings go to www.safersaner schools.org.

REFERENCES

Austin, G., & Skager, R. (2003). *Alcohol, tobacco, and other drug use among California students in grades 7, 9, and 11: Ninth biennial statewide survey.* Office of the Attorney General of California, Crime Prevention Center, Sacramento, California.

Baum, D. (1996). *Smoke and mirrors: The war on drugs and the politics of failure.* Boston: Little, Brown.

Beck, J. (1998). One hundred years of "just say no" versus "just say know." *Evaluation Review, 19*(1), 15–45.

Braithwaite, J. (1989). *Crime, shame, and reintegration.* Cambridge: Cambridge University Press.

Caulkins, J. P., Liccardo Pacula, R., Paddock, S., & Chiesa, J. (2004). What we can—and cannot—expect from school-based prevention. *Drug and Alcohol Review, 23,* 79–87.

Coggans, N., & McKellar, S. (1994). Drug use amongst peers: Peer pressure or peer preference? *Drugs: Education, Prevention, and Policy, 1*(1), 15–26.

Cook-Sather, A. (2002). Authorizing student perspectives: toward trust, dialog, and change in education. *Educational Researcher, 31*(4), 3–14.

Cuijpers, P. (2002). Effective ingredients of school based drug prevention programs: A systematic review. *Addictive Behaviors, 27*(1), 1009–1023.

Earleywine, M. (2002). *Understanding marijuana: A new look at the scientific evidence.* Oxford: Oxford University Press.

Fertman, C., Tarasevich, L. L., & Hepler, N. A. (2003). *Retrospective analyses of the Pennsylvania student assistance program online data: Implications for practice and research.* Available at http://www.nasap.org/.

Fertman, C. (2004). Student assistance program practitioners talk about how to link students to behavioral health care. *Report on Emotional and Behavioral Disorders in Youth, 4,* 87–92.

Flay, B. R. (2000). Approaches to substance use prevention utilizing school curriculum plus social environment change. *Addictive Behaviors 25*(6), 861–885.

Golub, A., & Johnson, B. (2001). Variation in youthful risks of progression from alcohol/tobacco to marijuana and to hard drugs across generations. *American Journal of Public Health, 23*(2), 225–232.

Gorman, D. M. (1995). On the difference between statistical and practical significance in school-based drug abuse prevention. *Drugs, Education, Prevention, and Policy, 2*(3), 275–283.

Gorman, D. M. (1996). Etiological theories and the primary prevention of drug use. *Journal of Drug Issues, 26*(2), 505–520.

Gray, M. (1998). *Drug crazy: How we got into this mess and how to get out.* New York: Random House.

Harris, J. R. (1995). Where is the child's environment? A group socialization theory of development. *Psychological Review, 102*(3), 458–489.

Hawks, D., Scott, K., McBride, N., Jones, P., & Stockwell, T. (2002). *Prevention of psychoactive substance use: A selected review of what works in the area of prevention.* World Health Organization, Mental Health: Evidence and Research, Department of Mental Health and Substance Dependence, Switzerland.

Hine, T. (1999). *The rise and fall of the American adolescent.* New York: HarperCollins.

Johnston, L. D., O'Malley, P. M., & Bachman, J. G. (2004). *National survey results on drug use from the Monitoring the Future Study. Overview of key findings* (NIH publication No. 94). Washington, DC: U.S. Government Printing Office.

Kandel, D., Yamaguchi, K., & Chen, K. (1992). Stages of progression in drug involvement from adolescence to adulthood: Further evidence for the gateway theory. *Journal of Studies on Alcohol, 53,* 447–457.

MacCoun, R., & Reuter, P. (2001). *Drug war heresies: Learning from other vices, times, and places.* Cambridge: Cambridge University Press.

Mailes, M. (1999). *Framing youth: Ten myths about the next generation.* Monroe, ME: Common Courage.

McCold, P. (2002, November). *Evaluation of a restorative milieu: CSF Buxmont School/Day Treatment programs, 1999–2001.* Paper presented at the American Society of Criminology annual meeting, Chicago, IL. Available at www.restorativepracticesorg/library/erm.html.

McNeely, C. A., Nonnemaker, J. M., & Blum, R. M. (2002). Promoting school connectedness: Evidence from the national longitudinal study of adolescent health. *Journal of School Health, 72*(4), 138–146.

Morrison, B. (in press). Restorative justice in schools. In E. Elliott & R. Gordon (Eds.), *Restorative justice: Emerging issues in practice and evaluation.* Devon, England: Willan.

Moshman, D. (1999). *Adolescent psychological development: Rationality, morality, and identity.* Mahwah, NJ: Erlbaum.

Paglia, A., & Room, R. (1998). *Preventing substance use problems among youth: A literature review and recommendations.* Center for Addiction and Mental Health, Toronto, Canada.

Resnick, M. D., Beaman, P. S., Blum, R. W., Bauman, K. E., Harris, K. M., Jones, J., et al. (1997). Protecting adolescents from harm. *Journal of the American Medical Association, 278*(10), 823–832.

Shope, J. T., Copeland, L. A., Kamp, M. E., & Lang, S. W. (1998). Twelfth grade follow up of the effectiveness of a middle school-based substance abuse prevention program. *Journal of Drug Education, 28,* 185–197.

Skager, R., & Brown, J. (1998). On the reconstruction of drug education in the United States. In J. M. Fish (Ed.), *How to legalize drugs.* Northvale, NJ: Aronson.

Tobler, N. S., & Stratton, H. (1997). Effectiveness of school-based prevention programs: A meta-analysis of the research. *Journal of Primary Prevention, 18*(1), 71–128.

Wachtel, T. (1997). *REAL Justice: How we can revolutionize our response to wrongdoing.* Pipersville, PA: Piper's Press.

Wachtel, R. (1999, February). *Restoring community in a disconnected world.* Adapted from *Restorative justice in everyday life: Beyond the formal ritual.* Paper presented at the Reshaping Australian Institutions Conference: Restorative Justice and Civil Society. The Australian National University, Canberra.

Weil, A., & Rosen, R. (2004). *From chocolate to morphine: Everything you need to know about mind-altering drugs.* New York: Houghton Mifflin.

Zinberg, N. (1984). *Drug, set and setting: The basis for controlled intoxicant use.* New Haven, CT: Yale University Press.

SECTION VI

Support for Prohibitions

Kevin Sabet shows how a comparable look at the same data can serve as a basis for dramatically different arguments. His view of research reviewed here and in other chapters leads him to argue that marijuana is more harmful than many suggest. In contrast to the views of previous authors, he sees the connections between marijuana and respiratory problems, mental health, and addiction as reasonable justification for continued prohibition. He makes an important distinction between the number of marijuana arrests per year and the actual number of people arrested. He also emphasizes his view that prohibition has succeeded in keeping the prevalence of regular marijuana use far behind that of legal drugs like alcohol and tobacco. He sees no problem with using the legal system or drug testing (when it is respectful of privacy) to motivate treatment. He also expresses strong views that a legal market in marijuana can be misinterpreted as tacit encouragement or as a message of harmlessness to youth.

Prohibitionists will find these arguments familiar; opponents of the drug war will see the point of view they're up against.

16   The (Often Unheard) Case Against Marijuana Leniency

Kevin A. Sabet

Marijuana is the most common illegal drug used in the United States, indeed the world. What we should do about marijuana use is the subject of count- less debate among policy analysts, community leaders, and even government agencies. Among academics, the call for marijuana legalization, or less drastic "reform" proposals such as depenalization, has become routine. These claims are usually based on some sound facts: It is difficult to persuade even half of all 18-year-olds not to try it, most people have generally mild (or no) reac- tions when beginning its use, and the drug is contained in an increasingly vi- olent $10 billion underground market that seems impossible to break up. Further, proponents of reform argue that marijuana laws unnecessarily waste sparse criminal justice system resources and that restrictions on mari- juana use have been relaxed elsewhere with few problems (Nadelmann, 1989; Stroup, 1999).

Hardly anyone claims that marijuana use is without problems. Propo- nents and opponents (and everyone in the middle) alike acknowledge that heavy marijuana use, especially among teens, is not a good thing. In addition, a myriad of troubling research on marijuana use and its link to mental illness hardly helps the liberalization effort. There is also credible evidence that marijuana can ease the way into use of other drugs.

In this chapter, I will explore these notions and conclude that pro- hibitory laws on marijuana are justified. I will present the case that restric- tive laws on marijuana—a harmful drug—have actually kept use levels low compared with levels for alcohol and tobacco, and though the public policy

of marijuana prohibition is not perfect, it is far better than a regime of legalization or depenalization. In this case, I argue that the status quo is about right. Its no open-and-shut case, but a more pertinent question than "Which is better, legalization or prohibition?" would go something like "How can we make restrictive policies work better?" This chapter hopes to establish why we should begin with having restrictive policies in the first place.

WHAT WE'RE DOING NOW

The United States is consistently described as having a policy of marijuana prohibition. That description is about half right. Yes, marijuana is an illegal drug, according to the federal government. And if you asked them, most Americans would tell you that marijuana use is prohibited.[1] But in practice the marijuana user is subject to different, sometimes confusing laws in various cities, counties, and states. In 12 states, for example, marijuana is actually decriminalized (a certain amount of use is subject to a fine only), and in dozens of localities, law enforcement turns a blind eye to simple marijuana use. For purposes of this chapter and for lack of a better term, I will (half wrongly) refer to the status quo as prohibition or a "restrictive policy," though readers should note that this characterization somewhat ignores the nuances of American marijuana policy.[2]

Since many drug policy analysts call for a radical change in the way marijuana is handled, are we doing something terribly wrong? Rather than take their word for it, let us look at the current scenario of marijuana use in the United States. Marijuana is the most common illegal drug used by the population, representing its popularity and strengthening the case for its legalization. But how many people actually use the drug? When asked, about 6% of Americans admitted to using the drug in the past month—what the U.S. government calls "current" marijuana users. Half of all drug users use marijuana only, and one quarter of drug users do not use it at all. Somewhat surprising is the fact that 12- and 13-year-olds use psychotherapeutics nonmedically and inhalants at rates higher than they smoke marijuana, but among all youths 12 to 17 in 2003, 7.9% used marijuana; rates of use were highest for the young adult age group (18 to 25 years), with 17% using marijuana (Substance Abuse and Mental Health Services Administration [SAMHSA], 2004). Using a different, more school-specific survey, 7.5%, 17%, and 21.2% of 8th, 10th, and 12th graders, respectively, used marijuana in the past 30 days—a significant drop from the mid-'90s, when drug-use rates in almost every major category skyrocketed (Johnston, O'Malley, Bachman, & Schulenberg). Since 2001, 600,000 less youths in the United States have used drugs. The declining popularity of MDMA and LSD contributed to this drop, but marijuana use has also dropped significantly.

The number of marijuana users is far lower than the number of people using tobacco or alcohol. Fifty percent of all Americans report being current drinkers (SAMHSA, 2004). Among young people, the prevalence of current alcohol use in 2003 increased with age, from 2.9% at age 12 to about 70% at ages 21 or 22. Thirty percent of all Americans report using tobacco currently (SAMHSA, 2004). Of people 12 to 17, 14.4% report using tobacco; the rate is 45% for people 18 to 25.

Even considering that self-reported data for marijuana use may undercount users, it is still a stretch to claim that "everybody is doing it"—a favorite catchphrase of people advocating legalization. The evidence shows that far more people use our legal substances. Still, marijuana use is widespread among the illegal drugs, and one could hardly argue that current American policy on marijuana is perfect. But the serious advocate of public health and public safety would ask how we can make our existing policies work before blindly walking into the uncertain territory of experimenting with legalization.

IS MARIJUANA HARMFUL?

This question continues to act as a starting point of discussions about loosening restrictions on marijuana. Legalization advocates and most depenalization advocates contend that using marijuana is relatively harmless, and that most people use it without any problems (Nadelmann, 1989). But an honest look at the scientific research tells us otherwise.

Nuttall and colleagues at the University of Birmingham found that smoking marijuana for even less than six years caused a marked deterioration in lung function and may rob the body of antioxidants that can lead to heart disease and cancer (Nuttall, Raczi, Manney, Thorpe, & Kendall, 2003). Additionally, marijuana affects alertness, which could in some circumstances lead to car crashes; that sort of tragedy takes using the drug only once to happen. (Though, as Kleiman has noted, it's plausible that a dependent user will more likely engage in risky activity [driving while stoned] than would a first-time or occasional user, who is more apt to be cautious about his behavior [personal communication, 2004].) The U.S. National Highway Traffic Safety Administration (NHTSA) noted that marijuana has a severely negative effect on driving, whether used alone or in combination with alcohol. The NHTSA reports that marijuana-intoxicated drivers pose a threat to others and that this alone kills many drivers and passengers every year (see Liguori, chap. 4, in this volume). The study also noted that when combined with marijuana, a blood alcohol level of .07 (legal in most states) gives driving performance similar to that of .14 (NHTSA, 1999). Other studies affirm the negative effect of marijuana on driving. For example, a

roadside study published in the *New England Journal of Medicine* conducted in Memphis, Tennessee, of reckless drivers not believed to be impaired by alcohol found that 45% tested positive for marijuana (Brookoff, Cook, Williams, & Mann, 1994).

Using the drug frequently (even if nondependent upon it) may contribute to respiratory problems and lung changes consistent with precancerous states (Tashkin, 1990). The British Lung Foundation, outraged at Britain's casual attitude about marijuana, published a report titled *A Smoking Gun* in 2002 showing that smoking three or four marijuana cigarettes is equivalent to smoking 20 tobacco cigarettes in terms of harm to the lungs (British Lung Foundation, 2002). And although marijuana users probably smoke less marijuana in one sitting than do habitual tobacco smokers, these studies are troubling. As expected, smoking tobacco and marijuana adds to the harm associated with lung damage (Taylor et al., 2002).

Marijuana also appears to contribute to other cancers. A study of more than 340 people in 1999 by Zhang and colleagues confirmed a previous study by other UCLA cancer researchers that smoking marijuana may contribute to head and neck cancer. Zhang also showed that people with a genetic defect may not have the ability to repair DNA damage brought on by habitual marijuana smoking. They showed that these people are 16 times more likely to develop head and neck cancers than are people with normal DNA who do not smoke marijuana (Zhang, 1999).

An active literature on the link between marijuana and mental illness, including psychosis and schizophrenia, has emerged in recent years (Ashton, 2001; Hall & Solowij, 1998; Jha, 2004; Johns, 2001; Patton, 2002; Zammit, Allebeck, Andreasson, Lundberg, & Lewis, 2002). In 2002, the cover story of an issue of the *British Medical Journal* was titled: "Cannabis and mental health: More evidence establishes clear link between use of cannabis and psychiatric illness." In the same issue, Zammit and colleagues looked at 50,087 Swedish conscripts to conclude that marijuana use in adolescence is a risk factor for schizophrenia, independent of the effects of other drugs or social personality traits. Also, in a New Zealand study, Arseneault and colleagues (2002) discovered that using marijuana as an adolescent increases a person's risk for schizophrenia even after adjustment for preexisting childhood psychoses. Meta-analyses have found that eliminating marijuana use could reduce incidence of schizophrenia by 8% among a nation's population (Arseneault et al., 2002). In the United States, that means that eliminating marijuana use could reduce schizophrenia by more than 19,000 people.

Additionally, heavy marijuana use also can lead to psychosis. Those who smoked marijuana at ages 18 or 15 were 60% and 450% more likely to achieve psychosis, respectively (Jha, 2004). Psychosis has even been linked with oral—not smoked—cannabis administration, leading Favrat and colleagues to conclude that "while the oral route of administration achieves

only limited blood concentrations, significant psychotic reactions may occur" (Favrat et al., 2005). Marijuana use is also linked with depression (Patton et al., 2002). These dire statistics about the link between mental illness and marijuana use have officials worldwide worried.

Nondependent marijuana users can quickly slide into dependency. Data show that about half of those who use marijuana daily become dependent for some period of time (use of the drug daily could itself bring major health problems regardless of users being scientifically diagnosed as "dependent"). About 1 in 10 people in the United States who have ever used marijuana become dependent at some time. In Britain, drug treatment centers have reported a rise in the number of marijuana cases they deal with (Jha, 2004).

Crowley and colleagues report that marijuana use by teenagers with prior antisocial problems can help escalate use to dependence (Crowley, Macdonald, Whitmore, & Mikulich, 1998). The study found that, for these troubled teenagers using tobacco, alcohol, and marijuana, progression from their first use of marijuana to regular use was about as rapid as their progression to regular tobacco use and more rapid than the progression to regular use of alcohol.

Though clearly not as habit-forming as smoking crack cocaine, marijuana does appear to have addictive potential, at least psychologically. In a study published in *Nature Neuroscience* in 2000, Tanda, Munzar, and Goldberg demonstrated that squirrel monkeys will self-administer the active ingredient in marijuana, THC, in doses equivalent to those used by humans who smoke the drug. Additionally, other findings published in 2001 showed that some heavy users of marijuana develop withdrawal symptoms—restlessness, loss of appetite, sleep disturbances, weight loss, and so on—when they stop using the drug (Budney, Hughes, Moore, & Novy, 2001). Budney's conclusions on withdrawal have been well established in the marijuana literature (Beardsley, Balster, & Harris, 1986; Holson, Ali, Scallet, Slikker, & Paule, 1989; Huestis, Gorelick, & Heishman, 2001; Jones, 1983; Kouri, Pope, & Lukas, 1999). Based on these recent assessments, Australian public health officials, once neutral on marijuana's role in mental illness, called high levels of marijuana use a "ticking time bomb."

MacCoun and Reuter (2001) touch on cannabis dependence and conclude that "(marijuana) dependence occurs frequently, almost as frequently as for alcohol amongst those who start using the drug. However, dependence seems to have modest adverse consequences." They base the latter notion on outdated research, much of it coming from the mid- to late 1980s and very early 1990s, when Jones (1987) showed that withdrawal symptoms were mild and generally passed in a few days and when Compton, Dewey, and Martin (1990) reported that dependence was not a major issue with marijuana. It appears that the literature on withdrawal has shifted in the past few

years; withdrawal is not only becoming a common phenomenon but a serious one. It is too bad MacCoun and Reuter didn't write their book a year or so later; we would have benefited from their analysis of these newer, troubling findings—findings that point in the direction of, not away from, the assertion that even some marijuana use is harmful.[3]

IS MARIJUANA A "GATEWAY" DRUG?

Anyone who has heard anything about marijuana has probably heard that it is a "gateway" drug, one that leads the user to other, more serious drugs such as cocaine or heroin. This assertion is confirmed by some who explain their downward spiral into drugs ("It all started with pot") and rebuked by those who claim they'd never try the hard stuff ("Marijuana is the most I've ever done"). But is marijuana really a gateway drug? Sometimes.

A quick analysis shows us that most people who smoke marijuana once *never* go on to other drugs. Every major data set used to gauge drug use tells us that. By the same token, there is evidence that of the people who have used drugs like cocaine and heroin, the vast majority of them started with marijuana (and tobacco and alcohol).

The gateway theory was first popularized by the founding director of the National Institute on Drug Abuse (a division of the National Institutes of Health), Robert L. DuPont. DuPont (1984) notes that "the connection of pot use to other illegal drug use is clear and indisputable. The most basic connection is the use of a drug (any drug, including, of course, pot) to stimulate brain reward. That is the same brain mechanism for all of these drugs. People who find drug use to be a good way to stimulate brain reward are more willing to try another drug to do it than are kids who never used drugs." To his critics he asks: "Would you think that the fact that not everyone who smokes tobacco cigarettes gets cancer means that smoking is not a significant risk factor for cancer?" (R. DuPont, personal communication, September 2004).

There does seem to be a correlation between marijuana and other drug use—most proponents and opponents of marijuana decriminalization agree on that (Golub & Johnson, 1994). But what is so special about marijuana? Indeed, people advocating legalization retort that most people who have used cocaine have also used milk. Does that make milk a gateway drug? Hardly, as MacCoun and Reuter point out, since there is no *correlation* between drinking milk and snorting/injecting/smoking cocaine (MacCoun & Reuter, 2001). But even they admit, in their support for a less restrictive marijuana policy, that "the evidence for a correlation between cannabis use and hard drug use is . . . overwhelming" (MacCoun and Reuter, 2001, citing Kandel, Yamaguchi, & Chen 1992).

So what causes the strong correlation between marijuana use and the use of other drugs? We're still trying to figure that out, but it appears that evidence has weakened for any kind of genetic effect on drug using by people who by their nature are rebellious. Australian researchers published in 2003 a major study in the *Journal of the American Medical Association* that followed 311 same-sex twin pairs; each pair had one twin that had used marijuana before age 17 and one who had never used the drug. The researchers found that the marijuana-using twins were five times more likely to go on to hallucinogens such as LSD, three times more likely to go on to cocaine, and twice as likely to go on to heroin (Lynskey et al., 2003). Lynskey and his colleagues claimed they found a causal relationship between marijuana and other drugs. Though this assertion was contested by an editorial in the same issue of the *Journal* written by a leading marijuana researcher, the study gives the gateway theory overwhelming force.

So marijuana can lead to other drugs. The Australian study still didn't tell us why, but the authors point out three of the most popular assertions: (a) Initial pleasurable experiences with marijuana may encourage other drug use; (b) innocuous early experiences with marijuana (little chance of running into the law and/or having a negative biological reaction) may reduce the barriers to trying other drugs; and (c) obtaining marijuana from the underground market, which is necessary when the drug is illegal, implies coming into contact with the underworld and dealers who sell drugs other than pot.

All of these seem plausible. Marijuana does not usually produce a negative reaction after the first puff. Indeed, for most people it is a pleasurable experience that does not cause the violence of smoking crack or the crazed feelings of injecting methamphetamine. Additionally, since most people rarely suffer great criminal justice consequences for smoking or possessing a few joints, this could lead to the impression that all drug use is easily concealable and that the omnipresence of the police is a myth. This latter thought may give fodder to those wishing to recriminalize marijuana in places where penalties have been eliminated. For example, after years of decriminalization, Alaska voters put a successful initiative on the ballot in 1990 stipulating penalties for marijuana possession.

This third plausible explanation is a favorite of legalization advocates. It is used profusely to argue for the legalization of marijuana and the separation of marijuana from other drug markets. They claim that if marijuana were brought out of the underground market, kids would have less contact with cocaine and heroin dealers and thus have a harder time than they do currently in obtaining those drugs. Indeed, many marijuana apologists cite the fact that cocaine use among those who have used marijuana is lower in the Netherlands than in the United States (22% vs. 33%, from MacCoun & Reuter, 2001). And although this is true as of 1996 (which is important to

note since drug use rose between 1992 and 1996 before leveling off in 1997 and falling in 2001), we don't know whether to attribute the difference to separate drug markets or the cultural and social differences that exist between the two countries. The use rates of cocaine in the United States and Netherlands do not control for other possible factors, and, as MacCoun says, "Cross-country comparisons are problematic" (MacCoun 2001). Reinarman, Cohen, and Kall's (2004) analysis comparing drug policy in Amsterdam and San Francisco, and concluding that San Francisco's policies are worse since more people go on to harder drugs there than in Amsterdam, completely ignores the obvious limitations of global city comparisons (which do not take into account cultural, social, and political climates, and, perhaps most important in this case, nuances in the law: San Francisco's marijuana laws are notoriously lax, even Dutch-like).

I am skeptical of the theory that says separating markets will lead to less prevalence of other drugs since people are usually introduced to marijuana by their friends, not by contact with aggressive dealers (Dupre, 1995; Simmons, Conger, & Whitbeck, 1988). Many dealers of marijuana sell just that and do not have contact with dealers of other drugs. Besides, evidence from abroad that American marijuana smokers use more cocaine than the Dutch, evidence of other drug use because of marijuana's legal status, is purely speculative. That argument loses even more credence when we consider that alcohol and tobacco—our two legal drugs—act as gateway drugs in a profound way.

Additionally, the normalization of marijuana in the Netherlands seems to have actually *attracted* dealers of other drugs. There may be evidence that a laissez-faire attitude on one drug (marijuana in this case) has a gateway effect of attracting dealers of other drugs. The Netherlands is the largest producer of MDMA (Ecstasy) in the world, according to the United Nation's International Narcotics Control Board. Law enforcement in Britain and France further attest to it. "Holland is Europe's drug supermarket. Drugs of all kinds are freely available there," says one British official (qtd. in Collins, 1999). French officials report that 98% of amphetamines seized in France in 1997 came from Holland, as did more than three quarters of the ecstasy tablets. A leading French law enforcement official laments, "The light sentences they hand out and the liberal attitude of their judges has resulted in an explosion in the number of international trafficking groups operating out of Holland." He continues: "Get arrested with 50 kilos of heroin or cocaine in France or England and you'll be sentenced to 20 years to life and serve at least 17 of those years. . . . In Holland . . . the most you'll get is eight years, of which you'll serve only four in prison, where you'll be in your own cell with color TV and a stereo and have the right to a conjugal visit twice a month from a woman who may—or may not—be your wife. Is it any wonder

then that the country has become the drug traffickers' preferred working place?" (qtd. in Collins, 1999).

DOES POTENCY MATTER?

Because of increasingly sophisticated growing methods, the amount of THC, the active ingredient, in marijuana is markedly greater today than it was in earlier decades. But what does this mean to the average marijuana smoker? It would appear that a more potent drug means a more dangerous drug, which gives us more reason to keep it illegal or at least quasi-illegal. The potency debate has enjoyed much fanfare in the marijuana discussion, with many governments claiming that today's stronger marijuana is another reason to keep people away from it. Opponents of that view claim that stronger marijuana does not make much of a difference in the relative harmfulness of the drug. They claim that drumming up the importance of potency is just another indefensible claim to further the "war" on marijuana users (e.g., Zimmer & Morgan, 1997).

The potency dispute reached a high mark in the summer of 2004 when newspapers and Internet news sites in the United States showcased a Reuters health story titled "Stronger Pot Causes Policy Shift" (Fox, 2004). It reported that "pot is no longer the gentle weed of the 1960's and may pose a greater threat than cocaine or heroin because so many more people use it." It went on to say that the National Institutes of Health and the White House hope to shift focus in research and enforcement from "hard" drugs to marijuana.

Whether a true policy shift in enforcement or research by federal officials truly takes place has yet to be seen. Thus far, on the enforcement side, the vast majority of those in federal prison are not there for marijuana possession. Research on illegal drugs is hardly marijuana-focused. But chief among the reasons cited by authorities to focus on marijuana comes from its image, that it is a harmless drug. "If you told people that one in five of 12-to-17 year olds who ever used marijuana in their lives need treatment, I don't think people would remotely understand that," explained Drug Czar John Walters, a longtime opponent of marijuana legalization (Fox, 2004).

Officials went on to explain that a rise in marijuana potency could have negative effects on the brain, especially for adolescents. They cite the fact that more young people are in treatment for marijuana (marijuana-dependent youths 12 to 17 years of age account for 60% of the treatment admissions in the United States) than for all other drugs combined as proof that more potency means a more dangerous drug. (See figures on increased potency and mentions of emergency room visits.)

The Reuters story attracted a critique by Bruce Mirken of the Marijuana Policy Project (an organization whose aim is to alter marijuana prohibition) claiming that prohibition is to blame for a perceived increase in treatment admissions and the harmfulness of marijuana (Mirken, 2004). Mirken claimed that: (a) more potent marijuana does not mean more dangerous marijuana; (b) the potency debate is erroneously portrayed as a battle between "scientists vs. legalizers"; (c) young people are forced into treatment after being arrested for smoking pot, and the government then uses admissions as proof of marijuana dependence; and (d) more than half of marijuana "abusers" used marijuana three times or less in the month prior to entering treatment.

This critique is helpful for my purposes here because it sums up the main arguments against any government's claim that today's more harmful marijuana has resulted in more youths suffering greater adverse consequences of the drug.

Though clearly not as dangerous as shooting heroin or smoking crack, marijuana is harmful, and data sets of real marijuana users (emergency room data, for example) expose the fact that today's more powerful marijuana probably leads to greater health consequences today than the marijuana of the 1960s. The proof of this correlation (between higher potency and increased danger) can be seen both in the consumption and in the selling of this drug.

Since 1990, marijuana emergency rates have been rising. Astonishingly, even controlling for the fact that many more people use marijuana than heroin, marijuana admissions now exceed those of heroin. Visits to hospital emergency departments because of marijuana use rose steadily during the 1990s, from an estimated 16,251 visits in 1991 to more than 119,472 in 2002 (SAMHSA, 2003). That has accompanied a rise in potency from 3.26% to 7.19% according to the Potency Monitoring Project at the University of Mississippi. If there's another explanation for this increased danger other than a rise in potency, I can't think of it.

More potent marijuana is also seen as more lucrative on the market. Customs reports, for example, claim that in San Diego, California, a dealer coming north with a pound of cocaine can and does make an even trade with a dealer traveling south with a pound of high-potency B.C. "bud"—the marijuana produced in British Columbia notorious for its high concentration of THC. It appears that people pay more for stronger pot because the high is better.

What do scientists say? Independent researchers have shown—in the literature on marijuana withdrawal, dependence, schizophrenia, and other conditions—that today's marijuana is more harmful than the marijuana studied a few decades back.

Many of the conclusions on the harmfulness of marijuana prior to the 1980s coincide little with the troubling findings established after that time,

as marijuana from that era was weaker and probably less dangerous. It is astonishing that legalization advocates obsessively cite the 1972 Shafer Report on marijuana, commissioned by President Richard Nixon, as evidence of marijuana's harmlessness almost religiously. The report did indeed call for decriminalization, but it based its conclusion on the data and experience conducted until that day (the commissioners did not have the luxury of foretelling the future), and thus cannot be seriously looked at today as a point of reference on marijuana. It is a dated document with outdated conclusions.

Back to the present. The May 5, 2004, issue of the *Journal of the American Medical Association* showed that in a study that dissected the National Longitudinal Alcohol Epidemiologic Survey (conducted from 1991 to 1992 with 42,862 participants) and the National Epidemiologic Survey on Alcohol and Related Conditions (conducted from 2001 through 2002 with more than 43,000 participants), the number of marijuana users stayed the same while the number dependent on the drug rose 20%, from 2.2 million to 3 million (Compton, Grant, Colliver, Glantz, & Stinson, 2004). Since the criteria used to determine dependence changed little from 1992 to 2002, what else could plausibly account for this finding other than the fact that today's marijuana is more harmful than it used to be?

The assertion that the U.S. government wrongly arrests kids for smoking pot, forces them into treatment, and then uses the admissions as "proof" of marijuana addictiveness should also be examined with a closer eye. A critical point missed by advocates of this line is that although a majority of youth in treatment were referred there by a judge or prosecutor, it is only a slight majority—about 54%. The rest are self-referrals, school referrals, or doctor referrals. To paint the picture that the reason marijuana dependence appears to be more common is because we're forcing that number to look higher via the criminal justice system is disingenuous. Most children enter treatment because they abuse marijuana or are dependent on it.

This point begs an even greater question: Is it wrong for youth to be filtered into treatment or intervention through the criminal justice system? Marijuana sympathizers argue that it is, for they portray it as Big Brother rearing his wielding hand once more. But getting kids help for their marijuana problem via the criminal justice system may do some good. It means that judges and prosecutors are turning to the treatment system and health care providers as opposed to prisons and jails for kids who do get caught smoking weed. In fact, the finding that since 1995 the number of admissions from the criminal justice system increased tells us that judges and prosecutors are using carrots and sticks wisely. This decision seems wise given the success of drug testing and sanctions for drug offenders (e.g., Huddleston, Freeman-Wilson, & Boone, 2004; Kleiman, 1997). Contact with the authorities can also wake a family up to the grim reality of dealing

with drug problems and other problem behaviors that can be too easily overlooked in denial. Though one can plausibly concede that some of the rising rate of admissions is probably explained by stronger law enforcement, it may also be explained by the fact that marijuana has become a stronger drug.

Stronger marijuana also seems to be having an effect in Europe. When *Foreign Affairs* chided "Holland's half-baked experiment," Professor Heather Ashton, "Britain's leading expert on the medical effects of cannabis," noted that the effect of THC is proportional insofar as the user develops a tolerance for high-level-THC marijuana. Ashton went on to say that this stronger marijuana "is not the benign product advocates would have us believe." British treatment expert Dr. Bryan Wells notes that "for the first time I am beginning to see something that resembles withdrawal symptoms produced by hard drugs in heavy cannabis users." In Holland's most popular drug-treatment center, doctors are noting withdrawal symptoms in marijuana users previously seen only in cocaine and heroin users (Greenfield, 2002). In all likelihood, this potent pot would remain on the market under any decriminalization or legalization scheme.

MARIJUANA AND THE CRIMINAL JUSTICE SYSTEM

Another chief argument for the decriminalization or legalization of marijuana is that vast criminal justice resources are used up to prosecute petty marijuana offenders. Legalization advocates claim that ending the war on marijuana would free up much needed prison space and police time (e.g., Nadelmann, 1989).

The real picture is, however, much different than the one painted by marijuana sympathizers. Most marijuana users are never caught by law enforcement. The ones who do get apprehended are usually large-scale offenders. According to the most recent survey of inmates in state and federal correctional centers, only 0.7% of those in state prison are there for marijuana possession. And for first-time offenders, that number drops to 0.3% (U.S. Department of Justice, 2000). Of the 7,401 marijuana offenders in federal prison in 2002, only 191 of them were there for simple possession (U.S. Sentencing Commission, 2002). Federal marijuana offenders served an average of 33 months in prison, the lowest of any drug (U.S. Sentencing Commission, 2002). Additionally, the median amount of marijuana for those convicted of marijuana possession is 115 pounds—or 156,000 marijuana cigarettes (U.S. Department of Justice, 2000). The U.S. government convicted only 27 federal marijuana offenders (possession and trafficking) having less than 5,000 grams of marijuana, with an

average of 3,906 grams—about 12,000 joints (U.S. Sentencing Commission, 2002).

The most often cited criminal justice statistic by legalizers is that, according to the FBI's Uniform Crime Reports, authorities arrest more than 700,000 people a year for marijuana (Nadelmann, 1989). This figure at first glance seems high, especially because the total number of drug offenses is roughly 1.5 million (U.S. Department of Justice, 2003). But a closer look reveals that the FBI numbers are a poor measure to gauge criminal justice outcomes. First, and perhaps most important, the report states, in fine print found in the appendix, that "an individual may be arrested several times during the year, so the arrest figures in this section should not be viewed as an annual accounting of the number of persons arrested, but rather, as the number of arrests reported by law enforcement." So the number of different people arrested for pot (or other drug violations for that matter) is completely unknown. All we might know is the number of actual arrests a year—and since marijuana offenders usually do not typically get thrown into jail, it is quite possible that one person would be arrested several times in one year.

The proposition that the Uniform Crime Reports even give us an accurate number of total arrests a year is questionable. The reports simply combine different jurisdictions (which have different data collection methods) into one number, giving us an arbitrary figure for "arrests." Additionally, arrest patterns vary widely among different local law enforcement agencies—as seen, for example, in the varying sentencing schemes across the country for marijuana (e.g., marijuana is decriminalized in 12 states).

Finally, the Uniform Crime Reports are unhelpful because the term "arrest" itself could mean very different things, including a citation (ticket) or summons—the former often invoked for simple marijuana possession. Additionally, if one person is arrested for multiple violations simultaneously, only the "most serious" offense is reported to the FBI—causing significant undercount or overcount (whichever you prefer) for actual drug arrests. Using these arrest data tells us little about the certainty, severity, or actual application of drug control laws. Honest drug policy analysts should cease using these misleading data.

LOCAL JAILS

In July 2004, the Bureau of Justice Statistics released for the first time in six years a profile of local jail inmates, covering the year 2002. It revealed that the number of inmates held for drug law violations rose by about 40,000 during those years, although drug violations were still just under violations for public order and violent offenses; to be fair, they each hovered around

25% (public order violations rose by 30,000; violent offenses rose by 24,000). And of the drug offenders in jails, they were about equally distributed for possession and trafficking (10.8% and 12.1%, respectively). A 40,000 rise in the number of drug violators, however, is no small number. This resulted because there was a steep increase from 1996 to 2002 in the time served for drug traffickers—not possessors (from 29 to 50 months). In fact, the average time drug possession inmates could expect to serve in jail was 6 months; for traffickers it was 16 months. Note that these local jail figures are for all drugs, not just marijuana, but that 58% of all inmates used marijuana regularly (James, 2004).

It appears, then, that the state and federal anti-marijuana effort is not targeting kids in college dorm rooms, but rather large-scale marijuana traffickers. Ironically, Daniel Polsby, who favors marijuana legalization, sums it up best when he writes: "Despite well-publicized declarations to the contrary, there is very little worthwhile evidence that the current prison population of drug offenders contains any appreciable fraction of temperamentally inert flower children, ensnared by happenstance in the war on drugs" (Polsby, 1997).

THE DUTCH FALLACY

"Do as the Dutch Do" has become a clarion call for legalization advocates, who fondly imagine a day when the world, or at least the United States, will treat marijuana the way the Dutch do. Almost every drug legalization discussion leads both sides of the debate focusing on drug policy to the Netherlands. It is fascinating that this tiny country of 16 million people is so often referenced in comparison to countries (including the United States and United Kingdom) with much larger populations. The reason for this comparison, of course, is that the Netherlands is one of the only places in the world where you can buy marijuana legally. (Even so, the Dutch have a tough time admitting that marijuana is "legal" because they are bound by international treaty obligations mandating that marijuana remain an illegal drug. When asked if the Dutch have legalized marijuana, MacCoun and Reuter [2001], two of the more prolific observers of Dutch marijuana policy, answer "No. Well yes and no. Sort of." They settle on the term "de facto legalization" which seems sensible.)

In 1976, as the counterculture swept through much of the Western world proclaiming free love and drugs (and as drug use was reaching historic levels in the United States), the Dutch approved a formal policy to allow the possession *and* sale of up to about 90 marijuana cigarettes (30 grams). The government allowed "coffee shops" selling marijuana to appear around the country, and it approved in 1980 guidelines allowing more local discretion

over commercial marijuana practices. As the Dutch got used to the idea of legal marijuana, coffee shops popped up in nicer parts of town, and the number of them grew elevenfold in eight years (9 in 1980 and 102 by 1988; Jansen, 1991). Currently, a lower-end estimate numbers coffee shops at about 1,200 (MacCoun & Reuter, 2001).

But not everyone has been pleased with the proliferation of coffee shops in the Netherlands. Pressures from residents to reduce the noise associated with marijuana vendors and patrons, and international bodies (such as the International Narcotics Control Board, an arm of the United Nations) calling for less drug tourism and drug trafficking led the country in 1996 to tighten its regulations. Now coffee shops are licensed, and one can legally possess no more than 15 joints (5 grams) at one time.

MacCoun and Reuter point out that between 1976 and 1984, marijuana use rates remained about the same for adults and youths. Thus the effect of legalization (or, "depenalization" as they put it) was minimal. From the mid-1980s to the mid-1990s, though, they observe that "surveys reveal that the lifetime prevalence of cannabis in Holland increased consistently and sharply." They report that the percentage of people 18–20 who had used marijuana in their lifetime was 15% in 1984 and 44% by 1996—a 300% increase. Indeed, they also cite past-month prevalence of 8.5% in 1984 and 18.5% in 1996. Why would marijuana use suddenly increase in the mid-1980s, after remaining relatively flat for nearly the first 10 years of lenient marijuana laws? MacCoun and Reuter point to "commercialization" as the culprit. That is, they contend that during this period between 1984 and 1996, the greater glamorization and more visible promotion of marijuana led to an increase in use. They claim that depenalization without commercialization does not increase use, as noted in steady use rates between 1976 and 1984 (MacCoun & Reuter, 2001).

Their analysis is tightly reasoned and highly plausible—the glamorization of cocaine in early 20th-century America probably led to a major increase in use during that time—but there are other possible reasons. Still largely unanswered is why the year 1984 is so special. What made that year such a tipping point for commercialization? Using MacCoun and Reuter's numbers (which they cite from Jansen), the number of coffee shops grew at a faster rate between 1980 and 1985 (9 to 71—an eightfold increase) than between 1985 and 1988 (71 to 105). Could the increase between 1984 and 1996 be more related to what I call "normalization," that is, the time where a drug is gradually accepted and brought into a culture to the extent where it becomes an established, oftentimes irreversible norm? Normalization by definition does not occur overnight—indeed, when a policy as obvious to the public as marijuana legalization is implemented, it makes sense that prior antidrug attitudes take time to soften—acceptance takes place gradually.

The approval of marijuana in the Netherlands seems to also have the effect of downplaying the known risks of the drug, resulting in the normalization of marijuana in that country. The former Dutch health minister, Dr. Ernest Bunning, is on record as saying: "The moment we say, 'there are people who have problems with soft drugs,' our critics will jump on us, so it makes it a little bit difficult for us to be objective on this matter." Even Amsterdam's police commissioner, Jelle Kuiper, notes: "As long as our political class tries to pretend that soft drugs do not create dependence, we are going to go on being confronted daily with problems that officially do not exist. We are aware of an enormous number of young people strongly dependent on soft drugs, with all the consequences it has" (Collins, 1998).

Additionally, the normalization of marijuana seems to have an effect on the production of the drug. Jansen notes that the annual Nederweit (high potency Dutch-grown marijuana) crop is about 100 tons a year—almost all grown illegally—of which 65 tons is exported. The Dutch Ministry of Justice reports that the Nederweit industry employs 20,000 people. And since sentences for even large-scale marijuana distributors are very low (the maximum prison sentence for a marijuana smuggler is four years, "two years–of which he would serve one–is more likely"; Collins, 1998).

The normalization of marijuana in Europe, especially in light of brand-new evidence on the strong link between marijuana use and mental illness, has officials increasingly worried. A European Union working group on drug policy issued a draft resolution in July of 2004 identifying marijuana as "European drug problem number one" and recommending that governments criminalize Internet sites that promote marijuana use or cultivation. There is also growing evidence that Britain and the Netherlands may soon reverse or review their weak marijuana policies.

ENVISIONING LEGALIZATION

Let us imagine that even knowing what we do about marijuana's harmfulness, and the experience of other countries that have legalized the drug, we still opted for marijuana legalization. A spike in marijuana-related violence on the street, for example, could prompt some well-meaning officials to reluctantly choose to repeal punitive laws.

What would that scenario look like?

Describing the results of legalizing drugs is almost impossible for a few reasons. First, with the exception of the Netherlands and some cannabis clubs in the United States, drugs have not been available on the legal market for almost a century. Though cocaine, heroin, and other drugs were once available in the United States, they offer little by means of comparison when

we fast-forward 100 years to today. Also, proponents of legalization have never really presented what their regime would look like. But let's briefly look at what it might look like under a few imaginable circumstances.

Treat It Like Alcohol and Tobacco

Alcohol and tobacco are a favorite reference point for those who wish to legalize drugs. Since those two killers are legal—indeed alcohol contributes to more violent crime than crack cocaine—why not just legalize other dangerous substances (or at least one more) and regulate their sale? Why the difference between alcohol and tobacco on one hand and marijuana on the other, especially when we know that alcohol use has a much greater association with violence than does marijuana use?

Even a cursory glance at the status of our two legal drugs shows us that to add a third drug to this list would exacerbate an already difficult public health problem. Tobacco kills half a million people every year. Alcohol is worse—not only is it responsible for negative health effects on the drinker but on people around them. If we are to look at these two legal drugs as indicators of behavior associated with legal drug use, we see a pattern: Legal drugs are by definition easy to obtain; commercialization glamorizes their use and furthers their social acceptance, their price is low, and high profits make promotion worthwhile for sellers. Subsequently—inevitably—more users occur, more addicts, and the increased use results in more social and health damage, increased deaths, and greater economic burden. When sellers rely on addiction for profit, there is not a strong case that drugs—even just marijuana—should be sold alongside alcohol and tobacco.

The alcohol/tobacco versus marijuana argument also falls apart because alcohol and tobacco have cultures surrounding them that are very different from that surrounding marijuana. For one, most people who use alcohol do so responsibly—it is a minority of drinkers that cost society greatly. Second, unlike marijuana, tobacco can claim no such role in potentially hurting the lives of nonsmokers (with the exception of secondhand smoke, especially to children)—in fact, marijuana is second only to alcohol in drugs implicated in driving accidents. Tobacco can claim no such infamous role in destroying the life of nonsmokers. Furthermore, unlike tobacco, cannabis is implicated widely in the loss of productivity at work, long-term reproductive system damage; and, like tobacco, long-term respiratory disease and cancer risk. As Kleiman has stated, "Until success is achieved in imposing reasonable controls on the currently licit killers, alcohol and nicotine, the case for adding a third or fourth recreational drug . . . will remain hopelessly speculative" (Kleiman, 1993).

Tax the Hell Out of It

An alternative to commercially selling marijuana through private industry is having the government regulate and distribute the drug. Many legalization advocates (including Vancouver Mayor Larry Campbell) urge the government to "tax the hell out of" drugs like marijuana in order to pay for the assumed increase in use and addiction costs. That way, new users will be deterred from starting because the price would be out of reach. The most vulnerable (i.e., the poor) would benefit from high costs, too.

Ironically, however, this scenario actually exacerbates some of the worst qualities of prohibition. High-cost drugs would ensure that an already well-established underground market would remain largely intact. If I can buy cocaine for $10 an ounce from my dealer or go to my government-sponsored "drug store" for 10 times that much, I would opt for the former scenario. Especially if drugs were still illegal for kids (no one has seriously proposed legalizing marijuana for children), an underground market would still have reasons to linger. This is precisely what occurred in Canada when they imposed steep taxes on cigarettes (Gunby, 1994).

In the United States, illegal drugs generate $160 billion a year in social costs like illness, accidents, and lost productivity. The amount would no doubt increase under legalization. Experience with taxing alcohol and tobacco show us that any attempt to pay for lost costs through taxes would be futile. Indeed the social costs of legalization outweigh any possible tax that could be levied against the drug. In 1999, state and federal governments gained about $11 billion from alcohol taxes—but health care costs related to alcohol use amounted to four times that much, notwithstanding the costs to the criminal justice system, federal entitlement programs, and loss of productivity (U.S. Census Bureau, 1999, 2000; Center on Addiction and Substance Abuse [CASA], 1996). Tobacco was worse—the $13 billion in federal and state tobacco tax revenue in 1999 was one sixth of the $75 billion in direct health care costs attributable to tobacco (U.S. Census Bureau, 1999, 2000; CASA, 1996).

Taxing drugs could feasibly increase street crime as well. As addicts frenzied for their next fix need to find more money to buy expensive drugs easily, they can be expected to engage in criminality. Taxing drugs would do no one good.

Make It Cheap—Cut Out the Underground Market

One way to doom the underground market for drugs is to beat the market down: Make drugs so cheap that the underground market will eventually wither away in the face of legal competition. That way, turf wars between

drug gangs and crime surrounding people's desire to get money for drugs would be eliminated.

This would be a good economic model to apply if we weren't concerned about the effects of drugs themselves. Certainly, drugs are dangerous because they rob people of making rational decisions. Cheap drugs would put a joint of marijuana well within the reach of a child's daily allowance. Additionally, it would dissuade users from stopping (thus giving them a greater chance to become addicted) because of the cheap price. The American tobacco experience shows us that the price of drugs greatly influences a person's decision to use.

CAN WE MAKE PROHIBITION WORK BETTER?

To say that legalization would increase drug problems doesn't imply that prohibition policies could not benefit from improvement (Reuter, 1997). This chapter was written with the intention of assessing the current marijuana problem and arguing against liberalizing American federal anti-marijuana policy. Still, I feel obligated to briefly mention some areas of current marijuana policies that need improvement. Making our restrictive policies work better, though, is easier said than done. Even so, some suggestions are worth mentioning.

First and foremost, the lack of research into law enforcement techniques and criminal justice measures continue to hamper the effectiveness of marijuana control policies (Manski, Pepper, & Petrie, 2001). A more concerted effort to collect accurate information about the price and purity of marijuana would help, especially the relationship between price elasticity and demand by certain high-use populations (Reuter, 1997). A simple way to begin to understand this important relationship would be for the attorney general to release federally restricted drug-price data to the public (currently, only federally funded researchers can access Drug Enforcement Administration drug-price data).

There should also be more resources dedicated to finding out how specific aspects of social policy relate to drug policy and problems (i.e., housing policies, welfare policies, education policies; the list goes on). In what aspects of society can we target those most at risk for marijuana use? How can courts and regimes of coerced abstinence work to reduce and stop marijuana prevalence, especially among the young (Kleiman, 1997)?

Education should be a chief component of any anti-marijuana effort. I do not just mean educating young people (that is obvious), but also the medical and community health clinic community, which is shockingly ignorant of the true dangers of occasional and heavy use of marijuana. Surveys indicate that physicians lack the skill and knowledge to deal with drug use

(Barthwell, 2004). As Dr. Andrea Barthwell, former deputy director for demand reduction at the White House Office of National Drug Policy, wrote in 2004:

> Often we write, "Patient is a 39-year-old white female alcoholic . . ." as if the diagnosis were a relevant descriptor, with the same value as religion or occupation. Descriptors help us understand more about a patient, but they confer no responsibility on the part of the physician to communicate life-saving advice. If the condition were diabetes, physicians would be responsible for drawing a blood level and managing the disease. Unfortunately, most of the time today the same standards do not apply when it comes to substance abuse. (p. A12)

To counter this, governments should include grants for screening, brief interventions, referral, and treatment (SBIRT) training aimed at primary care givers and community clinic workers. To elaborate:

- Screening—initial drug (including alcohol) screens by general primary care physicians or counselors to identify at-risk persons and overall prevalence in area/district
- Brief Advice—one-time intervention for short consultation and literature
- Brief Intervention/Brief Treatment—1 to 12 sessions of substance-use intervention
- Referral to Treatment—referrals for dependent users to receive specialized services, case management, and follow-up support in the community

Another way to identify people early in their drug-use careers for the purpose of getting them help is through drug testing in the school and workplace. Testing should respect a person's privacy and act as a filter for a brief intervention or treatment referral, whichever makes most sense.

Increased parental involvement in a child's life, and policies designed to encourage it, is a cornerstone of effective marijuana policy. An example of a promising program is the Parent Anti-Drug Corps, which trains parents to be effective antidrug leaders in their community. A parent effort in the 1980s contributed to massive declines in marijuana use in that decade.

Restricting anything by law—especially something that some people find pleasurable—surely does not guarantee success all of the time. But legalizing a harmful substance like marijuana would exacerbate our problems by signaling that the drug is relatively harmless and can be used with little danger. Compounding this with the problems accrued by our two legal substances, alcohol and tobacco, and the relatively minor costs attributed to a restrictive marijuana policy, the case for relaxing laws related to marijuana

remains weak, dangerous, and unconvincing. A more hopeful, reasonable solution to lowering rates of marijuana use and reducing the total harm that widespread marijuana use inevitably brings is found in a balanced strategy of research, prevention, education, treatment, and law enforcement.

NOTES

1. This question was posed to a class on drug policy in which I was a student, taught by drug policy analyst Robert MacCoun. When asked if they thought marijuana was illegal in California (it is by contrast decriminalized), the overwhelming majority of my fellow students believed that it was.

2. These important nuances have been only somewhat acknowledged (e.g., MacCoun & Reuter, 2001) and explored (e.g., Haaga & Reuter, 1990; ImpacTeen Illicit Drug Team, 2002; Kleiman & Smith, 1990; Sabet, 2002). More work in the area is needed.

3. I agree with MacCoun and Reuter when they state that bad news about a drug should be viewed "with regret, not relief" because it means that people are worse off than we thought.

REFERENCES

Arseneault, L., Cannon, M., Poulton, R., Murray, R., Caspi, A., & Moffitt, T. (2002). Cannabis use in adolescence and risk for adult psychosis: longitudinal prospective study. *British Medical Journal, 325,* 1212–1213.

Ashton, C. (2001). Pharmacology and effects of cannabis: A brief review. *British Journal of Psychiatry, 178,* 101–106.

Bammer, G. B., Dobler-Mikola, A., Fleming, P. M., Strang, J., & Uchtenhagen, A. (1999). Compass. *Science, 21,* 1277–1278.

Barthwell, A. (2004, May 12). War on drug addiction needs physicians on front line. *Chicago Sun-Times,* p. A12.

BBC News. (2005). *Heated debate over heroin report.* Retrieved February 3, 2005, from http://news.bbc.co.uk/2/hi/uk_news/scotland/4230985.stm.

Beardsley, P., Balster, R., & Harris, L. (1986). Dependence on tetrahydrocannabinol in rhesus monkeys. *Journal of Pharmacology and Experimental Therapeutics, 239*(2), 311–319.

Benedictus, L. (2005, February 3). Cocaine, anyone? *The Guardian.* Accessed February 3, 2005, from http://www.guardian.co.uk/g2/story/0,,1404499,00.html.

Bennett, W. (1989). Speech given at the Kennedy School of Government, Harvard University, USA. Accessed January 2, 2005, from http://www.drugtext.org/library/articles/901605.html.

Brady, L. (2002). *Unlocking the potential.* Performance Resource Press. Accessed January 25, 2005, from http://www.prponline.net/School/SAJ/Articles/unlocking_the_potential.htmon.

British Lung Foundation. (2002). A smoking gun: The impact of cannabis smoking on respiratory health. Accessed January 22, 2005, from http://www.ukcia.org/research/SmokingGun/ASmokingGun.pdf.

Brookoff, D., Cook, C., Williams, C., & Mann, C. (1994). Testing reckless drivers for cocaine and marijuana. *New England Journal of Medicine, 331,* 518–522.

Budney, A., Hughes, J., Moore, B., & Novy, P. (2001). Marijuana abstinence effects in marijuana smokers maintained in their home environment. *Archives of General Psychiatry, 58*(10), 917–924.

Boot, B., McGregor, I., & Hall, W. (2000). MDMA neurotoxicity: Assessing and communicating the risks. *Lancet, 355,* 1818–1821.

Caulkins, J., & Reuter, P. (1997). Setting goals for drug policy: Harm reduction or use reduction? *Addiction, 92*(9), 1143–1150.

Center on Addiction and Substance Abuse. (1996). *The cost of substance abuse to America's health care system.* Final report. New York: author.

Chapple, P. A. L., & Marks, V. (1965). The addiction epidemic. *The Lancet, 19,* 288–289.

Collins, L. (1999). Holland's half-baked experiment. *Foreign Affairs, 78,* 11–33.

Compton, D., Dewey, W, & Martin, B. (1990). Cannabis dependence and tolerance production. *Advances in Alcohol and Substance Abuse, 9,* 129–147.

Compton, W., Grant, B., Colliver, J., Glantz, M., & Stinson, F. (2004). Prevalence of marijuana use disorders in the United States: 1991–1992 and 2001–2002 *Journal of the American Medical Association, 291,* 2114–2121.

Condon, J., & Smith, N. (2003). *Prevalence of drug use: Key findings from the 2002/2003 British Crime Survey.* Research, Development, and Directorate.

Crowley, T. J., Macdonald, M. J., Whitmore, E. A., & Mikulich, S. K. (1998). Cannabis dependence, withdrawal, and reinforcing effects among adolescents with conduct symptoms and substance use disorders. *Drug and Alcohol Dependence, 50,* 27–37.

Department of Justice. (2000). Bureau of Justice Statistics estimates based on the 1997 Survey of Inmates in State and Federal Correctional Facilities. National Archive of Criminal Justice Data.DRC Net. (1997, August 22.). The Week Online with DRCNet, 8. Retrieved January 25, 2005, from http://www.bigeye.com/drugfree.htm.

DuPont, R. (1984). *Getting tough on gateway drugs: A guide for the family.* Washington, DC: American Psychiatric Press.

Dupre, D. (1995). Initiation and progression of alcohol, marijuana, and cocaine use among adolescent abusers. *American Journal on Addictions, 4,* 43–48.

Favrat, B., Ménétrey, A., Augsburger, M., Rothuizen, L. E., Appenzeller, M., Buclin, T., et al. (2005). Two cases of "cannabis acute psychosis" following the administration of oral cannabis. *British Medical Journal of Psychiatry, 5,* 17.

Fox, M. (2004, July 19). Stronger pot causes policy shift. Reuters wire service.

Frankau, I. (1964). Treatment in England of Canadian patients addicted to narcotic drugs. *Canadian Medical Association Journal, 90,* 421–424.

Frankau, I., & Stanwell, P. (1960). The treatment of drug addiction. *The Lancet, 2,* 1377–1379.

Golub, A., & Johnson, B. (1994). The shifting importance of alcohol and marijuana as gateway substances among serious drug abusers. *Journal of the Study of Alcohol, 55,* 607–614.

Gouzoulis-Mayfrank, E., Thimm, B., Rezk, M., Hensen, G., & Daumann, J. (2003). Memory impairment suggests hippocampal dysfunction in abstinent ecstasy users. *Progressive Neuropsychopharmacological and Biological Psychiatry, 27*(5), 819–827.

Gouzoulis-Mayfrank, E., Daumann, J., Tuchtenhagen, F., Pelz, S., Becker, S., Kunert, H., et al. (2000). Impaired cognitive performance in drug free users of recreational ecstasy. *Journal of Neurology, Neurosurgery, and Psychiatry, 68,* 719–725.

Greenfield, S. (2002, January 6). Why they call it "dope"—Pot can really blow your mind. *San Francisco Chronicle.*

Grove, D. (1996). *Harm Reduction Communication.* New York: Harm Reduction Coalition.

Gunby, P. (1994). Canada reduces cigarette tax to fight smuggling. *Journal of the American Medical Association, 271,* 647–651.

Haaga, J., & Reuter, P. (1990). The limits of the Czar's ukase: Drug policy at the local level. *Yale Law and Policy Review, 8,* 36–74.

Hall, W., & Solowij, N. (1998) Adverse effects of cannabis. *Lancet, 352,* 1611–1616.

Holson, R., Ali, S., Scallet, A., Slikker, W., Jr., & Paule, M. G. (1989). Benzodiazepine-like behavioral effects following withdrawal from chronic delta-9-tetra-hydrocannabinol administration in rats. *Neurotoxicology, 10*(3), 605–619.

Hornik, R., Maklan, D., Cadell, D., Barmada, C. H., Jacobsohn, L., & Henderson, V., et al. (2002). *Evaluation of the national youth anti-drug media campaign: Fourth semiannual report of findings* (report prepared for the National Institute on Drug Abuse [Contract No. N01DA-8-5063]). Washington, DC: Westat.

Hser, Y., Grella, C. E., Hubbard, R. L., Hsieh, S. C., Fletcher, B. W., Brown, B. S., et al. (2001). An evaluation of drug treatment for adolescents in four U.S. cities. *Archives of General Psychiatry, 58,* 689–695.

Huddleston, C., Freeman-Wilson, K., & Boone D. (2004). *Painting the current picture: A national report card on drug courts and other problem solving court programs in the United States.* Washington DC: National Drug Court Institute.

Huestis, M., Gorelick D., & Heishman S. (2001). Blockade of effects of smoked marijuana by the CB1-selective cannabinoid receptor antagonist SR141716. *Archives of General Psychiatry, 58*(4), 322–328.

ImpacTeen Illicit Drug Team. (2002). *Illicit drug policies: Selected laws from the 50 states.* Berrien Springs, MI: Andrews University.

Insel, T., Battaglia, G., Johannessen, J., Marra, S., & DeSouza, E. (1989). 3,4-Methylenedioxymethamphetamine (Ecstasy) selectively destroys brain serotonin terminals in rhesus monkeys. *Journal of Pharmacology and Experimental Therapeutics, 249*(3), 713–720.

James, D. (2004). *Bureau of Justice Statistics special report: Profile of jail inmates 2002.* Washington, DC: Department of Justice, Office of Justice Programs.

Jansen, A. C. M. (1991). *Cannabis in Amsterdam: A geography of hashish and marijuana.* Muiderberg, Netherlands: Coutinho.

Jha, A. (2004, January 29). Some patients don't realise cannabis is actually a drug. *The Guardian.*

Johns, A. (2001). Psychiatric effects of cannabis. *British Journal of Psychiatry, 178,* 116–122.

Johnston, L., O'Malley, P., & Bachman, J. (1991). *Drug use among high school seniors, college students, and young adults, 1975–1990: Vol. 1. High School Seniors.* Rockville, MD: National Institute on Drug Abuse.

Johnston, L., O'Malley, P., Bachman, J., & Schulenberg, J. (2004a). *Monitoring the Future national results on adolescent drug use: Overview of key findings, 2003* (NIH Publication No. 04–5506). Bethesda, MD: National Institute on Drug Abuse.

Johnston, L. D., O'Malley, P. M., Bachman, J. G., & Schulenberg, J. E. (2004b). *Overall teen drug use continues gradual decline; but use of inhalants rises.* University of Michigan News and Information Services, Ann Arbor, MI. Retrieved January 25, 2005, from www.monitoringthefuture.org.

Jones, R. (1983). Cannabis tolerance and dependence. In K. O. Fehr & H. Kalant (Eds.), *Cannabis and health hazards* (pp. 71–88). Toronto: Addiction Research Foundation.

Jones, R. (1987). Drug of abuse profile: Cannabis. *Clinical Chemistry, 33,* B72–B81.

Joshi, V., Hser, Y., Grella, C. E., & Houlton, R. (2001). Sex-related HIV risk reduction behavior among adolescents in DATOS-A. *Journal of Adolescent Research, 16*(6), 642–660.

Judd, A., Hickman, M., Jones, S., McDonald, T., Parry, J. V., Stimson, G.V., et al. (2004). Incidence of hepatitis C virus and HIV among new injecting drug users in London: Prospective cohort study. *British Medical Journal, 330,* 24–25.

Kandel, D., Yamaguchi, K., & Chen, K. (1992). Stages of progression in drug involvement from adolescence to adulthood: Further evidence for the gateway theory. *Journal of Studies on Alcohol, 53,* 447–57.

Kleiman, M. (1988, October 16). Quit dreaming of a drug-free America [Letter to the editor]. *New York Times,* p. E21.

Kleiman, M. (1993, June 12). Legalizing drugs [Letter to the editor]. *The Economist,* p. 8.

Kleiman, M. (1997). Coerced abstinence: A neopaternalistic drug policy initiative. In L. Mead (Ed.), *The new paternalism: Supervisory approaches to poverty*. Washington, DC: Brookings Institution Press.

Kleiman, M. (in press). Controlling drug use and crime among drug-involved offenders: Testing, sanctions, and treatment. In P. Heymann (Ed.), *Drugs and Addictions*. Cambridge: Harvard University Press.

Kleiman, M. A., & Smith, K. D. (1990). State and local drug enforcement: In search of a strategy. In M. Tonry and J. Q. Wilson (Eds.), *Drugs and crime* (pp. 69–108). Chicago: University of Chicago Press.

Kleven, M., Woolverton, W., & Seiden, L. (1989). Evidence that both intragastric and subcutaneous administration of methylenedioxymethamphetamine (MDMA) produce serotonin neurotoxicity in rhesus monkeys. *Brain Research, 488*(1–2), 121–125.

Kouri, E., Pope, G. Jr., & Lukas, S. E. (1999). Changes in aggressive behaviour during withdrawal from long-term marijuana use. *Psychopharmacology, 143*, 302–308.

Lester, B. M., LaGasse, L. L., & Seifer, R. (1998). Cocaine exposure and children: The meaning of subtle effects. *Science, 282*(5389), 633–634.

Little, K. Y., Krolewski, D. M., Zhang, L., & Cassin, B. J. (2003). Loss of striatal vesicular monoamine transporter protein (VMAT2) in human cocaine users. *American Journal of Psychiatry, 160*, 47–55.

Longshore, D., & Hsieh, S. (1998). Drug abuse treatment and risky sex: Evidence for a cumulative treatment effect? *American Journal of Drug and Alcohol Abuse, 24*(3), 439–451.

Lynskey, M., Heath, A., Bucholz, K., Slutske, W., Madden, P., Nelson, E., et al. (2003). Escalation of drug use in early-onset cannabis users vs. co-twin controls. *Journal of the American Medical Association, 289*(4), 427–433.

MacCoun, R. (2001). American distortion of Dutch drug statistics. *Society, 38*, 23–26.

MacCoun, R., & Reuter, P. (2001). *Drug war heresies: Learning from other vices, times, and places*. New York: Cambridge University Press.

Makris, N. (2004). Decreased absolute amygdala volume in cocaine addicts. *Neuron, 44*, 729–740.

Manski, C., Pepper, J., & Petrie, C. (Eds.). (2001). *Informing America's policy on illegal drugs: What we don't know keeps hurting us*. Washington, DC: National Academy Press.

Milne, D. (2003). Cocaine appears to damage brain's dopamine neurons. *Psychiatry News, 38*(3), 22.

Mirken, B. (2004a). *Getting the "potent pot" story wrong*. Retrieved January 25, 2005, from http://www.jointogether.org/sa/news/features/reader/0,1854,571035,00.html.

Mittleman, M. (1999). Triggering of myocardial infarction by cocaine. *Circulation, 289*, 2737–2741.

Morgan, M. (2000). Ecstasy (MDMA): A review of its possible persistent psychological effects. *Psychopharmacology, 152*, 230–248.

Nadelmann, E. (1989). Drug prohibition in the United States: Costs, consequences, and alternatives. *Science, 245,* 939–947.

National Highway Traffic Safety Administration. (2000). Marijuana and alcohol combined severely impede driving performance. *Annals of Emergency Medicine, 35,* 398–399.

Nuttall, S., Raczi, J., Manney, S., Thorpe, G., & Kendall, M. (2003). Effects of smoking and cannabis use on markers of oxidative stress in exhaled breath condensate. Birmingham, England: Division of Medical Sciences, University of Birmingham.

Patton, G., Coffey, C., Carlin, J., Degenhardt, L., Lynskey, M., & Hall, W. (2002). *British Medical Journal, 325,* 1195–1198.

Polsby, D. (1997). Ending the war on drugs and children. *Valparaiso University Law Review, 31,* 542–543.

Reinarman, C., Cohen, P. D., & Kaal, H. L. (2004). The limited relevance of drug policy: Cannabis in Amsterdam and in San Francisco. *American Journal of Public Health, 94,* 836–842.

Reuter, P. (1997). Why can't we make prohibition work better: Some consequences of ignoring the unattractive. *Proceedings of the American Philosophical Society, 141,* 3.

Rey, J., & Tennant, C. C. (2002). Cannabis and mental health. *British Medical Journal, 325,* 1183–1184.

Rusche, S. (1999). Prescribing heroin, *Science, 285* (5427), 531.

Sabet, K. (2002). *Defining American drug policy: Is all policy local?* Department of Comparative Social Policy, CSP Library, Oxford University.

Schechter, M. T., Strathdee, S. A., Cornelisse, P. G., Currie, S., Patrick, D. M., Rekart, M. L., et al. (1999). Do needle exchange programmes increase the spread of HIV among injection drug users? An investigation into the Vancouver outbreak. *AIDS, 12,* 45–51.

Schmued, L. (2003). Demonstration and localization of neuronal degeneration in the rat forebrain following a single exposure to MDMA. *Brain Research, 974*(1–2), 127–33.

Simmons, R., Conger, R., & Whitbeck, L. (1988). A multistage reaming model of the influences of family and peers upon adolescent substance abuse. *Journal of Drug Issues, 18*(3), 293–315.

Simpson, D. D., Joe, G. W., & Broome, K. M. (2002). A national 5-year follow-up of treatment outcomes for cocaine dependence. *Archives of General Psychiatry, 59,* 538–544.

Slikker, W., Jr., Ali, S., Scallet, A., Frith, C., Newport, G., & Bailey, J. (1988). Neurochemical and neurohistological alterations in the rat and monkey produced by orally administered methylenedioxymethamphetamine (MDMA). *Toxicology and Applied Pharmacology, 94*(3), 448–457.

Strang, J., & Gossop, M. (Eds.). (1994). *Heroin addiction and drug policy: The British system.* New York: Oxford University Press.

Strathdee, S. A., Galai, N., Safaiean, M., Celentano, D. D., Vlahov, D., Johnson, L., et al. (2001). Sex differences in risk factors for HIV seroconversion Among Injection Drug Users. *Archives of Internal Medicine, 161,* 1281–1288.

Stroup, K. (1999). Testimony of R. Keith Stroup, esq. executive director, NORML before the Subcommittee on Criminal Justice, Drug Policy, and Human Resources Committee on Government Reform, U.S. House of Representatives, July 13, 1999.

Substance Abuse and Mental Health Services Administration. (1993). *Preliminary estimates from the 1992 National Household Survey on Drug Abuse.* Rockville, MD: SAMHSA, Office of Applied Studies.

Substance Abuse and Mental Health Services Administration. (2003). *Emergency department trends from the Drug Abuse Warning Network, final estimates 1995–2002* (DAWN Series: D-24, DHHS Publication No. SMA 03-3780). Rockville, MD: SAMHSA Office of Applied Studies.

Substance Abuse and Mental Health Services Administration. (2004). *Results from the 2003 National Survey on Drug Use and Health: National findings* (NSDUH Series H-25, DHHS Publication No. SMA 03-3780). Rockville, MD: SAMHSA Office of Applied Studies. Accessed January 25, 2005, from http://dawninfo.samhsa.gov/old_dawn/pubs_94_02/edpubs/2002final/.

Tanda, G., Munzar, P., & Goldberg, S. (2000). Self-administration behavior is maintained by the psychoactive ingredient of marijuana in squirrel monkeys. *Nature Neuroscience, 3*(11), 1073–1074.

Tashkin, D. (1990). Pulmonary complications of smoked substance abuse. *Journal of Medicine, 152*, 525–530.

Taylor, R., Fergusson, D., Milne, B., Harwood, L., Moffitt, T., Sears, M., et al. (2002). A longitudinal study of the effects of tobacco and cannabis exposure on lung function in young adults. *Addiction, 97*, 1055–1061.

Tencer, D. (2004, October 8). City "abetting" drug users, Cullen Fears. *Ottawa Citizen,* p. C15.

Texas Department of Health, Commission on Alcohol and Drug Abuse. (2004). *GHB withdrawal syndrome.* Retrieved on January 25, 2005, from http://www.tcada.state.tx.us/research/populations/GHB.

U.S. Census Bureau (1999). *State government tax collections: 1999.* Retrieved on September 22, 2004, from http://www.census.gov/prod/2001pubs/statab/sec10.pdf.

U.S. Census Bureau (2000). *Statistical abstract of the United States: 2000.* Retrieved September 22, 2004, from http://www.census.gov/prod/2001pubs/statab/sec10.pdf.

U.S. Department of Justice. (1998). *Bureau of Justice Statistics estimates based on the 1997 survey of inmates in state and federal correctional facilities.* National Archive of Criminal Justice Data, Washington, DC.

U.S. Department of Justice, Bureau of Justice Statistics, and U.S. Department of Justice, Federal Bureau of Prisons. (1997). *Survey of inmates in state and federal correctional facilities, 1997.* Compiled by the U.S. Dept. of Commerce, Bureau of the Census, ICPSR ed. Ann Arbor, MI: Interuniversity Consortium for Political and Social Research.

U.S. Department of Justice, Federal Bureau of Investigation. (2003). *Crime in the United States 2002.* Retrieved September 22, 2004, from http://www.fbi.gov/ucr/03cius.htm.

U.S. Department of the Treasury, Bureau of Alcohol, Tobacco, and Firearms. (1995). *Statistical release: Alcohol, tobacco and firearms tax collections. Fiscal year 1995*. Washington, DC: Author.

U.S. Sentencing Commission. (2002). *U.S. Sentencing Commission's 2001 sourcebook of federal sentencing statistics*. Retrieved September 24, 2004, from http://www.ussc.gov/ANNRPT/2001/SBTOC01.htm.

Volkow, N. D., Fowler, J. S., & Wang, G. J. (1999). Imaging studies on the role of dopamine in cocaine reinforcement and addiction in humans. *Journal of Psychopharmacology, 13*(4), 337–345.

Voorhees, C., Broening, H., Morford, L., Inman-Wood, S., & Fukumura, M. (2001). 3,4–Methylenedioxymethamphetamine (Ecstasy)-induced learning and memory impairments depend on the age of exposure during early development. *Journal of Neuroscience, 21*, 3228–35.

Wikipedia. (2004). Online encyclopedia. Retrieved December 12, 2004, from http://en.wikipedia.org/wiki/Heroin.

Wood, E., Tyndall, M. W., Spittal, P. M., Li, K., Kerr, T., Hogg, R. S., et al. (2001). Unsafe injection practices in a cohort of injection drug users in Vancouver: Could safer injecting rooms help? *Canadian Medical Association Journal, 165*, 405–410.

World Health Organization. (1999). *Report of the external panel on the evaluation of the Swiss scientific studies of medically prescribed narcotics to drug addicts*. Geneva: Author.

Yao, W. D., Gainetdinov, R. R., Arbuckle, M. I., Sotnikova, T. D., Cyr, M., Beaulieu, J. M., et al. (2004). Identification of PSD-95 as a regulator of dopamine-mediated synaptic and behavioral plasticity. *Neuron, 41*, 625–638.

Zammit, S., Allebeck, P., Andreasson, S., Lundberg, I., & Lewis, G. (2002). Self reported cannabis use as a risk factor for schizophrenia in Swedish conscripts of 1969: Historical cohort study. *British Medical Journal, 325*, 1199.

Zhang, Z.-F., Morgenstern, H., Spitz, M., Tashkin, D., Yu, G.-P., Marshall, J., et al. (1999). Marijuana use and increased risk of squamous cell carcinoma of the head and neck. *Cancer Epidemiology, Biomarkers, and Prevention, 6*, 1071–1078.

Zimmer, L., & Morgan, J. (1997). *Marijuana myths, marijuana facts: A review of the scientific evidence*. New York: Lindesmith Center.

SECTION VII

A Call to Action

17   Values and the Marijuana Debate

Mitch Earleywine

Recent political arguments have turned to values in an effort to provide guiding principles for decisions. The information in the previous chapters raises several questions related to values. A few questions about values may help us decide sensible new directions for marijuana policy. People often change in small steps, and nations change in even smaller ones. A focus on the values of compassion and justice leads to a couple of simple conclusions, which suggest some small changes that might make our actions more consistent with our beliefs.

Do we value compassion?

Our own understanding of compassion is central to how we treat each other. Nearly every religious and humanitarian group claims compassion as a value. Treating each other as we wish to be treated serves as the Golden Rule. Most organized systems of values, whether they support the idea of a deity or not, emphasize our need to heal the sick and alleviate pain. Members of some religions see themselves as commanded to care for the suffering. As national polls reveal, more and more people extend this compassion to those in need of medical cannabis.

Nevertheless, this compassion worries some. Misunderstandings lead people to fear that only standard pharmaceuticals can heal the sick, and that medical cannabis will lead to addiction, create pulmonary problems, send a wrong message to our youth, and generate difficulties for distribution. Although several prohibitionists insist that pharmaceutical drugs would work

as well as medical cannabis, each of these actually. has drawbacks. The expense, the side effects, and the efficacy of these alternative medicines make them less than ideal.

Prohibitionists often point to dronabinol, a synthetic form of one of the active ingredients in cannabis (THC), as the appropriate medication for people currently using medical marijuana. But dronabinol is a pill. Patients must swallow it—a difficult task for those experiencing nausea and vomiting. It often takes a couple of hours to provide any relief. Because it contains only one active ingredient, those who benefit from medical cannabis because of some other component of the plant receive no relief at all from dronabinol. (The antianxiety and sleep-enhancing effects of marijuana seem more related to another chemical, cannabidiol, than to THC.)

Dronabinol is also expensive, up to $13 per pill. Some patients need three of these per day. The dosage is difficult to monitor because the pills are made in certain sizes. (They don't break in half like other tablets because the THC is suspended in oil inside a gelatin capsule.) The inability to alter dosage leads to intoxicating side effects or inadequate relief of symptoms. Those who take too much feel disoriented; those who take too little still feel ill. Inhaling vapor from the cannabis plant provides rapid relief, and the dosage is much easier to monitor. Medical cannabis is also markedly cheaper, often less than $5 per day.

No single medication works best for all people. Data reveal that we each have our own idiosyncratic reactions to chemicals. Anyone who has returned to a physician to try a second or third medication in an effort to solve some medical problem knows that finding the proper treatment can be as much an art as a science. Just as some people have certain biological characteristics that make them allergic to penicillin or responsive to one antidepressant but not another, some people respond to medical cannabis better than any other medicine.

Adding this ancient plant to our armament increases our options, improving our chances of eliminating suffering. Medical cannabis is not a panacea. It will never replace every other medicine for every other ailment. But some people with some illnesses do not respond better to anything else. Imagine the frustration of patients told that the one medicine that works best for them must be replaced with another, less efficacious one.

What about the negatives of medical cannabis like addiction and lung problems? Concerns about addiction to medical cannabis seem hypocritical given the widespread availability of pharmaceutical opiates, drugs with an addictive potential that dwarfs that of cannabis. As chapters throughout this book have emphasized, cannabis dependence is relatively rare and hardly debilitating. Worries about respiratory troubles are easy to combat with orally

administered cannabis, cannabis extracts, or vaporizers. (Vaporizers heat cannabis to a temperature that allows cannabinoids to escape in a fine mist without igniting the plant and creating carcinogens.)

What about the children? Fears that making medicine available to the sick will send the wrong message to teens are also misplaced. As Skager (chap. 15) emphasizes, medical marijuana laws do not alter teen use. Any message suggesting that we should show kindness to the sick should be most welcome. In fact, this message would appear novel and humane compared to many other messages teens get from media and industry.

How do we handle the problem of distribution? Distributing medical cannabis need not differ from distributing any other prescription medication. Those in need could present the appropriate paperwork to the pharmacist and purchase enough for personal use. A program like this has flourished in the Netherlands since 2003.

Thus, if we value compassion, we must legalize medical cannabis.

Do we value justice?

As Husak (chap. 10) has emphasized, justice rests on the idea that the punishment for any crime should fit its severity. No one wants murder to have the same penalty as trespassing. The severity of a punishment often parallels the harm that the crime creates. Arson likely creates more harm than shoplifting, and it has a larger penalty. But what harm does marijuana possession create? Although prohibitionists continue to split hairs about health risks to the user, the actual harm to another person is difficult to identify.

Those who wish to impose penalties on marijuana possession have a great deal to justify. How does marijuana possession compare to a traffic violation? How does it compare to possession of alcohol? Given the level of harm associated with marijuana possession, it is extremely unclear what, if anything, should be the penalty for this behavior.

When pressed, prohibitionists turn to some mental gymnastics to identify harms that stem from marijuana possession. Generally, they focus on impaired driving and other crimes. Although few prohibitionists state their arguments this bluntly, criminalizing marijuana possession is considered justified because it has the potential to limit impaired driving and other crimes. A brief look at data and logic reveals that these arguments are embarrassingly weak.

The effects of marijuana on driving are still unclear (see Liguori, chap. 4) but potentially negative. If this reason alone is enough to justify prohibition, then a host of other substances, including over-the-counter antihistamines (Verster & Volkerts, 2004) and our beloved alcohol, qualify for prohibition as well. In fact, driving impaired is already a crime. Impairments could arise from fatigue, illness, medications, licit and illicit drugs,

head injury, or a host of other sources. Focusing on drug use as the lone source of impaired driving is ill advised. Criminalizing marijuana possession because possession may lead to driving after using marijuana, and driving after using marijuana may be impaired, is illogical. It is simply too inefficient. Let's penalize impaired driving directly if it is the source of our concerns.

The idea that marijuana causes crime is laughable to anyone who has used it, including the millions of people who have tried the drug and never committed any other crime. The available research reveals that marijuana does not cause violent crime. Laboratory studies and epidemiological work confirm this finding again and again. Any association with other crimes probably arises because those who break the law while intoxicated are more likely to get caught (Pacula & Kilmer, 2004). It's not that people who are high commit crimes, it's that people who commit crimes and happen to be high are easier for police to apprehend.

Again, crime, by definition, is already illegal. Attempting to limit crime by prohibiting marijuana wastes time and effort because marijuana does not cause crime. If there are particular crimes that worry us most, let's increase their penalties rather than try to criminalize behaviors that are weakly correlated with them.

Given this evidence that marijuana causes little harm to most regular users and no harm to the people around them, the negative effect of marijuana possession appears too small to estimate. If we believe that the punishment should fit the crime, then there should be no punishment for owning a personal amount of marijuana.

Thus, if we value justice, we must remove penalties for possession of marijuana.

CONCLUSIONS

Truly valuing compassion and justice can lead us to legalize medical cannabis and remove penalties for possession of marijuana for personal use. A focus on some other values can lead to more dramatic changes. For example, a taxed, legal market for marijuana is consistent with the value of fiscal responsibility. Alternatively, a completely free market for marijuana is consistent with the value of liberty. But the United States may not be ready for such big steps. For now, let's focus on the fundamental values of compassion and justice; let's legalize medical marijuana and remove penalties for personal use. Religious, moral, and empirical arguments mandate these moves. Precedents from other countries offer further support. If we value justice and compassion, we must change marijuana policy.

REFERENCES

Pacula, R. L., & Kilmer, B. (2004). Marijuana and crime: Is there a connection beyond prohibition? (Working Paper 7982). Cambridge, MA: National Bureau of Economic Research.

Verster, J. C., & Volkerts, E. R. (2004). Antihistamines and driving ability: Evidence from on-the-road driving studies during normal traffic. *Annals of Allergy, Asthma, and Immunology, 92,* 294–304.

NAME INDEX

SUBJECT INDEX

Italicized page numbers refer to figures and tables.